JAPAN'S Shrinking Regions in the 21st Century

JAPAN'S Shrinking Regions in the 21st Century

Peter Matanle and Anthony S. Rausch
with the Shrinking Regions Research Group

CAMBRIA PRESS

Amherst, New York

Requests for permission should be directed to:
permissions@cambriapress.com, or mailed to:
Cambria Press
20 Northpointe Parkway, Suite 188
Amherst, NY 14228

Library of Congress Cataloging-in-Publication Data

Matanle, Peter C. D.
Japan's shrinking regions in the 21st century: contemporary responses to depopulation and socioeconomic decline / Peter Matanle and Anthony Rausch with the Shrinking Regions Research Group.
p. cm.
Includes bibliographical references and index.
ISBN 978-1-60497-758-5
1. Japan—Population.
2. Japan—Rural conditions.
3. Rural-urban relations—Japan.
4. Japan—Economic conditions—21st century—Regional disparities.
5. Japan—Social conditions—21st century.
I. Rausch, Anthony, 1960- II. Shrinking Regions Research Group. III. Title.

HB3651.M367 2011
304.6'20952—dc23

2011018367

For all of our children

Table of Contents

List of Figures

List of Maps

List of Photos

List of Tables

List of Abbreviations and Acronyms

ABM	Aomori Brand Management
ASEAN	Association of Southeast Asian Nations
BED	Business Enterprise Department
DEMIFER	Demographic and Migratory Flows Affecting European Regions and Cities
DPJ	Democratic Party of Japan
EMR	European Metropolitan Region
ETA	Eco-Tourism Association
EU	European Union
EUR	Euro
GBP	Great Britain pound
GDP	Gross domestic product
HIE	Highlands and Islands Enterprise
IAEA	International Atomic Energy Agency
INES	International Nuclear and Radiological Event Scale

ITP	Industrial Training Programme
JITCO	Japan International Training Cooperation Organization
JLGC	Japan Local Government Centre
JNR	Japanese National Railways
JPY	Japanese yen
JR	Japan Railways
KUT	Kōchi University of Technology
LDP	Liberal Democratic Party
MoE	Ministry of Environment
NINo	National Insurance Number
NIPSSR	National Institute of Population and Social Security Research
NPO	Nonprofit organisation
NRW	North Rhine-Westphalia
NUTS	Nomenclature of Units for Territorial Statistics
OAC	Oga Aquarium Corporation
OECD	Organisation for Economic Cooperation and Development
OTA	Oga Tourism Association
SIC	Socially Integrative City
SIT	Special interest tour
TEPCO	Tokyo Electric Power Company
TFR	total fertility rate
TIP	Technical Internship Programme
UNPD	United Nations Population Division
USD	United States dollar
WPUK	Work Permits UK
WRS	Worker Registration Scheme

Note on Romanised Japanese

Representing Japanese names in English language text is always difficult. In Japanese one's family name comes first, followed by one's given name. However, this presents problems when rendered into Romanised Japanese because some readers who are not familiar with Japanese naming conventions may become confused as to which part of the name is the family name. This is an important issue when people wish to use names in citations and references. Thus, while acknowledging that changing the order of names might appear disrespectful, simply to avoid confusion and to facilitate correct citation and referencing, we have rendered all names into the English format, with given names preceding family names.

Diacritics also present problems in Romanised Japanese and we have found there is no single method for representing the pronunciation of Japanese words in Roman script that can be followed in all cases. So, we have adopted the following convention which we hope is a good compromise between rigour and ease of understanding for those not familiar with the Japanese language. We have avoided using diacritics with personal names, as this makes following up on citations and references easier for readers. We have also avoided using diacritics for place names where these are commonly used in English without macrons: for example, Tokyo, Kyoto, and Osaka, rather than Tōkyō, Kyōtō, and Ōsaka. However for place names that are not commonly known in English we have used macrons; for example Tōhoku, Kyūshū, Kōchi and Yūbari, so that readers might know their pronunciation a little more clearly. However, there are a small number of exceptions to the basic approach we have adopted here, for various reasons particular to those cases. For all other prose, such as the names of laws and titles of books and articles, we have used macrons.

ACKNOWLEDGMENTS

The acknowledgments that must be noted in a book of this nature are too many to be listed fully. Beyond thanks to individuals and groups that have supported the members of our research team in their professional lives, we wish to make five specific acknowledgments. First, we would like to extend sincere thanks and appreciation to our research informants, who cannot be mentioned by name but who gave so much of their time, insight, and experience and without whose input this book would not have been possible. Second, we would like to acknowledge the generous financial sponsorship of the workshop and symposium held 3–5 July 2008 at the Yorkshire Artspace in Sheffield, which event provided the academic and organisational impetus for this book: the Daiwa Anglo-Japanese Foundation, the GB-Sasakawa Foundation, the British Association for Japanese Studies, and the White Rose East Asia Centre. Third, we wish to acknowledge and thank the Project Office Philipp Oswalt and Professor Philipp Oswalt (chief curator); the Japan Local Government Centre, London Office (JLGC) and Mr Shunsuke Mutai (director [2007-2008], JLGC); Sheffield City Council Council and Mr

Andrew Skelton (art officer); and Derbyshire County Council and Mr Nawaz Khan for their kind support and participation in the workshop and symposium. Fourth, we would like to extend a special thanks to Dr Kuniko Ishiguro, who organised the workshop and symposium and ensured that it was an enjoyable and worthwhile experience for all participants. Finally, we would like to thank the staff of Cambria Press, whose professionalism, efficiency, and good humour have contributed so much to making our vision for this book a reality.

Turning to acknowledgments by individuals:

- Peter Matanle thanks Professor Yasuyuki Sato of Niigata University for his support and co-operation in the research that they undertook on Sado Island. An earlier version of this research was published as 'Coming to a City Near You! Learning to Live Beyond Growth in Japan's Shrinking Regions,' in *Social Science Japan Journal* (2010). Peter also wishes to note that parts of the Epilogue are taken from 'The Great East Japan Earthquake, Tsunami and Nuclear Meltdown: Towards the (Re)Construction of a Safe, Sustainable, and Compassionate Society in Japan's Shrinking Regions,' in *Local Environment - The International Journal of Justice and Sustainability* (2011).
- Philomena de Lima would like to acknowledge the contributions of coauthors Maariyah Masud Chaudhry, Robert Whelton, and Rowena Arshad, of *A Study of Migrant Workers in Grampian* (2007), from which tables 2.3–2.5 of this book are drawn.
- Neil Evans acknowledges publication permissions for maps as follows: Maps 2.1 and 2.2 are reproduced with permission from the Council of Europe Directorate of Communication, Public Information Division; and map 2.3, with permission from the European Parliament.
- Christopher Hood's contribution to this publication is based upon 'The Shinkansen's Local Impact,' *Social Science Japan Journal* (2010).

- Sachie Mizohata is most grateful to Kimie Kitanaka, Tooru Kitanaka, the late Kumi Ohmori, Shigeo Ohmori, Isao Sawai, Okuji Nishijima, Nui Iwabuchi, Takehisa Okazaki, and Yuko Yamamoto for their support and thoughtful suggestions, as well as to all those who participated in her study for their generous time and insights. She also wishes to thank Masayuki Kunitomo of Shiga prefectural government for permission to use photo 6.3.
- Naofumi Nakamura would like to mention an Institute of Social Science, University of Tokyo, publication titled *Kibō no Saisei: Kamaishi no Rekishi to Sangyō ga katarumono* (Reproducing hope: What the history and industry of Kamaishi tell us), in Y. Genda and N. Nakamura (eds.), (University of Tokyo Press, 2009), which is related to the research on Kamaishi City presented in chapters 5, 8, and 9.
- Philip Seaton acknowledges that his contribution is based on the article 'Depopulation and bankruptcy in Yūbari: Market forces, administrative folly, or a warning to others?,' which appeared in *Social Science Japan Journal* (2010).

JAPAN'S Shrinking Regions in the 21st Century

Prologue

Throughout the post-Second World War era, depopulation has been occurring across almost the whole of rural Japan. In the 21st century this trend continues, broadening and accelerating to include most prefectural urban centres and even some metropolitan districts of the country. During the early postwar decades, this took place mainly in the more remote rural locales—namely, the mountainous hinterlands of Japan's four principal islands of Hokkaidō, Honshū, Kyūshū, and Shikoku, as well as in the hundreds of smaller populated islands that compose the Japanese archipelago. This process of rural shrinkage was occurring in the broader context of a rapid and continuous increase in the overall population of the country, and therefore much of the rural decline that took place at that time was simply a consequence of the emigration of younger people to urban areas in search of employment as well as educational and social opportunities. As remote rural areas shrank and the national population grew, urban areas experienced a commensurate increase in population and in social and economic vitality.

It is almost certain that social scientists interested in Japan, who on the whole have conducted their research in the country's industrial and urban settings (against the background just described), have contributed to the development of a normative understanding of postwar Japan as a country with an energetic and dynamic economy and society; a notion that is rooted in conventional progressive notions of modernisation, industrialisation, and permanent economic expansion. Rural depopulation and its associated outcomes have therefore come to be understood as unfortunate but unavoidable, or even necessary, consequences of national—read urban—success. In this way, misgivings surrounding the rural-urban relationship under Japan's spectacular postwar economic development may have come to be neutralised through incorporation in the unfolding narrative of Japan's modernisation and its so-called economic miracle. Despite the readjustments rural communities have undergone as their populations have thinned out, so far this story of Japan's postwar dynamism has largely been an optimistic one because, as was argued by the government at the time, all (or nearly all) Japanese have benefited from the improvements in living standards and longevity that have accompanied such a remarkable transformation. Indeed, historian Mikiso Hane (1996) referred to this period (somewhat tongue in cheek) as 'the greatest years of prosperity Japan had seen since the Sun Goddess Amaterasu shut herself up behind a stone door to protest her brother Susano-o's misbehavior,' and economist Kaname Akamatsu (1962) went as far as employing the flying geese metaphor from classical Chinese literature to suggest that through the judicious application of its development model, Japan could lead the rest of Asia out of poverty and into a new era of prosperity.

Japan in the 21st century, however, is a different society from what it was in the mid-1960s, when the population was expanding by approximately one million persons per year and the average annual growth in the country's gross domestic product (GDP) was more than 10 percent. Sometime between 2005 and 2010 the population of the country as a whole began to shrink, and it is projected to continue to do so for some decades. Since 1990 the country has suffered three economic recessions and intervening periods of stagnation, such that what was once described as the 'lost decade' of the 1990s (see, for example, Hayashi and Prescott, 2002) might now even be described as two lost decades—and counting. Moreover, the Japanese people are now becoming increasingly concerned about the appearance of a *kakusa shakai*, or a society of gaps, in which one gap is the widening gulf between the country's metropolitan and rural regions. Under these circumstances, it is no longer possible to subordinate regional shrinkage to the more visible story of urban and national success. Instead (and beyond performing the important task of describing and analysing depopulation and socioeconomic decline in Japan's regions on its own terms), might the examples of what we call *Japan's shrinking regions* be deployed to assist in evaluating, and even predicting, possible trajectories of experience for regional towns, cities, and some metropolitan urban districts as their populations also begin to shrink? The research presented here is a contribution first, to the growing academic conversation on shrinking communities worldwide; second, to recalibrating the terms of academic and public discourse surrounding the narrative of Japan's postwar development; and third, to developing effective evidence-based policy orientations for shrinking regional communities and urban districts in Japan and beyond in the years to come.

Any research team faced with the challenge of pulling together disparate themes and approaches into one coherent narrative will be faced with a number of tasks and dilemmas. In many cases, this will entail working out thematic groupings, ordering and sequencing papers, prefacing the various works with an introduction and weaving them together in a conclusion. What we have done here is different and is rather more ambitious in its scope.

Based on a workshop convened at the University of Sheffield in the United Kingdom in July 2008, we took the contributors' papers, along with some that originated later, and dissected them into their thematic and empirical subsections. We then reassembled and redrafted these into sections, from which emerged the story that we wish to relate. Once complete, we sent the manuscript to the publisher for review; the authors were then asked for revisions based on this review and on the project leaders' overall understanding of how and where each author's contribution fits into the overall schema. Though the bulk of each author's work may at times have been preserved more or less in one piece, constituting a notable section within a broader thematic chapter or part of the book, other segments are likely to be found in various places throughout the book and have been combined to provide additional detail and clarity. In addition, the project leaders have written both the introductions and conclusions to each chapter, this preface, and the volume's conclusion and epilogue; they have smoothed out the text and have rewritten some parts of it, and have inserted data and analysis into the body of each chapter to enhance theoretical continuity and empirical breadth across the whole volume. We therefore do not indicate the author of each and every contribution where it occurs; instead, we name the main contributors to each chapter in alphabetical order in a footnote at the base of the chapter's first page and provide an overall description of the book and our coauthors' contributions towards the end of this prologue. Rather than a conventional edited volume with discrete chapters by different authors, then, this book is a properly coauthored monograph, written by an unusually long list of authors that we have named *The Shrinking Regions Research Group*. Moreover, we believe that bringing together such a geographically diverse set of data and case studies at the macro, mezzo, and micro scales of analysis gives our volume a resonance and a representativeness that would be difficult, if not impossible, to achieve within the resource confines of a single-authored project. It is our hope that we have woven together a theoretically, methodologically, and empirically rich and textured narrative exploring the contemporary reality of Japan's shrinking regions.

This book is, first, an examination and evaluation of the contemporary demographic and socioeconomic decline of Japan's non-metropolitan rural regions and, second, an analysis of the responses to shrinkage that have been developed thus far at the national, regional, community, and individual levels. We present this research with a view to laying down a set of evidence-based markers that might serve to inform future research and action. To the degree that a solution can be brought to the fore in response to a complex and multifaceted problem, this is ours. Our book initially investigates the characteristics and impacts of the phenomenon of regional depopulation in Japan, its social and economic outcomes, and the implications of these outcomes—in short, *shrinkage*. This issue is becoming sufficiently common in developed regions worldwide to warrant the interest of a growing number of scholars and policy makers and is drastic enough for the places and peoples involved to justify close examination. However, our book is also about the various responses to regional shrinkage. If an issue warrants examination, then it necessarily warrants a response as well, and we offer responses to regional shrinkage as these are envisioned, organised, and put into practice in locales across Japan. Although we do at times use the term *revitalisation* as a conceptual tool for investigating and analysing the response to regional shrinkage in Japan, we do so because it is the English term that is currently most commonly being used with reference to the Japanese case. Nonetheless, one question raised by our research is whether revitalisation—to the extent that it means a return to growth—is ultimately possible within the context of the protracted depopulation that the Japanese nation has only just begun to experience. We therefore invite readers to consider others concepts, such as *stability* and *sustainability*, as replacements.

This book deals with concepts and phenomena that appear worldwide without reference to national or regional boundaries, but the study is also about mapping the particularities of a place—simultaneously and recursively. It is thus about mapping a contemporary phenomenon within Japan while also mapping Japan in terms of that phenomenon. We are talking about a place, but in truth, it is less a single place than a richly diverse mixture of places grouped together to constitute regional Japan—where shrinkage is being experienced and revitalisation is being attempted.

Though we need to make mention of the following issues, this book is *not* an exploration of the causes of Japan's low fertility, the ageing of society, or indeed Japan's industrial restructuring. Detailed research into these questions can be found in abundance elsewhere. Instead, what we do here is recount how demographic shrinkage is playing out across Japan's regions and how the people living in these areas are responding to the problems they are encountering. Moreover, neither is this book another study that seeks to describe Japan in a totalising and reductionist manner for the ease of outsiders' comprehension of things Japanese. This is not a book that carries a comprehensive treatment of the general phenomenon of either shrinkage or revitalisation. We firmly contend that such objectives cannot be realised, and therefore they should not be attempted. The nature of regional and place studies is presently being reconsidered by scholars as they encounter the distinctiveness that characterizes all regions and places and all case studies; so it is for our efforts in the study of regional Japan. We are focusing on a single issue, but one with diverse factors in its origin and compound factors in its process, and investigating it in a set of regions within the (it needs to be said) rather artfully and artificially constructed country that is Japan. What we offer is a heterogeneous collection of portraits and landscapes, of people and places experiencing shrinkage and proposing responses. This volume is a collection that describes a phenomenon that is itself unfolding against the portrait of a country that is being painted and repainted even as we vainly try to capture the moment of our research.

Nevertheless, Japan presents an instructive case of a phenomenon experienced elsewhere but unlikely to be replicated exactly anywhere else. As countries and regions develop, and are themselves affected by the development of other countries and regions, change inevitably occurs. As discussed in this study, many of Europe's regions are experiencing their own cycles of depopulation, and they are developing their own responses. Does Japan mirror this? Can we therefore argue that there is a degree of path dependency to the phenomena we are researching? Given that Japan's situation in many ways parallels the social and economic arcs that have been experienced in Europe, are there precedents for what regional Japan is experiencing today? Significantly, if there are path-dependent characteristics in the relationship between economic development and population change, then what of the lessons from Europe and Japan for China, whose own population is projected to age rapidly in the coming years and to begin its decline sometime around 2035 (Rostow, 1998, p. 29; UNPD, 2004, p. 31)? Asia is not Europe, however, and Japan is not identical to either Europe or China. Hence, this book seeks to present shrinkage in regional Japan as simultaneously a human, a Japanese, a local, and a personal experience.

What we present to the reader is at once a single study and a collection of stories that have been woven together; our intent is to examine a phenomenon and its human response and thence to develop a cohesive narrative for regional shrinkage in Japan and beyond. The scholars included in this book have all been to, lived in, and experienced the places about which they write, and many have an interest in the fate of the people they encountered. Looking at Japan's regions, one wonders whether shrinkage is a reality that the people in these places must accept, even embrace? Must one acquiesce and acknowledge this fate for rural regions in a globalising world? Or is there instead a different response—one of revitalisation, rebirth, and growth? Need we concede that we are using outdated dichotomies and paradigms? Should we seek not an endless cycle of growth and decline but, rather, stability and sustainability?

It is in their aggregate that these multiple narratives contribute to overall understanding. As much as one discovers in these stories simplicity and uniformity, one also finds complexity and particularity—and a mix of approaches that can be brought to bear on a range of different circumstances in the overall (but still developing) dynamic of shrinkage and revitalisation in regional Japan.

***

The places that we include in this book are scattered throughout Japan. They range from Hokkaido in the far north and Aomori and Iwate Prefectures in the northern Tohoku region, to Niigata Prefecture and Sado Island, which are part of the Hokuriku region on the west coast of Tōhoku. Locales vary from the mountains of Kyoto, Shiga, and Wakayama Prefectures in the Kinki region to Kōchi Prefecture in Shikoku, Kaminoseki Town in western Honshū's Yamaguchi Prefecture, and the southernmost point of Japan in the Ryūkyū archipelago of Okinawa Prefecture.

Map showing locations of authors.

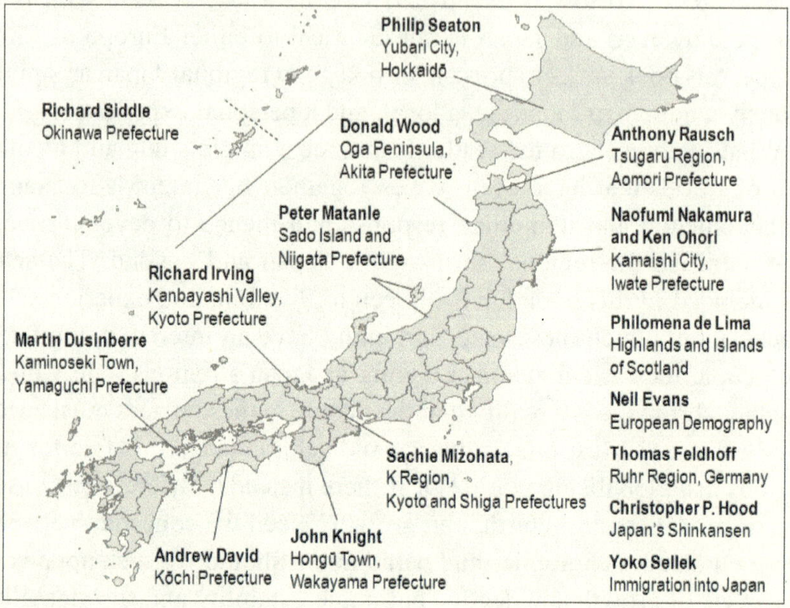

Though each location presents a particular context and perspective on regional shrinkage—some focusing on the contributing factors and others on avenues of revitalisation—this study also introduces themes that move beyond the limitations of place. What follows is a brief description of these places and themes, along with introductions to the contributors. Various parts of the book return to the places mentioned here, with the appropriate context accompanying each appearance. That said, the following introductions are important and necessary because, ultimately, it is the stories that these places provide which instruct us.

Part 1 begins with an introduction to regional shrinkage in Japan and elsewhere. Martin Dusinberre, Thomas Feldhoff, and Neil Evans provide the foundations of the first chapter with some historical and theoretical background to regional depopulation. Dusinberre's work focuses on Kaminoseki Town in Yamaguchi Prefecture, whereas Feldhoff and

Evans's research looks at regional depopulation and decline in Germany and continental Europe. Andrew David, Peter Matanle, and Sachie Mizohata then go on to provide some important definitional and contextual background for the investigation of shrinkage in Japan. Chapter 1 sets the scene for an overview of the European case, which comes in chapter 2. Neil Evans leads this off with continental-scale empirical data on European regional depopulation and its consequences, and then Thomas Feldhoff and Philomena de Lima present evidence from Germany and Scotland. In these two cases we ask readers to consider two contrasting options for resolving the crisis engulfing Japan's regions: either a continuation of a growth-first approach, which would almost certainly require the Japanese government to resort to repopulating regional communities by large-scale immigration from overseas; or the groping towards a solution that acknowledges depopulation as a fact and even embraces the opportunities that may derive therefrom.

Chapters 3, 4, and 5 examine in more detail the characteristics, impacts, and implications of shrinkage for Japan's regional communities. Sachie Mizohata begins chapter 3 by describing the policy context for Japan's shrinking regions, or *kaso* areas, and Peter Matanle follows this with a presentation of demographic data at the national, prefectural, and local levels and extrapolates these data using government projections. The chapter then begins the task of examining the implications of shrinkage in Japan's regions with Andrew David's analysis of economic trends in Kōchi Prefecture, one of Japan's most peripheral areas. In chapter 4, Christopher Hood and John Knight deepen this analysis by presenting contrasting perspectives on the recursive causes and effects of depopulation. Hood looks at the role of regional infrastructural development in the form of Japan's Shinkansen super-express train service, and Knight examines the deterioration of the living environment in a shrinking mountain village in Wakayama Prefecture. Chapter 4 then concludes with some qualitative research by Richard Siddle on settlement patterns in the outer islands of Okinawa, an unusual prefecture in that its population is forecast to continue to grow in the period 2010–2030. Chapter 5 focuses on the roles of geographical peripherality and industrial transformation in regional shrinkage. Sachie Mizohata's and Richard Irving's research focuses on peripherality in, respectively, the K Region of Kyoto and Shiga Prefectures and in the Kanbayashi River valley, showing the limitations of topographical isolation. Philip Seaton and Naofumi Nakamura then relate the stories of two regional cities that have undergone massive economic contraction due to the collapse of their industrial bases—namely, the former coal-mining town of Yūbari City in Hokkaido and the iron and steel centre of Kamaishi City in Iwate Prefecture.

Part II investigates how communities in Japan have responded to their circumstances as shrinking regions. Out of our research emerge four response themes: *redeveloping*, *repopulating*, *recovering*, and *reinventing* the region; these last two are based on notions of *rediscovery.* Chapters 6 and 7 examine the notion of revitalising the regions by attempting to regrow their economies and populations. In the former, Thomas Feldhoff, Sachie Mizohata, and Philip Seaton argue against the prevailing governmental response in the postwar era whereby governments and authorities at all levels attempted to regrow regional economies through infrastructure developments of increasingly questionable public utility and value. As a result, a complex and—we would argue, addictive—relationship of codependency among national, regional, and local actors has been developed around Japan's construction industry and become embedded in the fabric of the postwar national and regional political economies. Whereas chapter 6 deals with the past, in chapter 7 Yoko Sellek and Peter Matanle look to the future with an analysis of the potential for repopulating Japan's regions through immigration from overseas, a topic that is frequently debated in academic and policy circles. The chapter critiques the argument for replacement migration from both empirical and theoretical perspectives and ends with a pragmatic justification for acknowledging, accepting—even embracing—shrinkage as a fact of regional life in Japan. By presenting three cases at differing levels of geographical scale, chapter 8 takes a multilevel approach to the search for viable alternatives to redevelopment and repopulation by examining how regional actors are attempting to recover their economies from the ground up. John Knight's description of residents' attempts to keep nature from swallowing their mountain village leads to the sobering conclusion that many of these settlements will eventually disappear in the course of Japan's national depopulation and continued concentration in the capital region. At the city and prefectural levels, Naofumi Nakamura describes some hopeful developments in Kamaishi City as the community attempts to recover some stability after the steep decline in its economy, and Andrew David considers similar developments in Kōchi Prefecture. Both of these cases have met with some success, but these are small scale, and in the face of a very difficult external economic environment, they lack the vigour and sustainability required to be regarded as full-fledged recoveries.

In chapters 9 and 10, we examine in detail the regional tourism industry from the perspectives of current practice and theoretical potential. Tourism is emerging as the dominant industry in Japan's regions as government reforms take hold and the national economy continues its transformation from manufacturing to services and as communities strive to reinvent themselves for a new era of shrinkage and greater independence from the centre. In chapter 9, Donald Wood, Richard Siddle, and Ken Ohori present examples of regional reinvention through the development of cultural tourism, ecotourism, and green tourism in Akita's Oga peninsula, the peripheral islands of Okinawa Prefecture, and the former steel town of Kamaishi City. In chapter 10, Anthony Rausch and Thomas Jones explore the potential for regional tourism development in the operationalisation of a reinvented and rebranded identity around a region's cultural heritage and natural endowments. Peter Matanle and Anthony Rausch conclude the volume by first tying all of these themes to a review of the role of population growth and shrinkage in the development of Japan's postwar political economy and then by linking this review to the lessons that can be learned and applied—in Japan's urban locales as they encounter shrinkage, as well as across Asia and Europe in the years and decades to come. We conclude the book with the following research and policy recommendations:

1. That Japan's national, prefectural, and municipal authorities engage local commercial, nongovernmental, and nonprofit organisations and citizens' groups more fully in the area planning process so that residents may take greater ownership of and make greater commitments to the decisions that affect their communities and places.
2. That prefectural and municipal authorities build professional capacity in place branding and management in order to assist in the successful utilisation and management of local cultural and natural assets for the establishment of regional economic stability and environmental sustainability.
3. That an international centre be established for researching and developing effective strategies for dealing with the problems in shrinking regions worldwide and for sharing in the advantages that regional shrinkage may bring to light.
4. That more research be conducted into discovering the potential positive outcomes of shrinkage, including establishing the existence of possible relationships between depopulation and reducing human pressures on the natural environment.

Overall, Japan's regions are shrinking and under present trends and calculations will continue to do so through the coming decades. Recessions and recoveries will come and go, and what happens in Japan's regions will, of course, continue to be linked to wider developments in the national and international economies. How regional communities respond to their local circumstances and external contexts will to some extent depend, we argue, on how those communities understand the relationship between local, regional, and national depopulation. Acknowledging the inevitabilities that some villages will disappear and that local populations will age and decline in size and vitality will play a part in reaching pragmatic resolutions to the questions, issues, and problems that regional shrinkage and national depopulation reveal. If communities can embrace shrinkage as an opportunity to develop a new way of life that emphasizes economic stability and environmental sustainability and that replaces currently prevailing notions of permanent expansion and growth, then Japan's shrinking regions could become pioneers in achieving postindustrial solutions to some of the major questions facing humankind in the 21st century.

* * *

As the book was going to press, on 11 March 2011, the Great East Japan Earthquake, tsunami, and nuclear crisis occurred. In response to this disaster, we have added an epilogue that details the events of March and early April 2011 and provides some initial analysis of the Japanese government's response in terms of the dynamics of change in the Tōhoku region and Japan as a whole. In addition, we provide some recommendations for recovery from the disaster in terms of the research presented in this volume. The epilogue was completed in late April 2011 and, as the crisis is ongoing, provides just a preliminary snapshot of events. We extend our sincerest condolences and sympathies to all those affected and wish for a speedy recovery for the Tōhoku region.

Part I

Impacts and Implications

Chapter 1

Introducing Japan's Shrinking Regions*

Introduction: General Background to Population Shrinkage

Shrinking regions are a daily reality facing 21st-century Japan, bringing with them concerns for the state, society, and—most importantly—local communities, families, and individuals. Beyond the abstract demographic phenomena that describe shrinkage as a statistical fact, in people's lived experience shrinkage is most often associated with community and societal decline and with the eventual disappearance of previously thriving human settlements. Indeed, in its most extreme form, shrinkage can result in a complete societal collapse and the disappearance of an entire civilisation (Diamond, 2005; Tainter, 1990). Hence, population shrinkage is not solely a contemporary phenomenon; it has

*The principal contributing authors to this chapter are Andrew David, Martin Dusinberre, Neil Evans, Peter Matanle, and Sachie Mizohata.

been manifest throughout history in rural and urban locations in every major region of the world, including Japan (Rieniets, 2005). Writing in the 1970s, several scholars focused on regional decline as a key theme in Japan's social and economic history from the 18th through the 20th century. Yet for various reasons, the interplay between demographic atrophy and growth in Japan over the long term has, until recently, failed to gain the attention it deserves.

One reason for this may be related to the types of scholarship many prefer to write and read. Ward-Perkins (2005, p. 182) noted his puzzlement that 'the word 'decline' should be so contested in historical writing, when 'rise' is used all the time, without anyone ever batting an eyelid.' Perhaps, he continued, the problem is psychological, both in the 'strongly negative connotations' of the word *decline* and in its implicit sense 'that somebody can and should be blamed for the change.' Regardless of whether this is true of academic writing in general, the experience of Culter (1999), who was questioned during her research in Yūbari in the 1980s as to why she had chosen a topic—managing decline—that 'did not fit the reality,' suggests that there has at times been a particular aversion to the narratives of shrinkage which could be explored further.

Yet the general phenomenon of depopulation is comparatively under-researched. Until the closing decades of the 20th century, nearly all scholars and policy makers had assumed that the principal demographic question that the world faced was rapidly increasing populations, particularly in the developing world. Moreover, based on the research of Warren S. Thomson (1929), it had been assumed that development issues—principally declining infant mortality, rising female education and empowerment, and the high cost of raising multiple children to adulthood in modern urban settings—would bring birth and death rates into balance, such that countries' populations could remain stable for long periods after such a balance had been achieved. This change from a rapidly expanding to a stable population was termed the *demographic transition*. What had not been predicted, however, was that developed countries would go beyond this state into a *second demographic transition*, first identified in Europe by Van de Kaa (1987), whereby deaths would begin to exceed births and inward migration would not compensate for the resulting loss, leading to population shrinkage. Although suggestions of a *third demographic transition* and the establishment of stable populations have been put forward (Myrskyla, Kohler, & Billari, 2009), this has not yet occurred in a manner sustainable enough to enable replacement in Europe or Japan.

Population shrinkage is multidimensional and is a process that normally occurs within a cumulative self-reinforcing pattern of depopulation, economic disruption, and social deterioration, the outcome of which is a renewed—if not strengthened and accelerated—cycle of the emptying of local communities, the gutting of local economies, a collapse in local reserves of social and human capital, and a decline in the quality of life experienced by those who remain.

Although the research presented in this book offers a more complicated, if not occasionally contradictory, portrait of a challenging social phenomenon, as a starting point it is safe to say that population shrinkage in developed countries is fundamentally a relationship of cause and effect that is normally associated with a decline in fertility—specifically, when fertility remains for a long period below the base population reproduction level of approximately 2.1 births per woman over her lifetime, resulting in an eventual surplus of deaths over births. This is either tempered or exacerbated by net levels of migration that occur in an area, with this population decline also being a function of other social dynamics that alter the relationships in sometimes unpredictable ways. In a comprehensive study of depopulation in Europe, Bucher and Mai (2005) classified the phenomenon into either an 'old' or a 'new' pattern. The former is mainly caused when out-migration exceeds natural change, whereas the latter occurs when the component of change is a death surplus caused by a long-term decline in fertility. These two patterns can be further elucidated using the Webb classification, which identified eight different types of population change, as follows:

Population increase:

A: Birth surplus exceeds out-migration
B: Birth surplus exceeds in-migration

C: In-migration exceeds birth surplus
D: In-migration exceeds death surplus

Population decrease:

E: Death surplus exceeds in-migration
F: Death surplus exceeds out-migration
G: Out-migration exceeds death surplus
H: Out-migration exceeds birth surplus

Focusing on population decrease, types G and H represent the old type of depopulation, in which more people (usually young and with additional economic and reproductive capacity) leave than are replaced; types E and F representing the new pattern and are biological consequences of an ageing society.

These patterns usually do not occur in isolation as one-dimensional or unidirectional processes. For example, settlements with chronically low fertility rates but dynamic economies can be sustained by in-migration from surrounding areas—a type D pattern of population increase. This pattern, however, often ends when in-migration from areas with a birth surplus is no longer sufficient to outweigh the death surplus, thereby developing into an E pattern; what Bucher and Mai (2005, p. 15) referred to as the theory of 'regional-demographic shift of phases.' These two scenarios reflect the complexity of depopulation in particular. Moreover, patterns F and G reflect a demographic reality that is particularly devastating to rural areas, what might be referred to as a *double-negative demographic disequilibrium* (see Matanle & Sato, 2010), a situation in which both death and out-migration contribute simultaneously to shrinkage.

Beyond this demographic–migration dynamic, the shrinkage that takes place in rural locales is also a function of many interrelated, even mutually causative, factors. First and most notable is the loss of population due to natural decreases and out-migration (especially of younger people), which is both a cause and a consequence of demographic ageing and which results in reductions in a region's stock of social and human capital. Out-migration is often due to a variety of factors, including a decline in the availability of desirable local jobs and a rise in unemployment, which can then accumulate an additional loss in terms of reduced capabilities to attract investment in new and economically sustainable sources of employment. The consequent economic contraction leads to a decrease in individual purchasing power for rural residents and consequently a significantly lower potential for endogenous economic sustainability. This leads to decreasing municipal tax revenues and in turn less local investment in public and private infrastructure—which, over the long term, results in declines in the local quality of life and provokes feelings of geographical peripheralisation, social isolation, and exclusion among residents.

Population shrinkage is also visually apparent in the areas where it occurs. Accompanying the decline in economic fortunes is a tendency towards less new construction and renovation of residential and business properties, a trend that leaves the built environment appearing increasingly shabby and run down. Changes in local patterns of land use are an important issue in the character of rural places as well, one that often brings ecological consequences. As a result of the contraction of agricultural activities, there is an increase in the acreage of disused agricultural land and scrub vegetation. With the withdrawal of an agrarian human presence, human control of plant growth is reduced, and within a matter of years a pattern of succession resumes. Within decades, farmland and grassland give way to secondary forest and its fauna. In this way, the decline in the human population of remote areas comes to be associated with an increase in the numbers of insects, birds, and mammals living in proximity to and within sparsely populated human settlements, though possibly not a return to pre–human habitation levels of biodiversity (Jacob et al., 2008). Shrinking therefore implies a process in which development trends usually regarded as negative come to be cumulatively linked together (Heineberg, 2005; BMVBS & BBR, 2006, p. 27).

Consequences of Population Shrinkage

Whether a declining economy leads people to leave or an increasing number of people leaving results in a declining economy, it is clear that as the process advances, there are consequences. Some that have been identified in Europe include the following (Commission of the European Communities, 2005, 2006, 2007; Bucher & Mai, 2005; Council of European Municipalities and Regions, 2008):

- Potential for the intensification of regional disparities as a result of the decidedly uneven spatial character of demographic change and potential for revitalisation.
- Pressure on general services, which exist in low density in rural regions, and difficulty providing essential community services in the short term and maintenance and upgrade of infrastructure in the long term.
- Pressure on health care and social services in areas where caring for older people occupies an expanding share of overall health and care budgets.
- Changes in educational provision as smaller numbers of children lead to restructuring of educational systems, including school closures.
- Changes in transportation in areas where decreasing populations lead to reduced demand for and therefore provision of public transport. Concurrently, a rising proportion of older people, many without access to cars, means continued demand for such services from vulnerable individuals, with the consequence that many will experience feelings of isolation.
- Changes in housing needs as ageing populations contribute to trends towards smaller households, particularly single and two-person households, while causing an adjustment to the specific needs of older households.
- A challenge to the heretofore dominant growth paradigm in spatial planning, along with planning for shrinkage, and the adoption of a new paradigm that places novel demands on urban restructuring, such as finding new uses for abandoned land and buildings and encouraging the responsible conversion of disused land into environmentally sustainable ecosystems.

Ageing is one of the more apparent phenomena associated with depopulation. In 2002 the United Nations Population Division (UNPD) published its seminal report, *World Population Ageing: 1950–2050*, which described global trends and included indicators by major regions and countries. From this report emerge four important issues:

- Current population ageing is unprecedented and without parallel in the history of humanity.
- Ageing is pervasive. It is a global phenomenon affecting everyone.
- Ageing is profound, having major consequences and implications for all aspects of human life.
- Ageing is an enduring and long-term phenomenon. (UNPD, 2002, p. xxviii)

The report also reveals that each country is at different stages of the ageing process and that the pace of change differs significantly among countries. Though it is progressing slowly, ageing is largely irreversible.

Nevertheless, the story of rural and regional decline is not complete without the consideration that, from a broader historical perspective, shrinkage itself is not an endpoint; something always follows. Eisenstadt (1988) asserted that even social and community collapse, as devastating as it may seem to one who is involved, almost never means 'the complete end of those political systems and their accompanying civilizational frameworks,' a notion that leads to 'viewing collapse as a part of the continuous process' that ultimately may lead to some form of revitalisation (p. 242). It is, however, by no means certain that revitalisation will necessarily incorporate a human element, as examples of former settlements and civilisations now overrun by thriving populations of flora and fauna attest. As valuable as Eisenstadt's view is, experience is often a more awkward and complicated affair that also incorporates a great deal of human agency. Although natural succession may, at first glance, appear to require no input other than neglect, realising the potential of a cycle of rural decline and revitalisation requires foresight, imagination, and inspiration at the very least. Indeed, some consider even neglect to be a form of agency that eventuates in collapse (Diamond, 2005). In his review of the Schwartz and Nichols (2006) volume entitled *After Collapse*, Yoffee (2006) argued that ultimately 'regeneration doesn't just happen; it has to be engineered' (p. 225). Accordingly, one of the questions that emerges from our research is this: What would constitute a successfully engineered regional or community regeneration in the Japanese context?

INTRODUCING JAPAN'S SHRINKING REGIONS

In the postwar period, population shrinkage began in Japan's more remote rural areas just as the so-called baby boom peaked, in about 1950. As early as the 1960s, regional social and economic decline as a consequence of rural depopulation had been recognised on an official basis with regeneration initiatives such as the *jiba sangyō shinkō jigyō* (regional industry promotion projects) and the *isson ippin* (one village, one product) movement of the 1970s (Knight, 1994). However, although such revitalisation measures have been a constant feature of policy approaches to rural decline and depopulation (other elements aimed at reversing the declining birth rate having been pursued since the 1990s), in aggregate, they have had almost no success reversing either economic decline or demographic shrinkage (Masaki, 2006).

Exacerbating already difficult circumstances, both the global and the Japanese national economies have seen trends positive and negative over this long period, all of which have in general negatively affected Japan's rural regions. Positive trends have spurred economic growth in metropolitan regions (against which rural economies find it difficult to compete to retain investments in human and social capital), and periods of contraction and stagnation bring about a reduction in financial flow to rural prefectures and municipalities. The decline in the national population, combined with the continued concentration of activity in the capital region, are further accelerating regional depopulation, meaning that it has become inevitable that some communities are now collapsing and that settlements are being abandoned (see BBC Radio 4, 2007). As these factors accumulate and unfold, processes that previously had affected only isolated and remote hamlets and villages are now affecting a broader swathe of regional towns and cities (Flüchter, 2008; Matanle and Sato, 2010; Project Office Philipp Oswalt, 2008). Some have even argued that Japanese society will have to adjust to long-term economic contraction and that depopulation and its outcomes will be replicated even in the poorer inner wards of Tokyo itself (Matsutani, 2006; Nihon Keizai Shimbunsha, 2007, pp. 9–20).

Japan's shrinking regions at once both conform to and confound easy generalisation. In addition to the dynamics of rural depopulation, the last 20 years has seen increased international agricultural competition, rapid technological change, the collapse in the early 1990s of Japan's financial bubble, and changing Japanese business models, each of which has contributed to the long-term decline in Japan's regions. This decline has been accompanied by both declining fertility and continuing out-migration of predominantly younger people, and the average age of remaining residents has steadily increased. The ultimate consequences are a steady decline in the size of communities, a lower quality of life for those that remain, and their eventual loss of independence through merger with larger neighbouring settlements, or even their collapse and disappearance.

Kasochi, as defined under the 2000 Special Law Promoting Independence in Depopulated Areas (*kaso chiiki jiritsu sokushin tokubetsu sochihō*), which remained in effect until 2009, are depopulated rural areas that 'have experienced a significant population loss, whereby the area has experienced declines in its vitality and is in a lower level in terms of production functioning and infrastructures related to daily living, compared to other areas' (Kaso Taisaku Kenkyū Kai, 2004, p. 3). In April 2010 the law was revised once more for a period of six years and renamed the Revised Special Law Promoting Independence/Autonomy in Depopulated Areas (*kaisei kaso chiiki jiritsu sokushin tokubetsu sochihō*). The term *genkai shūraku*, coined by rural sociologist Akira Ohno, refers to the worst affected *kaso* communities, those which have experienced large-scale depopulation and dramatic demographic ageing such that more than 50 percent of the population is aged 65 and older, and thus the areas have diminished communal capacities—hence the implication of having 'reached their limits' (Ohno, 2005, pp. 22–23).

Previous out-migration and extremely low birth rates have compounded population ageing in many of these *kaso* communities, and many are now in terminal decline, from which point recovery is doubtful and collapse likely. According to a 2006 government report (Ministry of Land, Infrastructure, Transport, and Tourism, 2006), 7,878 *genkai shūraku* currently exist and 423 of these will disappear within 10 years. A similar report released in 1999 documented that 191 villages had disappeared during the decade leading up to its publication, of which 88 had not been previously projected; the implication is that the speed of these processes has accelerated. At present, the ministry estimates that 2,220 communities face the threat of collapse sooner or later (Ministry of Land, Infrastructure, Transport, and Tourism, 2006).

Characterised demographically by a low population density, a high proportion of older people, and a lower proportion of young adults, these *genkai shūraku* are also at a disadvantage because their reduced vitality has led to underdeveloped local infrastructure and limited availability of public and commercial services. These circumstances add difficulty to the daily lives of the people, who are often older and possess little economic surplus. *Genkai shūraku* are typically remote from urban economic centres and they are physically isolated, which also negatively affects access to opportunities and services. These communities typically lag behind the rest of the country in virtually all indicators, particularly economic; this ultimately exacts a cost nationally because financial resources are redistributed from metropolitan regions to these areas to compensate for local shortfalls.

Contemporary Economic Change and Regional Shrinkage in Japan

In the contemporary period, national-level economic transformations such as the collapse of the 1980s investment bubble, the pace and nature of technological advance, the outward globalisation of Japanese manufacturing, and changes in the agricultural sector—each in its own way and also in aggregate—have had dramatic impacts on Japan's regional economies. Hence, regional shrinkage is not only a story about chronic problems of depopulation in Japan's villages, but it is also the outcome of large-scale developments in the international and Japanese economies (which it affects, as well). For example, the drastic decline in Japan's heavy, extractive, and chemical-processing industries that has taken place through the late 20th and early 21st centuries has dramatically influenced the country's regions, such that whole communities have emptied out as coal mines have closed and steel mills have restructured, leading to loss of employment and income that had been the foundation of community prosperity (see, for example, Culter, 1999; Genda & Nakamura, 2009).

In agriculture, trade liberalisation has led to more intense international competition as well as reforms, albeit modest, in the structure of government support (Mulgan, 2006). At the same time, structural transformation in East and Southeast Asia from low- to middle-income economies has created opportunities for Japanese exports. Japanese agricultural products are often perceived as high quality and more expensive than locally produced products; Asian consumers are beginning to reward quality, and their ability to purchase such goods is growing. However, neither the increasing domestic competition for quality agricultural products within Japan nor the potential for Japanese products in Asia as a whole has altered the fundamental factors contributing to long-term negative employment trends in farming communities. Moreover, although government attempts to support the economy—in rural areas in particular—through public-works funding contributed to a 16 percent increase in construction employment nationally from 1990 to 1997, construction employment has steadily decreased from its 1997 peak, and it has not served as a permanent replacement for reduced agricultural employment (Statistics Bureau, 2010a).

Japan's regions have also been affected by the national shift in employment and economic output from primary industries and manufacturing to services, although this has not yet resulted in a decline in manufacturing production, as it has in the United States. Although firms have shifted low-value-added production to less costly locations overseas, much high-value-added manufacturing remains within Japan's borders. Over the 10-year period 1998–2007 (after the Asian financial crisis and the resultant drop in production, and prior to the onset of the 2008–2009 economic downturn), the index of industrial production (with 2005 = 100) increased from 93.7 to 107.4 (Statistics Bureau, 2010b). The economic downturn did lead to a severe pullback in Japanese industrial production, with the index of industrial production falling to 81.1 in 2009, but this appears to be a short-term decline due to the specific economic conditions prevailing in the global financial system at that time rather than the result of a sudden structural change in Japan's industrial competitiveness. In the second quarter of 2010, industrial production recovered to 92.2 (Ministry of Economy, Trade, and Industry, 2010).

Though companies continue to produce in Japan, technological changes—including increasing automation and alterations in the composition of Japanese industries—have significant implications for employment. Manufacturing employment in Japan decreased by about 2.8 million (19%) from 1990 to 2002, with another decline of half a million between 2002 and 2004. Manufacturing employment was relatively stable from 2004 to 2007 but declined by 700,000 from 2008 to 2009 as a result of the global economic downturn (Statistics Bureau, 2010a). In addition, there have been significant shifts in the composition of manufacturing. For example, production of electronic parts and devices increased by 126 percent from 1998 to 2007, and production of textiles declined by 48 percent (Statistics Bureau, 2010b). These shifts have implications for the regions, though the implications differ depending on the composition of local industry and whether regions benefit from growth in newer industries.

Hence, the service sector is an increasingly important segment of the Japanese economy, rising from 59.1 percent of value added in 1990 to 70.1 percent in 2007 (Organisation for Economic Co-operation and Development, 2010). The tertiary sector accounted for 70 percent of employment in 2009, compared to 25 percent in the secondary sector (manufacturing, construction, and mining) and 4 percent in the primary sector (agriculture, forestry, and fisheries; Statistics Bureau, 2010c). As the society ages, one area of service sector growth has been in medical care, health care, and social welfare. During the period 2002–2009, this sector added 1.5 million jobs, more than any other sector (Statistics Bureau, 2010a).

The shift in the structure of the Japanese economy has also coincided with a move by employers towards a greater reliance on nonregular employment (Ishiguro, 2008). The proportion of part-time, contract, and temporary workers (termed *nonregular workers*) increased from 20 to 34 percent between 1990 and 2009. Women are much more likely to be engaged in nonregular employment, with the proportion rising to 53 percent in 2009, whereas only 18 percent of men were classified as nonregular workers (Statistics Bureau, 2010a). However, nonregular female employment is not new to Japan's regions, for manufacturing industries have relied on the employment of part-time, temporary, despatch, and contract female workers to keep costs low throughout the postwar period (Chalmers, 1989; Macnaughtan, 2005). What is new is the steadily rising proportion of nonregular employees in the labour force, coupled with the fact that women and younger people make up a majority of these workers (Ishiguro, 2008).

In sum, it can be said that Japan's contemporary economic circumstances are not conducive to a return to general expansion in the country's regions. Because employment is the bedrock upon which regional economies rest, and regional employment faces continuous downward pressure from structural changes in the global and national political economies, Japan's regional—and particularly rural—communities face a difficult future as they confront the pressures of depopulation and economic change.

Consequently, the prospect of rural collapse for the residents of regional and rural communities, as well as the implications for Japan on broader measures, not only calls for special attention to the problems of regional shrinkage but also raises the question why these shrinking communities have been left behind by postwar Japan's rising prosperity.

Looking to the future, the Japanese people must inevitably consider how the central government will address regional decline on the one hand, and the prefectural and municipal governments will also be required to develop approaches that suit their own circumstances, on the other hand. Ultimately, therefore, the exploration of viable solutions to regional depopulation requires (1) the identification of gaps in understanding what shrinkage entails for a region and what it is like to live there and (2) the identification of implications that stem from this awareness. This inevitably begins with setting the problem of regional shrinkage within its proper historical and historiographical context.

Japan's Shrinking Regions in Historical Perspective

Why have shrinking regions in Japan until recently not received the attention and study they deserve? One of the earliest English-language discussions of demographic shrinking was published by Smith (1973) and focused on population dynamics during the Edo period (1603–1868). Smith argued that, unlike preindustrial patterns of economic growth in the West (patterns characterised by 'marked urban growth'), economic growth patterns in Japan during the 18th and early 19th centuries saw castle-towns generally stagnating or losing population. From a sample of 35 such towns, Smith identified 25 whose populations declined by 10 percent or more between 1700 and 1850, nine of which suffered declines of more than 30 percent. Although Smith omitted great metropolises such as Edo and Osaka from his data, he was aware that the population of the latter had also fallen from a high of 423,000 in 1765 to 313,000 in 1859 (McClain, 1999, p. 75). Whatever standard is used to measure shrinkage, these figures represent regional urban atrophy on a major scale.

Yet Smith's analysis of castle-town decline was only one part of a wider pattern, namely, that 'decline was ... a function of growth itself' (1973, p. 130). He identified 'scores—perhaps hundreds—of country places,' generally villages with fewer than 1,000 residents, where the population 'grew fairly rapidly through a major part of the century and a half after 1700, several doubling or tripling in that time' (1973, pp. 141–142). Among the factors accounting for such growth, he noted the incentives for rural producers and merchants to bypass urban merchants—who had monopoly rights on certain commodities and thus charged higher fees—and instead sell their produce to other dispersed rural markets. The precise implications of Smith's argument need not concern us here; suffice it to say that he read into this rural-centred mode of economic growth a different pattern from the urban-centred growth of premodern Western Europe.

For our purposes, the key point is that a 'negative' story of demographic shrinking (to borrow Ward-Perkins's psychological explanation) was subsumed under an implicitly positive story of premodern Japanese growth. This process of subsumption offers one possible explanation why shrinkage and decline were for many years relatively understudied in the historiography of Japan. As Smith later acknowledged about himself in the introduction to his *Native Sources of Japanese Industrialization*, in which 'Pre-Modern Economic Growth' was reprinted, the postwar generation of US-trained historians tended to slight 'much about the Japanese past that did not prove useful to the present' (Smith, 1988, p. 2).

> When I began studying Japanese history immediately after World War II, the dark side of the Japanese past needed no elaboration and had many distinguished analysts. What seemed to me to need study was how, in such darkness, so much that was admirable about Japanese life, even under the most trying postwar conditions, had flourished. (Smith, 1988, pp. 2–3)

This search for the 'admirable' in Japanese history, which by the 1960s had become intertwined with approaches inspired by modernisation theory, arguably led a generation of historians away from investigating what Smith called 'the cost of what occurred' (1988, p. 2). Their focus was to be on growth, not decline.

But if the themes of shrinkage and decline were avoided first because of their negative connotations in the light of postwar modernisation historiography, a second problem concerned the frame of enquiry itself. Whereas many modernisation historians focused on the development and growth of the Japanese nation, at the turn of the 1990s a new group of English-language scholars started calling for a more regional approach to Tokugawa Japan. Wigen (1992) argued, for example, that a greater understanding of the geographic imagination of early modern Japanese history would help reduce the 'importance of East/West (Orient/Occident) polarity as the definitive context for Anglo-American writing on Japanese history' (Wigen, 1992 p. 4). Noting Smith's conceptual division of rural Japan into broadly 'advanced' and 'backward' areas, Wigen proposed an analysis of specific geographical regions so as to define (among other things) their varied divisions of labour, their internal economic and political structures, and their sense of boundaries. Wigen (1995) later published an exemplar of such an approach—one of a number of books in that decade which reconstructed regional Tokugawa Japan in unprecedented detail and scope (see Howell, 1995). In it, Wigen traced the transformation of the Shimoina valley in present-day Nagano Prefecture from the mid-Edo period, when it served both as a trade corridor and as a producer of luxury crafts, to the new economy of the early 20th century, in which the capital and control of local industries were increasingly located outside the region. By 1920, she argued,

> not only had the Ina valley been reduced from a corridor to a cul-de-sac, and from a diverse protoindustrial center to a precarious industrial supply zone, its political hub had at the same time been demoted from domainal capital to country seat. Where in 1750 a relatively autonomous economy and polity had existed, a periphery was now in place. (Wigen, 1995, p. 12)

In geopolitical and economic terms, if not (yet) in demographic ones, such marginalisation was in many ways a story of regional decline—one which could be told thanks to Wigen's particular focus on the subnational frame of enquiry.

In a similar vein, Lewis (2000) examined the multiple ways in which one region's relationship to Tokyo changed during a period of modernisation and industrialisation. As the book's title, *Becoming Apart: National Power and Local Politics in Toyama, 1868–1945*, suggests, Toyama was also peripheralised—rendered apart from the concentration of politics and capital in Japan's new capital. One consequence, Lewis noted, was that agricultural workers fled the effects of higher taxes and the Matsukata deflation, leaving behind villages that in the 1880s and 1890s lost up to one third of their pre-1868 populations—a classic example of 19th-century shrinking regions, and one reflected in the early 20th-century moniker for Toyama and the surrounding prefectures: *ura Nihon* (backwaters of Japan). Once again, the regional approach created the discursive space in which a less 'admirable' history of decline and shrinking might be told, as in Soranaka's (1997) example of urban decline in the *ura Nihon* hinterland in his study of Obama port.

But Wigen and Lewis did not limit their studies to a subnational frame. At the same time, they also explored the interface between local and global history. Wigen showed how the economy of the Shimoina valley was transformed by the mid-19th-century opening of Japan to the West, in particular by the new international markets for silk. The increasing specialisation of Shimoina's residents in silk production was a response to these new trading opportunities and was also made possible by the importation of cheap fertilizer and grain from the Asian mainland—into which the Japanese state was expanding ever more aggressively. In this sense, the 'intersection between the local and the global' in Shimoina took on a wider significance in the story of early 20th-century Japan (Wigen, 1995, pp. 12–13). For his part, Lewis showed how Japanese imperialism on the Asian mainland—just on the other side of the Japan Sea from Toyama—suddenly made the prefecture a gateway to the empire; *ura Nihon* was transformed into a 'centrally important place, no longer apart from the nation but irrevocably a part of it' (Lewis, 2000, pp. 191, 212). Such an association between shrinking regions and the wider global economy is echoed by the research on contemporary Japan that we present in this volume.

Wigen and Lewis told tales not only of regional marginalisation per se but also of spatial boundaries reconstituted: There is a gerund in both their books' titles—*making* and *becoming*, respectively—which one would do well to note, and which we reaffirm in the term *shrinking regions*. Neither author understood marginalisation and decline as two-dimensional processes in which the regions were simply acted upon by the centre; rather, the people of the researchers' histories were active agents in reframing their everyday lives—even if that activity was occasionally expressed in the form of protest against economic change. Shrinking, in other words, is never merely a story of decline: scholars could also give ample voice to the process of *making*—that is, local participation in and response to the decline.

The question then arises how to connect the voices of the mid-19th-century regions to the voices of Japan's shrinking regions today? Bernstein (2005) has offered a richly nuanced account of one household's story from the mid-Tokugawa period to the present day, and the approach taken by Dusinberre (in press) has been to seek a middle ground between the regional and household levels by focusing on a single municipality.

Kaminoseki Town, an Inland Sea port located in the southeast of Yamaguchi Prefecture, was one of the hundreds of 'country places' identified by Smith (1973) that witnessed dramatic population growth in the second half of the Edo period; indeed, Smith himself used mid-19th-century data from Kaminoseki as the basis for a seminal article on by-employments in rural Japan (Smith, 1988, pp. 71–102). In 2010, by contrast, Kaminoseki is a quintessential shrinking community. Its population has declined by two thirds since 1950 to approximately 3,600 people, and the proportion of people over age 65 in the town has ballooned to 49 percent, making Kaminoseki a typical *genkai shūraku*. In 1970 the word *kaso* was used for the first time in official town publications. Just over a decade later, with local bureaucrats increasingly desperate to 'stop depopulation,' Kaminoseki volunteered itself as a candidate site for a new nuclear power station to be constructed by Chugoku Electric Power Company (Dusinberre & Aldrich, 2011). Although vociferous local opposition has delayed the planning and, following the 2011 crisis at the Fukushima Daiichi nuclear power plant, the site's future is uncertain—Kaminoseki now receives scholarly attention mainly because of its nuclear status (see Aldrich, 2008).

Like the many cases presented in this book, Kaminoseki is significant because of what its situation suggests both about shrinkage as a historical phenomenon and about the ways it might be studied. First, there is the temporal perspective. An analysis of Kaminoseki's story beginning with the 1950s would result in the mistaken impression that the town's depopulation was simply a postwar policy challenge. Although that may be true in strictly demographic terms—the zenith of Kaminoseki's residential population was indeed the early 1950s—it misses the point that the town bureaucrats of the 1970s and 1980s were men who in many ways had *decline* written in their DNA: They were the sons and grandsons of the generation that had experienced the economic upheaval of the post-1868 decades—in particular, the decline of early modern maritime trading routes in the 1880s and 1890s. These Inland Sea routes, which connected Kaminoseki to both the markets of Osaka and to those of the northern Japan Sea coastal regions, had been vibrant due to a proliferation of independent shippers and local merchants who betted on the price differentials between those markets (Nakanishi, 2009). When the advent of new shipping conglomerates and new forms of instant communication (the telegraph) undermined the foundations of interregional trade through the Inland Sea—playing a part in rendering the Japan Sea regions *ura Nihon*—Kaminoseki merchants made their frustrations known. In an 1894 petition, for example, four such merchants complained that

> world conditions have been transformed: the domains have been replaced by the prefectural system; the coming and going of official ships has stopped; most shipping has become steam-powered; goods are transported [directly] to meet demand; and both commercial shipping and merchants are no longer coming [to port]. Quite suddenly this has become a desolate area [*sekiryō no chi*]; our merchants have lost their work and now continually present us with the pitiful sight of bankruptcy, or with taking up fishing, or with descending [to the level of] day labour and out-migration to other provinces.... We wonder when will be the day that we see once again the prosperity [*seikyō*] of the old days. (Kaminoseki chōshi hensan iinkai, 1988, p. 450; translation by Dusinberre)

Kaminoseki's post-1950s decline, in other words, was not an entirely new phenomenon. Its demographic manifestation may have been novel, but town bureaucrats had in fact been concerned about the economic transformation of the port since the collapse of Inland Sea trading routes in the late 19th century.

It goes without saying that Kaminoseki's historical experience is not representative of every municipality and region in Japan that has suffered from shrinkage in the postwar decades. Nevertheless, the longer historical perspective facilitates a better understanding of the thinking of town bureaucrats in the late 20th century, both in the ways they perceived the demographic crisis and the ways they attempted to frame solutions. A microhistorical approach that gives names and personalities to those bureaucrats and that, moreover, attempts to trace their family histories back to the heyday of Inland Sea trade helps contextualise the reasons why such a radical proposal as an atomic power plant came to be seen by many as a panacea for the town in the early 1980s. When pronuclear lobby groups erected propaganda billboards in Kaminoseki that presented the power station plan as a way of restoring 'prosperity' (*uruoi*) to the 'old hometown' (*furusato*), they were echoing—sometimes consciously—the hope articulated by their 19th-century ancestors for a prosperous golden age to which the town might one day return (Dusinberre, in press, chapter 11).

In addition to contextualising the longer history of decline and shrinkage in Japan, the historical case study of towns such as Kaminoseki is significant as a reminder that just as the story of growth is not always 'admirable,' so the story of decline need not always be negative. As the 1894 document indicates, some townspeople responded to Kaminoseki's economic woes by migrating to other regions of Japan; large numbers went even further afield, to the distant lands of Hawaii and the United States of America, Peru, Brazil, Korea, Sakhalin, Manchuria, Taiwan, the South Seas, and mainland China. This diaspora has had an extraordinary impact on the Kaminoseki home community in terms of wage remittances, employment networks, education, social mobility, and material culture (Dusinberre, 2008). What needs to be reiterated here is that, as Slater and Higgins pointed out, periods of decline, decay, and destruction could thus equally be 'times of opportunity' (2000, p. 1)—even though the population of a particular community might begin to shrink and even though the opportunities presented to residents might lie outside that community.

Just as Smith identified a subtheme of population decline within a wider story of societal growth in the late Edo period, so it is equally possible to identify subthemes of growth and opportunity not only within the story of post-1868 Kaminoseki but also, it might be argued, within the wider story of shrinking regions in Japan today. Among the depressing statistics of demographic decline and an ageing population, therefore, these questions surely lurk: What can be *made* from this crisis? And what will the society we call Japan *become* in the 21st century?

Conclusion

As already alluded to in Eisenstadt's volume, *regional shrinkage*—depopulation, ageing, and the consequent decline in social and economic vitality (which itself contributes to a renewed cycle of depopulation and ageing)—need not be viewed as necessarily catastrophic. At a minimum, it may be understood as a step in a recurring process and, more positively, as the harbinger of opportunity renewed. History offers many examples of population decline creating possibilities for particular groups to improve their circumstances. However, it must be recognised that for the majority who now live in Japan's rural communities, the current situation is not a hopeful one. Many factors appear to be conspiring simultaneously against a general revitalisation of regional society, or at least against a stabilisation of living conditions, and population shrinkage is at the centre of this complex cycle of interrelationships. A chronically low birth rate and an ageing population; structured out-migration of the young to metropolitan areas in search of education, employment, and social opportunities; reduced local tax revenues and reductions in redistributed income from urban regions; obsolete public infrastructure and reduced investment in the rural economy; predatory substitution of independent local businesses with branches of national and international business chains; abandonment of residential and business properties;

decline in the quality of the built environment; and severe damage to the natural environment—these are some of the difficulties that local areas are tackling as they seek to sustain their communities and, in some cases, avoid collapse.

The next chapter looks at population decline in Europe and then focuses on two shrinking regions, the Ruhr region in Germany and the Highlands and Islands of Scotland. We consider these European locales in order to situate the problem of Japan's shrinking regions in the global context. From this context it becomes apparent that Japan's situation is not unique among developed countries. Moreover, the cases from Germany and Scotland show that contrasting experiences of shrinkage reveal contrasting approaches for managing its consequences.

CHAPTER 2

SETTING JAPAN IN THE GLOBAL CONTEXT

SHRINKING REGIONS IN THE EUROPEAN UNION*

INTRODUCTION

Japan's rural regions, like those of many European countries, are undergoing simultaneously both population shrinkage and difficult economic and social transformations; principal among these is the ongoing agglomeration and concentration of political, economic, social, and cultural activities—that is, urbanisation—taking place within what are now deindustrialising economies. All of these processes have had profound consequences for the societies in which they have occurred. Because of the particularities of geography, culture, and history, shrinkage has resulted in different outcomes for each locale. As discussed in what follows, an

*The principal contributing authors to this chapter are Philomena de Lima, Neil Evans, and Thomas Feldhoff.

assortment of policy agendas is being implemented across the various regions that are experiencing shrinkage, and each policy is underpinned by its own set of values and institutional foundations.

By initiating our enquiries with a presentation of the characteristics of contemporary regional population development in the European Union and by then moving on to present two case studies from Germany and Scotland, we wish to draw out the following: First, Japan and much of Europe are similar in that industrialisation and urbanisation have taken root within civilisations whose histories, cultures, and community practices were and are deeply rooted in medieval town and village life. Second, leading up to the contemporary period, shrinkage in the rural regions of both Japan and Europe has almost invariably occurred alongside the continuous growth of urban, and particularly metropolitan, centres; indeed, shrinkage has been the counterpoint to the urban dynamism in these countries. Third, regional shrinkage and urban concentration can be seen at all levels of geographical perspective: continental, national and regional, and local community levels. Fourth, alongside processes of deindustrialisation and under the scenario of national- and even continental-scale demographic decline, regional shrinkage is also now occurring in formerly dynamic urban locales. Thus, in preparation for discussing Japan, we introduce the Ruhr region of Germany as an example of regional deindustrialisation and shrinkage within the context of a declining national population. Fifth, thus far one part of the policy mix being adopted to counter declining birth rates and revitalise some European regions has been to encourage, or at least tolerate, immigration; and immigration is periodically discussed in Japan as a possible partial solution to demographic shrinkage and ageing there. We therefore round off this chapter with a discussion of the recent experience of rural Scotland with immigration from the countries of Eastern Europe.

Sixth and finally, in Europe and Japan the predominant response to shrinkage to date has comprised national and regional authorities' implementing regeneration measures aimed at once more setting regions on a growth trajectory that is founded on interdependent processes of economic and demographic expansion. However, in circumstances of a shrinking national or continental population, it is no longer possible to plan for expansion in one region without recognising that other regions will have to shrink in order to accommodate such growth. We therefore present here the contrasting cases of Germany and Scotland: Scotland continues to work towards the reestablishment of a growth regime that includes, or even requires, immigration from elsewhere in Europe; in Germany, governance structures are coming to accept the inevitability of continued future population decline and are establishing a new set of institutions and policies that view shrinkage either as something to be acknowledged and managed or as an opportunity to be grasped.

Population Shrinkage in the European Union

If the problem of shrinking regions is particularly acute in Japan, it is only slightly less so in Europe. Indeed, the countries of Eastern Europe have the most rapidly ageing and declining population profiles in the world, as a recent World Bank report, *From Red to Gray*, highlights (Chawla, Betcherman, & Banerji, 2007). Birth rates in most of Europe have been declining since the mid-1960s. By 2005 the natural population growth rate of the EU was down to 0.1 percent per annum (Commission of the European Communities, 2007, p. 42), and from 2015 births are expected to be outnumbered by deaths (Eurostat, 2010a). However, the effects of low birth rates have been masked to a large extent by substantial immigration. Initially, this was mostly from outside Europe in the form of immigrants from the former colonies of the European imperial powers. More recently, however, there has been substantial intra-European migration, principally from the states of the former Soviet bloc to the countries of Western Europe; moreover, higher birth rates among immigrant populations, particularly first-generation immigrants, have contributed to this masking effect. In addition, Europe's population is ageing, and even allowing for continued substantial immigration from outside the EU, it is increasing slowly and is projected to go into decline from about 2035 (Eurostat, 2010a)—echoing Japan's shift to a shrinking population beginning in 2005. At the EU level, the issue has come into particularly sharp relief since 2004 with the accession of 10 new countries, followed by 2 more in 2007; most of these were former communist countries of Eastern Europe. In Eastern Europe population decline has already begun. A combination of very low birth rates since the 1980s and large-scale emigration since the end of communism, and particularly since joining the EU, has reduced the populations of all these countries in a decline that in some cases has been quite dramatic.

The problem has become an issue of great concern for the European Commission, prompting the publication in early 2005 of the Green Paper *Confronting Demographic Change* (CEC, 2005). This was followed by a further communication, *The Demographic Future of Europe—From Challenge to Opportunity*, in October 2006 (CEC, 2006), together with the initiation of a biannual series of conferences on Europe's demographic future to highlight the issues and promote discussion around policy responses.

Within the overall pattern of an ageing (and in some parts an already declining) population throughout Europe, there are significant spatial disparities at the national and subnational (i.e., regional) levels. Significant numbers of regions in most, if not all, European countries are shrinking in population and declining in vitality. As in Japan, these are predominantly rural areas that have lost population to urban areas, but they are also regions with urban areas dominated by declining industries, such as mining, steel, and other heavy industries. This contrast between declining regions, often on Europe's geographical periphery and regions that are growing in Europe's more prosperous and more central areas strikes at the heart of the European dream and its goal of achieving broad social, economic, and territorial cohesion. Even though regional policy is a major part of the EU policy arsenal—and the focus of much of its budget—there has been little policy explicitly directed at shrinking regions per se, although such regions have been among those that have benefited indirectly from a wide range of EU policy instruments and funding mechanisms, a process likely to continue in the future. The following data provide an overview of the current structure and dynamics of Europe's demography using data and maps produced by the European Spatial Planning Observation

Network (ESPON), Eurostat (the EU's Statistics Office), Bucher and Mai (2005), and the European Parliament.

Current Demographic Characteristics in Europe

At the national level, population decline in some parts of Eastern Europe had already started to set in by the 1980s, and by the 1990s most Eastern European countries were losing population. By the turn of the millennium, Estonia, Latvia, and Bulgaria in particular were losing population very rapidly, with numbers decreasing almost as rapidly in Lithuania and Romania; decreasing population was also a reality in Hungary and the Czech Republic.

At the regional level, by the 1990s almost 40 percent of NUTS (Nomenclature of Units for Territorial Statistics) 3 regions[1] had declining populations (European Spatial Planning Observation Network, 2005, p. 16), and most countries have at least one region with a declining population. Latvia, Lithuania, most of eastern Germany, Bulgaria, Hungary, and parts of Romania, Croatia, central Finland, and Poland are experiencing particularly rapid decreases in population. Whereas moderate or slight rates of decline can be seen in most of the rest of eastern Europe, with significant pockets also in southern European countries and some of the more remote regions of Scandinavia (Eurostat, 2010b). The case of Germany, the European Union's most populous country, is particularly noticeable. Not only are all the regions of the former East Germany (with the exception of the Berlin region) losing population rapidly, but much of the rest of the country also has either declining populations or only sluggish growth. Like Japan's experience in the postwar decades, shrinking regions in Europe since the 1990s have tended to be, though they are not exclusively, rural and relatively remote.

As already mentioned in chapter 1, population change is a product of two components: natural change (the balance between birth and death rates) and net migration (the difference between the numbers of in-migrants and out-migrants). Total fertility rates (TFR) have been falling throughout Europe since the 1960s and are now below the population replacement rate of approximately 2.1 per woman in all countries. Almost all regions in eastern, central, and southern Europe have a TFR below 1.5, with some regions in northern Spain, Portugal, and southern Italy, as well as a number of areas of eastern and southeastern Europe showing a TFR below 1.25 (ESPON, 2010, p. 72).

This sustained period of low fertility rates has resulted in negative rates of natural population change in almost 50 percent of Europe's regions (Eurostat, 2010b). Particularly high negative rates are to be found in Germany, the Baltic states, and much of southeastern Europe, northern Spain, Portugal, and Italy. In Germany, the regions with the highest negative rates are those in the east, and there are only a couple of regions in the south of the country that have positive rates. All regions of Scotland, meanwhile, now have negative rates of change, though values are not high.

Negative population change is the result not only of declining fertility but also of the age structure of the population. For example, even though fertility is much lower in Spain than in France, much of southern Spain (as well as Italy) exhibits a natural population increase, whereas parts of central France are experiencing population shrinkage, a legacy of an older age structure there. With low fertility rates and negative natural population growth in most of Europe, immigration has been the prime driver behind population increases where they have occurred in recent years.

Not surprisingly, net migration patterns vary considerably across Europe's regions. In recent years, particularly high rates of net in-migration have been found in Ireland, Spain, the northern half of Italy, much of southern France, and parts of the United Kingdom and Belgium (Eurostat, 2010b). This reflects the booming economic conditions in these countries prior to the economic downturn in 2008; consequently, the long-term sustainability of these recent high levels of in-migration must be in doubt. All of Scotland had moderately high positive rates of in-migration, but in Germany such conditions prevailed in much of the south of the country and in some parts of the north and the Rhine Valley. In contrast, most of eastern Europe (particularly eastern Germany) and economically depressed northeast France were characterised by negative rates as people moved to Europe's more prosperous regions in search of jobs, particularly as a consequence of the 2004 expansion of the EU (though movement to Mediterranean regions and some other coastal regions for retirement or leisure purposes was also a significant factor).

Regions with both a negative migratory balance and a negative natural balance are primarily located in eastern Europe, particularly Romania and Bulgaria and including much of eastern Germany (ESPON, 2008, p.7). To a large extent these coincide with the regions with severe or moderate population decreases described above, though there are some exceptions. Capital-city regions in all countries, for example, are excluded from this category because they tend to draw migrants from the more rural regions of the country.

In addition, there are areas that, although they have positive scores for immigration, this is more than offset by negative rates of natural growth. These can be seen in some of the more economically buoyant parts of eastern Europe, such as parts of eastern Germany, Hungary, and Estonia, as well as northwest Spain and parts of Greece and Portugal. These are areas that have had persistently low birth rates but, at least until 2009 in the cases of Spain, Greece and Portugal, relatively dynamic economies attractive to migrant labour (international in Spain's case, but generally domestic in the case of Eastern European countries).

In contrast, other regions have a positive natural balance but a negative migratory balance: parts of southern Italy, eastern France, the far north of Scandinavia, and southern Poland. These areas have had relatively high birth rates (often corresponding to Roman Catholic majorities in these countries) but that are now losing population to more economically dynamic areas.

Most of Germany outside the east is characterised by a positive migratory balance and a negative natural balance, with the exceptions of the relatively depressed Ruhr Basin, where migration is negative, and parts of the south of the country that have a positive natural balance.

Bucher and Mai (2005), in their study of depopulation in Europe, distinguished between what they described as the 'old' type of depopulation, in which the overriding cause is out-migration, and the 'new' type of depopulation, in which the primary factor is the negative rate of natural population change. Map 2.1 shows the regions of Europe that suffer from the old type of depopulation, with the darker areas indicating regions where out-migration exceeds a birth surplus and the lighter shade where it exceeds a death surplus. These are regions that suffer from emigration, often as a result of weak economic development and high unemployment, as in segments of eastern Europe and in peripheral parts of Europe. Much of the eastern area of Germany is characterised by this type of depopulation, as is much of Scotland, including the Highlands and Islands.

According to Bucher and Mai, eventually the regions highlighted in map 2.1 will shift to the 'new' type of depopulation shown in map 2.2. Here, the darker areas indicate regions where death surpluses exceed out-migration, and the lighter shade shows where it exceeds net in-migration. Here, the age structure is the crucial factor driving the process, and most of these regions are in eastern and southern Europe. Most of the rest of eastern Germany falls into this category, but no region of Scotland did at that time. Of the 448 European regions with declining populations analysed by Bucher and Mai (2005, p. 30), 44 percent fell into the category of *old* and 56 percent into the category of *new*.

As already discussed, increasing concern is being shown at the European level regarding the potential problems of an ageing and ultimately declining European population, both in general European terms and in specific relation to currently declining regions. As well as being the subject of the two communications from the European Commission referred to earlier (CEC, 2005, 2006), the issue occupies a significant portion of the most recent Cohesion Report (CEC, 2007). Additional reports have been commissioned by the Council of Europe (Bucher & Mai, 2005), the Council of European Municipalities and Regions (CEMR, 2006), the European Parliament (2008), and ESPON (2010), among others.

The primary perspective from which the ageing of Europe's population is viewed has generally been financial, considering the financial implications for national pensions and health budgets for Europe's increasing old-age dependency rate. However, as already indicated, demographic

MAP 2.1. 'Old' Type of Depopulation.

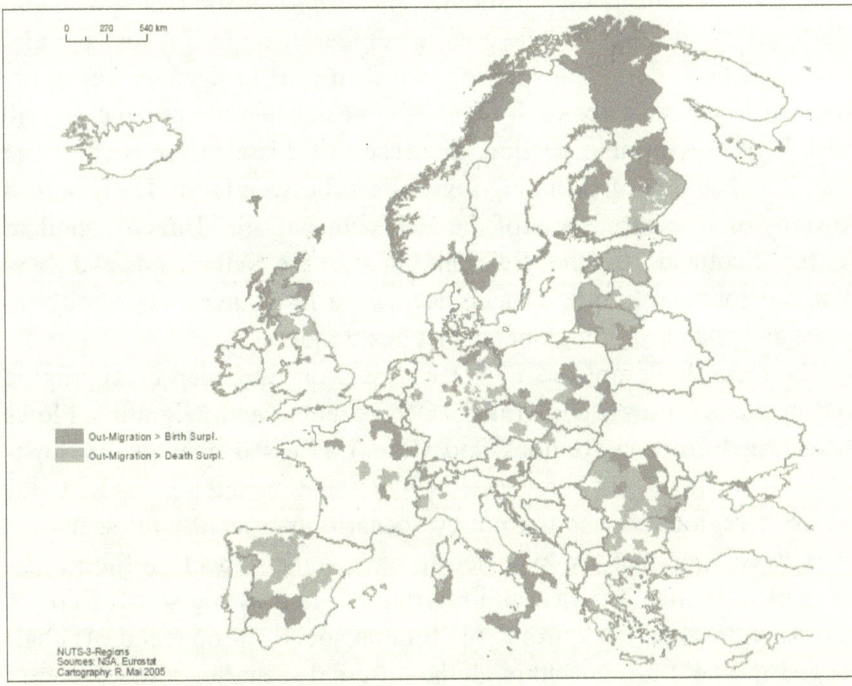

Source. Bucher and Mai (2005, p. 69).

decline in Europe is a profoundly uneven process and is also likely to intensify regional disparities. This will pose a massive challenge for EU regional policy, which is based on the overarching aim of reducing regional disparities. Consequently, many of these recent studies have been concerned with trying to forecast where and when this problem will be felt most severely.

The European Parliament study looked at the period 2005–2030, during which the population of the EU is not expected to vary a great deal within an overall trend of a gradual increase followed by a gradual decline. It is forecast that 42 percent of regions in the EU-27 will experience a decrease in population over the period (European Parliament, 2008, p. 30). Though this is only a slightly greater proportion than are declining today, it does not include a large number of regions whose populations will peak during this period and then start to decline. The study goes on to estimate for each region the year when the population will peak before going into decline. The result of this exercise is shown in map 2.3. The tide of shrinking regions can be seen to gradually spread towards more central parts of the EU, with only the United Kingdom (except Scotland), Ireland, Belgium, most of the Netherlands and Sweden, the southwestern half of France, and a few other isolated city-regions and islands holding out against this trend.

The recently completed ESPON project on European demographic and migratory flows, DEMIFER (Demographic and Migratory Flows Affecting European Regions and Cities) assessed changes in population growth, labour-force size and population ageing to 2050 for NUTS 2 regions by using a policy scenario approach. Four scenarios were developed that are expected to have some impact on future patterns of mortality, fertility, and migration: (1) growing social Europe, (2) expanding market Europe, (3) limited social Europe, and (4) challenged-market Europe. Although the different scenarios result in somewhat divergent forecasts, the general trend of a declining population at some point in the future (but with very significant regional differences) is clear. The study also notes the considerable influence of migration on population size. In much of Eastern Europe, intra-European migration is the primary driver of change, but in most of Western Europe, extra-European migration is more significant. In most of the western regions, extra-European migration reduces population decline or even effects an increase. Migration also affects the population age structure and size of the labour force; it tends to reduce ageing in affluent regions and increase it in poorer ones, thus increasing regional disparities. Regardless of which policy scenario is considered, old-age dependency ratios will increase steadily everywhere. Increases are expected to be greatest in central and eastern regions; many regions will face increases in the ratio of more than 200 percent.

MAP 2.2. 'New' Type of Depopulation.

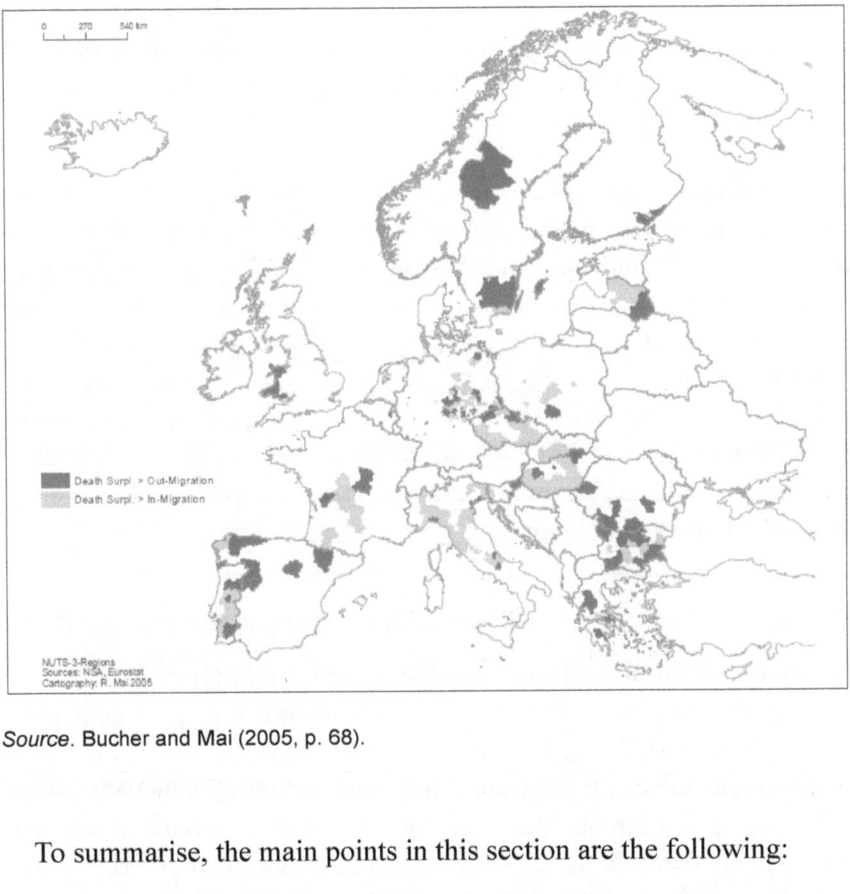

Source. Bucher and Mai (2005, p. 68).

To summarise, the main points in this section are the following:

- Although the population of the EU is still increasing (slowly), this growth masks considerable regional disparities, with at least 40 percent of regions in long-term decline.
- These declining regions are located predominantly in eastern parts of the EU and in more peripheral areas of the rest of the EU.
- Populations are ageing rapidly in all parts of the EU.
- The effects of sustained low birth rates have been masked to a large extent by continued in-migration from outside the EU.

- Europe's ageing profile means that continued immigration will be insufficient to prevent a decline in absolute population in the near future. Likewise, old-age dependency rates will increase, as will regional disparities between dynamic urban regions and declining, generally rural, regions.

What follows is a consideration in more detail of the effects and implications of depopulation in two regions of Western Europe. The treatment also examines the contrasting policies that have been crafted in each region in response to its particular circumstances. The first case addresses industrial decline and transformation in a regional urban setting—the Ruhr area in western Germany—and how imaginative policy orientations have developed out of the expectation of continuing population shrinkage. In the second case—the Highlands and Islands of Scotland—traditional growth-oriented approaches are being maintained, as yet with uncertain outcomes.

SHRINKING REGIONS IN GERMANY: DEINDUSTRIALISATION IN THE RUHR

Policy Implications of Demographic Shrinkage in Germany

In Germany, demographic changes and urban shrinkage provide considerable challenges for regional policies. Until the first half of the 1990s these policies were still determined by growth options (Heineberg, 2005). However, unfavourable demographic and socioeconomic conditions have had an increasingly negative impact on cities and their urban structures, especially in the eastern parts of the country, where urban development was characterised by out-migration, economic shrinkage, and social decline in the aftermath of German reunification. More recently, similar conditions have also been observed in former West Germany, especially in deindustrialising regions like the Ruhr area and the Saarland. With regard to urban and regional planning policies and cultures, shrinking cities are already a fact and are on occasion even propagated as something like an incentive. Several urban-renewal subsidy programmes have been launched by the federal and state governments since the early

Map 2.3. Projected Spatial Distribution of Demographic Decline in Europe

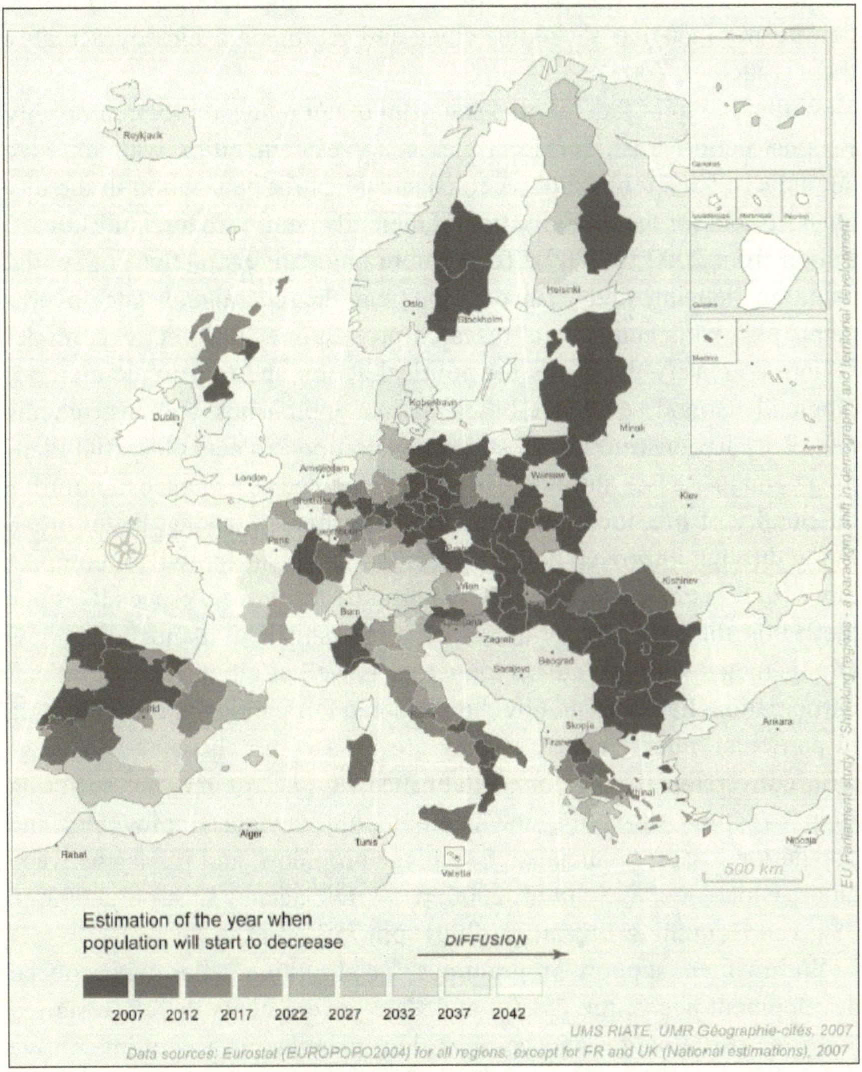

Source. European Parliament (2008, p. 32).

1990s, and this change of direction contrasts with countries such as Japan or the United States, in which the growth paradigm still predominates, despite the fact that shrinking cities and regions are already a reality there (Flüchter, 2005).

Within the joint federal- and state-run urban renewal programme City Reconstruction East, for example, many eastern cities with massive amounts of vacant housing received subsidies for demolition in the city outskirts and for the revitalisation of their city centres (a total of EUR 2.5 billion from 2002 to 2009). To promote innovative strategies of spatial planning, housing, and urban development, the federal and state governments also launched several research programmes that focus on model regions to clarify the needs for political action and to provide methodologically sound, evidence-based action approaches and instruments (e.g., City Reconstruction West, Demonstration Projects of Spatial Planning). In these cases shrinkage is being promoted as a chance to improve the quality of life, including providing affordable housing, better urban living through improved public spaces (from 'urban sprawl' to 'compact city'), and better environmental conditions. Moreover, especially since the 1990s, the necessity for increased partnership activity, including new arrangements with private sector actors as well as citizen activation and participation, has become obvious. Old-economy cities in the Ruhr area in particular, characterised as they are by a comprehensive and long-term conversion from a long-established Fordist regime, are suffering from structural economic and demographic change, employment and population losses, financial stress, image problems, and rivalry between cities (Blotevogel & Schmitt, 2006, p. 57; DiGaetano & Strom, 2003, p. 384; van Houtum & Lagendijk, 2001, pp. 757–761).

Within their support programmes for shrinking cities with special development needs, the federal and state governments therefore started to foster participation and co-operation, postulating a new integrative political approach to urban development linked to the 'communicative turn' in spatial planning that Blotevogel (2000) observed. Traditional spatial planning characterised by the hegemonic claim of planners to scientific superiority and authority is being replaced by the communicative rationality of open planning discourses. As the demographic changes are particularly pervasive and are taking place comparatively early in an ongoing process of structural economic change, the Ruhr area can be seen as a model for what might happen in other parts of Germany some two decades on.

One major problem related to Germany's decreasing population is the accompanying change in the population's age structure. As the absolute number of older people (65 years and over) increases, the proportion of the total population they represent is also increasing. Particularly, the number and proportion of the very old (80 years and over) is growing rapidly and is presenting major challenges for social and health-care systems. Demographic research refers to these aspects as the *threefold process of demographic ageing,* which is also associated with the 'singularisation' and 'feminisation' of old age (Tews, 1993). That the number of older persons increases more rapidly in the higher the age ranges is a general feature of ageing populations in Europe. Among the subregions of the world, Europe already has the oldest population, with a median age of nearly 39 years in 2005 (Germany: 42.1; Japan: 42.9) that is expected to reach 47 years by 2050 (Germany: 49.4; Japan: 54.9; United Nations Population Division, 2007).

Population projections are a key instrument for appraising future development processes, and they provide information for political decision making. At the regional and local levels in particular, these projections can enhance decision makers' awareness of problems in advance by indicating the need for action. The results of Germany's demographic future cited here are based on two variants of development scenarios produced by the Federal Statistical Office (2006) referred to as the 'medium-aged' population's lower and upper limits. The 11th coordinated population projection is based on the assumptions that birth rates will remain nearly constant, at the present level of 1.4 children per woman; that life expectancy will increase by about seven years; and that the migration balance will amount to 100,000 or 200,000 people per year. According to the Federal Statistical Office (2006, p. 5), 'these variants define the limits of a corridor, within which

FIGURE 2.1. Estimates of the 11th Coordinated Population Projection for Germany (until 2050).

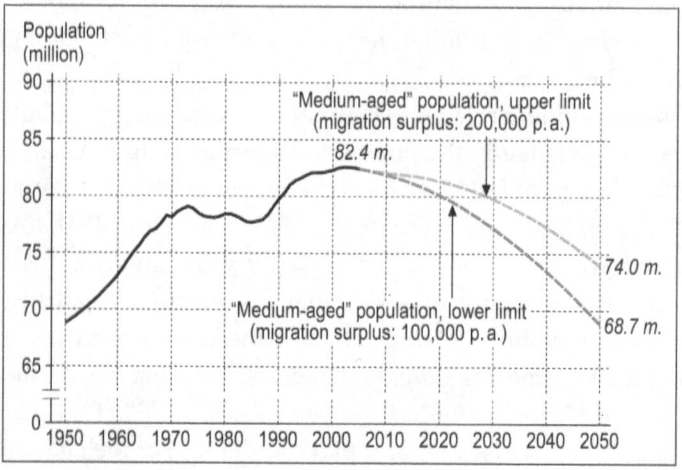

Source. Federal Statistical Office (2006, p. 15).

population size and age structure will evolve, if the currently observed demographic trends continue to be effective' (figure 2.1).

In late 2005, some 82.4 million people lived in Germany. Assuming a rise in life expectancy of 7.6 years for men and 6.5 years for women and a positive migration balance of 100,000 people, the size of the total population will drop to 68.7 million by 2050 (medium-aged population, lower limit). An increased annual migration balance of 200,000 people (medium-aged population, upper limit) will slow the decrease to about 74 million people by 2050. Accordingly, the population will decrease by between 10 and 17 percent during the period 2005–2050, unless there is a fundamental change in current demographic trends. Population pyramids display graphically that the proportional relationship between older and younger people will change dramatically as the working-age population (aged 20 years to under 65) decreases and ages. Looking at broader age groups, the proportion of older people (65 years and over) will increase from 19 percent of the population in 2005 to 29 percent in 2030 and 33 percent in 2050 (Federal Statistical Office, 2006, p. 37). Demographic research has indicated two major reasons for population ageing and shrinking in Germany: declining fertility and increasing longevity. In the case of Germany, the TFR fell below 2.1 children per woman in the mid-1960s (in both parts of the formerly divided country) and has been fairly constant at a low level of about 1.4 children since reunification. In 2006 the TFR was 1.31, that is, less than two thirds of replacement rate. In addition to consistently low fertility rates, age-specific changes occurred because women are postponing the moment of couple formation and first birth and, on average, are now giving birth for the first time in their early thirties (Federal Statistical Office, 2006, p. 27). The problem is that the postponement of the first birth shortens the length of a woman's fertile phase, and if the birth rate is generally low, there is no full compensation for the children not born when women are at a younger age. It is noticeable here that, as with Japan (Coulmas, 2007, p. 9), the percentage of children born out of wedlock is relatively low in Germany compared to percentages in countries like Sweden, Norway, France, or Iceland where higher 'illegitimacy' rates correlate positively with higher fertility rates.

The rapid increase in average life expectancy in Germany recorded until the mid-20th century can to a large extent be attributed to infant and childhood mortality reduction (Federal Statistical Office, 2006, p. 37). Statistical surveys show that in 2004–2006, life expectancy at birth for both sexes combined marked a record high of 79.36 years, with women living longer than men by an average of nearly 5.5 years. According to the base assumption of the 11th coordinated population projection, the average life expectancy at birth in 2050 will be 83.5 years for men and 88.0 years for women (Federal Statistical Office, 2006, p. 41). This future life-expectancy increase has much to do with the continuous improvement of living conditions and improved health care in old age. The population projection shows that the population aged 80 years and over will continuously grow, from about 3.7 million in 2005 to more than 10 million in 2050 (Federal Statistical Office, 2006, p. 23).

Deindustrialisation and Shrinkage in the Ruhr Region: The Socially Integrative City Programme

In accordance with spatial disparities of economic power, until the late 1980s, employment trends in the former West German states were subject to a clear north–south divide (Braun, 2005). The Ruhr region in North Rhine-Westphalia, in particular, has been suffering from long-term changes in its regional economic structure and substantial job losses in the aftermath of the coal and steel crises. After many years of a steady influx of 'guest workers,' the massive restructuring processes required by deindustrialisation have raised issues of population decline and accompanying social problems.

Consisting of 15 mandatory members (11 independent cities, and 4 counties), and comprising a total area of 4,435 km^2 and about 5.3 million people, the Ruhr region is one economic-geographical unit that has experienced these problems firsthand. Since 1993 its population has been declining continuously, and according to estimates by the North Rhine-Westphalian State Office for Data Processing and Statistics (Landesamt für Datenverarbeitung und Statistik Nordrhein-Westfalen, 2006), this trend will continue in the future. Whereas the population in North Rhine-Westphalia (NRW) on average is projected to decline by 2.6 percent, the Ruhr area is scheduled to lose about 9.3 percent of its 2005 population by 2025. The maximum predicted relative population decline can be observed in the city of Gelsenkirchen (-16.3%). Like the situation in many of Japan's regions, the demographic situation of the Ruhr area is notable for its extremely low fertility rates, increasing mortality rates among older people, and ongoing out-migration of well-educated and highly-skilled young people. Hence, the population structure is changing dramatically, with the percentage of people 65 years and older projected to increase from 20.9 percent (NRW: 19.12%) in 2006 to 25.1 percent (NRW: 23.7%) by 2025. These processes show that population decreases in the Ruhr area are not only a quantitative phenomenon; the qualitative effects are even more problematic with regard to endogenous potentials, such as innovation and knowledge, which are critical for maintaining prosperity within a deindustrialising economy.

Concerning the long-lasting and wide-ranging effects of the demographic shift, it is noteworthy that the economy, employment patterns, family structures, health and social care, and education and learning are all affected in one way or another. Moreover, individual and group actors in the political, economic, and social spheres have to be aware of the profound and wide-ranging consequences for spatial development processes and planning policies because growing and shrinking cities and regions within national and continental spaces are on diverging paths. Locally specific pressures require flexible and creative problem-solving strategies and measures—for it is well known among demographers that due to the demographic momentum in Germany and Japan today, population decrease will probably continue for decades even if fertility rates rise again. The management of shrinking processes is therefore not a question of choice, but a challenge that must be met (and that is not new in its historical dimensions; Schwartz, 2006).

Consequently—and within the wider context of a shrinking national population—as both sparsely populated rural-peripheral and old-industrialised regions with severe structural weaknesses (such as the German Ruhr) suffer from the loss and ageing of population, new spatial visions and strategies as well as new forms of regulation are becoming necessary. However, as Sorensen (2007) explained, 'new challenges and demands often require new governance arrangements and institutions, as existing institutions are often unable to carry out new functions, and can even inhibit the establishment of new institutions that can' (p. 60). State authorities in Germany face difficult financial problems and, unable to solve pressing national, regional, and local issues, they have come to realise that a new balance between state action and the self-organisation of citizens is necessary.

In this way, the German federal government's Socially Integrative City (SIC) programme (Becker, Franke, Löhr, & Rösner, 2002) is a major driving force of public-private interaction across Germany and is a possible model for regional governance under conditions of deindustrialisation and shrinkage elsewhere. The programme can be characterised as a district-oriented, participatory, co-operative, and integrative approach to urban regeneration that is based on neighbourhood management, the elaboration of integrated action plans, and the implementation of measures and projects that have a stabilising effect on local economic and social conditions. Because the drafting of integrated action plans is still a domain of bureaucratic actors, however, DiGaetano and Strom's characterisation of the typical German mode of urban governance as 'managerialism' with some elements of corporatism still seems convincing (2003, pp. 384–387). That does not necessarily affect governance functionality adversely, as long as local administrative and political leadership remains open to communicative and collaborative problem-solving strategies (Knorr-Siedow, 2006, p. 482). In urban districts where such important local players as housing companies, local businesses and associations, and neighbourhood citizens have been adequately involved, notable improvements in housing, living, and environmental conditions are being achieved. Hence, it seems appropriate that the federal and state governments in 2007 decided to continue and even extend their financial support for the SIC programme.

Communicative and collaborative problem solving requires (1) the establishment of effective coordination and efficient management institutions, (2) the development of integrated action plans; (3) district-related interdepartmental cooperation within local administration; (4) the establishment of local development agencies coordinating horizontal networking with local actors and vertical networking between 'system' and 'living' worlds, and (4) participatory forums like round-table talks and workshops (Becker et al., 2002). Hence, the strategic objectives of the SIC programme include the following (Roggenthin, 2001, pp. 84–86):

1. Activation and participation of inhabitants and local actors in programme and project planning, implementation, and evaluation.
2. Strengthening of the local economy and improvement of employment within the urban district as a prerequisite for its social stabilisation.
3. Redevelopment and strengthening of urban district centres.

4. Supply of infrastructure for the cultural and social integration of native and immigrant population groups.
5. Improvement of local housing and living conditions.
6. Exchange of experience, evaluation of programme success, and accompanying research.

New neighbourhood-management systems based on horizontally and vertically integrated networks of actors and integrated action plans taking into account all necessary policy and activity fields are essential elements of the SIC programme. Figure 2.2 reveals the case of the city of Duisburg. With regard to neighbourhood management, the 2005–2006 survey conducted by the German Institute of Urban Affairs on the degree of programme implementation within the programme districts reveals that 80 percent of the municipal respondents assess as a critical success factor effective neighbourhood-management structures as a prerequisite for motivating neighbourhood citizen involvement (see Difu, 2007,

FIGURE 2.2. Fields of Activity of the Duisburg Development Agency (EG DU).

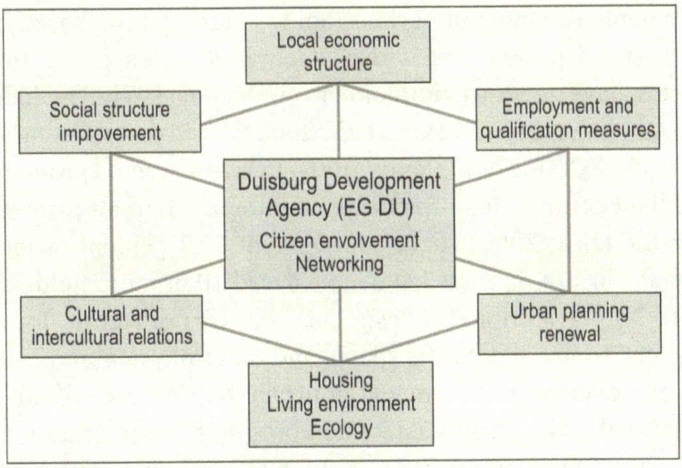

Source. Modified from EG DU (2008).

p. 147). Organisational forms of neighbourhood management are diverse, ranging from traditional top-down approaches with limited local actor participation to bottom-up approaches with grassroots neighbourhood experts playing a central role. The process of citizen activation primarily involves 'project-unrelated, informal procedures, mostly addressed directly to people' (Becker et al., 2002). In the case of Duisburg, this kind of neighbourhood management (*Ortsteilmanagement*) has proven to be quite effective. *Ortsteilmanagement* initiates and coordinates neighbourhood meetings, it organizes festivals and campaigns, counselling services, talks, information stands and public relations work, contact and networking with residents; and it takes responsibility for conflict management. Thus far, however, some population groups, such as in-migrants, ethnic German immigrants and long-term unemployed persons have hardly been reached. These groups require special attention, for example in developing group-specific modes of participation and counselling services tailored to their particular requirements (Difu, 2007, p. 167).

Community empowerment and participation are strengths of the programme, which follows a social-space-centred approach integrating different policy fields rather than a sectoral approach to urban improvement. The most important tool for participation based on more or less planned procedures is the 'integrated action plans' that local authorities have to draft, implement, and update with residents and other local players (see Becker et al., 2002). Even for planning experts, however, the extreme complexity of the task is a serious problem. Concerning the central fields of activity of integrated urban district development, the Difu (2007) survey shows that 77.3 percent of integrated action plans in 174 districts have considered 10 or more fields of activity (table 2.1). Traditional investment measures related to local housing markets, living and public space, and other physical improvements as tools to develop enhancements in urban districts are still necessary, but individual skills improvement and progress on integration and networking by means of noninvestment measures are becoming much more important (Difu, 2007, p. 165). Moreover, measures to soften the

TABLE 2.1. Fields of Activity Considered in the Integrated Action Plans of the Socially Integrative City Programme Districts 2005/2006.

Field of activity	Absolute figures	Relative figures
Living and public space	217	96.4
Social activities and infrastructure	216	96.0
Image and public relations	198	88.0
Neighbourhood coexistence	182	80.9
Employment, qualification and training	180	80.0
Local housing market and housing industry	176	78.2
District schools and education	174	77.3
Integration of migrants	173	76.9
District culture	168	74.7
Local economy	160	71.1
Transportation	159	70.7
Sports and leisure	154	68.4
Empowerment, articulation, political involvement	108	48.0
Security and crime prevention	107	47.6
Promotion of disadvantaged people	89	39.6
Environmental protection	84	37.3
Health care and health promotion	75	33.3
Evaluation of process and result	59	26.2
Monitoring	57	25.3
Others	16	7.1

Source. Difu (2007, p. 44).

negative images of disadvantaged neighbourhoods and to counteract stigmatisation and social exclusion are also significant aspects of the process of improvement.

The interconnection of the different fields is quite well developed in some of the problematic Duisburg districts, but the city fails to systematically implement district-specific integrated action plans and strategies in citywide development approaches, so as to avoid isolated planning. The possibility that tendencies towards fragmentation and exclusion will be further strengthened should be considered within a citywide context. Integrating activities need to be further intensified because the integrative approach is the centrepiece of the programme.

The Difu (2007) evaluation of the degree of programme implementation within the Socially Integrative City programme districts also hints at finance as the third crucial success factor. The complexity of problems in many programme districts requires strong financial support. Because of the precarious financial situation of most municipalities and the limited resources available directly through the SIC programme, gaining additional resources from various European Union and federal state-support programmes associated with investment and noninvestment measures for urban district development and related policy areas is essential; this is *resource pooling* on the basis of integrated action plans, a key element of the SIC programme (Becker et al., 2002). Evaluation results show that the municipal and urban district levels are most important for such resource-pooling activities, but local neighbourhood-management organisations in charge of fundraising coordination are frequently understaffed and unable to cope with the variety of claims on their attention. One reason is that funding programmes lack harmonisation because the vertical organisation of government departments still dominates administrative behaviour. Because this is a difficult structural problem, more detailed information about how to obtain additional funds and pool resources through targeted counselling—as well as further training services provided by the states—appears to be needed in order to sustain programme financing (see Difu, 2007, p. 166). The awarding of financial resources should encourage creative ideas and concepts and thus contribute to enhancing quality standards that are subject to continuous programme evaluation and monitoring. Good-practice analysis and evaluation are, of course, essential to making the necessary programme adjustments on the basis of municipal experiences true to the current spatial planning principle of 'more campaigns and projects instead of programmes and planning' (BMVBS & BBR, 2006).

Because the future liveability of regional environments is a highly complex issue, accepting 'shrinkage as a new potential' (Oswalt, 2005, p. 13) and propagating development approaches (such as the SIC programme) offer ways out of the shrinkage dilemma that do not equate to a restoration of the growth paradigm. Measures and projects can be embedded within a broader vision for a citywide—and even regionwide—managed stability. In fact, problems such as unemployment, welfare dependence, and education and qualification deficits are not necessarily and exclusively caused locally. Many policy areas affected by these problems are beyond municipal jurisdiction and must be tackled by overarching macroeconomic and macrosocial policies in areas like labour, business, education, housing, immigration, and integration that only programmes like the SIC can include. Because the problems are complex and interrelated, the focus is not on isolated subjects or districts but on their integral place in the broader context of citywide, regionwide, and nationwide structures and processes. Thus the discussion about shrinking cities in Germany is illustrative with respect to the search for local and structural causes of shrinkage in Japan and with respect to the opportunities and limits for action strategies at the district level.

With regard to issues relating to social and ethnic cohesion, socially integrative development programmes are an important instrument for overcoming negative neighbourhood externalities and preserving the city as an integrating entity. In terms of sustainability, these development programmes must counteract problematic local economic conditions (job losses, poor infrastructure services, urban blight), social conditions (education, vandalism, insecurity), and environmental conditions (noise and air pollution, lack of greenery)—including neighbourhood mood, lack of individual perspectives, and image and perception problems.

Consequently, in terms of regional planning, the emerging discourse about the Rhine-Ruhr area as a European Metropolitan Region (EMR) is closely connected with the accelerating processes of European integration and globalisation (BMVBS & BBR, 2006, pp. 40–44; Blotevogel & Schmitt, 2006). Individual cities pursuing national and international competitiveness are in need of coordination and co-operation within a context of urban agglomeration in order to develop joint responsibility and solidarity. Against this background, the concept of European metropolitan regions has an outstanding strategic role for future economic growth and global competitiveness. Blotevogel and Schmitt (2006, p. 69) argued that the Rhine Ruhr area is 'a complex arena covering multiple interests, identities and prospects,' often resulting in rivalry between cities. The various potentials for conflict do indeed complicate intermunicipal co-operation and networking. But within the worldwide competitive economic environment, there is a great need for collaboration and joint strategic action that will benefit the region as a whole (van Houtum and Langendijk, 2001, p. 759). For the cities along the Ruhr, the *metropoleruhr* business-development agency coordinates such joint action, at least to some extent. This agency is an RVR–associated (*Regionalverband Ruhr*, Ruhr Regional Association) limited company responsible for all kinds of regional marketing and economic promotion activities that contribute to the restructuring and modernisation of the economic base of the Ruhr area. It is also involved in the European Capital of Culture Ruhr.2010 project, which envisions the building of a new metropolitan identity. That the economically strong cities along the Rhine are not included in these activities makes clear that the potential for a European Metropolitan Region Rhine-Ruhr is not yet fully recognised by the local and regional stakeholders (Blotevogel & Schmitt, 2006).

Apart from that struggle, the concept of European metropolitan regions is a two-sided vision of spatial planning. On the one hand, it identifies new chances for regions like the Rhine-Ruhr area that are part of a particular metropolitan region in the context of globalisation. On the other hand, it is risky with regard to the long-lasting general principle of equivalent regional living conditions as laid down in the Spatial Planning Law in accordance with the Basic Law of the Federal Republic of Germany (BMVBS & BBR, 2006).

Having explored the effects of and responses to shrinkage in a deindustrialising urban area in central Europe, and having considered evidence of a shift in consciousness towards viewing depopulation as a possible incentive to improve the quality of life for remaining residents,

we now turn to analysing approaches to regional shrinkage in Europe's rural periphery: the Highlands and Islands of Scotland.

Creating Thriving Communities? Migration in Rural Scotland

The impact of globalisation, population changes, and the growth in urban populations all raise important questions for scholars and policy makers, including questions about the relationship between urban and rural locales and about spatial disparities at the supranational—that is, continental and global—scale. Changes in the size and structure of populations are closely linked to economic development, education, social welfare, health, and other services, which in turn affect peoples' lives irrespective of their places of residence. As in Japan, in Germany and Scotland (and in the European Union more generally), the growing population of older people, fertility rates below the replacement level, a potential shortage of working-age population, and the tendency for younger people to leave rural areas all have a particular resonance (de Lima & Wright, 2009).

Many rural areas in the United Kingdom are characterised by the prevalence of sectors such as agriculture, tourism, and food processing, which offer seasonal work, low pay, and poor employment conditions to local people (Commission for Rural Communities, 2007; Green & Hardill, 2003). When juxtaposed with negative overall population trends, these labour-market characteristics have consequences for the economy, welfare policies, and the sustainability of rural communities (particularly in remote rural areas such as the Scottish Highlands and Islands), and they have given rise to a range of debates and policy responses. On the question of strategies for creating thriving rural communities or fostering—to use the Japanese expression—revitalisation, a wide spectrum of proposals has emerged in the Scottish rural context. These have included strategies for stemming the outflow of younger people and for encouraging immigrants and migrant workers to fill labour-market shortages, as well as strategies to encourage older people to extend their labour-force participation. Overall, these approaches fit within a traditional growth paradigm which, to a great extent, assumes that improvements in material living standards are

an essential and basic priority for government and communities and that, moreover, continued economic expansion is dependent on an unbreakable relationship with a stable or growing labour supply.

Context: Demographic Trends and Policy

The population of the United Kingdom was 61,792,000 in mid-2009, representing an increase of 394,000 (0.6%) since mid-2008 (Office for National Statistics, 2010a); much of this increase is attributable to net inward migration. In the 12 months between 1 July 2008 and 30 June 2009, Scotland also experienced a 25,500 person (0.5%) increase in its population, reaching 5.19 million, due mainly to net in-migration from the rest of the United Kingdom and (increasingly) from overseas (ONS, 2010a, p. 7; General Register Office for Scotland, 2010, p. 9). Leaving aside the contribution of immigration, to the extent that the United Kingdom's and Scotland's general population development echoes both those of Japan and those of other European countries, there are currently an ageing population and below-replacement fertility rates combined with high levels of out-migration by younger people, and these trends affect remote rural areas of Scotland in particular (table 2.2; Jamieson & Groves, 2008; ONS, 2010a; ONS, 2010b; ONS, 2010c). Overall, the Scottish fertility rate is currently lower than the UK average, at 1.77 children per woman in 2009, in contrast to the provisional UK Total Fertility Rate of 1.94 (ONS, 2010c). The UK population is projected to increase by 4.3 million by 2018 (ONS, 2009). However, the Scottish increase is predicted to be the lowest in the United Kingdom at 4 percent, in contrast to 7 percent for England and Northern Ireland and 5 percent for Wales; this discrepancy stems from lower fertility and life-expectancy rates in Scotland. Most of the natural increase is assumed to be due to net inward migration, whereby first-generation immigrants are expected to have higher fertility rates than indigenous populations.

In contrast to Germany, where there is greater emphasis on developing adaptation approaches to shrinkage, policy discourses in Scotland have consistently privileged strategies for promoting regional and national growth. Since 1999 policy-led discussions on emigration and immigration

TABLE 2.2. Internal Population Change and Migration in Scotland by Geographic Area, 2007.

	Remote Rural	Accessible Rural	Rest of Scotland
Natural Reproduction (2007)			
Births(2007)	2,957	6.508	48,316
Crude Birth Rate (per 1,000 pop.)	9	11	11
Deaths (2007)	3,284	4,207	48,495
Crude Death Rate	10	7	12
Migration (2007/8)			
Net migration	2,274	10,021	7,681
Net Migration as % of population	0.7%	1.6%	0.2%
Total Immigration	20,661	44,064	109,061

Source. Scottish Government (2010), table 3. Data from General Register Office for Scotland (using Scottish Government Urban Rural Classification, 2007–2008).

in Scotland generally, and in Scottish rural areas in particular, have taken place against a background of concerns about the consequences of a declining and ageing population for the economy—skills gaps and labour shortages in particular (Crichton, 2004; Denholm, 2004). These concerns have led to a strong emphasis since the late 1990s on growing the population in Scotland and on developing initiatives and conducting research into ways people from overseas might be attracted into Scotland and its rural regions (de Lima & Wright, 2009; Wright, 2006). A number of high-profile campaigns such as Fresh Talent (Scottish Executive, 2004) and One Scotland, Many Cultures were funded by the then Scottish Executive to address skills shortages and to counter negative attitudes towards overseas migrants and minority ethnic groups living in Scotland. Launched in 2004, the Fresh Talent Initiative included collaboration with Work Permits UK (WPUK) and provided opportunities for overseas students studying at Scottish universities to stay in Scotland for two years after they had graduated (Scottish Executive, 2005). This scheme was incorporated into the UK Border Agency's revised immigration scheme, called Tier 1 Post-Study Work, which allows international students who have studied in the United Kingdom to stay on after graduation and look for work (United Kingdom Border Agency, 2010). With a new Coalition Government elected in the UK in 2010 and continued economic uncertainty, this scheme is liable to be discontinued.

Alongside initiatives at the UK and Scottish levels, regional development agencies such as Highlands and Islands Enterprise (HIE) have also emphasised the importance of attracting and retaining people in remote and rural regions of the Highlands and Islands. It identified five factors as crucial to success: 'population, place, productivity, pay and prospects' (HIE, 2005, p. 9). HIE aspires to increase the population of the region to half a million by 2025, noting that 'more people living, working and studying in the Highlands and Islands are essential to sustaining our long-term progress' (HIE, 2005, p. 9). These discourses and strategic developments coincided with European Union enlargement in May 2004 and the entry of Accession 8 country nationals (Czech Republic, Estonia, Latvia, Lithuania, Hungary, Poland, Slovakia, and Slovenia) and Accession 2 country nationals (Romania and Bulgaria) in January 2007 into the UK labour force (de Lima & Wright 2009; Rolfe & Metcalf, 2009).

In May 2007, following the election of a minority government in Scotland led by the Scottish Nationalist Party, the Scottish government's focus on what it refers to as 'increasing sustainable economic growth' has provided the organising framework for its activities and target setting, including promoting population growth (Scottish Government, 2007). Population growth is presented as 'a key contributor to, and consequence of, a more vibrant society and a more dynamic economy' and the government has set itself a target 'to match average European (EU-15) population growth over the period from 2007 to 2017, supported by increased healthy life expectancy in Scotland over this period' (Scottish Government, 2007, p. 16). In addition to exploring issues such as influencing fertility rates, encouraging inward migration has played a central role in policy discussions (Wright, 2006). The assumption that a successful economy is predicated on a growing population, and vice versa, is deeply embedded in Scottish policy discourses, as are concerns about the consequences of a declining population—leading to the 2009 announcement by the Economic and Social Research Council that it would promote research into these issues.

> While many European countries are experiencing falling birth rates and an ageing population, the demographic challenges facing Scotland are particularly demanding. An ageing and declining population has important implications for public services, the labour market and the quality of everyday life. Current population trends therefore pose important policy questions, argues Professor Ian Diamond, Chief Executive of the ESRC: 'What implications does changing population have for the Scottish economy? Why is the population in Scotland falling when no other EU country is experiencing a similar decline? What can the government do to influence trends of migration and childbearing, to enable people to have the children they want at the time they want?' (Economic and Social Research Council, 2009)

Migration Experiences in Rural Scotland

Scotland is the United Kingdom's northernmost country and is considered highly rural in character, home to many small and remote communities. With its very diverse geography, rural Scotland accounts for 19 percent of the country's population dispersed across 94 percent of its land area. The rest of Scotland accounts for 82 percent of the population but only 6 percent of the land area (Scottish Government, 2010, p. 6). Though it is recognised that immigration into the United Kingdom and Scotland is largely an urban phenomenon, there is some acknowledgement of the changing trends in general UK migration settlement patterns.

> New immigrants with less established networks and patterns of settlement tend to be drawn to locations with a wider range of employment opportunities—principally to London but also to small towns and mid-sized cities (for instance to work in construction), coastal and other leisure-centred localities (where they might engage in hospitality and catering services) and rural areas

> (usually for short-term jobs in agriculture and food processing). (Vertovec, 2006, p. 22)

May 2004 marked an important turning point for inward migration from outside the United Kingdom into rural areas, largely due to the European Union's enlargement and the inclusion of Eastern European countries from the former Soviet bloc. In contrast with previous predominant migration trends to urban centres, rural areas (hitherto unused to immigration from overseas) began attracting migrant workers from Eastern Europe on a scale not previously experienced. Hence, inward migration has played a larger part in Scotland's demographic change than in previous decades. Moreover, this immigration trend has increased the importance of high-quality statistics on migration and the population, for policy development and for planning and providing public services (GROS, 2010, p. 61).

In the context of a current lack of robust and reliable data on migration in Scotland and its impact, much of the research has tended to focus on qualitative research and overall UK data where available (GROS, 2010; Rolfe & Metcalf, 2009). Research on migration in rural areas of Scotland since 2004 has suggested that EU enlargement has led to a strong flow of migrant workers from Central and Eastern Europe, more specifically from Poland to northern Scottish rural areas such as Grampian, the Highlands and Islands, and the Scottish Borders (Aitken, 2006; BSolutions, 2005; Citizens Advice Bureau, 2005; CRC, 2007; de Lima, Jentsch, & Whelton, 2005; de Lima, Chaudhry, Whelton, & Arshad, 2007; Scottish Economic Research, 2006). Drawing on data gathered for a study undertaken in Grampian (table 2.3; de Lima et al., 2007),[2] National Insurance registrations (NINo) in Scotland had increased by 185 percent, with registration by the Scottish proportion of UK overseas nationals increasing from 4.2 percent (14,520) in 2002/2003 to 6.2 percent (41,370) in 2005/2006. This increase occurred mainly in 2004/2005 with an almost 50 percent increase from 2003 to 2004 and in 2005/2006 with a 73 percent increase from 2004 to 2005 (de Lima et al., 2007, p. 21). The biggest increase was attributed to the Accession 8 immigrants. The majority of Accession 8 immigrant workers were of Polish origin, with

TABLE 2.3. NINo Registrations in Scotland and Selected Regions.

	UK	Scotland	Grampian	Aberdeen City	Aberdeen-shire	Moray
2002/3	349,240	14,520	1,850	1,430	330	90
2003/4	370,750	15,500	2,120	1,530	420	170
2004/5	439,730	22,850	3,450	2,220	920	310
2005/6	662,390	41,370	5,980	3,860	1,590	530
Total	1,822,110	94,240	13,400	9,040	3,260	1,100

Source. de Lima et al. (2007, p. 21).
Note. Department for Work and Pensions NINo data were rounded at source, to the nearest 10 for 2002/2003, 2003/2004, and 2005/2006, and to the nearest 5 for 2004/2005.

smaller numbers from the other countries (Lithuania, Latvia, Slovakia, and the Czech Republic), as well as from outside the European Union (table 2.4). This trend is confirmed by others using Worker Registration Scheme (WRS) data for the United Kingdom, such as Gilpin, Henty, Lemo, Portes, and Bullen (2006, p. 14), who found that migrants from Poland formed the majority (58%) of WRS applicants, followed by those from Lithuania (14%) and Slovakia (11%). The predominance of Polish workers can be attributed to the fact that Poland is the largest accession state with the weakest labour market in the European Union.

The Grampian and other studies (Aitken, 2006; BSolutions, 2005; Gilpin et al., 2006; de Lima et al., 2005) also confirmed that the majority of migrants from the Accession 8 countries have tended to be single and aged between 20 and 45 years. Though the main motivation for migration is economic, learning English and experiencing a different culture are also important motivations. However, despite their good qualifications, many migrants end up employed in semiskilled and unskilled work in a limited range of sectors—typically food processing, agriculture, construction, hospitality and tourism, and social and health care—as reflected in the Grampian study, which was based on a small sample of employers (table 2.5).

Thus most migrant workers have worked in sectors and jobs for which employers have encountered difficulties in recruiting local labour due

TABLE 2.4. NINo Registrations in Grampian by Selected Nationalities, All Study Years.

	2002/3	2003/4	2004/5	2005/6	
				No.	Percent
Czech Rep	0	0	70	140	2.3
Latvia	0	0	240	390	6.5
Lithuania	0	10	220	520	8.7
Poland	20	60	490	1720	28.8
Slovak Rep	0	0	40	130	2.2
Estonia	0	0	50	50	0.8
Hungary	0	0	10	60	1.0
Eire	100	100	120	120	2.0
France	110	90	120	130	2.2
Germany	60	70	90	120	2.0
Italy	30	50	20	50	0.8
Netherlands	60	80	50	80	1.3
Portugal	70	150	140	120	2.0
Spain	30	50	70	80	1.3
China	80	130	180	210	3.5
India	180	180	270	480	8.0
Malaysia	60	100	80	100	1.7
Philippines	20	70	80	60	1.0
Nigeria	90	130	190	260	4.3
S. Africa	100	70	80	120	2.0
Australia	110	80	70	120	2.0
Canada	70	70	90	80	1.3
USA	80	80	90	90	1.5

Source. de Lima et al. (2007, p. 26).

to the perceptions amongst potential local employees of such work as dirty, difficult, and poorly paid. Qualitative research shows that employers in rural areas perceive migrant workers as an important part of the

TABLE 2.5. Immigrant Workers as a Proportion of the Workforce by Area and Industry.

Industry	Grampian	Aberdeen	Aberdeenshire	Moray
All Industries	18 (1,573)	11 (444)	18 (676)	23 (453)
Tourism/Hospitality	23 (236)	21 (163)	28 (67)	24 (6)
Construction	6.4 (81)	6.0 (38)	4.5 (19)	11 (24)
Food Processing	31 (924)	41 (123)	34 (501)	25 (300)
Nursing & Care	7.6 (99)	7.9 (34)	7.5 (65)	-
Agriculture	80 (82)	-	-	80 (82)
Oil & Engineering	3.4 (28)	5.6 (7)	3.0 (21)	-
Other	8.9 (123)	7.8 (79)	20 (3)	12 (41)

Source. de Lima et al. (2007, table 4, p. 30).
Note. Survey sample: 61 employers. Source: de Lima et al., 2007, table 4, p. 30.

workforce and in some cases attribute their own ability to stay in business to the availability of migrant labour. The productivity and work ethic of migrant workers was also viewed positively by employers when compared to the potential workforce locally, as reflected by the following comments made by an employer in Grampian: 'The Poles are so hard-working they put the British workers to shame. It's so sad that they are qualified nurses who have to hide their training and skills to work as carers. The care sector could not manage without them' (de Lima et al., 2007, p. 35).

However, on the question of whether migrant workers benefit the local economy, the evidence is mixed. The same Grampian employer also said, 'The economy of the North-East of Scotland has definitely been helped by migrant workers. However, they send most of their money home so do not spend it here' (de Lima et al., 2007, p. 35). Overall, employment for migrant workers has been characterised by short-term contracts, minimum pay, and long and irregular patterns of working. Although the short-term nature of employment makes planning difficult, in general it would appear that some migrant workers have been prepared to participate in low-skilled and underwhelming work tasks in order to earn more than they would in their own countries (Anderson, Ruhs, Rogaly, & Spencer, 2006). One migrant worker commented, 'Money is the main reason, the situation in Poland is not so good … many people can't get jobs. There are so many adverts in the local newspapers that Scotland needs us, so I think to myself I can come here and earn more money' (de Lima et al., 2007, p. 41). However, others expressed serious dissatisfaction because their qualifications are not being recognised; another migrant worker commented, 'It is depressing to be in this situation. I have a degree in systems engineering and this qualification is needed in Scotland but they will not take me because I have a degree from another country' (de Lima et al., 2007, p. 40).

In addition to their labour-market-entry difficulties, migrant workers tend to have access to a limited range of services and to experience social exclusion, in particular in the following three areas:

1. There is a general lack of easily available information on entitlements and services for immigrants and a lack of understanding about how to navigate systems and procedures in a new country.
2. Language and communication issues presented one of the main barriers to accessing information and services. Overall, accessing language provision in rural areas can be problematic due to limited provision and lack of transport, as well as difficulties in attendance at classes given long and irregular working hours.
3. Accommodation is often inadequate, with migrants experiencing overcrowding, multiple occupancies, and generally poor quality accommodation (including being housed in low-demand areas), as well as the tendency for landlords to charge high rents for poor quality housing. (Aitken, 2006; CAB, 2005; de Lima et al., 2005; de Lima et al., 2007; McKay & Winkelman-Gleed, 2005)

Accommodation issues are exacerbated particularly in areas where severe housing shortages already exist. Qualitative research in local rural communities in the North of Scotland (de Lima et al., 2005; de Lima & Wright, 2009) has shown that migrant workers tend to live in privately rented accommodation that is often overpriced. Furthermore, a review of research suggests that tied accommodation (provided by the employer) is particularly relevant in rural areas (Rolfe & Metcalf, 2008, pp. 32–33) and can expose migrants to sudden homelessness if their employment ceases (de Lima et al., 2007). Rolfe and Metcalf also suggested that there has been some evidence of homelessness for short periods amongst Accession 8 migrants (2008, p. 33). Service providers involved in the Grampian study suggested that there needed to be more central support from the then Scottish Executive with the injection of more funds to councils to improve the housing situation, as the following service provider stated: '[The local authorities] are overwhelmed … I hear horror stories of fifteen, twenty people living in small flats, swapping beds as shifts end … the Executive is not pumping enough money, this is secondary discrimination, migrant workers are being treated differently' (de Lima et al., 2007, p. 73). This potentially conflicting position between local authorities at the regional level and the national government in Scotland in relation to extra funding of services as a result of increased migration is taken up in what follows.

Migrants' work patterns often leave them limited time for activities involving interaction with local communities outside their workplace. In areas such as the Grampians and the Scottish Highlands and Islands, communication issues, distance, lack of transport, and a 'drink culture' prevalent in some communities also pose barriers for social interaction, despite the friendliness of local individuals (de Lima et al., 2005; de Lima et al., 2007). One migrant worker stated that 'parties are better in Slovakia … people don't just sit around and eat and drink but play music and dance … we like to dance a lot. People in Scotland are a bit conservative' (de Lima et al., 2007, p. 52). There are, however, examples of migrants socialising with others from within their ethnic groups—for example Poles meeting through church attendance (de Lima et al., 2007)—but this requires a critical mass of people from similar ethnic or cultural backgrounds living within a specific area.

Rural service providers have themselves faced particular challenges in responding to an increase in migrant workers. In Grampian, service providers were concerned that the increased number of migrants was not leading to a commensurate increase in resources from the government for specialist service provision, such as interpretation and translation and English language instruction, and that the government also did not take into consideration the extra staff time required to address migrants' needs (de Lima et al., 2007). Although data on the increased resource needs and provision posed by migration on local authorities in general are difficult to come by, this has not stopped some authorities from lobbying for extra funding, as reflected in the statement made by Sandy Bruce-Lockhart, chair of the Local Government Association (2006) in England: 'This [lack of accurate figures on migrant numbers] could pose severe problems in the future as services get cut, or council tax has to rise disproportionately for the growing migrant population' (BBC, 2006).

Increased migration to areas in Scotland with little experience of dealing with overseas migrants has also led to varying views on the Scottish government's policy of encouraging immigration and the realities of providing services at regional levels. A service provider commented, '[The Scottish Executive] are very keen to call people here but there is nothing, no support for them when they get here' (de Lima et al., 2007, p. 66). Responding to these debates about the impact on public services, Sriskandarajah (2006) argued that it is important to acknowledge local authorities' point about central government funding formulas being unresponsive to the arrival of new immigrants, but he also suggested that it is equally important to acknowledge that immigrants have been critical to the delivery of public services, such as health and education.

In addition to issues of funding, a combination of a lack of established networks and the nature of work patterns (long and irregular hours, shift working) has been cited by service providers as creating particular challenges in their capacity to access migrant workers and develop relationships with them. Developing language provision based on economies of scale for all skill levels and recruiting appropriate staff also pose particular challenges in rural areas, given the issues related to funding constraints already described. Overall, service providers also struggled to understand the service entitlements and rights of migrant workers due to changing immigration rules and associated entitlements and rights. The challenges faced by rural authorities have been reinforced by the lack of infrastructure for addressing the needs of a growing and culturally diverse population and lack of experience and skills for dealing with migration amongst rural service providers compared to urban authorities. Despite these challenges and despite the funding constraints, rural local authorities have been making efforts at responding to the changing situation through the development of 'welcome packs' intended to increase provision of English language instruction for immigrants, for example (de Lima et al., 2007).

Nevertheless, the dominant policy discourses on social inclusion and integration in relation to migrants have tended to emphasise the need for migrants themselves to adapt to their new circumstances, while ignoring the relational aspects of social exclusion. Thus social inclusion has to be perceived as a two way process requiring migrants to adapt and the communities to ensure that barriers to inclusion are removed (Rudiger & Spencer, 2003). Initiatives designed to attract migrants into rural areas are not in themselves enough, and there is a need for greater focus on retention strategies that address social exclusion and on positive, successful inclusion in communities. This means focusing on economic as well as social, political, and civic inclusion; recognising the economic and wider contributions that migrants are making; and focusing on capacity building within communities in rural areas for living in increasingly diverse and changing conditions. Evidence suggests that current circumstances have some way to go before achieving successful inclusion of migrants (de Lima & Wright, 2009; Rolfe & Metcalf, 2008), and in this context it is difficult to predict the extent to which migrants will be willing to tolerate such unfavourable circumstances. This is reflected in concerns expressed about the capacity of local authorities to provide a wider range of employment and services that would make rural areas attractive to migrants (de Lima & Wright, 2009; Rolfe & Metcalf, 2009). In addition, the frequently changing legislative context of immigration is often confusing and itself influences the nature of the migrant population (e.g., skilled or unskilled, from Europe or elsewhere, and so on). The dominant tendency until now has been to focus on migrant workers as a homogenous and needy group and direct little effort at understanding or acknowledging the impact of migration on the quality of life for local rural residents, or at considering the resulting quality of life for migrants, especially where there is competition for resources such as housing and well-paid local employment (de Lima & Wright, 2009).

The effect migrants have on the economy and on society in general is highly contested and difficult to assess without robust numerical data or consistent time-sensitive measurement methodologies. Overall, evidence for the real impact of migration-driven population growth for the United Kingdom and Scottish economies in general, and of rural areas in particular, is scarce, but when it exists it tends to be equivocal (Select Committee on Economic Affairs, 2008). Macrolevel studies and reviews suggest, variously, that migration affects unemployment, wages, and output and that inflation may result in lower prices for consumers (Rolfe & Metcalf, 2009). The House of Lords Select Committee on Economic Affairs, in an assessment of the economic impact of migrants, recognised both sides of the argument about the impact of migration but concluded 'that the economic benefits to the resident population of net immigration are small, especially in the long run. Of course, many immigrants make a valuable contribution to the UK. But the real issue is how much net immigration is desirable' (Select Committee on Economic Affairs, 2008, p. 6).

Rolfe and Metcalf (2009) also acknowledged that it is difficult to assess the economic impact of migrant workers at local levels. In general, the evidence seems inconclusive; a small number of studies have suggested there are no significant adverse impacts on the employment of local workers or wage levels, whereas other studies have suggested some small downward pressures on local wage levels. Much of the discussion of the positive effects of migrant workers in many of the locally commissioned studies on the subject by public bodies (Aitken, 2006; de Lima et al., 2005; de Lima et al., 2007; SER, 2006) has tended to privilege the views of employers and policy makers in government and in regional development agencies that have a strong interest in promoting and supporting research that reinforces their continuing attachment to the growth paradigm. Voices promoting alternative paradigms, such as planning for shrinkage and enhancing quality of life and equity for the existing rural population and communities, are inaudible or absent in Scottish discourse. Overall, therefore, the situation of rural migrants in Scotland is dynamic and remains dependent on local labour-market needs, as well as on global and national events and policies arising from, for example, the 2009 economic crisis and the implications of the UK Government Spending Review in October 2010.

Accordingly, the extent to which migrants—Accession 8 migrants in particular—are making a vital contribution to sustaining or creating thriving rural communities in Scotland is difficult to assess; the necessary data are simply not available. Even the evidence that does exist is often ambiguous and equivocal, leading to the conclusion that as many problems as benefits arise from a strategy of attracting overseas migrants to depopulating and predominantly rural locales, even if incomers are from relatively proximate countries and cultures. Inevitably, these problems come with associated economic and social costs, both to the indigenous and immigrant communities, and it is therefore by no means clear that immigration could be an effective revitalisation strategy for managing the difficulties experienced by shrinking regions in Europe or Japan.

Conclusion

In the coming decades, as the population in Japan's regions ages and declines still further, and as regional urban centres come under increasing strain due to the overall ageing and shrinking of the national population and the continuing concentration of functions in core metropolitan regions, immigration to Japan will increasingly be seen as a necessary and perhaps even as an unavoidable tool within a policy mix geared towards revitalisation and growth. Indeed, immigration may come to be seen as a necessary policy response simply in order to keep some regions functioning and to avoid collapse. If immigration to Japan's regions becomes widespread, then the immigrants themselves will almost undoubtedly come from nearby Asian countries, such as China. The case of Scotland is instructive here because, in contrast to the wave of immigration into Europe from the former colonies during the 1960s and 1970s, most recent immigrants to rural Scotland have come from Eastern Europe and, like Chinese immigrants to Japan, share some superficial cultural and ethnic similarities with their new communities.

In both Scotland and Japan, the emptying out of rural communities predates the arrival of immigrants. In Scotland, this population decline has in some locales produced a situation in which service providers, themselves previously run down economically, are unable to provide adequate services for incoming groups, opening up space for disagreements over local resource allocations and preventing proper integration of immigrant groups into local communities. From the perspective of policy makers and some resident populations in Scotland, increased immigration into their communities has often been seen as a welcome opportunity for regenerating regional economies. This approach has, among some residents and service providers, set up an unfortunate frame of mind in which immigrants are welcome only in so far as they can provide useful solutions to local labour shortage and economic problems. Communities are sometimes surprised to find themselves in the position of having to provide additional social services for these incoming groups.

Conversely, immigrants will almost certainly have recently left regions of the world where the social, economic, and political problems are more pressing than those of their new communities. Many will have left behind families and friends who are themselves in need of help; others will wish to bring dependent family members with them. In these circumstances, it is therefore understandably jarring for immigrants who need assistance to find themselves excluded from both full access to local services and warm acceptance into their new locales. If not properly and sensitively handled, this situation is likely to become a possible source of resentment and even of conflict between communities and immigrant groups because of differences in the expectations each group holds in terms of their social and economic roles.

Regional Japan faces various trajectories of future experience; the cases of Germany and Scotland represent only two of these. The Scottish approach, on the one hand, is growth oriented and carries with it possibilities already discussed. Germany, on the other hand, has taken another route and realistically accepted current circumstances by managing decline in order to stabilise communities; discussions are even taking place as to the potential opportunities and advantages that might accrue from shrinkage (Gatzweiler, Meyer, & Milbert, 2003; Kil, 2004; Oswalt, 2005).

In this book we argue, therefore, that within the worldwide context of shrinking regions, the most important requirement is confronting and considering in a dispassionate, realistic, and humane manner the underlying assumptions that guide strategies for dealing with depopulation and its associated economic and social outcomes. In Japan, as well as in Europe, is rigid adherence to economic expansion appropriate as the fundamental guiding principle for regional policy and its implementation in an age when concerns for quality of life extend beyond the economic domain to the significance—for individuals and communities—of culture and human and ecological relationships? Is it possible that the quality of regional, community, family, and individual life can be enhanced by fracturing the apparently unbreakable bond between population growth and economic expansion and by accepting, even embracing, the inevitability of regional shrinkage and treating it as an opportunity to be seized?

In the following chapters, we approach the issue of Japan's shrinking regions from the perspectives outlined here and in the introductory materials, thus making our contribution to answering the following questions: What are the characteristics, impacts, and implications of regional shrinkage for Japan's government and people? What have been some of the responses proposed thus far? And what is the most appropriate response to regional shrinkage for Japan in the 21st century?

CHAPTER 3

THE HISTORICAL ARC OF REGIONAL SHRINKAGE IN JAPAN*

INTRODUCTION

This is the first of three chapters that examine the characteristics, impacts, and implications of depopulation in Japan's regions. We focus here on the history of regional shrinkage in the modern and contemporary periods; we relate this to the wider context of Japan's political economy and to present-day economic conditions in peripheral areas. The chapter opens with a description of the general circumstances and national policy context that frames the emergence of rural and regional depopulation as a national problem in postwar Japan. We then introduce demographic data on Japan's population development, starting at the time of the country's emergence as a modern industrial nation-state in the late 19th and early 20th centuries and finishing with population

*The principal contributing authors to this chapter are Andrew David, Peter Matanle, and Sachie Mizohata.

projected through 2030. From there we consider in more detail the regional level by examining the case of Niigata Prefecture, which at the start of the country's modernisation was Japan's largest prefecture by population. The data and analysis lead us to conclude that, in the context of a rapid and sustained postwar expansion of the national population, an interdependent process of urban concentration and regional decline has been taking place simultaneously at the national, prefectural, and local settlement levels, as comparatively larger and more densely populated centres draw people in from peripheral areas of the country, the prefecture, and the community. The chapter closes with a description of general economic and employment trends in Kōchi, one of Japan's most peripheral prefectures and one that, like many similar regions, is experiencing simultaneous population ageing and shrinkage and relative economic decline.

Our research suggests that the postwar circumstances of urban growth and regional shrinkage are now reaching their limits, and a new dynamic is beginning to emerge. The analysis from Niigata shows that as the national population decline becomes manifest, local depopulation processes appear to be broadening geographically from outlying rural areas and small towns to regional urban centres, as well. Moreover, the data from Kōchi appear to indicate that this dynamic is accompanied by declines in overall economic performance and worsening employment conditions that together form a recursive downward spiral of depopulation and economic contraction. This prompts us to propose that the experiences of Japan's rural areas may be instructive for regional urban settlements as their populations also begin to shrink in the years to come. Needless to say, because Japan is the most rapidly ageing society in the world and because its population decline is more drastic and has come earlier than in many countries in Europe and Asia, worldwide implications may also emerge from a detailed examination of Japan's shrinking regions under national depopulation. For Japan, the question to be posed is not *whether* some of the phenomena associated with depopulation will manifest themselves in regional cities and metropolitan districts, but *when*, *where*, and *how* they will appear.

Contextualising Shrinkage: Demographic Trends and National Policy

In the postwar era, large-scale rural-urban migration can be traced back to the 1950s, when Japan embarked on what came to be known as a period of high-speed economic growth (*kōdō keizai seichō-ki*), which lasted through the early 1970s. Despite economic growth that slowed from the early 1970s and then stagnated in the 1990s, this rural exodus has continued unabated until today, to the point that few younger people reside in many of Japan's rural locales. There is no need here to reprise a detailed examination of Japan's industrial transformation and its impact on regional society because much has been written already (see, for example, Harris, 1982; Fujita & Tabuchi, 1997). In this section, we therefore provide a brief contextual outline of the principal economic and political trends that have affected Japan's regions in the postwar period.

As a result of a concentrated and nationally coordinated focus on fostering and developing the heavy, chemical, and manufacturing industries in areas along the Pacific coast industrial belt (stretching from Tokyo to Osaka-Kobe via Nagoya), Japan realised its so-called economic miracle and achieved an economic growth rate of approximately 10 percent GDP per annum through the 1960s and into the early 1970s (Johnson, 1982). The combination of a rapidly increasing population with an increasing demand for workers in urban industry and poor employment conditions in rural regions, particularly in agriculture, initiated a massive flow of rural population into these cities. Throughout the 1950s, 1960s, and 1970s, large numbers of young men from the regions were routinely absorbed into, for example, heavy industry, construction, and manufacturing, and young women were recruited into textile and consumer electronics factories (BBC, 2000; Fujita & Tabuchi, 1997; Kase, 1997; Macnaughtan, 2005). The demand for labour from the peripheral regions was so great that special trains were put into operation in April each year to take the thousands of fresh high school graduates into Tokyo to start their working lives, and public ceremonies were organised at the railway stations so that families and communities could bid their young ones goodbye and wish them well (see Jones, 1995; Kase, 1997). Although Japan's accelerated economic expansion proved the 'success' of this approach on a national scale (as well as to an international audience), the central government became concerned about the massive rural exodus that was taking place and by the fact that neither the country's economic development nor its benefits were being distributed evenly.

In order to counteract some of the negative effects in rural areas of the concentration of urban population and wealth, the government sought spatially balanced and integrated development, through which the country's land areas and natural resources would be used in a manner that would ensure economic growth based also on primary industries. One of the major interventions organised to achieve this has been the local allocation tax (*chihō kōfuzei*). With its origins in the 1940 local distribution tax (Mochida, 2001), *chihō kōfuzei* was established in 1954, and through it the national government redistributes a fixed percentage of the nationally collected revenues to the local administrative units in the form of subsidies and grants (Thompson, 2003). Its purpose was and is to provide fiscal equalisation between local authorities in urban and rural regions with different revenue-raising capabilities and expenditure responsibilities. For example, in 1992 the share of government expenditure taken by subnational government was 69.2 percent, whereas the revenue share was 36.5 percent, creating a fiscal imbalance of 32.7 percent (Mochida, 2001, p. 87). The level of the local allocation tax was derived from the national tax base, including income tax, corporate tax, and liquor tax, and the subsidy funding amount for each municipality was determined by the difference between a municipality's expected local tax income and the estimated income needed to operate local facilities and services (Thompson, 2003, p. 95).

As the period of high-speed economic growth continued and brought further concentration in industrialised areas, the amount of *chihō kōfuzei* redistributed to local areas increased, providing local governments with substantial resources that they used for development purposes, encouraging local governments to utilise public-works spending as a means of developing their locales. By 2001 the redistributive impacts of the tax had amounted to JPY 21.7 trillion in transfers and was the second-largest source of revenue for local governments at 22 percent of total revenue (Shirai, 2005, p. 217).

Demographic Trends and Local Economies

In 1960, then prime minister Hayato Ikeda launched the National Income Doubling Plan, which focused on enormous public investment, allocating JPY 452.2 trillion in 1961, a spending increase of 56.5 percent over the previous year (Ozawa, 2003). Then in 1962, during the first half of Japan's rapid-growth period (1954–1964), a comprehensive national development plan (*zenkoku sōgō kaihatsu keikaku*) was adopted under the slogan 'Improvement of Regional Disparity' (Mochida, 2001, p. 102) in order to address interregional disparities and to introduce stable, balanced growth across the country. This plan was based on what was termed a *foothold-development approach*, which involved deploying a 'foothold' industry in a suitable regional city, in the hope that the benefits of the resulting economic expansion would spread and thus contribute to the economic development of the wider area and to an increase in the incomes of local residents. The effect of these policies was a rapid and substantial equalisation of revenues and expenditures between rural and urban regions by the second half of the high-speed growth period (1965–1974). Although (as discussed in what follows) the uses that municipalities have made of these transfers is a matter for debate, Mochida calculated that the Gini coefficient for interregional disparities dropped rapidly, from 0.18 in the late 1950s to 0.6 by the 1970s, indicating that fiscal equalisation measures were having a positive impact on the economic and governmental capacities and finances of local areas in those years (Mochida, 2001, p. 102).

During this period, in addition, regional municipalities worked to attract industries to their areas by drafting special regulations to accommodate corporations considering relocation and offering special allowances, such as long-term tax breaks. Though these efforts did in fact entice many corporations to relocate to the regions, the outcome was not as successful as had been hoped, because firms' decisions were ultimately based on efficient business models and profit-maximising calculations. Most companies ended up creating a dichotomised corporate model, in which Tokyo served as the location of the corporate headquarters, with various combinations of general and specialised facilities and factories relocated to outlying areas. In addition, as specific corporations sought advantageous sites in capital-intensive heavy industries (e.g., iron and steel, petrochemicals, and shipbuilding), locations were chosen so as to maximise profit and minimise cost, necessitating proximity to a combination of raw materials, labour supply, transportation infrastructure, and potential markets. The central government attempted to ensure a wider distribution of further growth by selecting 13 industrial cities and 6 special areas for state-funded infrastructural development projects (Uchino, 1983), but these efforts merely fuelled a secondary urbanisation in areas set apart from Tokyo but still within the Tokyo-Nagoya-Osaka Pacific coast industrial belt (see Mutai, 2008). Although these efforts were attempts to entice corporations to relocate to outlying prefectures, the reality was continued industrial and urban agglomeration: A huge workforce relocated to the emerging cities, further weakening smaller local enterprises, which became even more isolated in rural regions.

The oil shocks of the 1970s slowed Japan's economic growth rate as domestic labour and other costs increased relative to costs elsewhere in the world. At that time, Japan's major corporations began to enter and then dominate overseas markets, and automobile and consumer-electronics manufacturing started to relocate overseas, to the United States and Western Europe in the 1970s and 1980s, and then to Asia and Eastern Europe from the 1980s and 1990s (see Fujita & Hill, 1989; McCormick, 2006). The demand for industrial labour in Japan slowed, and urban employment opportunities shifted gradually from secure long-term, skilled, factory-based work to white collar managerial positions for male university graduates and work as part-time, temporary, and despatch workers in retail and other services for non–university graduates and the growing proportion of female workers (Brinton, 1996).

As a result of slower economic growth rates, of the restructuring of industry and employment, and of the reduced numbers of younger people migrating to urban areas due to the declining birth rate, out-migration from rural areas steadily slowed. Although birth rates continued to decline and the ageing of Japanese society brought with it increases in death rates, however, the demographic impacts of even minimal out-migration were significant for rural communities. Consequently, from the late-1980s, outlying prefectures' populations began to shrink. It is notable, nevertheless, that during the worst years of Japan's 'lost decade' of the 1990s, migration into rural regions was in some cases net positive because severe employment conditions in Japan's cities pushed people to return to their home prefectures and towns or discouraged school and university leavers to emigrate from their home regions. Many of the returnees were younger people who swelled the ranks of *freeters*—the freelance, part-time, and temporary employees—who work without long-term employment at any one company, and NEETs, those 'not in employment, education or training' (see Kosugi, 2008; Genda, 2005). Since that time, however, net out-migration has resumed as the economy gradually recovered in the early 2000s.

As these multilayered and self-reinforcing processes were taking place, numerous new and globally competitive export industries were expanding, industries that in many cases pushed existing traditional industries further to the rear of the growing national economy (Ozawa, 2003). These industries were often situated in rural regions, usually rooted in the circumstances of a particular place, and in many cases they provided the foundation for employment and stability in an area. The policies crafted in response, and the decisions that these yielded, have contributed to a pervasive dualism in the Japanese economy: One sector is outward-focused, efficient, internationally competitive, and located in metropolitan regions—a sector symbolised by Japan's automobile and electronics manufacturing—whereas the other sector remains inward-oriented and deals primarily with domestic products, is inefficient and protected from foreign competitors. This sector comprises such fundamental industries as agriculture, transportation, banking, insurance, construction, real estate, and food processing, and is the economic mainstay of Japan's regional cities, towns, and villages. In the emergence of the former sector, the latter has come to its dismal state (Katz, 1998; Pempel, 1998). The government initially tried to redress regional and income disparities and to ensure equal distribution of the benefits of economic growth but by funnelling resources from Tokyo to the countryside, '[the domestic-oriented sector] was soon made into a pork-barrel sector by the ruling party, the LDP [Liberal Democratic Party]' (Ozawa, 2003, p. 525). This development reflects the well-documented issue of government spending for public-works projects, which have played a significant role in the nation's economy and legendary pork-barrel politics (Igarashi, 1999; McCormack, 2001; Feldhoff, 2002a).

Hence, despite research showing that Japan's economic expansion has been achieved—at least until the 1990s—in a more egalitarian and progressive manner than in the Anglo-American world (Coates, 2007; Dore, 2003; Hein, 2008), rural areas have not shared in the country's material gains to the extent that urban regions have. This reality has been the principal factor pulling internal migrants towards metropolitan regions in search of the social and economic mobility that can be gained through educational advancement and improved labour market connections (Fujita & Tabuchi, 1997). It might therefore be argued that a major policy failure of successive Japanese governments through this period of 50-plus years has been the lack of success in addressing the negative consequences for rural areas of Japan's otherwise progressive industrial and postindustrial transformations.

In sum, the postwar Japanese government and business elites have pursued an economic development policy in a single-minded fashion—what Johnson (1982) has called the 'capitalist developmental state'—with the result that the country was able to attain a high-growth economy between 1950 and 1973 and able to maintain steady growth in the following years through the 1990s. However, this process resulted in a massive exodus of population from Japan's rural regions and inevitably contributed to their relative economic and social decline. The government initially sought to mitigate the worst effects by encouraging spatially and socially integrated development so as to make the economy more efficient and yield an equal distribution of industries throughout the country. However, the country's selective industrial policies led to a concentration of the state's investments on strategic industries, mostly built along the urban Pacific coast—and therefore left the rural sector behind. The irony has been that the spectacularly long economic boom that Japan experienced was made possible only by the labour of rural migrants who left their homes in towns and villages, communities, and families behind.

National and Regional Population Change in Japan and Niigata Prefecture Since 1884

Located on the northwestern coast of Honshū, Niigata is the fifth largest of Japan's 47 prefectures (12,582 km^2). In the 19th century, it had probably the largest population of any prefecture, at approximately 1.5 million persons in 1884 (Statistics Bureau, 2010d). However, just as growth in Western Europe led to a population shift towards urban areas, so in Japan: as economic development gathered pace and Japan became an urbanised modern industrial state centred on the Tokyo metropolis, so Niigata's population gradually became smaller relative to the rapidly expanding city regions of the Pacific industrial belt. At 2.4 million persons in 2005, Niigata ranked 14th in population among Japan's prefectures.

Although the relative contribution of agriculture to the prefectural economy has been steadily falling for many decades, Niigata remains one of Japan's most recognizably agricultural prefectures, producing the nationally famous *koshi hikari* rice brand, as well as remaining a centre for fishing, food processing, and saké production. Typical of many regional prefectures, Niigata has a broad range of settlement types, ranging in size from the large urban prefectural capital, Niigata City (estimated population on 1 September 2010: 811,935) to intermediate cities such as Nagaoka (282,810), Jōetsu (203,290), Shibata (101,856), Sanjō (101,544), Kashiwazaki (91,589), and Murakami (66,419) (Niigata ken, 2010) and to towns, villages, and isolated hamlets located in the mountainous inland areas, along the rugged coast, and on the wide agricultural flood plains of the Shinano and Agano rivers (see map 3.5).[3] Sado (62,447), also part of the prefecture, is Japan's sixth-largest island and is located in the Japan Sea some 20 kilometres from Niigata City.

We first address the broad trends of Japan's population development since the beginning of the country's industrial development in the second half of the 19th century and locate Niigata Prefecture in these terms: Japan as a whole has experienced almost continuous rapid growth in urban and industrialising regions throughout the 20th century (table 3.1). This growth has been matched in regional prefectures by steady but slower growth in the prewar period and by stability, even shrinkage, after 1945. Although 40 out of 47 prefectures experienced massive out-migrations of their populations to the industrialising Pacific coast from 1920 through 1935 (Harris, 1982, p. 70), on the whole these prefectures maintained a positive rate of population growth due to very high rates of reproduction, which also resulted in a rapid and sustained increase in the national population. The massive growth of the Japanese population through the early and postwar decades of the 20th century resulted in a comparatively young population and provided the Japanese economy with a substantial demographic dividend to support and fuel the country's rapid economic expansion, as well as to reduce pressures on government services during these crucial foundational decades (Bloom, Canning, & Sevilla, 2003).

Table 3.1 shows that among non-metropolitan prefectures, only Hokkaidō and Okinawa grew significantly in the postwar period, a trend consistent with the state's 'internal colonization' (Weiner, 2004) of these regions and in part also in order to consolidate the country's territory and bolster Japan's strategic defence. The growth in metropolitan regions was commensurate with Japan's almost continuous economic expansion since the late 19th century and accords with standard expectations and understandings of the demographic shifts that occur under the urban agglomeration processes of industrialisation and modernisation. Table 3.1 also shows reductions in rural populations in the 1960s, more balanced growth in the 1970s and 1980s, and a steady increase in the number of prefectures experiencing shrinkage from the 1990s, reflecting the phases of Japan's postwar economic and population development. In 2009 only 7 of Japan's 47 prefectures showed growth for that year, and Okinawa and Shiga Prefectures were the only two non-metropolitan prefectures in this group, and the national population also indicated shrinkage between 2005 and 2008. Okinawa continues to grow due to resettlement of retirees and those seeking a gentler life in warmer climes, and Shiga is growing as a new satellite region of the Kyoto-Osaka-Kobe metropolitan conurbation.

Figure 3.1 tells a similar story, this time in graphic form, depicting the relative growth of the national population of Japan overall and the relative growth of selected regional and metropolitan prefectures from 1884 to 2009. The graph demonstrates that Japan's population has expanded approximately 240 percent to 127 million and that the metropolitan

FIGURE 3.1. Populations of Selected Prefectures (left-hand scale) and Japan (right-hand scale), 1884–2010 (in millions).

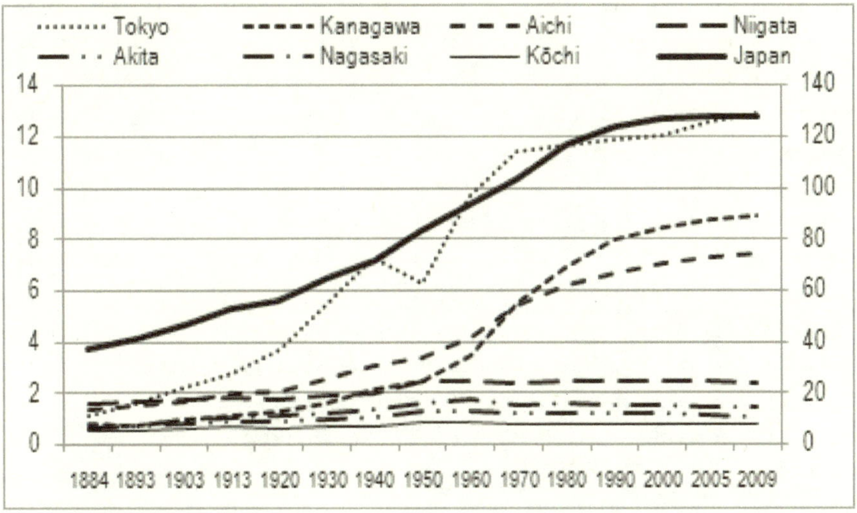

Source. Statistics Bureau (2010d, 2010e).

TABLE 3.1. Population of Japan and Prefectures, 1884–2009 (in millions).

	Japan	Hokkaidō	Aomori	Iwate	Miyagi	Akita	Yamagata	Fukushima	Ibaraki	Tochigi	Gunma	Saitama	Chiba	Tokyo	Kanagawa	Niigata	Toyama	Ishikawa	Fukui	Yamanashi	Nagano	Gifu	Shizuoka	Aichi	Mie
1884	37.5	0.2	0.5	0.6	0.6	0.6	0.7	0.9	0.9	0.6	0.6	1.0	1.1	1.2	0.8	1.6	0.7	0.7	0.6	0.4	1.0	0.9	1.0	1.4	0.9
1888	39.6	0.3	0.5	0.7	0.7	0.7	0.7	0.9	1.0	0.7	0.7	1.0	1.2	1.4	0.9	1.7	0.7	0.7	0.6	0.4	1.1	0.9	1.0	1.4	0.9
1893	41.4	0.5	0.6	0.7	0.8	0.7	0.8	1.0	1.0	0.7	0.7	1.1	1.2	1.6	0.8	1.7	0.8	0.8	0.6	0.5	1.2	0.9	1.1	1.5	0.9
1898	43.7	0.8	0.6	0.7	0.8	0.8	0.8	1.1	1.1	0.8	0.8	1.1	1.2	1.9	0.9	1.7	0.8	0.7	0.6	0.5	1.2	0.9	1.2	1.6	1.0
1903	46.6	1.0	0.6	0.7	0.9	0.8	0.9	1.1	1.2	0.9	0.9	1.2	1.3	2.3	1.0	1.7	0.8	0.7	0.6	0.5	1.3	1.0	1.2	1.7	1.0
1908	49.3	1.3	0.7	0.8	0.9	0.9	0.9	1.2	1.2	0.9	0.9	1.2	1.3	2.7	1.1	1.8	0.7	0.8	0.6	0.6	1.4	1.0	1.3	1.8	1.0
1913	52.9	1.7	0.7	0.8	0.9	0.9	1.0	1.3	1.3	1.0	1.0	1.3	1.4	2.8	1.1	1.9	0.8	0.8	0.6	0.6	1.4	1.1	1.5	2.0	1.1
1918	55.7	2.0	0.8	0.8	0.9	1.0	1.0	1.3	1.4	1.1	1.0	1.3	1.4	3.3	1.2	1.9	0.8	0.8	0.6	0.6	1.5	1.1	1.6	2.1	1.1
1920	56.0	2.4	0.8	0.8	1.0	0.9	1.0	1.4	1.4	1.0	1.1	1.3	1.3	3.7	1.3	1.8	0.7	0.7	0.6	0.6	1.6	1.1	1.6	2.1	1.1
1925	59.7	2.5	0.8	0.9	1.0	0.9	1.0	1.4	1.4	1.1	1.1	1.4	1.4	4.5	1.4	1.8	0.7	0.8	0.6	0.6	1.6	1.1	1.7	2.3	1.1
1930	64.5	2.8	0.9	1.0	1.1	1.0	1.1	1.5	1.5	1.1	1.2	1.5	1.5	5.4	1.6	1.9	0.8	0.8	0.6	0.6	1.7	1.2	1.8	2.6	1.2
1935	69.3	3.1	1.0	1.0	1.2	1.0	1.1	1.6	1.5	1.2	1.2	1.5	1.5	6.4	1.8	2.0	0.8	0.8	0.6	0.6	1.7	1.2	1.9	2.9	1.2
1940	71.9	3.2	1.0	1.1	1.2	1.0	1.1	1.6	1.6	1.2	1.3	1.6	1.6	7.3	2.2	2.0	0.8	0.7	0.6	0.7	1.7	1.2	2.0	3.1	1.2
1945	72.0	3.5	1.1	1.2	1.5	1.2	1.3	2.0	1.9	1.5	1.5	2.0	2.0	3.5	1.9	2.4	1.0	0.9	0.7	0.8	2.1	1.5	2.2	2.9	1.4
1950	83.2	4.3	1.3	1.3	1.7	1.3	1.4	2.1	2.0	1.6	1.6	2.1	2.1	6.3	2.5	2.5	1.0	1.0	0.8	0.8	2.1	1.5	2.5	3.4	1.5
1955	89.3	4.8	1.4	1.4	1.7	1.3	1.4	2.1	2.1	1.5	1.6	2.3	2.2	8.0	2.9	2.5	1.0	1.0	0.8	0.8	2.0	1.6	2.7	3.8	1.5
1960	93.4	5.0	1.4	1.4	1.7	1.3	1.3	2.1	2.0	1.5	1.6	2.4	2.3	9.7	3.4	2.4	1.0	1.0	0.8	0.8	2.0	1.6	2.8	4.2	1.5
1965	98.3	5.2	1.4	1.4	1.8	1.3	1.3	2.0	2.1	1.5	1.6	3.0	2.7	10.9	4.4	2.4	1.0	1.0	0.8	0.8	2.0	1.7	2.9	4.8	1.5
1970	103.7	5.2	1.4	1.4	1.8	1.2	1.2	1.9	2.1	1.6	1.7	3.9	3.4	11.4	5.5	2.4	1.0	1.0	0.7	0.8	2.0	1.8	3.1	5.4	1.5
1975	111.9	5.3	1.5	1.4	2.0	1.2	1.2	2.0	2.3	1.7	1.8	4.8	4.1	11.7	6.4	2.4	1.1	1.1	0.8	0.8	2.0	1.9	3.3	5.9	1.6
1980	117.1	5.6	1.5	1.4	2.1	1.3	1.3	2.0	2.6	1.8	1.8	5.4	4.7	11.6	6.9	2.5	1.1	1.1	0.8	0.8	2.1	2.0	3.4	6.2	1.7
1985	121.0	5.7	1.5	1.4	2.2	1.3	1.3	2.1	2.7	1.9	1.9	5.9	5.1	11.8	7.4	2.5	1.1	1.2	0.8	0.8	2.1	2.0	3.6	6.5	1.7
1990	123.6	5.6	1.5	1.4	2.2	1.2	1.3	2.1	2.8	1.9	2.0	6.4	5.6	11.9	8.0	2.5	1.1	1.2	0.8	0.9	2.2	2.1	3.7	6.7	1.8
1995	125.6	5.7	1.5	1.4	2.3	1.2	1.3	2.1	3.0	2.0	2.0	6.8	5.8	11.8	8.2	2.5	1.1	1.2	0.8	0.9	2.2	2.1	3.7	6.9	1.8
2000	126.9	5.7	1.5	1.4	2.4	1.2	1.2	2.1	3.0	2.0	2.0	6.9	5.9	12.1	8.5	2.5	1.1	1.2	0.8	0.9	2.2	2.1	3.8	7.0	1.9
2005	127.8	5.6	1.4	1.4	2.4	1.1	1.2	2.1	3.0	2.0	2.0	7.1	6.1	12.6	8.8	2.4	1.1	1.2	0.8	0.9	2.2	2.1	3.8	7.3	1.9
2008	127.7	5.5	1.4	1.4	2.3	1.1	1.2	2.1	3.0	2.0	2.0	7.1	6.1	12.8	8.9	2.4	1.1	1.2	0.8	0.9	2.2	2.1	3.8	7.4	1.9
2009	127.5	5.5	1.4	1.3	2.3	1.1	1.2	2.0	3.0	2.0	2.0	7.1	6.1	12.9	8.9	2.4	1.1	1.2	0.8	0.9	2.2	2.1	3.8	7.4	1.9

Shiga	Kyoto	Osaka	Hyōgo	Nara	Wakayama	Tottori	Shimane	Okayama	Hiroshima	Yamaguchi	Tokushima	Kagawa	Ehime	Kōchi	Fukuoka	Saga	Nagasaki	Kumamoto	Oita	Miyazaki	Kagoshima	Okinawa
0.6	0.8	1.6	1.4	-	0.6	0.4	0.7	1.0	1.3	0.9	0.6	-	1.5	0.5	1.1	0.5	0.7	1.0	0.8	0.4	0.9	0.4
0.7	0.9	1.2	1.5	0.5	0.6	0.4	0.7	1.1	1.3	0.9	0.7	0.7	0.9	0.6	1.2	0.6	0.7	1.0	0.8	0.4	1.0	0.4
0.7	0.9	1.3	1.6	0.5	0.6	0.4	0.7	1.1	1.3	0.9	0.7	0.7	0.9	0.6	1.3	0.6	0.8	1.1	0.8	0.4	1.0	0.4
0.7	1.0	1.5	1.7	0.5	0.7	0.4	0.7	1.1	1.4	1.0	0.7	0.7	1.0	0.6	1.4	0.6	0.9	1.1	0.8	0.5	1.1	0.5
0.7	1.0	1.7	1.8	0.5	0.7	0.4	0.7	1.1	1.5	1.0	0.7	0.7	1.0	0.6	1.5	0.6	1.0	1.2	0.8	0.5	1.2	0.5
0.7	1.1	1.9	1.9	0.5	0.7	0.4	0.7	1.2	1.5	1.0	0.7	0.7	1.0	0.6	1.6	0.7	1.0	1.2	0.9	0.5	1.2	0.5
0.7	1.2	2.2	2.0	0.6	0.8	0.5	0.8	1.2	1.6	1.1	0.7	0.7	1.1	0.7	1.8	0.7	1.1	1.3	0.9	0.6	1.4	0.5
0.7	1.3	2.6	2.2	0.6	0.8	0.5	0.7	1.3	1.6	1.1	0.7	0.7	1.1	0.7	2.0	0.7	1.2	1.3	0.9	0.6	1.4	0.6
0.7	1.3	2.6	2.3	0.6	0.8	0.5	0.7	1.2	1.5	1.0	0.7	0.7	1.0	0.7	2.2	0.7	1.1	1.2	0.9	0.7	1.4	0.6
0.7	1.4	3.1	2.5	0.6	0.8	0.5	0.7	1.2	1.6	1.1	0.7	0.7	1.1	0.7	2.3	0.7	1.2	1.3	0.9	0.7	1.5	0.6
0.7	1.6	3.5	2.6	0.6	0.8	0.5	0.7	1.3	1.7	1.1	0.7	0.7	1.1	0.7	2.5	0.7	1.2	1.4	0.9	0.8	1.6	0.6
0.7	1.7	4.3	2.9	0.6	0.9	0.5	0.7	1.3	1.8	1.2	0.7	0.7	1.2	0.7	2.8	0.7	1.3	1.4	1.0	0.8	1.6	0.6
0.7	1.7	4.7	3.2	0.6	0.8	0.5	0.7	1.3	1.8	1.3	0.7	0.7	1.2	0.7	3.0	0.7	1.3	1.3	1.0	0.8	1.6	0.6
0.9	1.6	2.8	2.8	0.8	0.9	0.6	0.9	1.6	1.9	1.4	0.8	0.9	1.4	0.8	2.7	0.8	1.3	1.6	1.1	0.9	1.5	-
0.9	1.8	3.9	3.3	0.8	1.0	0.6	0.9	1.7	2.1	1.5	0.9	0.9	1.5	0.9	3.5	0.9	1.6	1.8	1.3	1.1	1.8	0.7
0.9	1.9	4.6	3.6	0.8	1.0	0.6	0.9	1.7	2.1	1.6	0.9	0.9	1.5	0.9	3.9	1.0	1.7	1.9	1.3	1.1	2.0	0.8
0.8	2.0	5.5	3.9	0.8	1.0	0.6	0.9	1.7	2.2	1.6	0.8	0.9	1.5	0.9	4.0	0.9	1.8	1.9	1.2	1.1	2.0	0.9
0.9	2.1	6.7	4.3	0.8	1.0	0.6	0.8	1.6	2.3	1.5	0.8	0.9	1.4	0.8	4.0	0.9	1.6	1.8	1.2	1.1	1.9	0.9
0.9	2.3	7.6	4.7	0.9	1.0	0.6	0.8	1.7	2.4	1.5	0.8	0.9	1.4	0.8	4.0	0.8	1.6	1.7	1.2	1.1	1.7	0.9
1.0	2.4	8.3	5.0	1.1	1.1	0.6	0.8	1.8	2.6	1.6	0.8	1.0	1.5	0.8	4.3	0.8	1.6	1.7	1.2	1.1	1.7	1.0
1.1	2.5	8.5	5.1	1.2	1.1	0.6	0.8	1.9	2.7	1.6	0.8	1.0	1.5	0.8	4.6	0.9	1.6	1.8	1.2	1.2	1.8	1.1
1.2	2.6	8.7	5.3	1.3	1.1	0.6	0.8	1.9	2.8	1.6	0.8	1.0	1.5	0.8	4.7	0.9	1.6	1.8	1.3	1.2	1.8	1.2
1.2	2.6	8.7	5.4	1.4	1.1	0.6	0.8	1.9	2.8	1.6	0.8	1.0	1.5	0.8	4.8	0.9	1.6	1.8	1.2	1.2	1.8	1.2
1.3	2.6	8.8	5.4	1.4	1.1	0.6	0.8	2.0	2.9	1.6	0.8	1.0	1.5	0.8	4.9	0.9	1.5	1.9	1.2	1.2	1.8	1.3
1.3	2.6	8.8	5.6	1.4	1.1	0.6	0.8	2.0	2.9	1.5	0.8	1.0	1.5	0.8	5.0	0.9	1.5	1.9	1.2	1.2	1.8	1.3
1.4	2.6	8.8	5.6	1.4	1.0	0.6	0.7	2.0	2.9	1.5	0.8	1.0	1.5	0.8	5.0	0.9	1.5	1.8	1.2	1.2	1.8	1.4
1.4	2.6	8.8	5.6	1.4	1.0	0.6	0.7	1.9	2.9	1.5	0.8	1.0	1.4	0.8	5.1	0.9	1.4	1.8	1.2	1.1	1.7	1.4
1.4	2.6	8.8	5.6	1.4	1.0	0.6	0.7	1.9	2.9	1.5	0.8	1.0	1.4	0.8	5.1	0.9	1.4	1.8	1.2	1.1	1.7	1.4

Source. Statistics Bureau (2010d, 2010e).

Note. Shaded areas show population decrease from the previous census or estimate. Figures in bold are for prefectures shown in figure 3.1.

populations of Tokyo, Kanagawa (Yokohama), and Aichi (Nagoya) have expanded by up to 10 times during the same period, but that the populations of the predominantly rural and peripheral prefectures of Niigata, Akita, Kōchi, and Nagasaki have remained comparatively stable—even stagnant—by comparison, particularly in the postwar period. The graph also shows growth in the national population flattening in the period 1990–2010, with metropolitan prefectures continuing to grow, albeit less rapidly, confirming that Japan's regional prefectures are now shrinking more rapidly than previously.

A similar pattern of urban concentration has also been manifest on the intraregional scale as prefectural capitals grew through the long boom of Japan's industrialisation. Figure 3.2 shows population growth in Niigata Prefecture, Niigata City, and Sado Island between 1920 and 2009,

FIGURE 3.2. Population Growth of Niigata Prefecture (right-hand scale, in millions) and Niigata City (left-hand scale, in thousands), 1920–2009.

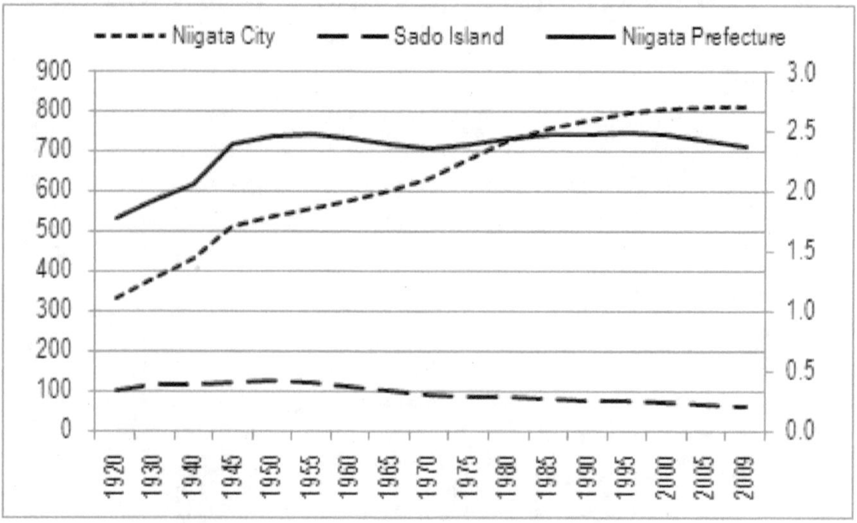

Sources: Statistics Bureau (2010d); Niigata ken (2011).
Note. Figures are adjusted backwards for municipal boundary changes to 2009.

indicating substantial growth for the first two prior to 1940 and a more mixed picture in the postwar decades. Adjusting backwards for municipal boundary changes since 1950, Niigata City's population increased by 51 percent from 1950 to its high point in about 2007, from 539,000 to 813,000 people (Niigata ken, 2011), whereas the prefecture's population remained steady at under 2.5 million and began to shrink again from about 1995 (Niigata ken, 2011). Sado Island's population, by contrast, has been declining since 1950, with part of that decline contributing to the increase in size of Niigata City as younger people have migrated in search of employment and other opportunities in the prefectural capital (see table 3.5).

Niigata Prefecture in the National Context

Maps 3.1–3.4 consolidate and extend the information presented thus far on Japan's postwar population development, showing national population change for prefectures and prefectural capitals throughout Japan over four 20-year periods since 1950 and projecting through 2030. All projections presented in this chapter employ the government's National Institute of Population and Social Security Research (NIPSSR) data, with national prefectural projections and municipal level projections for Niigata Prefecture employing the medium variant projections based on the 2000 population census (NIPSSR, 2002, 2003). For maps 3.1–3.4, grey shaded areas represent growth, and speckled and hatched areas show shrinkage in prefectures; the circles show population change in prefectural capitals.

It is important to note that, although the preliminary results of the 2010 census were published in the Spring of 2011 and the data indicate an increase in the national population of 288,032 persons (0.2 percent) to 128 million, this expansion is a statistical reflection of changes to census data collection methods and should not be interpreted as showing a continued expansion in the country's population. Indeed, the Japanese government acknowledges that the 2010 census is the first to have been conducted under a declining trend in the national population (see: Statistics Bureau, 2010e). Hence, in order to preserve statistical and methodological consistency, in

MAP 3.1. Population Change in Japan by Prefecture and Prefectural Capital City, 1950–1970.

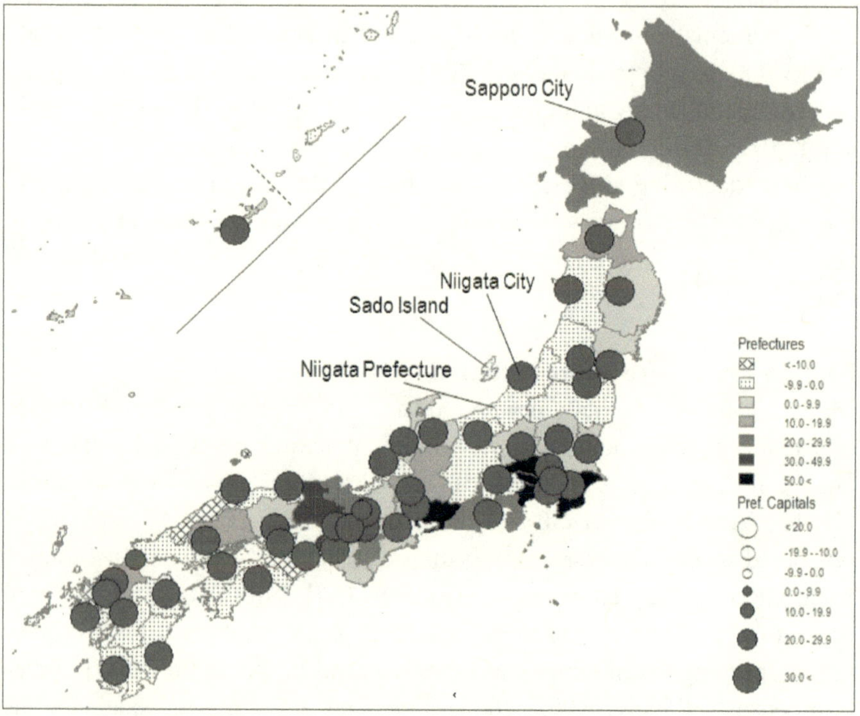

Source. Statistics Bureau (2010d). Maps 3.1–3.8 by Peter Matanle.

this volume we refer to census data up to and including 2005, and thereafter to population estimates and projections based on the 2005 census, as well as prefectural and municipal data where necessary. Statistics Bureau (2010j).

Map 3.1 (1950–1970) displays the pattern of rapid population growth in metropolitan areas already described and shrinkage in outlying prefectures, and in addition shows growth occurring in all 47 prefectural capitals during the early postwar high-speed growth phase of Japan's modernising economy and society. Underlying these trends was a comparatively

Map 3.2. Population Change in Japan by Prefecture and Prefectural Capital City, 1970–1990.

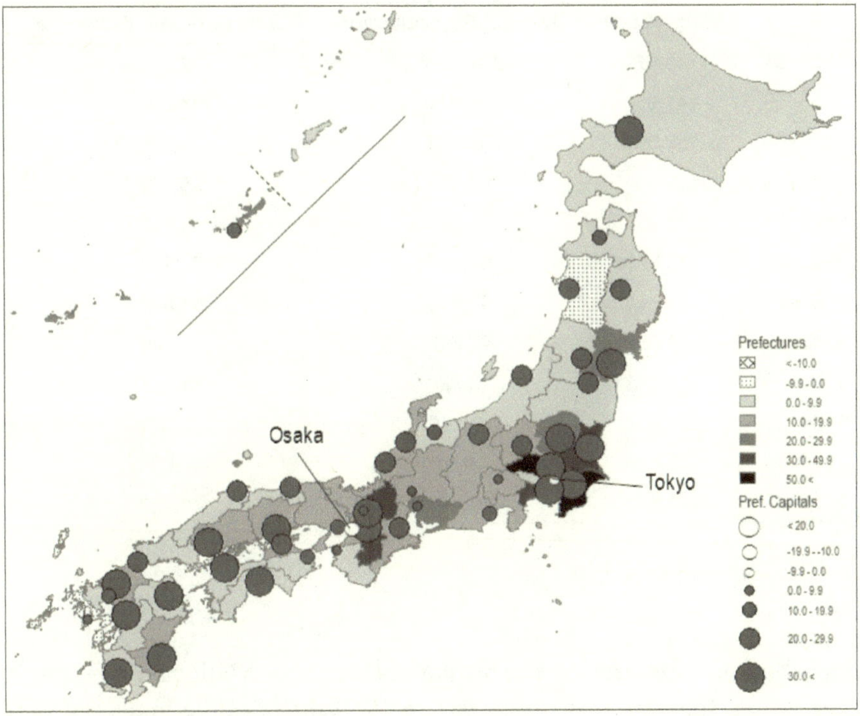

Source. Statistics Bureau (2010d).

rapid and steady natural growth in the national population, fuelled by a high reproduction rate towards the start of the period. Nevertheless, Japan's birth rate had already slowed dramatically by the beginning of the 1960s. Although many non-metropolitan regions experienced during this time the positive impact of a high natural growth rate, for outlying areas (unlike in the prewar period), this was more than offset by the negative effects of intraregional rural-urban migration; hence many provincial prefectures such as Niigata show a declining overall population and a growing prefectural capital between 1950 and 1970. Table 3.2 compares the

TABLE 3.2. Contributions of Migration and Natural Increase to Niigata Prefecture's Population, 1951–2008.

	Migration	Natural Reproduction	Total Population Change
1951–54	–145,579	143,314	–2,265
1955–59	–141,978	127,370	–14,608
1960–64	–158,371	97,451	–60,920
1965–69	–122,139	92,452	–29,687
1970–74	–96,938	99,149	2,211
1975–79	–36,686	93,807	57,121
1980–84	–36,714	68,806	32,092
1985–89	–40,669	46,665	5,996
1990–94	–13,988	20,920	6,932
1995–99	–1,404	6,740	5,336
2000–04	–18,625	–9,310	–27,935
2005–08	–22,871	–17,612	–40,483

Source. Niigata ken (2011).

contributions of migration and the natural increase to Niigata Prefecture's population, showing that from 1951 to 1969 the negative impact of out-migration was greater than the positive impact of the natural increase.

Map 3.2 (1970–1990) shows nearly all prefectures' populations growing. However, the data indicate that most growth took place in the late 1970s and early 1980s, when out-migration to metropolitan regions slowed in the wake of the economic consequences of the oil shocks (see table 3.2 for Niigata Prefecture) and when the government intensified its implementation of spatially balanced growth policies by attempting to disperse economic gains towards the rural periphery (Ishikawa, 1992). A large part of the financial transfer that took place between metropolitan and rural districts took the form of infrastructural developments, such as the laying of the Shinkansen super-express train lines and the construction of stations, expressways, and regional airports; the development

MAP 3.3. Population Change in Japan by Prefecture and Prefectural Capital City, 1990–2010 (projected).

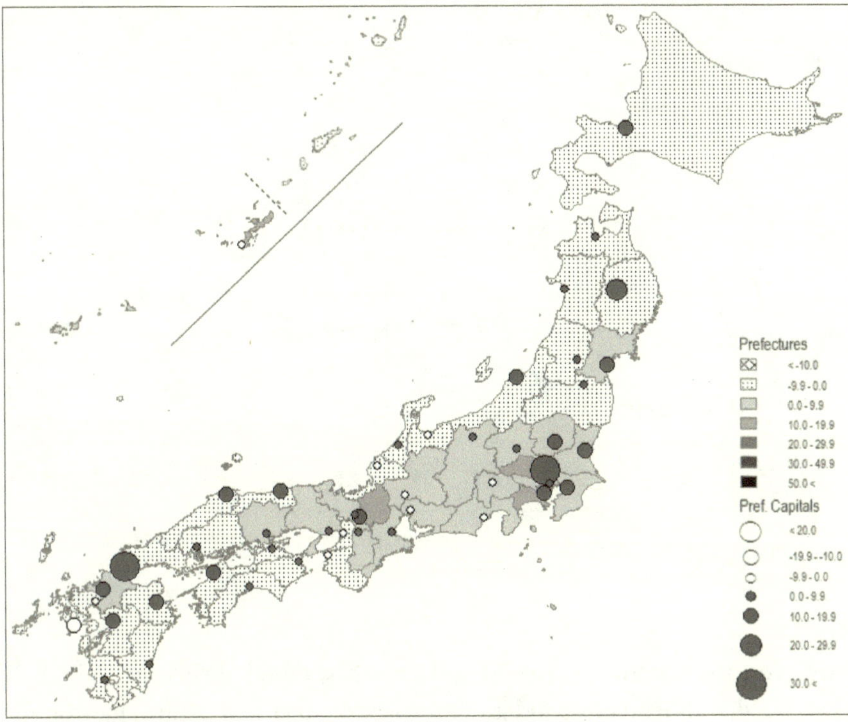

Sources. Statistics Bureau (2010d, 2010e); NIPSSR (2002).

of telecommunications and electric-power generating and transmission facilities; and the (re)construction of regional schools, hospitals, and other public facilities. Moreover, despite the fall in the nation's total fertility rate to below the replacement level in 1973–1974 (NIPSSR, 2006), life expectancy continued to rise rapidly throughout Japan, resulting in a masking 'tempo effect' of continuing positive natural growth for most regional prefectures until the late 1990s. Like map 3.1, map 3.2 shows that all prefectural capitals grew in size between 1970 and 1990, indicating continued (though slower) intraregional rural-urban migration.

FIGURE 3.3. Births and Deaths and Net Migration in Niigata Prefecture, 1955–2008 (in thousands).

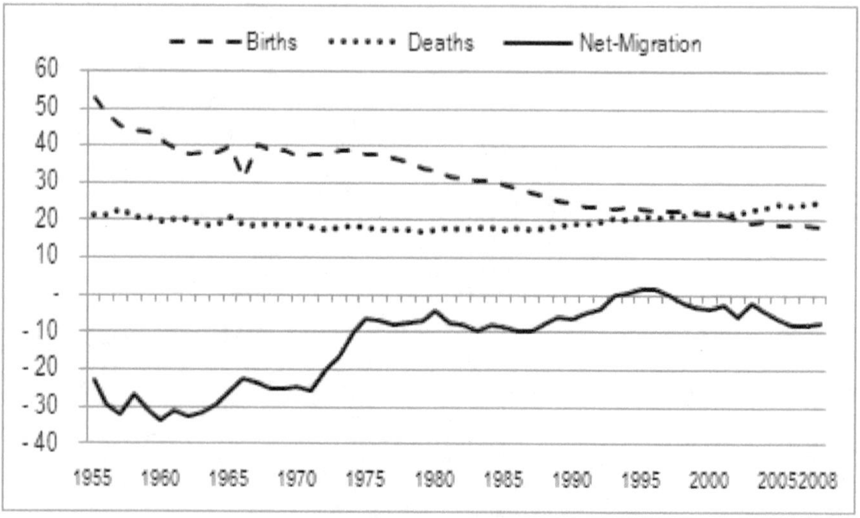

Source. Niigata ken (2011).

However, the centres of Tokyo and Osaka showed shrinkage, which is associated with land consolidation, the restructuring of central metropolitan functions (Waley, 2000), and the flight to the suburbs in response to skyrocketing urban residential land prices during the bubble economy.

Figure 3.3 consolidates the data from tables 3.2 and 3.3 for Niigata Prefecture and shows this masking effect. Throughout the 1970s, 1980s, and 1990s the number of births continued to fall, as did deaths, until about 1985. The number of deaths began to increase from the 1990s and did not overtake births until the early 2000s. Despite drastic falls in the numbers of children being born, steady increases in life expectancy had created a temporary structural natural increase in the population that more than mitigated continuing out-migration, and the prefectural population consequently shows an apparent equilibrium, or even a small amount of growth, from 1970 to 1990. Figure 3.3 makes clear that in reality no such equilibrium

TABLE 3.3. Crude Birth and Death Rates (per 1,000 population) for Niigata Prefecture, 1957–2008.

	Births	Deaths	Balance
1957–59	17.8	8.6	9.2
1960–64	16.1	8.1	8
1965–69	15.8	7.9	7.9
1970–74	16.2	7.7	8.5
1975–79	15	7.3	7.7
1980–84	12.7	7.2	5.5
1985–89	11	7.3	3.7
1990–94	9.6	8	1.6
1995–99	9	8.6	0.4
2000–04	8.4	9.2	–0.8
2005–08	7.6	10.2	–2.6

Source. Niigata ken (2011).

existed, however, and that improvements in life expectancy had masked a structured disequilibrium between births and deaths as well as a structured disequilibrium between in- and out-migration, or a *double-negative demographic disequilibrium*, which became manifest in sustained depopulation in Japan's rural regions from the closing years of the 20th century.

Beginning in 1990, a new dynamic of national-scale demographic shrinkage made its appearance (map 3.3), with metropolitan growth weakening and shrinkage broadening to include greater numbers of prefectures. Although out-migration from the regions resumed in the late 1980s, it dropped again in the 1990s due to the prolonged economic slowdown. It is in this period that the transition to the new regional population dynamic can be identified, a transition that, as mentioned, had been showing signs of its imminence in the period 1970–1990. From 1950 to 1990 there was a steady and ultimately drastic decrease in the positive contribution from natural reproduction, as well as high but decreasing net out-migration from

MAP 3.4. Population Change in Japan by Prefecture and Prefectural Capital City, 2010–2030 (projected).

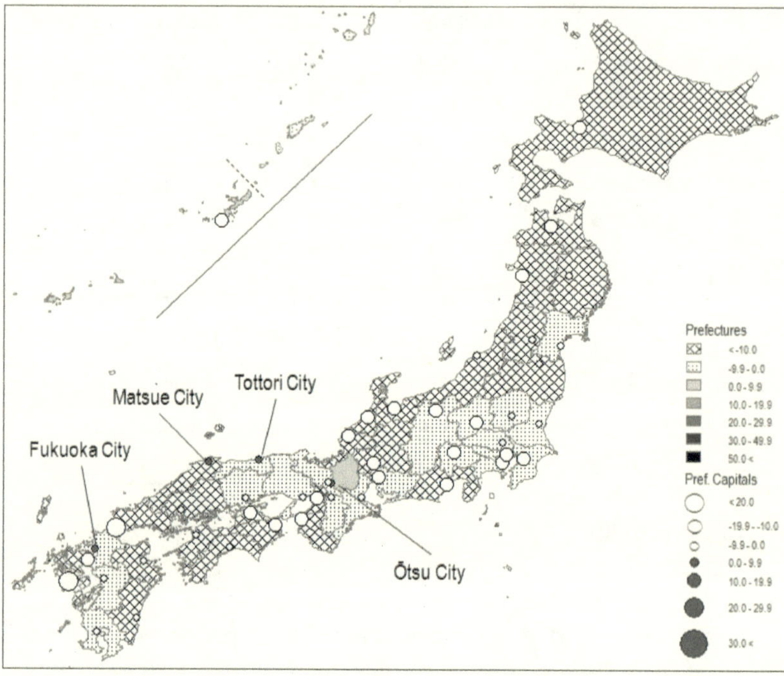

Source. NIPSSR (2002).

rural areas to metropolitan regions and prefectural urban centres—due to the government's spatial equalisation measures, a slower rate of economic growth in metropolitan regions, and a reduction in the number of younger people being born in rural areas. From about 1990 to 2000 a transformation to the double-negative demographic disequilibrium of negative natural and migratory contributions appeared in rural prefectures and is expected to appear in increasing numbers of prefectural urban centres after 2010.

Map 3.4 (2010–2030) anticipates that all prefectures (including the capital region but excluding Okinawa and Shiga) will soon be experiencing shrinkage, with Akita projected to shrink by approximately

18.7 percent and Wakayama by 14.8 percent. A small number of prefectural capitals (Matsue, Tottori, Fukuoka, & Ōtsu Cities) are projected to continue growing, but the majority of regional urban centres will also begin to shrink after about 2010.

The following presents a stylised representation for Japan's non-metropolitan regions of the Webb classification presented in chapter 1, taking into account the national and prefectural population data introduced thus far. Typically, the country's outlying regions will have passed through the following phases of demographic development since 1950:

- 1950–1969 Pattern H: Out-migration exceeds birth surplus
- 1970–1999 Pattern A: Birth surplus exceeds out-migration
- 2000–2010 Pattern G: Out-migration exceeds death surplus
- 2010–? Pattern F: Death surplus exceeds out-migration

As can be seen, in 2000–2010 the transformation to the present double-negative demographic disequilibrium began to appear in non-metropolitan prefectures more or less nationwide, though signs of its appearance had been present in outlying locales prior even to the 1990s. In the first phase of this disequilibrium, outlying regions are currently experiencing the so-called old type of depopulation, characterised by an excess of out-migration over deaths (Pattern G). However, the next phase, which is expected to appear in many regional prefectures after about 2010, will be the new type—that is, an excess of deaths over out-migration (Pattern F)—because only small numbers of younger adults will remain and be able to migrate away to metropolitan and urban districts.

It is from this period, therefore, that regional urban and some metropolitan districts' populations will probably begin to shrink as well, for their birth rates have been low for some decades and their death rates are rising, and they will no longer receive large numbers of in-migrants from the countryside. An examination of the experience of rural regions in the postwar period against the actual and projected experience of urban districts indicates that the past patterns of population increase and then decrease in rural areas will almost certainly be repeated in Japan's regional urban districts in the years to come.

Population Change in Niigata Prefecture: 1950–2030

It is noteworthy that for the period covered by the national population maps, both Niigata Prefecture and Niigata City conform in their absolute and relative growth patterns to the normative pattern for provincial prefectures across Japan. In this way we put forward Niigata as a 'typical' (Donmoyer 2000, pp. 56–59) and therefore 'transferable' (Gerring, 2007, pp. 89, 96) case study of regional depopulation within the overall context of Japan's actual and projected demographic development from 1950 to 2030. In the discussion that follows, we analyse population change within Niigata Prefecture at the municipal level, concentrating attention on inter- and intraprefectural migration.

Rural-urban migration by younger people through the pre- and postwar periods can be characterised by both push and pull factors, with both of these consequences of simultaneously high rates of population and economic expansion in the 20th century. Prior to World War II, large numbers of younger people had migrated out of Niigata Prefecture for reasons of family structure, because Japan's *ie* system allowed only the eldest son to inherit the family assets and subsequent children were required to move away. Prefectural out-migration peaked in 1927 at 196,223 persons, with 149,003 migrating in 1919, and 123,712 in 1938. Despite this, the prefecture's population grew, for natural reproduction remained very high. In addition to pursuing urban opportunities in Tokyo and elsewhere, during the prewar period many out-migrants worked as farm labourers in other rural areas, and Niigata Prefecture also received agricultural labourers from neighbouring prefectures. However, with land ownership readjustments, productivity improvements in agriculture, Japan's rapid economic expansion, and industrial agglomeration and expansion in metropolitan areas, rural-urban migration continued during the postwar era (see table 3.2)—though there were fewer migrant agricultural labourers and the majority of out-migrants have been younger people moving to the Pacific industrial belt in search of long-term skilled blue-collar

Map 3.5. Population Change in Niigata Prefecture by Municipality (2000 boundaries), 1950–1970.

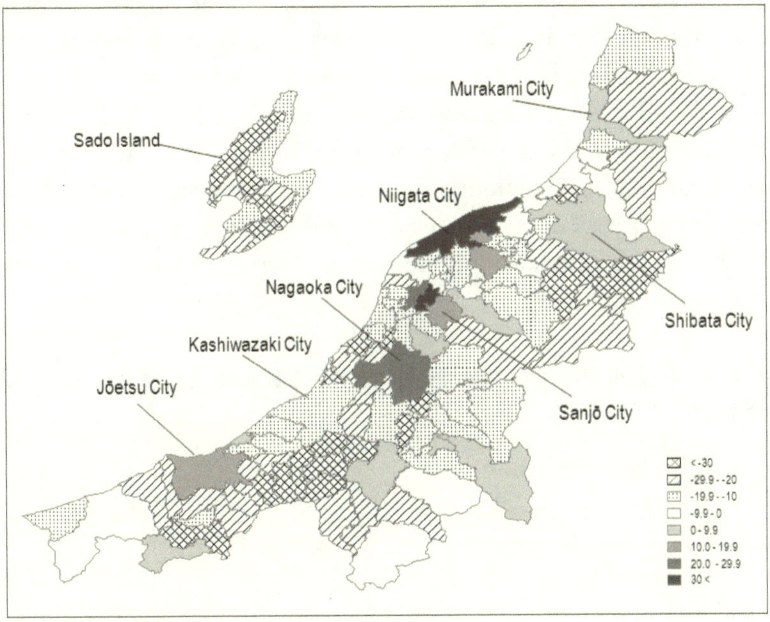

Sources. Niigata ken (2010); Niigata Prefecture website (http://www.pref.niigata.lg.jp/); Higashide (2008).

and clerical work and seeking advancement into tertiary education in preparation for professional and white-collar employment and marriage. Indeed, in recent decades, the percentage of the youth cohort attending full-time post-secondary educational institutions has been rising and it now stands at approximately 76 percent of 18-year-olds (Ministry of Education, Culture, Sports, Science and Technology, 2006). Although post-secondary education can be seen as an intermediate stage between school and employment, it is correct to say that university education is also an end in itself. Nearly all universities are located in urban areas; it can therefore be argued that higher education has become at least as important as employment and marriage or social opportunities in terms of reasons for rural-urban migration among adolescents and young adults. Hence, the relative lack of tertiary opportunities in rural areas pushes younger people away to urban areas, and the relative abundance of educational institutions in urban locales pulls younger people in to the cities. The same is true for employment and social opportunities.

Maps 3.5–3.8 describe demographic change in Niigata Prefecture at the municipal level from 1950, projecting through 2030, with municipal totals adjusted back to include municipal mergers prior to the Great Heisei municipal mergers (see Rausch, 2006).[4] Future projections to 2030 are based on the Japanese government's December 2003 estimates for

MAP 3.6. Population Change in Niigata Prefecture by Municipality (2000 boundaries), 1970–1990.

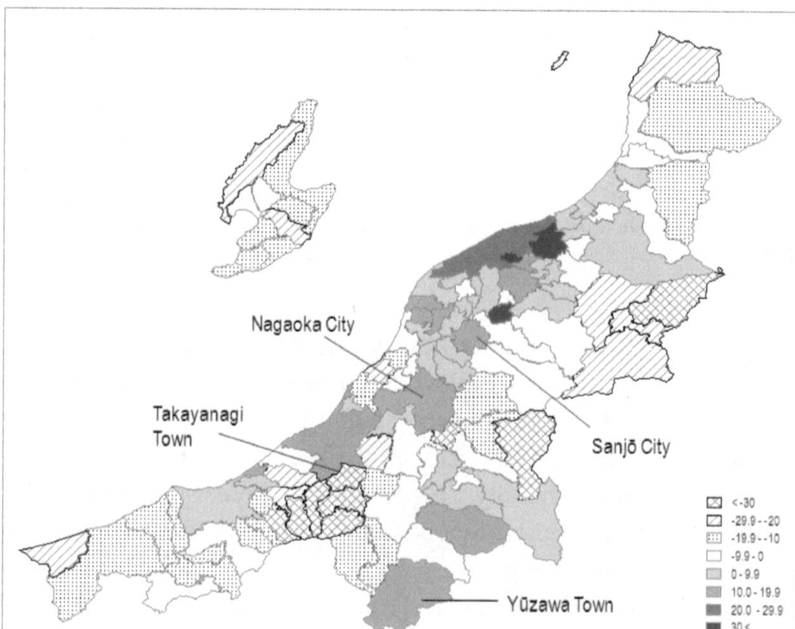

Sources. Niigata ken (2010); Niigata Prefecture website (http://www.pref.niigata.lg.jp/); Higashide (2008).

municipalities rather than the 2008 projections (NIPSSR, 2003) because these are approximately 5 percent less pessimistic than the 2008 projections (Kaneko et al., 2009) and because they offer a more detailed examination of local and regional population trends based on pre-2003 municipal boundaries. Maps 3.5–3.8 exhibit the following points:

- In addition to provincial-metropolitan migration, intraprefectural rural-urban migration has taken place as younger people especially have taken up educational, employment, and marriage and social opportunities in prefectural urban centres such as Niigata and Nagaoka Cities.

Map 3.7. Population Change in Niigata Prefecture by Municipality (2000 boundaries), 1990–2010 (projected).

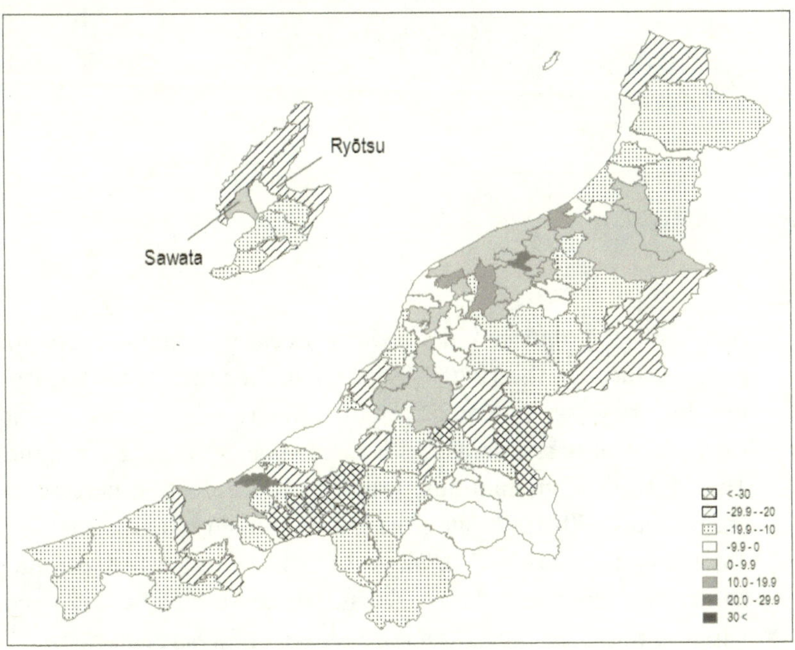

Sources. Niigata ken (2010); Niigata Prefecture website (http://www.pref.niigata.lg.jp/); Higashide (2008); NIPSSR (2003).

MAP 3.8. Population Change in Niigata Prefecture by Municipality (2000 boundaries), 2010–2030 (projected).

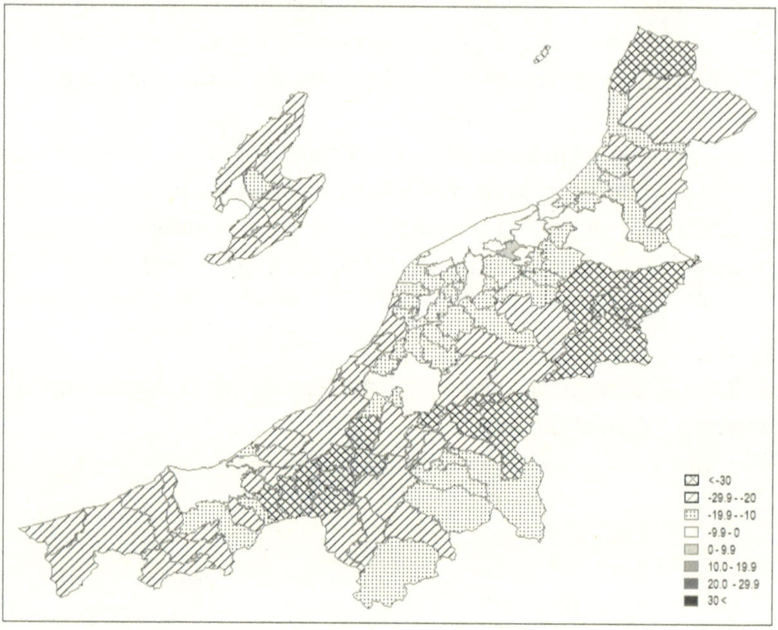

Source. NIPSSR (2003).

- Although the national data show even provincial prefectures growing through the 1970–1990 period, the prefectural data refine this by showing that most population growth in these decades took place in urban areas, with rural areas shrinking throughout. Twelve rural municipalities shrank by more than 50 percent over the period 1970–1990, with the maximum shrinkage occurring in Takayanagi Town (70.1%; map 3.6). The most-affected municipality in Sado was Aikawa Town, which shrank by 52 percent, whereas the other nine shrank by less than 50 percent.
- Even large prefectural urban centres such as Niigata City are now on the verge of shrinkage. Although the national census does not

yet recognise this, as already mentioned, Niigata City reached its population peak of 813,117 in December 2007, and this has now fallen back to an estimated 811,641 (Niigata ken, 2010). By 2030 the city is expected to have shrunk by 9.8 percent to 733,301 (NIPSSR, 2008).

- Some of the strongest growth, or slowest shrinkage, has taken place in the municipalities that have built a Shinkansen super-express railway station (map 3.6). Though very mountainous and remote, Yūzawa Town grew in the period 1950–1990 even as other municipalities with similar geographical circumstances experienced shrinkage. Sanjō City also grew more than the similar settlements Shibata and Murakami.
- Sado Island, despite its separation from the mainland, does not represent the most extreme example of population decrease in Niigata Prefecture. Four areas in mainland Niigata Prefecture are projected to show population declines of more than 30 percent in the 2010–2030 period (map 3.8), but Sado is expected to shrink by 21.4 percent, declining to approximately 52,000 people (NIPSSR, 2003).
- Rural-urban migration is present at the local level even within Sado Island, with the comparatively urbanised district of Sawata either growing more rapidly or shrinking less rapidly than the surrounding mountainous and agricultural areas (map 3.7). On the other side of the low-lying central agricultural plain from Ryōtsu port, Sawata has undergone development as Ryōtsu has declined. Much of this growth has centred on the construction of large-scale chain stores and restaurants with ample car parks, something that the traditional arcades of Ryōtsu, with their small, independently owned stores, have lacked.

Before moving on to examine migration and population change in Sado Island, it is worth briefly considering NIPSSR's various projections for Japan's prefectures and municipalities and comparing them to 2010 government population estimates in order to determine their relative

TABLE 3.4. Population Projections for October 2010 (various years and various locations) and Estimated Actual Populations on 1 October 2010.

	1997 Projection for October 2010	2002/3 Projections for October 2010	2007/8 Projections for October 2010	Estimated Actual Pop. 1 Oct. 2010
Japan	127,630,000	127,473,000	127,176,000	127,380,000
Tokyo	10,906,000	12,431,000	12,906,000	13,048,873
Niigata Prefecture	2,463,000	2,414,636	2,365,819	2,371,046
Niigata City	1)	2)	809,934	811,641
Sado Island	1)	65,790	62,332	62,394

Sources. NIPSSR (1997, 2002, 2003, 2007, 2008); TMG (2010); Statistics Bureau (2010f).
Note. No data available at the municipal level in the 1997 projections. Niigata City projections in 2003 based on pre-2003 municipal boundaries and therefore not comparable with 2008 projections and actual population in 2010.

accuracy in projecting population change and for assessing the degree of future divergence from projected trends.

Table 3.4 shows the Japanese government projections made in 1997, 2002/2003, and 2007/2008 for population in 2010. Each national census in Japan in the modern period takes place in October, and table 3.4 also shows the estimated population on 1 October 2010. The table shows that the 2002/2003 projections for Japan, based as they were on the 2000 census, were not pessimistic enough, whereas the 2007/2008 projections are somewhat too pessimistic. Only in the case of Tokyo were the 2002/2003 projections too pessimistic, probably due to underestimates as to the degree of urbanisation in Japan. It is too soon to make firm conclusions as to the accuracy of the Japanese government's population projections, let alone attribute much meaning from them. Nevertheless, seven to eight years since the 2002/2003 projections, it is becoming clearer that if anything, those projections underestimated the rapidity of Japan's population decrease as well as the degree of continuing concentration of population in the Tokyo metropolis. Both of these trends, if they continue, will have somewhat negative consequences for the degree and pace of population decrease in Niigata Prefecture and Sado Island in the years and decades to come, and it is possible that regional depopulation will be deeper and more widespread than the figures presented in this chapter suggest.

Population Change in Sado Island

Like Niigata Prefecture, of which it is a part, Sado Island has a varied geography and exhibits most of the basic characteristics of Japan's rural locales; indeed, some locals refer to it as a 'mini-Japan.' The island's two forested mountainous zones run parallel from the northeast to the southwest and are divided by a central populated agricultural flood plain, where most economic and political functions have been centralised under the 2004 merger of the island's former 10 municipalities into a single 'Sado City.' In addition, various smaller settlements are scattered along the island's coastal perimeter. Despite its prominent place in the Japanese people's nostalgic and romantic imaginings of the *furusato* (hometown), Sado is sometimes considered a rather remote island; however, this was not always so. Possessing the third-largest gold mine in the world during the Tokugawa period (1603–1867), Sado at that time provided much of Japan's financial wealth and was one of the country's most dynamic regions. It attracted immigrants in addition to the political enemies, criminals, and vagrants that had been despatched there by the Edo government. The settlement at Aikawa on the west coast, which in 2005 had a population of 8,601 (Sado shi, 2010), numbered about 120,000 at the height of the early 19th-century boom. Nevertheless, once the mine ceased large-scale production during the Meiji period (1868–1912) the economy declined, and by the interwar years Sado had stabilised as a regional centre for agriculture, fishing, and processing, with a population of about 100,000; that number briefly increased to over 120,000 in the early 1950s.

Sado has experienced both continuous out-migration of younger people and a reduction in fertility rates to below replacement level—that

TABLE 3.5. Population Change in Sado Island: Selected Years 1961–2008 (migration and natural contributions).

Year	Net Migration	Net Migration to Capital Region	Net Migration to Other Prefectures (including the Capital Region)	Net Migration to Niigata City	Net Migration Within Niigata Pref. (including Niigata City)	Net Natural Contribution	Crude Birth Rate	Crude Death Rate	Population Change	Total Population Previous Year
1961										113296
1963	–2575		–2176		–399					
1966	–1886	–1398	–1478	–430	–641					102925
1971	–1975	–769	–1492	–387	–544	136	11.17	9.7	–1839	92558
1976	–732	–484	–569	–171	–171	94	11.57	10.49	–638	87555
1981	–732	–469	–532	–261	–201	–10	9.79	9.91	–742	84941
1986	–733	–423	–454	–220	–279	–133	8.97	10.59	–866	81939
1991	–288	–217	–137	–192	–153	–282	8.42	12.03	–570	78061
1996	–288	–22	8	–167	–289	–433	7.66	13.44	–721	74949
2001	–241	–59	–34	–170	–205	–404	7.67	13.27	–645	72173
2006	–302	–100	–135	–90	–173	–554	7.12	15.34	–856	67386
2007	–652	–216	–346	–237	–305	–611	6.68	15.98	–1263	66530
2008	–378	–178	v245	–118	–145	–579	6.57	15.64	–957	65267

Sources. Niigata ken (1963); Niigata ken (1964–2009).

Note. Figures for net migration may not tally because of incomplete data. Calculations for crude birth and death rates and for net migration to the capital region and Niigata City were done by the authors using prefectural data sets. As defined by the National Capital Region Planning Act of 1956 (Shutoken seibi-hō), the capital region comprises Ibaraki, Tochigi, Gunma, Saitama, Chiba, Tokyo, Kanagawa, and Yamanashi Prefectures.

is, a double-negative demographic disequilibrium—since at least 1981 (table 3.5). At the local level, these two phenomena are interrelated because out-migration, particularly among young adults, reduces the aggregate reproductive capacity of the remaining community and produces a downward spiral of population ageing and shrinkage (Münz & Reiterer, 2009). Figure 3.3 shows that the largest proportionate population fall has been among the 0–14 age group, which shrank by 79 percent between 1960 and 2009, whereas the over-65 age group has more than doubled in size, increasing from 9,799 persons (8.6% of the total population) to 23,514 (36.3%) between 1960 and 2005, before falling to 23,244 (36.7%) in 2009. A steadily falling birth rate, rising life expectancy, and continuous out-migration of younger people from the island have created the circumstances whereby Sado has become a 'hyper-aged society' (see Coulmas, 2007; Matsutani, 2006).

Table 3.5 shows the migration and natural increase data for Sado Island for selected years between 1961 and 2008. Net migration has been negative for every year presented in the data, but the natural contribution shows a negative figure for the first time in this data in 1981—hence the appearance of the double-negative demographic disequilibrium at that time. Although the crude birth rate dropped continuously during the early decades, the crude death rate did not begin to increase until the 1980s. With the emergence of a hyper-aged society, the difference between the crude birth and death rates is now considerable and is set to increase in the coming decades as the population ages still more.

Figure 3.4 and table 3.5 show that, in addition, population shrinkage in Sado has begun to accelerate, due in part to the cumulative effects of ageing. First, increasing numbers of the over-65 age group are reaching advanced old age and are passing away. This age group has ceased its long-term upward trend and turned negative for the first time, by 270 persons between 2005 and 2009. Second, the rate of out-migration of 15- to 29-year-olds has also accelerated since 2000, almost certainly as a result of renewed economic growth in metropolitan regions and continued difficult economic circumstances in Sado. Thus in the five years between 2000 and 2005, Sado Island's population declined by 4.4 percent, but this decline

FIGURE 3.4. Population Change in Sado Island by Age Group (left-hand scale) and Total Population (right-hand scale; in thousands).

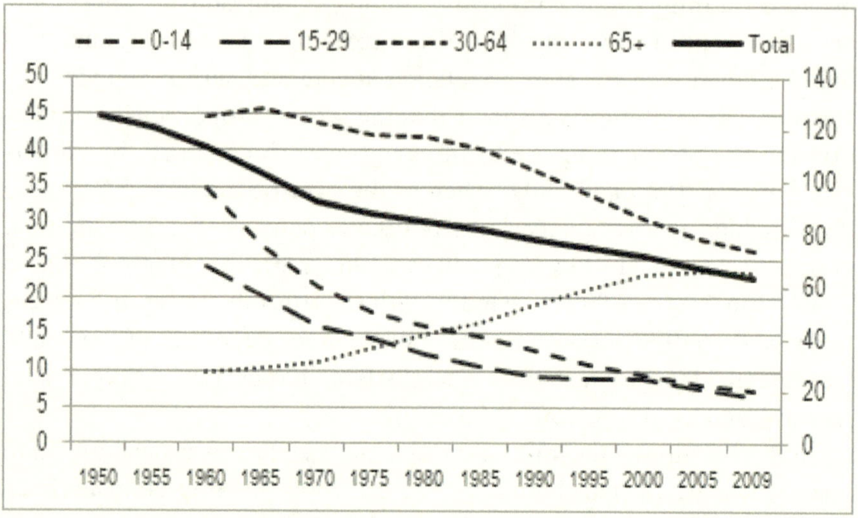

Sources. Sado shi (2006); Niigata ken (2011).

increased to 6.8 percent for the three years to 2008. Moreover, the average annual population loss for the three-year period 2006–2008 rose to 1,025 persons, compared to an average annual loss of 555 for 1995–2000 and of 635 for 2000–2005 (figure 3.4 and table 3.5).

The migration data for Sado Island show that net out-migration is a feature of the island's demography for every year presented, with the net figure steadily decreasing in size and in its proportion of the population as the total number of younger people able to migrate has declined drastically over the decades since the 1950s and as the proportion of young adults in the population has also declined (see figure 3.3). Analysis of the data shows that, for the years presented, the capital region has attracted more than 50 percent of all interprefectural migrants from Sado Island. For migration within Niigata Prefecture, the same pattern emerges but on a smaller scale, with more than half of all intraprefectural net out-migration from Sado accounted for

Photo 3.1. A shrinking village on the isolated northwestern coast of Sado Island.

Photo by Peter Matanle (April 2008).

by the prefectural capital, Niigata City. The following section explores in some detail people's reasons for migrating away from Sado.

Reasons for Emigrating

In recent decades, prefectural governments have been collecting self-reported data by municipality from individuals on their reasons for migrating, indicating that this has become a major issue of concern for the central and regional authorities. The raw data for Niigata Prefecture show out-migration from Sado Island following a regular pattern for at least the previous 30 years, with the largest numbers migrating for reasons of employment. The majority have been in their late teens and 20s, and numbers migrating to other prefectures have been slightly greater than those moving to other parts of Niigata, with Tokyo the most favoured destination (Niigata ken, 1964–2009). A 1996 government report matches this data, finding that 17.4 percent of those born in the

PHOTO 3.2. Many older people in regions such as Sado Island now live solitary and difficult lives with neither family nor neighbours nearby to rely on.

Photo by Peter Matanle (April 2008).

Chūbu-Hokuriku region (where Niigata is located) were currently resident in the Tokyo area (Ministry of Agriculture, Forestry, and Fisheries, 2007), with Nagoya at 3.6 percent and Kinki (Kyoto-Osaka-Kobe) at 3.0 percent. The report also finds that the two most significant migration patterns in the 1960s and 1970s were younger people moving to metropolitan regions, especially Tokyo, for educational advancement and labour-force entry. In this subsection, we focus on recent migration statistics for employment and education because these reasons have produced the largest contributions to net out-migration from Sado Island and have featured most prominently in government reports as being important factors in achieving community sustainability in regional areas (see, for example, MAFF, 2007; NIPSSR, 1996).

Figure 3.5 traces net out-migration from Sado for selected years from 1980 to 2005. Between 1980 and 2000 educational advancement was the largest contributor to net out-migration from the island and work

Figure 3.5. Net Out-Migration from Sado Island, Including Reasons for Migration (selected years: 1980–2005, number of persons).

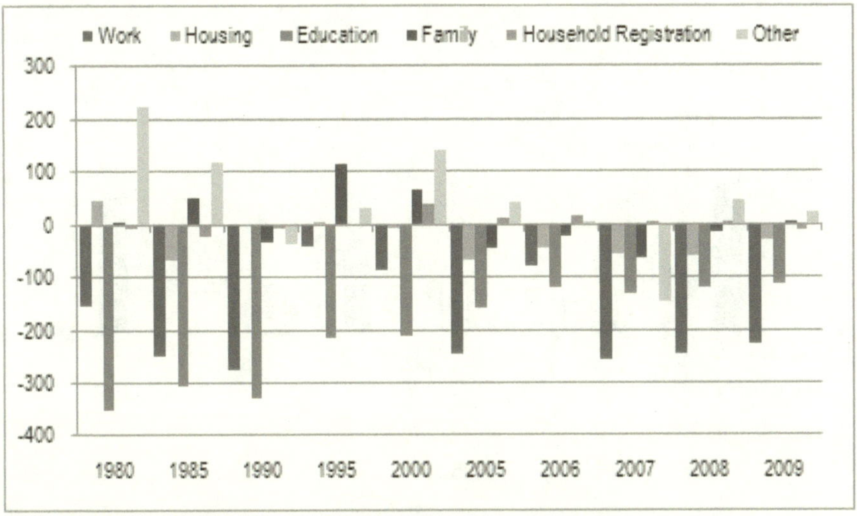

Source. Niigata ken no jinkō idō (Population change in Niigata Prefecture; Niigata ken, 1964–2009).

was second in significance. In 2005 these roles reversed, almost certainly because of the fall in the number of children being born in recent decades and because of the consequent reductions in the migration of adolescents to high schools and universities on the Japanese mainland. A detailed reading of the data shows, as expected, that among educational migrants nearly all are in the 15–19 and 20–24 age cohorts, emphasising standard educational advancement patterns to higher secondary schools (ages 15–18) and post-secondary institutions (Niigata ken, 1964–2009). Institutions outside the prefecture attract the largest numbers; the majority of these schools are universities and colleges for students aged at least 18 years in the Tokyo region. In 2005 some 141 persons migrated from Sado outside of Niigata Prefecture for educational reasons, and 47 migrated to institutions inside the prefecture. This pattern had been repeated, with larger numbers of migrants, in earlier years. Aggregate

FIGURE 3.6. Migration To and From Sado Island, 2005 (absolute and net totals).

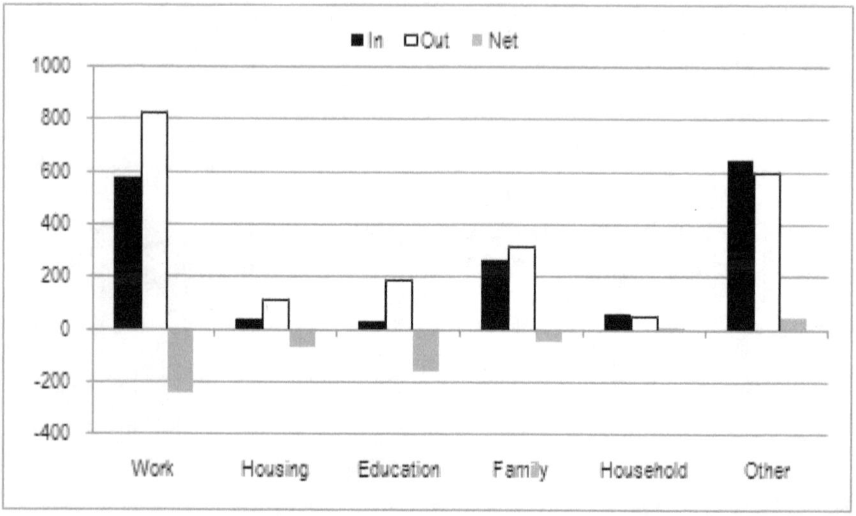

Source. Niigata ken (1964–2009).

figures for 2007 for the whole prefecture show that 62.8 percent of those who emigrated for educational reasons went to Tokyo—80.5 percent of educational migrants were 15–24 years old—and despite the fact that the number of younger people has drastically fallen in recent years, the number of people migrating from Sado to destinations outside the prefecture for educational reasons increased by 39 persons (Niigata ken, 2008, pp. 26–27). Education does not produce high total numbers of outward migrants compared to other reasons, especially employment. However, net figures show that education was the largest contributor to population loss through emigration for the whole period 1980–2005. Moreover, not all reasons produced net outward migration; *family* (mostly children under 15) and *other* both showed an inward trend.

Figure 3.5 provides details on absolute and net totals for migration to and from Sado Island in 2005. The three most common reasons for out-migration were *work*, *other*, and *family*. The majority of those migrating for family reasons were children under 15 (86% percent of out-migrants and 51% percent of inward migrants). Whereas in 1985 there was a net inward migration to Sado of 51 children (48 of these cited family reasons), in 2005 there was a net outward migration of 65. Because nearly all migrants under age 15 would have relocated because of parental employment transfers, it is almost certainly the case that for rural areas similar to Sado Island, migration for employment is bidirectional, with potential for attracting migrants and their children to both employment and educational institutions.

In 2005 the total number of out-migrants for educational reasons was low, but net out-migration was the second highest, after work. This pattern is even stronger for earlier years, when education was the largest contributor to net out-migration from Sado. Some 822 people emigrated for work and 578 immigrated, marking a net loss of 244; whereas 188 people emigrated for educational reasons, only 31 immigrated, showing a net loss of 157. When calculated by age, 57 percent of outward migrants were 15–29 years old, and these made up 4.3 percent of the total population aged 15–29 years in Sado Island in 2005 (Niigata ken, 1964–2009).

Figures 3.7, 3.8, and 3.9 illustrate the impact of rural-urban education and employment migration in Japan by comparing the age structure of the populations for Sado Island, Niigata City, and Tokyo. Sado Island generally experiences a sudden and marked reduction of population aged 20–29 years, due to education- and employment-related out-migration, but Niigata City and especially Tokyo experience gains in their populations in these age groups. Although Sado sees a small recovery after age 30, this gain is by no means commensurate with the initial losses, and Niigata City and, again, especially Tokyo experience growth among these cohorts. Tokyo's working-age population is enormous by comparison to Sado's, and it is notable that Sado shows a clear tendency towards being a hyper-aged society whereas Tokyo sees a marked reduction in its proportion of older people. Moreover, there are strong gender disparities in the Sado population—leaning

FIGURES 3.7, 3.8 AND 3.9. Population Pyramids Showing the Population Structures of Sado Island, Niigata City, and Tokyo, Respectively.

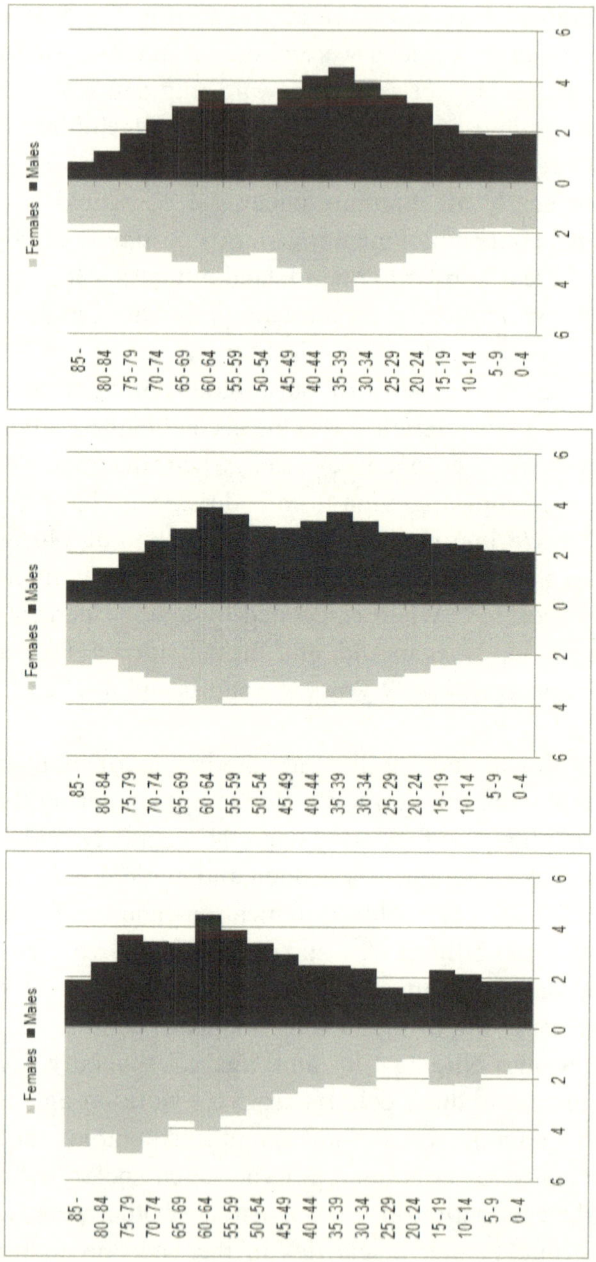

Sources. TMG (2010); Niigata ken (2010).

towards greater female longevity—probably related to the nature of male employment in Sado, which could result in earlier deaths among males. Finally, all three settlements, but especially Sado, see a long-term downward trend in the numbers of children being born. In aggregate, these graphs show the potential impact of rural-urban migration, which creates and exacerbates differential capacities for human and economic reproduction among settlements within the same national space. They also show the way that metropolitan and, to a lesser extent, regional urban centres benefit at the expense of rural regions from such population shifts.

Ageing and depopulation have been taking place across Japan's non-metropolitan regions for more than five decades already. Though Japan's overall economic performance through the postwar years has been nothing short of spectacular, especially in the earlier postwar decades, it appears that the fortunate convergence of population growth and economic expansion is nearing its limits and that a new dynamic of shrinkage—that is, population decline and economic contraction—is beginning to extend from rural locales to include prefectural urban centres and even some metropolitan districts. Having looked at the characteristics of depopulation in Japan as a whole and having considered one typical region and locale, we now begin the process of examining the broader impacts and implications of regional shrinkage, starting with an examination of the economy of one of Japan's most peripheral prefectures.

The Economics of Peripherality in Kōchi Prefecture

Located in south-central Shikoku, Japan's fourth-largest island, Kōchi is one of the country's most remote prefectures, far from Japan's urban and industrial centres. Though it is not representative of every prefecture on Japan's periphery, Kōchi does provide a good case study of those prefectures that have been hardest hit by the combination of demographic and economic changes that have taken place in regional Japan in recent decades. The economic changes occurring there are the result of both domestic and international factors, including (1) the collapse of Japan's 1980s economic bubble, through the 1990s, contributed to more than a decade of recession and slow growth; (2) increasing competition in the agricultural sector; (3) the globalisation and hollowing out of Japanese manufacturing; (4) technological changes to and automation in manufacturing; and (5) demographic changes of the type described earlier with respect to Niigata.

Demographic and Employment Trends in Kōchi Prefecture

Out-migration and declining fertility have created a severe demographic challenge for Kōchi. As with Niigata, Kōchi's population has fluctuated throughout the postwar period, peaking at 883,000 in 1956; declining to 787,000 in 1970; and once again increasing to 840,000 in 1985 (see figure 3.1). Since 1985, Kōchi's population has steadily declined, reaching a postwar low of 766,000 in 2009 (Statistics Bureau, 2010b, 2010d). Kōchi City is the largest city in the prefecture, with a 2005 population of 333,484; Nankoku City, located just outside Kōchi, is the second-largest, with a population of 50,758. Twenty-six percent of the population was 65 years or older in 2005, above the national average of 20 percent. In 2007 Kōchi had the third-lowest birth rate in Japan and the third-highest death rate, and net out-migration among Japanese nationals in 2009 was 2,178 people (Statistics Bureau, 2010b). Kōchi's population will likely continue to decline, for these data give no indication that a reverse trend in the prefecture's demographics might appear in the near future. Indeed, government projections through 2030 show Kōchi's population shrinking to approximately 634,000 people, representing a drop of 28.2 percent from the prefecture's postwar high (NIPSSR, 2007).

A lower percentage of high school graduates in Kōchi go on to universities and junior colleges than in the nation as a whole, a factor that could compound Kōchi's economic development challenges. Although there is little difference between Kōchi and Japan with respect to enrolments at secondary schools (the percentages of students who go to high school are similar), in 2009 some 38.2 percent of male secondary school graduates in Kōchi (compared to 52.3 percent nationally) and 48.7 percent of female graduates (compared to 55.5 percent nationally) advanced to universities and junior colleges, placing Kōchi 45th out of 47 prefectures nationally in the percentage of men and 32th in the percentage of women. 24.5 percent of males and 12.6 percent of females who graduated in March 2009 found employment by 1 May, as compared to national figures of 21.1 percent and 15.2 percent, respectively (Statistics Bureau, 2010b). It is difficult for Kōchi to retain high-quality human capital in the prefecture not only because academically good students have a tendency to emigrate but also because the ratio of job offers to job seekers in Kōchi is among the lowest in the country. This creates a difficult problem for policy makers—the prefecture does not have the educational and employment opportunities necessary to retain qualified workers, but it needs these workers to build its economy.

Kōchi is one of the poorest prefectures in Japan, with a per capita income that was the 44th out of Japan's 47 prefectures in 2006. Prefectural per capita income decreased from JPY 2.4 million in 2000 to JPY 2.2 million in 2006. One explanation for these income differentials may be related to higher rates of part-time employment in Kōchi Prefecture, particularly among women. This is consistent with higher national rates of part-time employment among women and generally higher rates of part-time employment among women in rural areas, and it is also consistent with legal changes that have made it easier to hire part-time workers. Women make up a slightly larger percentage of the labour force in Kōchi than they do nationally, and this is also true in seven of the eight largest industries in the prefecture (Statistics Bureau, 2010e). Over the three-year period from 2004 to 2007, while the Japanese economy was growing, Kōchi's real gross domestic expenditure decreased by 3.1 percent in 2004, by 1.1 percent in 2005, and by 1.2 percent in 2006. Kōchi's economy is not reflective of the Japanese economy overall, though like many peripheral prefectures it has a higher percentage of economic output coming from the primary and tertiary sectors and a lower percentage from the secondary sector. In 2006 the primary sector accounted for 3.9 percent of Kōchi's output, the secondary sector for 15 percent, and the tertiary sector for 81 percent (Statistics Bureau, 2010e). Employment and the size of the labour force in Kōchi both significantly declined over the period 1990–2005, with the labour force declining from 422,000 persons in 1990 to 402,000 in 2005 and employment declining from 402,000 to 370,000 (Statistics Bureau, 2010d, 2010e).

The primary sector continues to be an important part of Kōchi's economy even though it only accounts for 3.9 percent of economic output. Agriculture, forestry, and fisheries accounted for a combined 13 percent of employment in Kōchi Prefecture in 2005. Examination using a location quotient analysis to assess the concentration of employment by industry in Kōchi compared to the nation as a whole (table 3.6) indicates that Kōchi also has a high concentration of employment in these sectors. Kōchi has a location quotient (LQ) of 2.44 in agriculture, 7.98 in forestry, and 4.00 in fisheries (see note to table 3.6).

Kōchi also has a high concentration of employment in government and public sector positions, as measured by a location quotient of 1.11 for education, 1.23 for other government employment, and 1.45 for medical, health care, and welfare, the fastest growing industry in the prefecture. This concentration of employment in the education, government, and medical, health-care, and welfare sectors, which together account for 21.7 percent of all prefectural employment, points to a significant role for the public sector in the Kōchi economy despite the overall decline in government funding for public works. Medical, health care, and welfare is the second-largest employment sector in Kōchi, accounting for 47,000 jobs, and is an area in which Kōchi has a high concentration of employment (LQ = 1.45; Statistics Bureau, 2005). Recent growth in this sector and the high location quotient are to some extent consequences of the ageing of the population in Kōchi Prefecture, as in the periphery in general, but this sector should not be overlooked in terms of its importance to the local economy. It provides a large number of job opportunities for younger workers to earn relatively stable and satisfactory incomes. The medical, health-care, and welfare sector boasted the second-largest percentage of workers under the age of 40 among sectors in Kōchi in 2005,

Table 3.6. Location Quotient for Sector of Employment in Kōchi Prefecture (2005).

	Japan		Kōchi		Location Quotient
	Employment	Percent	Employment	Percent	
Agriculture	2,703,360	4.4	39,766	10.7	2.44
Forestry	46,618	0.1	2,239	0.6	7.98
Fisheries	215,813	0.4	5,193	1.4	4.00
Mining	26,921	0.0	575	0.2	3.55
Construction	5,391,905	8.8	38,073	10.3	1.17
Manufacturing	10,646,362	17.3	32,496	8.8	0.51
Electricity, gas, heat supply and water	279,799	0.5	1,395	0.4	0.83
Information and communications	1,624,480	2.6	4,017	1.1	0.41
Transport	3,132,712	5.1	13,567	3.7	0.72
Wholesale and retail trade	11,018,413	17.9	67,738	18.3	1.02
Finance and insurance	1,537,830	2.5	8,415	2.3	0.91
Real estate	859,635	1.4	2,752	0.7	0.53
Eating and drinking places, accommodations	3,223,451	5.2	19,886	5.4	1.02
Medical, health care and welfare	5,353,261	8.7	46,822	12.6	1.45
Education, learning support	2,702,160	4.4	17,991	4.9	1.11
Compound services	679,350	1.1	7,551	2.0	1.85
Other services	8,819,754	14.3	41,986	11.3	0.79
Other government	2,098,148	3.4	15,528	4.2	1.23
Other establishments	1,146,001	1.9	4,405	1.2	0.64
Total	61,505,973		370,395		

Source. Statistics Bureau (2005).
Note. The location quotient is the share of employment by industry divided by the share nationally. A location quotient greater than 1 indicates that the sector accounts for a larger share of employment than it does nationally, and a location quotient less than 1 indicates a share of employment lower than the national share

and in 2004 wages per employee that were 28 percent higher than wages in the service sector in Kōchi overall (Statistics Bureau, 2004, 2005).

Apart from medical, health care, and welfare, the service sector presents a very mixed picture. Employees in wholesale and retail trade numbered 68,000, the largest sector in terms of employment in 2005 (18% of employment), and employees working in eating and drinking places and accommodations numbered 20,000 (5% of employment). Both sectors had location quotients of 1.02 and were therefore close to the national average in the share of employment. However, although 42,000 people were employed in other services (11% of employment), the location quotient for this sector was only 0.79 (Statistics Bureau, 2005).

Kōchi has not benefited from the postwar growth in manufacturing to the extent that other prefectures have, and manufacturing in Kōchi is smaller and has struggled more than the industry nationally (figure 3.10). In 2005 only 9 percent of Kōchi's population was employed in manufacturing, compared to 17 percent nationally (LQ = 0.53; Statistics Bureau, 2005). Manufacturing employment in Kōchi closely followed national trends from 1992 to 1997, with manufacturing employment generally declining, and with Kōchi faring better than the nation as a whole in some years and worse in others. Starting in 1999, however, manufacturing employment in Kōchi declined more rapidly than in the nation as a whole—though it started to rebound in 2006, a year after manufacturing employment nationally started to grow (Ministry of Economy, Trade, and Industry, 2010a; Statistics Bureau, 2010e). Unfortunately for Kōchi, this was just before the global recession that led to a sharp drop in manufacturing production and employment across Japan.

After performing well relative to the nation as a whole in the 1990s, Kōchi's manufacturing production now lags behind the rest of Japan in terms of both its rate of growth and its yen value (figure 3.11). This lag is also reflected in the fact that Kōchi ranked 46th of 47 prefectures in shipments and value added in 2007. Furthermore, by value Kōchi's shipments were only 52 percent of Tottori Prefecture's

FIGURE 3.10. Manufacturing Employment in Kōchi (left-hand scale, in thousands) and Japan (right-hand scale, in millions), 1985–2008.

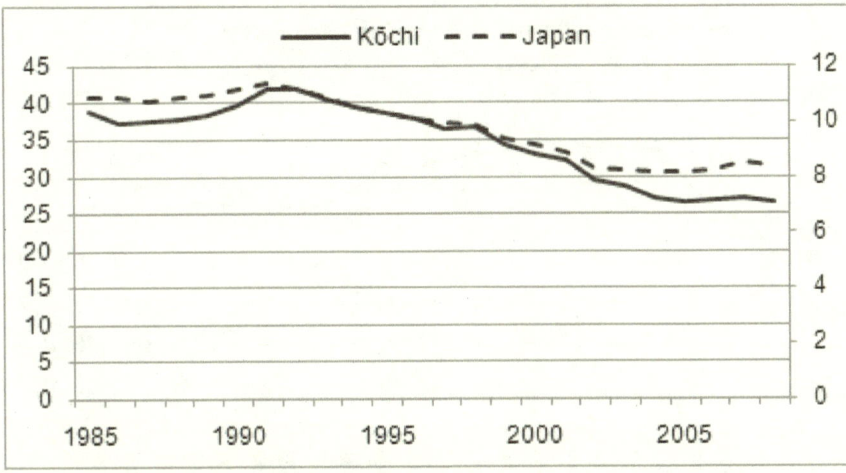

Sources. METI (2010); Statistics Bureau (2010e).
Note. The discussion and charts in these paragraphs are based on data from METI's Census of Manufacturers. Employment data from the Census of Manufacturers is not comparable to employment data from the national population census. Value added is gross value added for establishments with 9 or fewer people until 2000; from 2001 value added is gross value added is for establishments with 29 or fewer. Other slight changes in methodology or classifications may affect year-to-year data comparisons.

shipments (ranked 45th), and Kōchi's manufacturing value added was only 62 percent of Tottori's in 2007 (METI, 2010). From 1988 to 1995, Kōchi's shipments significantly increased, and Kōchi's manufacturing shipments frequently did better than the shipments of the nation as a whole. After 1996, however, shipments by companies in Kōchi fared worse than shipments across the nation as a whole. Like its employment, Kōchi's shipments did not recover in the 2000s as quickly as Japan in general, and when they did significantly recover it was not until just before the 2008–2009 recession, only to take a significant hit thereafter. Similarly, the value added of Kōchi's manufacturing increased from 1987 to 1995 but then declined in all but three years

FIGURE 3.11. Manufacturing Shipments and Manufacturing Value Added in Kōchi (left-hand scale) and Japan (right-hand scale), 1985–2008 (JPY billions).

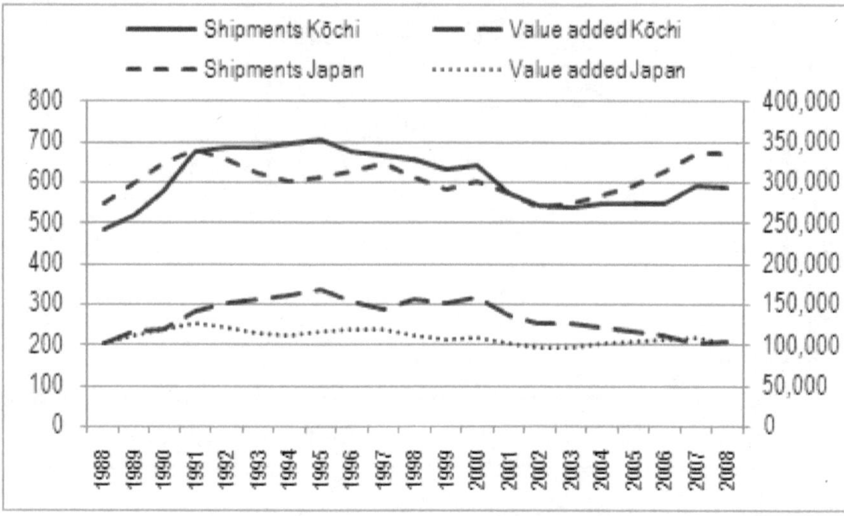

Sources. METI (2010); Statistics Bureau (2010d).

from 1996 to 2008 (METI, 2010; Statistics Bureau, 2010d). Despite the manufacturing sector's relatively small size and its struggles in Kōchi, manufacturing still accounts for a significant portion of Kōchi's economy. Shipments totalled JPY 587 billion in 2007, and the Kōchi manufacturing sector employed 27,000 people the same year (METI, 2010). Manufacturing was the sixth-largest sector in terms of Kōchi's employment in 2005, and parts of the manufacturing sector there are closely tied to the locale's traditional strength in the agricultural sector—indicating the continuing importance of the primary sector to the Kōchi economy (METI, 2010; Statistics Bureau, 2010d).

In sum, therefore, Kōchi Prefecture is worse off economically than many prefectures in Japan, and its peripheral location has a significant impact on its ability to attract and retain industry and to generate employment, both of which are crucial for the establishment of stable communities within the region. The prefecture is struggling to adapt to economic changes brought about by globalisation and technological change, and though its manufacturing sector was starting to recover after 2005, this recovery has been slowed by the global recession and financial crisis that significantly affected most of Japan's manufacturing sector. Though some service sectors have been growing of late, growth in these sectors has not been significant enough to revitalise Kōchi's economy. As elsewhere in Japan's more peripheral regions, Kōchi's poor economic performance (both in relative and absolute terms) has been a major factor in Japan's regional shrinkage over the long term, helping to set up a recursive downward spiral of out-migration, depopulation, and ageing, on the one hand, and a lacklustre economic performance, on the other—which then contributes to a secondary decline in the prefecture's economic and demographic indicators.

Conclusion

Niigata presents a useful case study of regional shrinkage in Japan for various reasons, of which four stand out. First, a closer reading of population change refines the understanding of the dynamics of shrinkage in Japan over the course of the postwar decades. In particular, the data show that population shrinkage and agglomeration have been taking place simultaneously at national, regional, and local levels. The research also demonstrates that depopulation has been spreading from rural and remote areas to affect larger and more densely populated settlements in the course of its advance. Second, the figures show that the relationship between changing birth and death rates temporarily masked a structural decline in the population, and this masking effect is now disappearing to reveal a double negative demographic disequilibrium in an increasing number of locales and on a progressively larger scale. Whereas Sado Island encountered this stage in its demographic development in the early 1980s, it appeared in Niigata Prefecture as a whole beginning in the late 1990s. Third, the migration data indicate that because the nationwide participation rate in post-secondary education has risen to approximately three-quarters of each youth cohort, rural-urban migration for educational attainment has joined employment as one of the most significant underlying causes of the migration contribution to rural and regional shrinkage, especially among older adolescents and younger adults.

Kōchi Prefecture's geographical circumstances have had a major influence on the long term-loss of employment opportunities there. The argument made here is based on this question of geographical peripherality, in terms of both distance and inaccessibility, which we analyse in subsequent chapters. We maintain that low fertility and rural-urban migration are major contributors to the recursive spiral of ageing, depopulation, and social and economic decline in Japan's shrinking regions. The introduction of Niigata and Kōchi Prefectures here sets up the discussions that follow and emphasizes that there are no simple diagnoses and, consequently, no simple solutions to the issues presented herein. The question that arises from this research, therefore, is this: What are the implications for Japan's urban areas as they also begin to experience depopulation?

CHAPTER 4

CONTRASTING EXPERIENCES OF GROWTH AND DECLINE IN REGIONAL JAPAN*

INTRODUCTION

This chapter and the next focus on the impacts and implications of population change in Japan's rural and suburban settlements. In aggregate, the three descriptions that follow present a stylised portrait of the historical development and decline of Japan's regions in the postwar period—including examples of the country's extraordinary economic expansion and the less well-known but equally dramatic long-term decay of the countryside as a site for human settlement—and finally raise the question of how those living throughout the islands that make up the Japanese

*The principal contributing authors to this chapter are Christopher P. Hood, John Knight, and Richard Siddle.

archipelago can maintain a decent quality of life under circumstances of population shrinkage.

The three very different and contrasting cases discussed in this chapter exemplify the often visually powerful transformations that have taken place in urban, rural, and island communities throughout Japan. Construction, particularly infrastructure development, has had a profound impact on the course of development in Japan's regions and is a recurring topic in this book. Thus in the first section, we look at the case of Japan's world-renowned Shinkansen super-express train system and investigate some of the system's spatial and demographic effects on regional urban and suburban districts. This research reminds us that depopulation has not been a uniform experience. Some settlements, particularly suburban ones, have been expanding whereas others, sometimes within the same region, have been shrinking. Whether one lives in a growing or a shrinking community can often simply be a matter of whether a high-speed train station has been built nearby. Population movement then becomes a story of governmental and commercial decisions being matched by the considerations of individuals and families within a rapidly changing economy and society.

In the second section of this chapter we move away from regional urban districts to introduce some of the cause-and-effect relationships between depopulation and natural succession in a rural mountainous area of Wakayama Prefecture. Despite empty buildings, abandoned houses, and vacant lots with weeds growing through pavements—powerful visual clues to the changing fortunes of urban areas—the more extreme and recursively experienced causes and consequences of community decline in Japan present themselves most dramatically and clearly in remote rural areas. Although these visual indicators may sometimes go unremarked, often because they are unseen by the majority of urban dwellers and opinion formers in society, they are nevertheless distressing, if not depressing, for the remaining residents in these locales, who themselves may feel compelled to leave by the atmosphere of a slowly collapsing community that surrounds them daily. (It is within this prevailing cultural context of hopelessness in communities that we consider the ultimate costs of depopulation in later chapters.)

The third section of this chapter presents an overview of the circumstances of Okinawa Prefecture and its focus on the relationship between peripheral communities and the decision-making processes in the prefectural and national government centres. Superficially, Okinawa presents an exceptional case in Japan, for the prefecture's population is expected to continue to grow. Moreover, the island prefecture's geographical circumstances prevent easy comparison with other places in Japan. Its uniqueness notwithstanding, however, a less superficial, more detailed look at local circumstances reveals that many of the issues present in the rest of Japan's regions also pose difficult problems in Okinawa. Okinawa's demography exhibits the same dynamic of peripheral shrinkage and concentration in the centre as elsewhere in Japan. Economic and social transformations within and beyond the prefecture present policy makers and citizens with a set of challenging and often contradictory problems. Okinawa's peripheral islands need investment in new businesses, infrastructure, and technology, as well as continued participation by the public sector to ensure the survival of its more isolated and distant communities and to maintain Japan's national area. Yet the precarious circumstances of many of these island communities raises this question: At what point does a community become no longer viable, and what does the state do under these circumstances?

Growth and Shrinkage Under Infrastructure Development: The Shinkansen in Japan's Shrinking Regions

An area of vital importance at the national and local levels that carries deep implications for social and economic stability in Japan's regions is the relationship between depopulation and infrastructure development. One factor that has long been identified as contributing to geographical peripherality is a relative lack of transportation infrastructure connecting regional settlements to larger population centres. Though potentially devastating in its ramifications for the out-migration of younger people in search of education and employment, over the long-term, this lack of connecting transportation infrastructure effectively separates family members, making frequent trips difficult and inconvenient; in addition, the lack of transport handicaps the potential of outlying areas to attract visitors from elsewhere. However, a somewhat unexplored area of research on shrinkage, especially with respect to Japan, is the effect that regional transportation infrastructure has actually had either in stemming out-migration or in accelerating the phenomenon.

On 1 October 1964, the Shinkansen began operating between Tokyo and Osaka, ushering in a new era of high-speed railways for the world. For Japan, this was a moment of historic national importance that, alongside the staging of the Olympic Games in Tokyo that same year, signalled the country's emergence from the shadow of the Second World War as a peaceful, modern, and technologically advanced democracy. In the subsequent 40 years, the system has steadily expanded into a nationwide network extending across Honshū and Kyūshū. Its careful and diligent operation has also made the Shinkansen synonymous throughout the world with high-speed, punctual, and safe transportation. Yet the far-ranging impact of the system as it has expanded, the implications of this process, and the reality it yields are rarely discussed. This discussion might begin with the Jōetsu Shinkansen connecting Niigata with Tokyo, which was initiated in 1971 by the then prime minister Kakuei Tanaka and which began service in 1982. This railway line could be viewed as a metaphor for Japan's postwar history, its construction and outcomes as emblematic of both the country's political structure and the government's unwavering pursuit of national economic expansion and infrastructure development—notions emphatically outlined in Johnson's (1982) accounts of the capitalist developmental state and in McCormack's (2001) depictions of the construction state, Japan's *doken kokka*. Although Japan had largely caught up with the so-called advanced industrialised nations of the world by the 1980s, the reality of this policy process proved both positive and negative in its outcomes, producing a complex reality that even today affects Japanese people's lived experiences.

Rail Transport in Japan's Regions: Measuring the Demographic Impacts of Infrastructural Development

Two of the most obvious means of quantifying the Shinkansen's impacts on Japan are measurements of changes in population and of changes in economic output—measures which can be taken at the level of the town, city, prefecture, region, or even of the country as a whole. In addition, in the context of depopulation, these levels of analysis are not unrelated. A population increase in one locale might be expected to lead to an increase in economic output. Similarly, a rise in economic activity will often lead to a subsequent rise in population as people move in search of employment opportunities, which then results in an expansion in local demand and contributes to generating a positive self-reinforcing cycle of economic and population growth.

Although transportation plays a significant role in this relationship, it may also have a negative effect on economic output and population change. If local transportation links are good, for example, people may choose not to live in the city where they are employed but to commute. In this case, the local economic benefits of industrial expansion may be less than expected because employees and their families spend their incomes elsewhere. Then again, if transportation links are inefficient or costs are high, the impact on the overall area may be significant, for industry may resist locating in the area or move out, affecting local demand negatively and contributing to a spiral of shrinkage and decline.

The reality of these interrelated measures is that there is rarely a win-win outcome, particularly in contemporary Japan, with respect to local economies and population change. The overall national population has started to decline, and the working population is scheduled to shrink more rapidly as the consequences of population ageing are felt more deeply. As a result, when there is significant population growth in a city, growth that could in part be attributed to transportation links provided by the Shinkansen, another area, often rural or without access to the Shinkansen, will inevitably experience shrinkage. This is economically significant because normally the most economically active individuals, or at least those with the most economic potential, migrate away, and this emigration will have a proportionately larger negative influence on demand in affected locales. This process can snowball once cities and affected settlements reach a point at which business and retail premises are forced to close, subsequently encouraging others in the working population to migrate away or to commute greater distances in order to work elsewhere. What ensues is a cycle of economic and demographic decline that can potentially lead to more severe declines in local economic activity; there is the additional danger that local government finances may reach a point at which the provision of essential services is threatened and whole communities come under imminent threat of collapse. Nevertheless, people's choices to commute greater distances can, of course, benefit the railway company, which can expect to see increased revenue—albeit concentrated at peak intervals—that will have implications for corporate profitability and service provision.

These scenarios of depopulation and economic output influence society in numerous important ways at the micro level and also require consideration. Because of migration, many family members live apart from relatives; most noteworthy are the many examples of elderly parents living alone in isolated and half-deserted hamlets and small towns. These circumstances create a disproportionately increasing reliance on—and therefore cost to—local authorities to provide support services for older persons, ranging from relatively simple tasks such as assisting with shopping or providing home help to the more complex provision of barrier-free housing and infrastructure and specialist health care in remote areas. In addition, migration may negatively affect the development of social capital among children, who will have reduced interactions with their elderly family members. In families with children without older relatives nearby, it will also be harder for both parents to work full time. Although compared to many European countries, dual-income families are less numerous in Japan, they have become more common (Asahi Shimbun, 2005, p. 10), and this trend is likely to continue as more middle-class families struggle to raise the funds necessary to cover the costs of modern life and as pricing mechanisms based on affordability adapt to a dual-income household as standard.

Those families with children but no local relatives will, in addition, become reliant on the availability of child-care facilities, both public and private. Child care has hitherto not been used extensively in Japan, where only 13 percent of 3-year-olds are in day-care, compared to 54 and 34 percent in the United States and the United Kingdom (Asahi Shimbun, 2005, p. 11). The reason for the lower Japanese figure is likely related not to the economic costs of such provision but rather to the social expectations for Japanese mothers and the willingness and availability of grandparents to aid in looking after children. Even without relatives nearby to help, many families will be able to meet the costs of child care; others, however, will need to raise additional money, and in these families both parents will need to work longer hours. The end result for such families will be that the children will have less interaction with their own family members, and the development of social capital may become more difficult in such households (see Bassani, 2003).

Complicating any examination of the Shinkansen's impact upon regional settlements are two important factors. The first is changes in the numerical level of train service and the quality of service, considered not only in terms of immediate impacts but also as harbingers of future change. Local train service is an important issue for any rural locale, but it is one that must be considered together with other public and private transportation options, such as cars and buses. For the purposes of this chapter, the changes considered focus on the opening of new Shinkansen lines in areas throughout Japan.

The second factor that must be considered comprises the recent changes in the Japanese municipal administrative structure, which have occurred with the so-called *Heisei dai-gappei* wave of municipal mergers that swept through Japan in 2003–2004 (see Rausch, 2006). These mergers were part of a process initiated by the Japanese government in order to address a host of financial problems evident at the municipal level throughout the country, many of which were and are a consequence of the drastic ageing and shrinking of rural communities. By the start of 2007, the number of municipalities in Japan stood at 1,822, a 40 percent decrease from 1999 (Rausch, 2010), but still well above the national government's eventual target of 1,000. The consequence of these mergers is that in some cases it is difficult, if not impossible, to gather accurate figures allowing a comparison of economic and population changes over several years. By way of example, on 1 October 2006, Haruna Town in Gunma Prefecture (population approximately 22,000) was merged with the larger and more historically significant city of Takasaki. In terms of the Shinkansen links, this merger was particularly interesting: as a result of the merger, the new Annaka-Haruna station was built on the recently completed Nagano Shinkansen line—with a new road and tunnel linking these previously unconnected cities. But measuring the implications of these changes on the local area is difficult because population data is no longer kept for Haruna and it is quite likely that the population growth Takasaki is currently experiencing may be masking other population movements between Haruna and Takasaki.

The JNR Shinkansen

We now turn to the impacts of particular Shinkansen lines and their stations. Four lines were operating by 1987 when Japanese National Railways (JNR) was broken up and privatised. These were the Tōkaidō Shinkansen (Tokyo-Osaka), the San'yō Shinkansen (Osaka-Hakata), the Tōhoku Shinkansen (Tokyo-Morioka), and the Jōetsu Shinkansen (Tokyo-Niigata).

The first section of the Tōhoku Shinkansen, running between Ōmiya and Morioka, opened in 1982, some 11 years after the initial approval of the line's construction. An extension between Ueno in the capital and Ōmiya opened in 1985. This extension met with much local opposition (Groth, 1986, 1996), an indication that not everyone considers a Shinkansen in their locale desirable. It should, however, be noted that opposition by local homeowners has sometimes been leveraged in order to increase the compensation received when they have been forced to relocate (Konno, 1984, p. 76; Hood, 2006, pp. 86–87). Another extension between Ueno and Tokyo opened in 1991, and at the northern end of the line, an extension between Morioka and Hachinohe opened in 2002. The final section between Hachinohe and Shin-Aomori, completing the connection between Tokyo and Aomori City, which opened in 2011.

MAP 4.1. Japan and the Shinkansen Network in 2008.

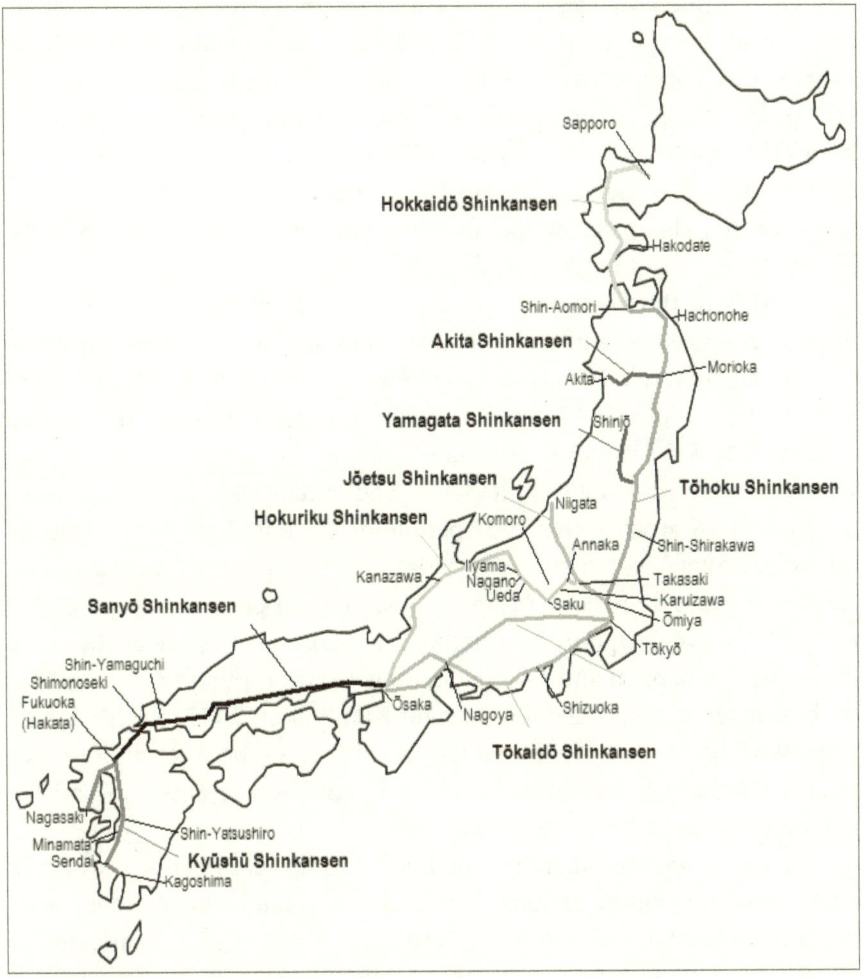

Source. Map by Christopher Hood.
Note. The Hokkaidō Shinkansen is currently under construction between Shin-Aomori and Hakodate. No route has been confirmed between Hakodate and Sapporo. The Hokuriku Shinkansen is currently under construction between Nagano and Kanazawa. No route has been confirmed between Kanazawa and Osaka. At the time of writing the Kyūshū Shinkansen was under construction between Shin-Yatsushiro and Hakata. It opened on 12 March 2011. No route has been confirmed between Hakata and Nagasaki. The route of the Chūō Shinkansen, initially to be built between Tokyo and Nagoya, has yet to be confirmed (Hood, 2006).

Population change between 1975 and 1995 along the Tōhoku Shinkansen line indicates that those cities with a station saw an average increase in their populations of 32 percent. This compares to a national average of 12 percent over the same period and a below-average increase of 7 percent in cities along the line where a Shinkansen station was *not* built (Kōsoku Tetsudō Kenkyūkai, 2003, p. 44). It is important, however, to note that the Shinkansen-line cities that did not have a station had seen population growth above the national average prior to 1984, barely 18 months after the opening of the line.

In terms of the changes in the number of companies located in the various cities, those with a Shinkansen station saw an increase of about 46 percent between 1975 and 1991. This compares to a national average of 21 percent and 17 percent for those cities without a Shinkansen station (Kōsoku Tetsudō Kenkyūkai, 2003, p. 45). Again, those cities in which stations were not built had seen above-national average increases until about 18 months after the opening of the line. Finally, the state of municipal finances indicates that those cities with a Shinkansen station saw an increase in income of approximately 155 percent between 1980 and 1993. This compares to a national average increase over the same period of 110 percent and to 75 percent increases for those cities without a Shinkansen station (Kōsoku Tetsudō Kenkyūkai, 2003, p. 45). Again, 1984 was the critical year in which the difference between those cities with a Shinkansen station and those without became apparent and the gap between them began to grow.

These data together demonstrate that a multiplier effect is at work. In cities with Shinkansen stations, improvement of public finances occurred more quickly than did either increases in the number of companies or expansion of the population. The conclusion from these data is also clear. During the initial development and operation phase of the Shinkansen system, if a line was built through a region, a city would develop and grow more rapidly than the national average only if it had a station; nevertheless, not having a station did not spell disaster. All cities, on average, saw improvements, although it should be remembered that the figures cover periods of general economic and demographic growth in

Japan, unlike the situation that has followed. However, lacking a Shinkansen station meant that a city would likely experience relatively less growth than neighbouring cities with stations. After all, even though Semmens (2000, p. 46) pointed out that 400 companies, many from outside of the region, opened branch offices in Fukuoka in preparation for the opening of the San'yō Shinkansen extension to the city in 1975, what is less clear is how many other offices in other cities were downsized or closed as a consequence of the new investments.

Before considering two lines constructed in the post-JNR era, we must consider two other cases on the original Shinkansen line, both of which illustrate the complexity of issues that emerge with the determination of a station-city. The example of Shizuoka, located on the Tōkaidō Shinkansen and now a city of over 700,000 people, highlights municipal reaction to the city's not being designated a station site. At only 167 km from Tokyo, Shizuoka City is on the edge of the commuting perimeter to the capital and to Japan's second-largest city, Yokohama. However, the fastest train service on the Tōkaidō line, the *Nozomi*, does not stop there. The prefectural governor concluded that this was likely hindering further investment in the city and deterring more people from moving to the area (because the travel time to the local station is often a significant part of the total journey time) and so suggested introducing a JPY 100 'tax' on nonstop services. This levy, whether paid by JR Tōkai or passed on to the passenger, would have raised an estimated JPY 3.1 billion annually (Shizuoka Shimbun, 2002) and was a clear sign that though having a Shinkansen station has almost certainly helped Shizuoka develop, still further development might occur if its transportation links were improved. Shizuoka Prefecture has also been arguing (so far unsuccessfully) that a station be built under Mt. Fuji Shizuoka Airport, which opened in 2009. This would not only make Mt. Fuji Shizuoka the only airport connected to the Shinkansen network—remarkable in itself given the inter- and intraministerial turf wars that go on within the Japanese state bureaucracy and political parties—but also significantly improve the connections to the airport and the airport's currently dire financial situation (see *Japan Times*, 2009). This development might also ease the negative environmental impacts arising from transportation because a large proportion of the CO_2 emissions and environmental pollution produced by airports is caused by the connecting land-based transportation available to airport users.

The naming of stations has also been a revealing issue, one connected to the likelihood that any particular station will be used as a Shinkansen station. For example, during the development of the San'yō Shinkansen connecting Osaka with Hakata in the late 1960s and early 1970s, the Yamaguchi prefectural government had initially hoped that one of the original stations, which would act as a gateway to the prefecture and to its capital, would be named Shin-Yamaguchi. The use of the character *shin*, meaning *new*, appeared as a prefix to identify the station as a new Shinkansen station and probably also helped to suggest a degree of freshness and progress occurring within Yamaguchi City. However, following a local mayoral election, the station was named after Ogōri City, in which the station was located (Umehara, 2002, p. 50). Not until 2003 did the station become Shin-Yamaguchi; at the same time, it also became a station at which some of the fastest *Nozomi* services made stops. It is noteworthy in this respect, therefore, that Yamaguchi City is one of only three prefectural capitals that is expected to grow more than 30 percent in the period 1990–2010 (the other two are Tokyo and Yokohama; see chapter 3, map 3.3).

Whereas the people of Ogōri initially opposed the exclusion of their town's name from the Shinkansen station's title, the people of the comparably sized Nishigō (Fukushima Prefecture) were apparently not concerned when their local station was renamed Shin-Shirakawa as a result of the development of the Tōhoku Shinkansen in 1982—even though the station was actually located in Nishigō and not in neighbouring Shirakawa City (Yamanouchi, 2000, p. 41). The significance of this station has taken another form in recent years: The local government of Izumizaki, three stops from Shin-Shirakawa on a local railway line, offered to pay up to 60 percent of passengers' commuting costs to Tokyo for three years as an incentive for people to move to the area, which was battling local population decline (Hood, 2006, p.14). Shin-Shirakawa is about 180 km north of Tokyo, a distance that reveals how far some Japanese are prepared to commute to work. Indeed, the Shinkansen operating companies have had to respond either through the addition of more frequent shorter-distance (as opposed to terminal-to-terminal) services or through the innovative use of rolling stock—namely, using double-decker trains and trains that can be easily separated so that the entire train does not cover the less-used sections of the line. Of course, such developments are likely to have increased the demand for housing in the commuting belt around the capital—a huge radius of some 200 km.

The argument can therefore be made that, whereas former prime minister Kakuei Tanaka and others may have viewed the Shinkansen as a means to connect the Japanese archipelago as part of the government's spatial equalisation and regional development measures, the construction of the Shinkansen has possibly increased the concentration of economic activity in the capital region by attracting more people to intermediate cities on the Kantō plain, from which they can easily access both the capital and their *furusato* (hometown), where their elderly relatives still live.

The JR Shinkansen

Two of the newer Shinkansen lines have been built in the JR (Japan Railways) era since the breakup and privatisation of JNR, revealing a different set of circumstances. The Hokuriku Shinkansen was initially planned to connect Takasaki and Karuizawa only, with passengers set to use the Jōetsu Shinkansen and Tōhoku Shinkansen in order to connect with Tōkyō, but this decision was changed and the line was actually extended to cover the distance between Takasaki and Nagano, opening in time for the 1998 Nagano Winter Olympic Games. Consequently, the line is now commonly referred to as the Nagano Shinkansen, even by JR East. Moreover, this line is currently being extended to Kanazawa; this stretch is due to open in 2013. Additional plans are pending for the construction of the Seibi Shinkansen (linking Kanazawa with Osaka), but the necessary agreements have not been reached and questions remain as to whether it will be built.

FIGURE 4.1. Change in Train Services Between Takasaki and Nagano.

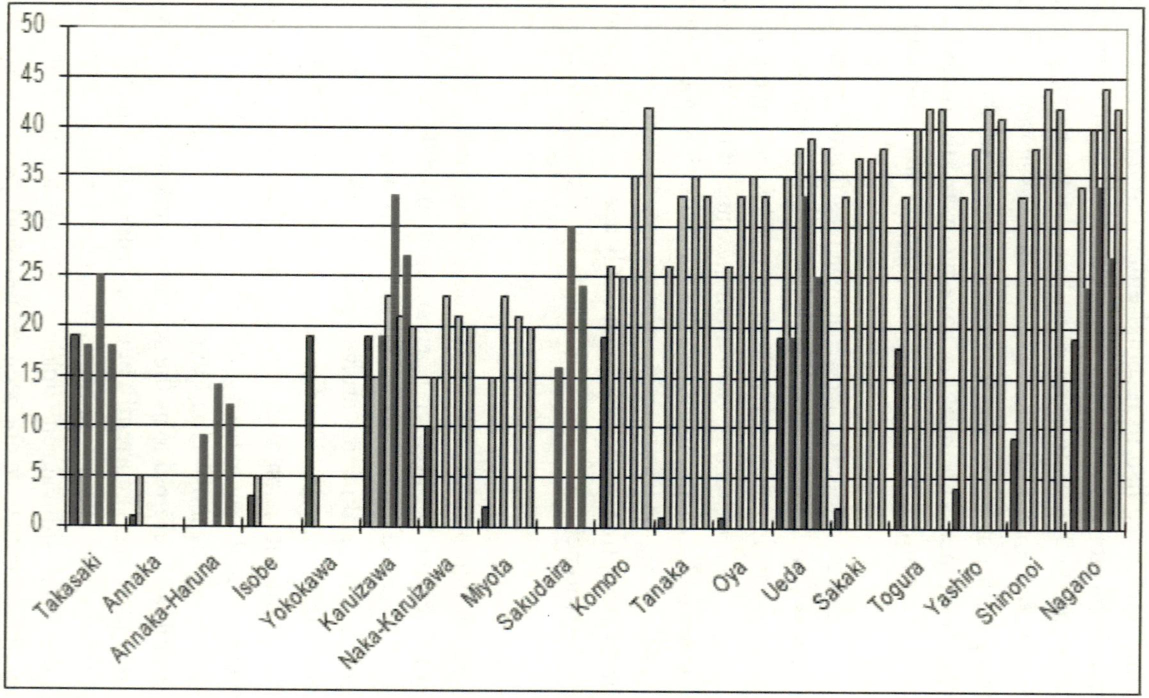

Note. Dark columns indicate the number of express trains (*tokkyū*) for 1996 and Shinkansen for 1997 onwards. Light grey columns indicate the number of local (*futsū*) trains. Data are for 'down' trains (i.e., those travelling from Takasaki to Nagano) only. Data based on railway timetables from May 1996, December 1997, October 2004, and January 2006.

Those living in towns and cities served by the Hokuriku Shinkansen have benefited from substantial time savings since its opening. Whereas the express train services between Tokyo and Nagano used to take nearly 3 hours, the Shinkansen completes the journey in 1 hour 40 minutes. However, for those who do not live in or visit a town or city served by the Shinkansen, the change has brought about numerous disadvantages. Much of the conventional railway is no longer operated by the regional JR company but by a third-sector company called Shinano Railways. Its income is primarily derived from fares and local government grants, which were also required to provide about one third of the finances for the construction of the Hokuriku Shinkansen within their respective prefectures. As figure 4.1 shows, whereas Komoro in 1996 had 19 'down' (i.e., from Tokyo to Nagano) express services stopping there each day, Komoro was taken off the Shinkansen route altogether in favour of Saku (served by Sakudaira station), which was not on the main line between Tokyo and Nagano. Similarly, Naka-Karuizawa has gone from having 10 express trains to none; the Shinkansen stops at the nearby Karuizawa station, which is actually farther from the main sites and shops in the town. Furthermore, the train service between Karuizawa and Yokokawa has been terminated and replaced by a bus service. However, it should be noted that in many rural areas, a bus service is not only cost-effective but

Table 4.1. Costs of Using the Hokuriku Shinkansen.

Route	May 1996	Dec. 1997	Jan. 2006
Takasaki – Nagano using express train/shinkansen	¥4,100	¥4,920 (+20%)	¥4,920 (+/-0%)
Karuizawa – Ueda using express train/shinkansen	¥1,260	¥3,040 (+127%)	¥3,040 (+/-0%)
Karuizawa – Ueda using local train	¥640	¥680 (+6%)	¥760 (+12%)

Note. Data based on railway timetables from May 1996, December 1997, and January 2006.

also more convenient than trains for customers because the number and locations of stops often make the bus services more convenient for those who are unable to travel very far in order to reach the nearest station.

In addition, table 4.1 shows that the number of local trains along the Shinano line has increased; this might appear to be a positive development, but it has come at a price. Table 4.1 also shows how the fare changed between selected stations along the Hokuriku Shinkansen route in 1996 (before the Shinkansen opened), December 1997 (when the line opened), and January 2006 (nearly a decade on). To put this table into context, one must remember that consumer prices for this period actually fell, albeit by small amounts, with the general consumer price index showing 100.8 in 1996 and 100. 3 in 2006 (Base year [100] = 2005; Statistics Bureau, 2010g).

If one considers the impact on population in Nagano Prefecture since the opening of the Shinkansen, a similar pattern to that of the Tōhoku Shinkansen appears. Since the decision to build the line was taken in 1987, those areas that have a Shinkansen station have seen population increases above the national average every year. However, those towns and cities without a Shinkansen station have seen increases below the national average. By 2001 the average increase for the group with Shinkansen stations was about 6 percent, compared to 2 percent for those without and a national average of 4 percent. However, such summary figures are misleading, for within the prefecture there are not only examples of more exceptional growth but also locations where the population has not simply grown at a slower rate but has fallen. For example, Saku's population increased from 62,003 in 1992 (five years before the Shinkansen line opened) to 67,025 in 2003 (five years after the Shinkansen opened), a change of 8 percent (Nihon Tetsudō Kensetsu Kōdan, 2002, p. 48). By 2005 the population of Saku had reached 100,457. However, much of the additional increase was due to mergers with other local municipalities, and when this is taken into account, the growth since 1999 is a more modest 1.41 percent (Tauninfo, 2009). Even Nagano and Ueda saw their populations fall, and the population of Nagano Prefecture has also started a gradual decline after peaking in 2001. Other than the notable exceptions of Karuizawa

Photo 4.1. The new Shinkansen station in the centre of Ueda City, Nagano Prefecture.

Photo by Peter Matanle (June 2009).

(which still remains a small town, so percentage changes are relatively exaggerated), Takasaki, Saitama, and Taitō Ward in Tokyo, there is little recent evidence of any obvious correlation between the population of the municipalities along the Hokuriku Shinkansen route and the presence of a Shinkansen station.

In Ueda City centre, for example, where there is a Shinkansen station just metres away (photo 4.1), the familiar sights of shuttered and vacant shops, and vacant weed-infested land (photos 4.2 and 4.3) have recently begun to appear due to reduced footfalls as a result of depopulation and ageing and of the construction of out-of-town shopping centres with ample car parking.

However, Komoro, which had lost out to Saku as a site for a Shinkansen station in that part of Nagano, has seen its population fall from 45,711 in 1995 to 44,559 in 2003, a drop of about 2.5 percent. Economic activity has also slowed in the city. Whereas the occupancy

PHOTOS 4.2 AND 4.3. Closed and shuttered shops, with 'to let' signs pasted on the front (photo 4.2), and disused land with weeds covering the ground (photo 4.3) are located just a few metres from Ueda City's new Shinkansen station; an increasingly familiar sight in non-metropolitan urban areas as communities age and shrink.

Photos by Peter Matanle (June 2009).

rate of shops in the city was 85 percent in 1992, by 2003 it had crashed to a mere 46 percent (C.P. Hood, interview with Komoro City officials, October 2004). The number of visitors to the city has also dropped by over 500,000 per year, and a shift to day-trips rather than longer stays has also been seen (C.P. Hood, interview with Komoro City government officials, October 2004). There is a real concern that one day the city will effectively cease to exist as an independent municipality.

Furthermore, the conventional train service between Yokokawa and Karuizawa in place prior to the opening of the Hokuriku Shinkansen was terminated when the new line began operations; it was replaced by a bus service. This is one example of why highways in many areas see significant increases in road-transport volume with the opening of a Shinkansen station in the area, some by more than 30 percent (Kōsoku Tetsudō Kenkyūkai, 2003, p. 50). The nature of the changes varies. For example, there has been an increase of between 10 and 30 percent in vehicle usage along the route between Komoro and Saku, likely due in part to the need of those visiting Komoro and those residing there to use Sakudaira Shinkansen station in Saku for an express service. There has also been an increase of over 30 percent in road usage within Karuizawa, likely in part because those in Naka-Karuizawa need to travel to Karuizawa station. Of course, in both cases one cannot ignore the impact of the transportation of visitors by taxis and minibuses. Some of the other increases seen across the prefecture are less obvious unless additional traffic in the form of goods vehicles is considered, including vehicles used in the construction industry, now more common because of increased investment generated by new Shinkansen stations.

One city included in figure 4.2 that is not currently on the Hokuriku Shinkansen is Iiyama. When the line is extended to Kanazawa, Iiyama will have a Shinkansen station; this connection will make Iiyama barely two hours from Tokyo. This is a significant change from the city's current circumstances: The main line from Nagano to the Japan Sea coast does not go via Iiyama on the Iiyama line but does so by way of the Shin'etsu line. In fact, the Iiyama Line trains travel so slowly that riding it at times it feels like stepping back in time (indeed, at one point the

FIGURE 4.2. Population Changes of Towns and Cities Along the Hokuriku Shinkansen Route.

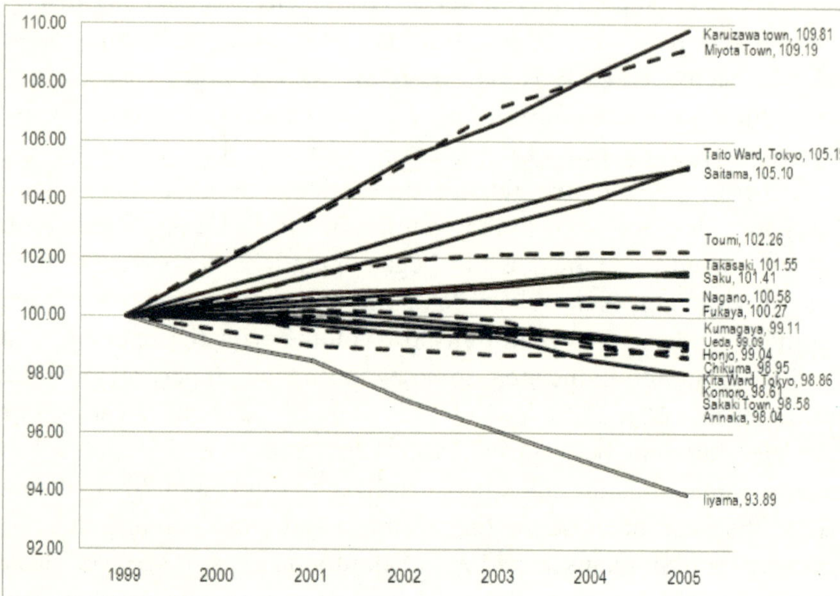

Source. Nihon rettō wo kuni jiman (http://www.towninf.co.jp/).
Note. 1999 = Base year (100). Municipalities are cities unless stated otherwise. Those marked with a red line have a Shinkansen station; those marked with a blue line do not. Iiyama is not currently on the Hokuriku Shinkansen, but will be when the extension to Kanazawa is completed. Other than Iiyama, only those municipalities with at least one station where express trains stopped, on the main line between Ueno in Tokyo and Nagano, are included. Honjō has only had a Shinkansen station (Honjō-Waseda) since March 2004.

train even appears to pass through the courtyard of a shrine). But the Iiyama City government is hoping that a Shinkansen station will make it possible to arrest the fall in the city's population, which in 2005 reached 26,000—a drop of nearly 2,000 in just seven years and about half what it was in 1950—and that other investment will also come into the city (C.P. Hood, interview with Iiyama City officials, December 2006). Whatever the current experiences of other cities located along the Hokuriku

Shinkansen, Iiyama is clinging to the hope that the Shinkansen can make a positive change in the town's fortunes.

This hope, however, may be optimistic, judging by the experience of Yūzawa Town. Yūzawa is significantly closer to Tokyo than Iiyama is, and it is also very well connected as the starting point and terminus for some Jōetsu Shinkansen services. Yet the town's population remains below 9,000 despite the Shinkansen station on the Jōetsu Shinkansen line that has been in place since operations began in 1982—a time when the overall Japanese population was still growing quite rapidly. There are undoubtedly many reasons for this, including the relative lack of space due to the mountainous terrain, and the harsh conditions during winter, when snow accumulations of five metres are not uncommon. It is notable, however, that other towns and villages nearby that are not so well connected have shrunk considerably and are scheduled to do so more rapidly than Yūzawa (see chapter 3). Although Iiyama possesses more space for development than Yūzawa, it also suffers from a harsh winter and heavy snowfalls. Combined with the extra distance

TABLE 4.2. Kyūshū Shinkansen Distances and Operating Times.

	Conventional Line		Shinkansen		Reduction	
	Distance	Time	Distance	Time	Distance	Time
Hakata ↔ Kumamoto	118.4	1:15	98.2	0:35	20.2 (17.1%)	0:40 (53.3%)
Kumamoto ↔ Shin-Yatsushiro[a]	35.7	0:20	31.8	0:10	3.9 (10.9%)	0:10 (50.0%)
Shin-Yatsushiro[a] ↔ Kagoshima-Chūō[b]	165.7	2:05	126.8	0:35	38.9 (23.5%)	1:30 (72.0%)
Total (Hakata ↔ Kagoshima-Chūō[b])	317.1	3:40	256.8	1:20	60.3 (19.0%)	2:20 (63.6%)

Source. Nihon Tetsudō Kensetsu Kōdan (2002).
Note. [a] = Distance/time calculated to Yatsushiro for conventional line data. [b] = Nishi-Kagoshima prior to opening of Kyūshū Shinkansen. Shinkansen journey time based on original operating speed of 260 km/h.

FIGURE 4.3. Change in Train Services between Kumamoto and Kagoshima.

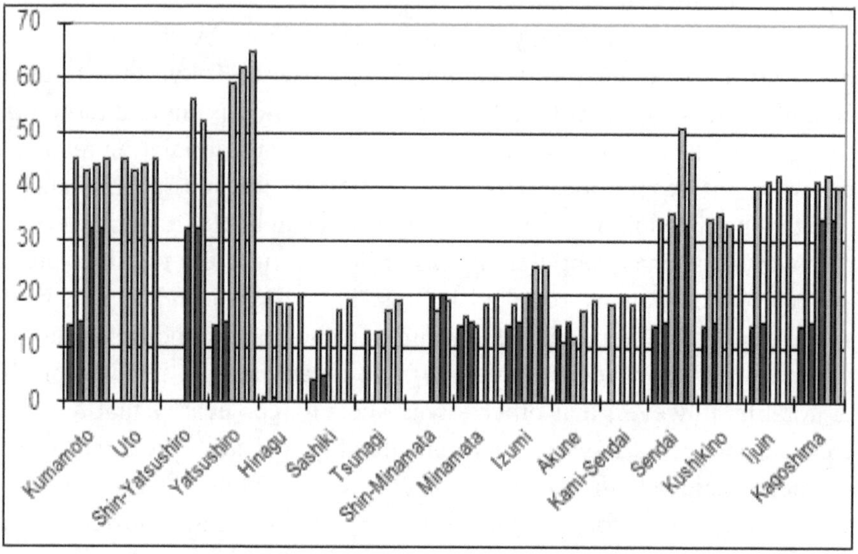

Note. Dark columns indicate the number of express trains (*tokkyū*) for 1992, 1996, and 1997 and Shinkansen for 1997 onwards. Light grey columns indicate the number of local (*futsū*) trains. Data are for 'down' trains (those travelling in the direction from Kumamoto to Kagoshima) only. Data based on railway timetables from May 1996, January 2004, April 2004, and January 2006.

from Tokyo and a falling national and regional population, it is therefore unlikely that Iiyama will see significant changes in its fortunes as a result of the opening of the Shinkansen station within its boundaries.

As table 4.2 indicates, those using the Kyūshū Shinkansen line have experienced substantial time savings since its opening, with further gains expected now that the line has been completed. However, for those who do not visit or live in a town or city served by the Shinkansen, the line's development has brought disadvantages. Whereas JR Kyūshū used to operate the entire conventional line between Yatsushiro and Nishi-Kagoshima, since the opening of the Shinkansen line, the conventional line has been split into three sections. Shin-Yatsushiro to Yatsushiro is still operated by JR Kyūshū, with most services operating between

TABLE 4.3. Costs of Using the Kyūshū Shinkansen.

	January 2004	January 2006
Kumamoto – Kagoshima using express train/shinkansen	¥5,960	¥6,350 (+6.5%)
Yatsushiro* – Kagoshima using express train/shinkansen	¥5,330	¥5,330 (+/-0%)
Izumi – Sendai using local train	¥1,080	¥1,330 (+23.1%)
Sendai – Kagoshima using local train	¥910	¥910 (+/-0%)
Sendai – Kagoshima using express train/ shinkansen	¥2,010	¥1,740 (-13%)

Note. *Shin-Yatsushiro in the case of the Shinkansen service. Data based on railway time-tables from January 2004 and January 2006.

Kumamoto and Yatsushiro. Yatsushiro to Sendai is operated by a new third-sector company, Hisatsu Orange Railway; and Sendai to Kagoshima-Chūō continues to operate under JR Kyūshū. Needless to say, the two sections operated by JR Kyūshū are the busiest and have the greatest potential to make a profit.

The opening of the Shinkansen line has also had a major impact on some cities reliant upon frequent train services because they are either popular tourist destinations or commuter towns for Kagoshima. For example, figure 4.3 shows that whereas 15 'down' (i.e., from Kumamoto to Kagoshima-Chūō) express services stopped in both Akune and Ijuin each day immediately before the Shinkansen opened, the towns now have no express services because they are not on the Shinkansen route. The number of local trains along the Hisatsu Orange Railway line has generally increased slightly, but as with the Hokuriku Shinkansen, this increase has come at a price (see table 4.3). Meanwhile, JR Kyūshū has tried to make fare adjustments so as to encourage locals to use the Shinkansen service while charging those travelling longer distances (i.e., connections to and from Kumamoto and farther north) extra.

In terms of population change in cities on the Kyūshū Shinkansen route, it is noticeable that most cities in Kagoshima and Kumamoto prefectures saw population decreases between 1999 and 2005. Even those cities with Shinkansen stops, other than Kagoshima (the regional centre of southern Kyūshū), saw their populations fall compared to previous years. Clearly the Shinkansen is no longer influencing population growth as it used to. In a Japan where there is a long-term trend to move from smaller cities to metropolitan conurbations, the Shinkansen is not only *not slowing* this trend—it may actually be *accelerating* it by increasing the ease with which people can return to their *furusato* at appropriate times for short visits.

Depopulation and Village Transformation: Abandoned Houses, Encroaching Forests, and Aggressive Wildlife

What becomes of the rural settings that people leave behind when they migrate to Japan's urban and suburban areas? One conspicuous feature of the depopulated villages that is increasingly seen in many rural areas is *akiya*—literally, *empty houses*. In extreme cases, most of the houses in a village are uninhabited, and only a handful are still occupied. In many cases, the absent owners of these houses return once or twice a year for a short spell—such as at the mid-August *obon* festival, during which they pay respects to family and ancestors; or at New Year—and in between these visits, a neighbour or nearby relative may mind the property. Insofar as residential areas still appear well looked after, visitors passing through may erroneously assume that the society of the area or village is not experiencing severe depopulation. However, as the number of residents in these villages decreases and as extended families are separated by work and marriage, houses increasingly remain uninhabited year round without anybody to maintain them. In such cases, these houses become run down, covered with vines, and—in extreme cases—infested with insects, rodents, birds, feral cats, and even monkeys; the land around them becomes overgrown with weeds and shrubs, and trees grow unchecked. Houses near the edges of forests, those that are peripheral even to their small village site, are particularly difficult for neighbours to maintain and are therefore vulnerable to weather- and

FIGURE 4.4. Population Change in Towns and Cities Along the Kyūshū Shinkansen Route.

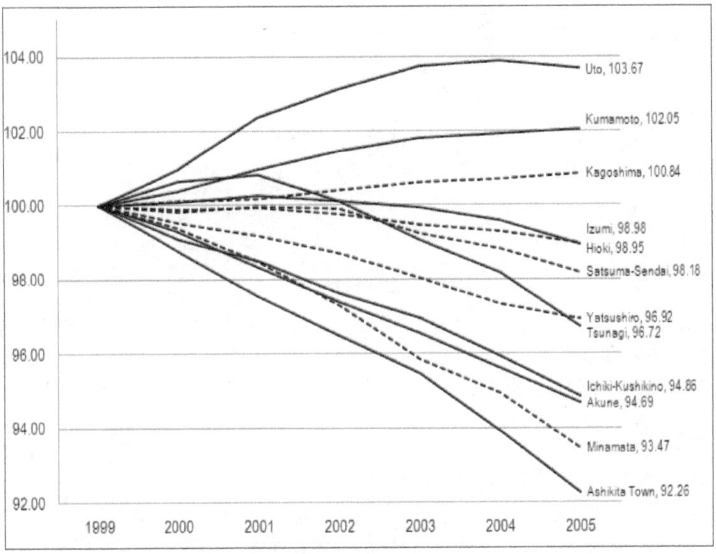

Source. *Nihon rettō wo kuni jiman* (http://www.towninf.co.jp/).
Note. 1999 = Base year (100). Municipalities are cities unless stated otherwise. Those marked with a dotted line have a Shinkansen station. Only those municipalities with at least one station on the main line between Kumamoto and Kagoshima are included.

nature-related deterioration. The accompanying photographs of abandoned (photo 4.4), overgrown (photo 4.5), and vine-covered (photo 4.6) houses, and of a collapsed school building (photo 4.7) depict the dramatic and all-too-common impacts of depopulation, abandonment, and collapse on the living environment in small mountain villages.

In addition to the appearance of such *akiya*, other signs signal village depopulation. In the village area, these include run-down village halls, village grounds covered with weeds, village paths overgrown with grasses, crumbled walls and broken fences left unrepaired, and large cobwebs suspended between standing objects, as well as abandoned cars and empty cans, bottles, and other trash littering the roadsides. Farther out from village centres, one can see unused and overgrown fields,

PHOTOS 4.4 AND 4.5. An abandoned house (photo 4.4) and an overgrown house (photo 4.5) in Hongū Town, Wakayama Prefecture.

Photos by John Knight.

blocked irrigation channels, graves that are overgrown in cemeteries that have become dark and dingy as the surrounding tree stands are allowed to close in. In areas where timber was once harvested, depopulation is revealed in the neglect of previously worked areas—forest paths thick with vegetation, fallen rocks and trees, and other kinds of uncleared damage caused by earlier storms and typhoons. As disused fields become overgrown, the clearing between remaining fields and the forest's edge disappears.

There is often a conspicuous pattern of wild vegetation that comes to mark depopulated areas. One common plant is *susuki*, or pampas grass (*Miscanthus sinensis*), which grows to a height of over two metres. In the past, *susuki* was put to use as roof thatch or as fodder for animals, but lacking any such use in modern times, it is now considered an undesirable weed. Another ubiquitous weed is *awadachisō*, or goldenrod (*Solidago altissima*)—a tall, slim plant that grows to more than two metres in height and produces a striking yellow flower in the autumn. This is an exotic weed species that was introduced from the Americas in the postwar period but is now widely found in old fields and along roadsides. *Kuzu*, along with a number of other vines, often comes to cover roadside guardrails, roadside signs, road-bend mirrors, lamp-posts, electricity cables, the protective fencing around fields, and even abandoned farm machinery and vehicles.

Depopulating Villages and Forest Encroachment

Another significant factor contributing to village decline is forest encroachment. Timber forestry is an important industry in upland Japan, but one major consequence of rural depopulation is the neglect of timber trees. Conifer plantations make up a large part of the Japanese forest, largely as a result of the afforestation policy of the postwar period. This policy consisted, on the one hand, of the replacement of slow-growing mixed and broad-leafed trees that had formerly been used locally for firewood with fast-growing, more economically productive conifers, and on the other hand, of the planting over of village-edge farmland with conifers.

PHOTO 4.6. Vine-covered houses in Hongū Town, Wakayama Prefecture.

Photo by John Knight.

Much of the afforestation that has taken place more recently has been carried out by people in the process of leaving the village. Farmland that is converted to timber forest requires a greatly reduced labour input, allowing people to live and work outside the village while continuing to put their land to an economically productive use. An additional consideration on the part of these landowners was that the planted trees would improve the value of the land, a boon if and when the owners decided to sell it (Shimotori, 1981, p. 90). This trend is illustrated by statistics from Hongū-chō in Wakayama Prefecture, located on the Pacific coast of Honshū at the end of the Kii Peninsula, directly south of Osaka. Since the administrative merger in 2004, Hongū has become a part of a newly expanded Tanabe City. Between 1960 and 1995 the area of farmland in Hongū Town diminished by two thirds (from 508 to 179 ha), and the area of rice fields halved. As might be expected, it is the more remote, less accessible farmland that has been abandoned.

The woodland around the village, known as the *satoyama*, was in the past relatively open and bright. It contained a certain amount of tree cover in the form of coppice forest, as well as timber forest, but it was traditionally associated with a patchwork of spaces such as rice fields, dry fields for vegetables, thatch fields, fruit orchards, grasslands, and swidden fields. The traditional *satoyama* landscape is often praised for its beauty, and central to this aesthetic appreciation is its comparatively open character. But a combination of timber plantation expansion and secondary forest succession has transformed the character of the *satoyama* space; the earlier mixed forest has been replaced by the tall mono-cultural tree growth of the plantations, and the open, bright *satoyama* has given way to a closed, dark conifer forest.

The village itself—as a clearing—is also subject to encroachment. Even though the increase in the forest area is proportionately small (in the case of Hongū, only 2%, this added forest area has had a considerable visual impact on the settlement. This conversion of village-edge farmland into forest adversely affects the remaining farmland on the forest's edge by reducing the amount of sunlight it receives, and the reduction of direct

PHOTO 4.7. A collapsed school building in Hongū Town, Wakayama Prefecture.

Photo by John Knight.

sunshine reduces the productivity of the fields adjacent to the forest. It is common knowledge among villagers in these areas that the harvests from fields that receive only late morning sunshine because of tree shade are much smaller than harvests from sunnier fields. Another villager complaint is that the reduction in sunshine hours makes it harder for washing to dry. The sun-blocking effect of conifer trees also tends to lead to higher fuel bills, either because it takes longer for the house to warm up on winter mornings or because solar warmth stops abruptly in the early afternoon.

This change is often represented as a *darkening* of the village environment. After a visit to his former village, Ue Toshikatsu of Nakahechi (which borders Hongū to the west) recorded the following impressions:

> In the thirty or more years since I left Okidaira for Nonaka, the landscape has completely changed. As a result of the so-called plantation boom, places where there was grassland and mixed woodland have been completely buried in cedars and cypresses. The fields and other parts of the settlement are in ruins, and there is only half the old arable area now left. The forest has been encroaching, little by little, from the edge to the centre, like it is trying to *swallow up the village* [emphasis added]. In the past this village was bright and would shine with green leaves in the spring, while in the autumn the mountains appeared like a woodblock colour print, but now the whole of the village is covered in conifer trees and has a black appearance throughout the seasons, while its old features can no longer be seen. (Ue, 1983, p. 204)

In applying the expression 'like it is trying to swallow up the village' (*sato o nomikomōtoshiteiru*) to the advancing plantation forest, Ue highlighted a recurring theme in accounts by residents of the environmental effect of the conifers: The village is shrinking and is in the process of disappearing. Another expression that is sometimes used by local people to refer to this change in the landscape is *yama ga sato ni haittekita*, or 'the forest has entered the village' (see Yukawa, 1988). On the island of Shōdoshima (Kagawa Prefecture), a former municipal councillor referred to the problem of forest encroachment affecting the depopulated village of Nakayama, recounting, 'You get the sense that the forest is rapidly descending [into the village]' (*yappari yama ga dondon ochite kuru to iu kanji*). This state of forest encroachment has also been described by Adachi (1998) in relation to mountain villages in Ehime Prefecture.

> Villages have been turned into places where old people live on their own.... As the years pass, the old people find themselves struggling to breathe as they become besieged by the circle of timber plantations around them that have replaced the rice fields and the dry fields. (Adachi, 1998, p. 163)

Given these effects of afforestation, it should come as no surprise that some farmland afforestation initiatives have been thwarted by the opposition of villagers. One recent example of this occurred in a village in Hongū-chō. At the western entrance to the village, there are six large rice fields below the village road. These were rented out to a local man, but in 2000 he gave up farming them. The landowner decided to afforest them and sought the approval of the villagers for his plans. But the villagers opposed the plan, complaining that it would darken the village. Leading this opposition was a 75-year-old former forestry labourer who offered the following comments during a 2002 interview:

> We asked the landowner not to go ahead with plantations there because if plantations are established in that place they would be right next to houses which would end up in their shade and so cause problems about their rights to sunshine. That's why we asked him to stop it.... If it went ahead, the village would become desolate. If trees are planted in that place then eventually, as those trees grow to this size [gesture] and it would become grim and dark over there.... Although there are people in those houses now, in thirty or forty years' time when those trees had become tall you don't know if human beings would want to live there any more, as they would find themselves covered and hidden.... For someone like me who has been born and raised in this village, to allow trees this thick [gesture] to grow at the entrance to the village would be just the same as if I had decided to strangle myself! ... I think that the residents of the village have to protect it against plantations that come close to houses. That's vital. If we don't do that, it would be no different from strangling ourselves. (J. Knight, interview, 21 December, 2002)

It should be noted that this man was not directly affected by the proposed afforestation plan; the land in question is not visible from his house, which lay in another part of the village. Thus he was not opposing the plantation of trees that would affect the amount of sunshine received by his own house. Rather, at issue was the future of the village—albeit a village in which there were only 16 households left, a drastic drop from the 40 that had composed the village in this man's youth. He feared that if the village became dark with tall plantation trees, those former villagers who had left for the city would be much less likely to return to live there again. In the end, the landowner reluctantly agreed not to proceed with the afforestation plans.

There are many examples of remote, upstream villages in Hongū that have undergone particularly heavy depopulation in recent decades and that have, as a result, become enclosed by tall plantation growth on abandoned farmland at the edge of the village. There is a well-known vicious circle: Out-migration is followed by forest succession and farmland afforestation, which in turn—by making that village that much less comfortable to live in—lead to further out-migration, and so on. Some of these outlying villages have already become deserted and are now part of the wider forest, whereas others are expected to be abandoned in the coming years. Given the scale of depopulation in recent decades, the village of Hoshinbo faces an uncertain future. The intensity of the former forestry labourer's reaction to the prospect of farmland afforestation in a part of the village should be understood in relation to these fears about the future of the village as a place fit for human habitation.

Depopulating Villages and Aggressive Wildlife

Depopulation and forest encroachment create the conditions in which another problem arises for the remaining villagers—namely, wildlife intrusion into the village environment. The progress of this development is as follows. First, as the *satoyama* forest floor is no longer cleared by human hands, the process of forest succession resumes, hastening the replacement of pine forest with deciduous oak forest. Second, as a result of the neglect of timber plantations by the absent owner, the amount of edible undergrowth within these plantations increases, and they become more attractive feeding sites for wild animals. As the village perimeter becomes increasingly thick with undergrowth, it provides cover for wild boar, monkeys, and deer.

Wild boar and monkeys are the most problematic of the animals. As a farmer in Hiroshima Prefecture attested, 'When people don't enter it [anymore], the forest becomes heaven for the wild boar' (Chūgoku Shimbun, 2000). Abandoned farmland becomes overgrown with wild vegetation, which provides effective cover for the wild boar as it raids adjacent still-productive fields. So emboldened, wild boar find the depopulated village itself an easy target for raids, for the decline in villager numbers, especially of younger people, tends to diminish human resistance to boar encroachment. In his book on wild boar in rural Japan, Isao Suto cited a 1969 newspaper report from Nagano Prefecture that describes depopulation as having reduced the number of village 'soldiers resisting the wild boar' (Suto, 1991, p. 163). Seemingly aware of this change in the village, wild boars have become more brazen in their raiding: 'As if foreseeing this [population decline], wild boars now calmly emerge, even when there is somebody around, and proceed to raid the field without any hesitation' (Suto, 1991, p. 163). This new boldness is reflected in the headline of one newspaper article: 'Arrogant Wild Boars—Beasts Rule' (Chūgoku Shimbun, 2000).

Yet if wild boar damage is exacerbated by depopulation, it can also contribute to rural depopulation. Reports from western Japan indicate that wild boars, through their recurrent raiding of farms, accelerate the depopulation and abandonment of remote hamlets (Palmer, 1983, p. 332; Suto, 1991, pp. 163–164), and surveys of depopulated villages have shown that wild boar damage is one of the main reasons given by families for migrating to the city (Takahashi, 1995, p. 38). One writer even suggested that wild boars' incursions represent 'the final blow to mountainous regions [of Japan] suffering from depopulation and agrarian abandonment' (Tokida, 2001, pp. 244–245).

Monkeys pose another serious problem for residents of depopulated villages in many parts of Japan. As depopulation progresses and the number of abandoned houses in Japan's upland villages grows, these old buildings attract monkeys, which have been known to occupy empty houses or to sleep under the eaves of houses. An old woman in a village in Yamagata Prefecture who has suffered many monkey raids on her own house, complains that 'it's just like the monkey area of a zoo around my house. There are monkeys which play on the roof of the empty house next door, treating it as a slide' (Kahoku Shinpō, 1996). Similar complaints were voiced by Taniguchi Soichi, a retired carpenter in Hongū, who described in an interview the way monkeys have taken over a nearby outbuilding:

> That building over there is my carpentry hut. The monkeys all gather on that roof and form a line along it, and as they eat and play about among themselves they look out towards us. They're clever—they're not worried about us anymore. They sit up there and just groom each other…. They defecate up there on the roof and it gets all dirty. When things reach this stage it really is the end—when human beings and their houses become surrounded like this, and you reach the point where you are desperate to try and escape from the monkeys! (Knight, 2003, pp. 102–103)

This spatial convergence of humans and monkeys is stigmatising for the communities affected. An 80-year-old woman, Naka Fumiko, in the Hongū village of Bujū, which has endured serious monkey harassment, commented: 'Everybody [around here] will become monkeys! We'll all become monkeys' (J. Knight, interview, 25 December 2000).

On the Inland Sea island of Shōdoshima in July 2007, Tsunehisa Yada, a construction company boss and former town councillor, described the connection between monkey damage and depopulation in the village of Nakayama as follows:

> For them [Nakayama villagers], monkeys are frightening…. As villagers get older, they no longer want to grow things in the fields, and as there are few young people, then they come to think there's no point in farming the fields. They give up farming early. Gradually, because of the monkey damage, the fields become abandoned and the village as a whole is becoming abandoned. Of course, as there are fewer people, then houses that were inhabited fall empty. Houses with nobody living in them are increasing. And where you have houses with nobody in them, the surroundings become covered in tall grass. When that happens, monkeys and deer obviously come around more, and so you get the sense that the mountain forest is rapidly descending. As the places of tall grassy growth in the village increase, monkeys and deer come around a lot. And when this happens, these abandoned areas lead other people who were cultivating their fields to stop cultivating

> them. At its worst, it could mean that, in decades from now, it will become a place where human beings can no longer live! Because people are steadily decreasing in number. J. Knight, interview, 6 July 2007

This is not simply a matter of there being fewer villagers but a matter of wild animals seeing the remaining villagers as less of a threat. Primatologists point out that a key factor in the rise of *engai*, or *monkey damage*, is that monkeys have shed their habitual fear of people (Wada, 1994, pp. 183–184; K. Watanabe, 1995, p. 49). Hence one often comes across newspaper reports such as the following one from Shiga Prefecture: 'Recently, [monkeys] have lost their fear of humans and raid the fields as though they own them' (Chūnichi Shimbun, 1997). Why is it that wild animals have become so bold? In the case of monkeys, one factor is the cessation of hunting. Monkeys were removed from the list of game animals after the Second World War. But even for animals that are still hunted, the rate of hunting—hunting pressure—tends to be much less than previously, owing to a decline in the number of hunters in upland areas in recent years. Consequently, wild boar and deer no longer associate humans with predatory danger to the extent they did in the past. Thus even if hunters are spotted in the field, these animals may not react with immediate flight. In short, in Japanese mountain villages, human presence no longer deters animal intrusion as it once did.

Wild animals feed on human crops and thus adversely affect human livelihoods, but in their forays into villages they also breach important human boundaries. When animals from the forest invade farms, graveyards, and houses in the village, they threaten the spatial order of remote rural areas. The status of forest animals as signs of an elemental disorder is expressed in the comments of villagers in the Okutama region, reported by Matoi Iguchi.

> With a worried look on her face, the grandmother said, 'It's frightening when the things from the forest come down to the village. I hope that something bad is not about to happen.' … Animals now commonly appear in the village, whereas before they could not be seen even if one tried to see them.… For the grandmothers

> and grandfathers who live in this land, as well as for a city dweller like myself, when the wild beasts that are supposed to live in the forest start to appear in the village to such an extent, it suggests that 'something bad' is happening. (Iguchi, 1990, p. 14)

Iguchi was struck by the old woman's suggestion that the unprecedented intrusion of forest animals in the village was a bad omen that presaged impending disaster. He takes these comments as evidence that, in addition to the material damage villagers in remote communities sustain from crop-raiding, they also suffer from what he calls *shinritekina appaku* (psychological oppression) because of the invasion of their everyday living space by forest animals (Iguchi, 1990, p. 14).

Shrinking Islands in the 'Other' Okinawa

Compared to other rural regions in Japan, such as the forested mountainous areas of the Kii peninsula described previously, on the face of things the island prefecture of Okinawa appears to be bucking the trend towards depopulation. Instead of shrinking, the population of Japan's most outlying prefecture continues to increase. With an approximate population of 1.39 million in 2009, Okinawa is the only prefecture in Japan that is expected to continue to grow in the period 2010–2030, to 1.43 million (National Institute of Population and Social Security Research, 2003; Okinawa ken, 2009a). On closer inspection, however, it is clear that the prefecture is experiencing in microcosm the problem that Japan as a whole faces and that we described in the previous chapter with respect to Niigata Prefecture and Sado Island. The main island of Okinawa, where the principal social, economic, political, and cultural activities of the prefecture are concentrated, is growing at the expense of a shrinking and ageing periphery—the *ritō*, or outlying islands, of the prefecture. As a result, it is becoming increasingly difficult to maintain stable communities, since the critical mass of population necessary for the construction and maintenance of public infrastructure and the provision of commercial goods and services is disappearing in many of these remote island communities—raising the question of what kind and quantity of support local residents can expect from the national, prefectural, and municipal authorities in preserving their communities as viable settlements.

As Japan's only prefecture made up entirely of an island archipelago, Okinawa occupies a huge swathe of the South China Sea, extending some 1000 km east to west and 400 km north to south. Within this vast area of ocean there are over 40 inhabited islands and many more uninhabited ones. The main island of Okinawa (Okinawa *hontō*) is the largest and has been the focus of considerable media and academic inquiry regarding the presence of large and intrusive US military bases and their attendant problems (see Hook and Siddle, 2003). In contrast, the issues facing the 39 inhabited islands that compose the rest of the prefecture (where there are no US military facilities) have been largely overlooked. This chapter presents an overview of the circumstances of Okinawa Prefecture because it exemplifies the facts that, first, each region is unique in its history and geography, but that, second, even Okinawa—with its growing population—exhibits many of the issues addressed in this volume in terms of the impacts and implications of shrinkage throughout Japan.

Socioeconomic and Political Conditions in Okinawa's Outlying Island Settlements

The 39 outlying islands (*ritō)* can be classified into three main types. First, there are those clustered around the main island of Okinawa (e.g., Zamami), which are within an hour's journey by ferry from the prefectural capital, Naha. Next are the distinct island groups within the archipelago, the Ishigaki and Iriomote clusters (known collectively as Yaeyama), and Miyako. Finally, there are the more isolated islands that are more than an hour's ferry ride from Okinawa or one of the other hub islands (e.g., Yonaguni, Tarama, Kume, or the Senkaku and Daitō islands). The *ritō* are served by vehicle and passenger ferries, high-speed passenger boats for short-haul journeys within island groups, and a more limited network of air transport to the major or most isolated islands. As this classification indicates, relative isolation has a major influence on conditions on any given island and also accounts for many of the differing characteristics between the islands themselves (Okinawa ken chiiki ritō ka, 2009. Unless otherwise attributed, information in the following subsection is compiled from this source).

Population

The demography of the *ritō* follows a pattern similar to that in other regions in rural Japan as it simultaneously shrinks and ages. About 130,000 people live in the *ritō*—that is, about 9.5 percent of the prefecture's residents. In contrast, the population of Okinawa Island itself (hereafter Okinawa) has virtually doubled in the last 50 years, whereas that of the *ritō* has declined by 40,000 over the same period. Much of this loss occurred between 1965 and 1975, when many migrated away from their home islands to find work in base-related construction or servicing in Okinawa. Although the *ritō* population has remained roughly stable since then, it has also aged; only 15.2 percent of its population fell into the 15–29 age group in 2005 (compared to 20.1 percent in Okinawa), so it is expected that further declines in the *ritō* population will occur as the age structure changes still further and the progressively larger population of older people become very old and pass away.

It is important to remember, however, that the outer islands were never completely isolated and unchanging, but have experienced periodic population movements and forced transfers from the time of the Ryūkyū Kingdom (15th to 19th centuries) through the prewar period as a result of natural disaster, disease, and government policy. Ishigaki, for example, includes a number of communities that originated on other islands, including the descendants of 600 villagers from Taketomi (population in 2010: 344; Ishigaki shi, 2010) sent there after the great tsunami of the 18th century. The majority of villagers from the small islands of Aragusuku (population in 2010: 6; Ishigaki shi, 2010) have relocated to Ōhara, on nearby Iriomote. In contrast, the population of Yonaguni was dramatically boosted in the 1940s to about 20,000—that is, 10 times its current level—by smugglers running black market goods from Taiwan, only 125

MAP 4.2. Okinawa Prefecture and the Principal Island Groups.

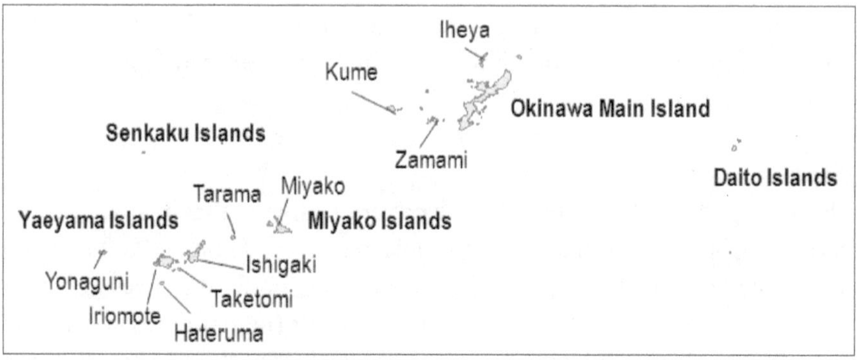

Source. Map by Richard Siddle.

km away. Nevertheless, the scale and nature of the current population movement and of the ageing of the islands' residents are unprecedented.

Economic Structure and Conditions

The economic base of the prefecture's outlying islands is fishing, agriculture, and tourism. Fishing and agriculture occupy 19.9 percent of the *ritō* working population, in contrast to only 4.1 percent on Okinawa and 5.9 percent nationally (2005 figures; statistics and other data for this subsection are taken from Okinawa ken chiiki ritō ka, 2009). Agriculture—in particular, sugarcane and beef production—is the most important productive industry in the islands but is facing an uncertain future as the existing farming population ages and few younger people appear willing to succeed their parents in the traditional manner. This is despite the fact that beef production is very profitable; local beef (*Ishigakigyū*) enjoys a premium reputation, and locally bred calves are sold on to Kobe for rearing as Matsuzaki beef.

The secondary sector in the outlying islands is little different from that in Okinawa or across Japan as a whole, representing 16.1 percent of employment. Though it is predominantly construction, it includes some small-scale agriculture-related industrial plants—for instance, Okinawa's second-largest sugar factory on Hateruma (though employment is seasonal with 70 workers between November and April; only maintenance staff work year-round), the specialist *awamori* (Okinawan rice liquor) distillery on Yonaguni (which imports its rice from Thailand), and a rum distillery on Minami Daitō. The tertiary sector, comprising mainly resorts and other tourism-related activity, now employs 62.9 percent of working islanders. This is fewer than in Okinawa itself (78%), but this number is expected to increase—although the extent to which locals can realistically take advantage of such opportunities is debatable. The levels of per capita income vary among islands, but in some cases can actually be considerably higher than the prefectural average; on Yonaguni, for example, the average per capita income is 33.5 percent above the prefectural average, and in Taketomi Town, which includes the tourist island of Taketomi itself, incomes are 19.8 percent higher. On smaller islands that see few tourists and are heavily reliant on sugarcane, incomes are lower, with Iheya and Tarama at 80.2 and 87.6 percent below the prefectural average, the lowest in the prefecture (Okinawa ken, 2006). This is only true for those in work, of course; in an ageing population, higher numbers of residents live on retirement incomes and are supported by working relatives. But even where incomes are higher than average, this is offset by higher prices for everyday items.

The cost of transportation is a key factor in the local economies of the islands. Prices for goods imported from Okinawa are typically some 10–50 percent higher than those of goods produced locally. The price of gasoline and other fuel products is of such crucial importance that transportation costs are subsidised by the prefectural government; nevertheless gasoline remains 14 percent more expensive in the islands than in Okinawa. Overall, the combination of low incomes and high prices clearly affects islanders' standard of living.

Local Government and Finance

A shrinking and ageing population means reduced revenues from taxation for the prefecture and municipalities. The situation is further complicated on Ishigaki, for example, where there is a temporary population of retired people from other parts of Japan who stay for long periods and consume local services but pay no municipal taxes because their official *honseki* (family residence) registrations are elsewhere in Japan. Estimated at about 5,000 persons (a considerable number compared to Ishigaki's official 2008 population of 46,657), they are referred to by local officials as 'ghosts' (*yūrei*) (R. Siddle, interview at Ishigaki Town Office, April 2008). On average, local administrations in Okinawa's outlying islands can raise only 21 percent of the income they require and therefore remain heavily dependent on regional subsidies from the prefectural (37.2%) and central (15.4%) governments. Unsurprisingly, most of the local authorities that administer the islands face considerable financial strains. Annual expenditures (per municipality average of JPY 5.9 billion) are just over one third of an equivalent municipal authority on the main island (Okinawa ken chiiki ritō ka, 2009).

Although local finances are weak, however, considerable public investment has been made in infrastructure. This partly reflects the patterns of infrastructure investment found throughout rural Japan and its links to pork-barrel politics, but there is an additional factor at work. As one prefectural official explained, even though some islands have very small populations and are not able to maintain their communities independently of public support, it is very much in Japan's strategic interests to maintain a population on these islands, especially those closest to Taiwan, and particularly in light of the recent history of local territorial disputes over the Senkaku Islands, small uninhabited outlying islands that are part of the prefecture but claimed also by Taiwan and the People's Republic of China (R. Siddle, interview at Ishigaki Town Office, April 2008). Thus each island has to replicate a full set of facilities that on the mainland could service or at least be shared between larger populations in geographically contiguous settlements. Waste collection and disposal facilities, sewage treatment plants, road improvement, educational and medical facilities, and so on, though somewhat less dense in the *ritō* than in Okinawa and nationally, are nonetheless not far behind. An exception is connection to sewage systems: Only 13.7 percent of households are connected in the *ritō* (in contrast to 68.9 percent in Okinawa). Generally, electric power is generated by oil-fired plants, although there are also some wind turbines. (An attempt to harness wind power on Hateruma suffered a major setback when the massive wind turbine was knocked out of action by lightning in 2007; it was still under repair in April 2008. Frequent typhoons also make reliance on this technology a challenge.) In terms of medical facilities, the figures for the islands may seem close enough—with 0.9 doctors and 12.7 beds per 1,000 persons in the *ritō*, compared to 1.5 and 15.8 in Okinawa (Okinawa ken chiiki ritō ka, 2009)—but the issues faced by an ageing population in geographically remote locations make this gap more problematic.

Issues and Policies

The Okinawan prefectural government takes the view that the special geographic characteristics of the *ritō* demand policies different from those aimed at other municipalities within the prefecture and moreover that they make the official national policy of the merger and integration of local authorities (*shichōson gappei*) inappropriate. The prefecture has developed an overall plan, the New Okinawa Prefecture Outlying Islands Development Plan (2002–2011), drawing upon a mixture of state and prefectural funds, fiscal policies, and special measures.

The Section for the Regions and Outlying Islands (Chiiki ritō ka) within the Okinawan prefectural government identified the following key issues facing the islands (see Okinawa ken chiiki ritō ka, 2009): First, there is the need to maintain and promote local industries by addressing the ageing agricultural workforce, improving production and stabilising harvests, lowering distribution costs, and improving the infrastructure and human resources for tourism development.

Second, the maintenance and improvement of communications and transport networks is considered a vital function of local government in these areas, one that should not be left to the private sector. Hateruma, for instance, suffered a major blow when its only regularly scheduled flight was cancelled in 2007. At present, six local island authorities (e.g., Iheya Village) run ferry services, whereas others (e.g., Kume Town) work independently with air carriers to subsidise fares. The effort to improve transport links is not without controversy; a major struggle raged for years between conservationists and developers in Ishigaki over the need for a bigger airport that could handle large jets. This was finally resolved with the new airport now under construction and scheduled to be completed by 2013. The new facility will have a runway large enough for 280-seat medium-sized jets and airfreight-handling facilities; it is expected to be a major engine of development, bringing in tourists and stimulating local industry (Okinawa ken, 2009b). The extension of broadband and mobile phone coverage is another aspect of this development; hope is expressed that these developments will encourage younger people to stay. However, just as with the Shinkansen trains (discussed earlier), such developments could have the opposite effect—they could actually accelerate the departure of younger people as information about the possibilities available in the outside world becomes even more accessible and as opportunities to make short visits and to keep in touch after emigrating increase in availability and decrease in cost.

A third need on the islands is improvement of the infrastructure that affects residents' quality of life. Water supply has always been an issue on the smaller islands (except Yonaguni, the limestone substrata of which have a high water-bearing capacity). Taketomi, for instance, received a safe and stable water supply only after the construction of a pipeline from Ishigaki in 1976. Environmentally friendly waste disposal, too, is becoming more urgently required. Add to this the other facilities needed to sustain community life in a modern state (health, education, emergency services, etc.), and the cost to small communities merely to maintain these services is enormous. Tonaki Island, for instance (population 487 in 2008), runs (among other community services) a desalination plant, a wind-powered electricity generator, a waste disposal plant, and an elementary and a junior high school. A fourth and related issue is the improvement of medical, welfare, and educational facilities. The recruitment of medical personnel, medical emergency provision such as air ambulances, nursing care for older persons, and the maintenance of schools in the face of a declining birth rate are pressing concerns.

A final policy area concerns the natural environment. The scenery and wildlife of the islands, from the abundant coral reefs to the virgin forests of Iriomote, are a vital resource for the tourist industry. Measures are required in order to counter the phenomenon of *red earth* (*akatsuchi*, run-off from construction and farming, which is a major problem in Okinawa in particular, where the effluent from intensive pig farming runs into the rivers and thence the sea, where it destroys coral reefs). Likewise, local governments must work to 'typhoon proof' the local infrastructure. The islands lie in a major typhoon zone and storms cause significant damage every year to roads, ports, and electric power networks. It is considerably more expensive, for instance, to bury electric power cables rather than use the overhead power lines common in the rest of Japan, and private electric power companies have to be subsidised to undertake this work.

For the prefectural government, maintaining a state presence in these islands is crucial for several reasons in addition to the strategic concern over national territorial rivalry already mentioned. Local services, the municipal office, and the school system also provide virtually the only employment opportunities for young people outside tourism; there are islands on which the only residents between the ages of 15 and 30 are civil servants or schoolteachers. The local offices and schools also provide a focus for the maintenance of community life. Many smaller islands are facing a dramatic cultural impoverishment as the distinctive old ways of life and community rituals are no longer being transmitted and are gradually being abandoned. On Yonaguni, for instance, there used to be fourteen *tsukasa* (community priestesses, a role that is exclusively the preserve of female elders in Okinawan traditional religion); now there is only one, and the separate village festivals that used to take place at various points in the agricultural cycle have been amalgamated into one annual event. In Hateruma, too, the masked dramas and festivals of the six hamlets on the island are now combined into one performance a year. In such an environment, small government-run local museums and the sponsorship of cultural preservation provide important forums and personnel for the work of transmitting local cultural practices and rituals. The fear is that the ongoing process of municipal mergers could deprive some smaller islands of their local offices, thus not only leaving them politically disadvantaged in terms of representing their interests but also effectively eliminating the core of the community, resulting in its collapse and disappearance. Yonaguni Town, for instance, is fiercely resisting any merger; indeed, the mayor there has called forthrightly for the abolition of the prefecture itself so that he can deal directly with Tokyo (R. Siddle, interview at Yonaguni Town Office, April 2008).

CONCLUSION

Shrinkage is occurring in Japan, and will continue to occur, nationwide—from the relatively affluent and heavily populated urban and suburban settlements along Japan's network of Shinkansen super-express train lines, to the sparsely populated and forested mountainous villages of Hongū Town on the Kii Peninsula, and to the remote islands of Okinawa Prefecture in Japan's far southwestern province. These descriptions illustrate some of the recursive impacts that play out through the decisions and actions of social and economic actors at the national, regional, and community levels and that work to illuminate some of the implications of shrinkage for Japan's regions. These illustrate both the breadth and depth of shrinkage and its consequences for the country as a whole.

That national policies were crafted in response to recognizable trends of depopulation as early as the 1960s is significant not only because such actions were taken at all but also because the measures did not significantly alter trends of regional depopulation; in fact, as discussed in chapter 3, depopulation is accelerating in some regions. The outcomes of these trends are clearly evident in their effects on regional urban settlements as well as in the relatively unseen and unmeasured areas of local rural life, highlighting the importance of addressing shrinkage not simply as a matter of economics or regional administration but rather as a matter closely tied to achieving a decent and dignified quality of life for all Japanese, whether urban or rural, old or young. Finally, that decisions—taken by actors such as those organising transportation networks or developing infrastructure in distant and underpopulated islands—bring such clear implications for the areas affected by those decisions, both to their advantage and to their disadvantage, highlights that foresight is necessary to mitigate and minimise such impacts.

Along with these past and present microlevel processes, one must constantly keep in mind that in the context of a decline in the overall national population, any future increase in the size of one settlement will necessarily require a proportionately greater decrease in the size of another. Regional Japan is therefore at a major turning point in its history. For example, it will prove more difficult in the future for government intervention (in the form of, for example, infrastructure projects) both to gain the necessary funding and to generate the desired regional and community revitalisation. Hence, the population downturn will likely cause wider spatial disparities than have been experienced hitherto. One question that emerges from this chapter is this: How do national and regional actors adapt their policies to the changing circumstances that depopulation brings to Japan's regional communities—whether urban, suburban, or remote rural and island settlements—in order that all Japanese continue to share equitably in the country's prosperity?

CHAPTER 5

GEOGRAPHICAL PERIPHERALITY AND INDUSTRIAL TRANSFORMATION IN JAPAN'S SHRINKING REGIONS*

INTRODUCTION

In this concluding chapter to part I, we add to the information submitted thus far a presentation of four case studies that exemplify the two principal processes affecting Japan's shrinking regions. First is the steady and continuing thinning of rural populations due to low fertility and the out-migration of younger people. Second is the sudden loss of population that comes with the collapse of a locale's primary economic functions. In the first part of the chapter, we focus on the K region of Kyoto and Shiga Prefectures and the Kanbayashi River valley area and on their relative geographical peripherality in terms of both their distance from

*The principal contributing authors to this chapter are Richard Irving, Sachie Mizohata, Naofumi Nakamura, and Philip Seaton.

population centres and their topographic isolation. As we describe, the limitations of place inherent to these locations has led to, if not necessitated or encouraged, long term out-migration. Linked to the decline of the timber industry in K region, the depopulation of Yūbari and Kamaishi Cities represent a dramatic contraction in the local economic base, contraction that has resulted in a rapid—and in the case of Yūbari, disastrous—community shrinkage.

We view these two themes as interconnected factors in regional shrinkage. Geographical peripherality is itself often a function of an extractive economy that in its earlier stages of industrialisation was built on developing primary and secondary industries for the purposes of consolidating the nation-state and growing its economy. These then give way to the internationalisation and globalisation of the national industrial base and the domestic transition to a service-oriented economy, though the structure of the extractive relationship between the metropolitan core and regional periphery remains in place. The resulting stagnation in regional and local economies and the collapse in employment that ensues set off recursively combinative impacts of increasing severity, even as local communities seek to develop fresh opportunities, such as tourism, that have themselves been initiated by the economic, social and cultural transformations taking place in the metropolitan core. The consequences for individuals and families are severe and long lasting, presenting few if any opportunities to return to a growth trajectory.

As an analytical framework for understanding the characteristics, impacts, and implications of regional shrinkage that the first part of this volume presents, McGranahan's idea of 'conceptual distinction between sustenance and maintenance activities' in communal systems is useful for analysing the processes of regional shrinkage in Japan:

> Sustenance activities bring money or goods into a household or community, while maintenance activities keep it circulating within the community. Both are necessary for survival.... [A]t the community or area level, we can distinguish between what economists call 'economic base' activities (agriculture, mining, manufacturing, and services for people or business outside the

> community), which bring money or goods into the community, and services that support the community and its members. These support activities include not only the maintenance of 'social institutions' such as health care, education, churches, and local government, and civic activities ... but also services for local businesses and households. Paid work in these areas is sustenance activity for households, but maintenance activity at the community level. A community cannot survive on services alone, unless outsiders such as tourists are making the purchases and/or residents have considerable transfer income (e.g., welfare, social security, pension income). (McGranahan, 2003, p. 136)

An understanding of the tension between sustenance and maintenance at the family and community levels can be adopted in an analysis of shrinkage in Japan's regions in the postwar period, as sources of income have declined or even vanished and as individuals responsible for supporting their dependents feel compelled to fall back on service and dependency activities. In rural villages, home to a large number of older residents and limited opportunities for remunerative nonagricultural employment, many households have come to be sustained by income sources derived from outside the region; these include pensions, remittances from their family members, wage employment in the public sector (e.g., working as a local teacher or for a village office), and the income from, for example, apartment rents in urban locales. Moreover, in the regional settlements presented in what follows, once their source of economic sustenance has shrunk or disappeared, local people are barely able to maintain the existence of their community by developing new sources of income, few if any of which provide the means of sustenance that such a settlement requires in order to exist in its current size and form. The consequence is that resilience to external risks is compromised and a spiral of decline and shrinkage ensues as productive individuals leave and households disappear. All these factors contribute to the suspicion that many communities in Japan's shrinking regions have been dependent on maintenance income for their sustenance and are therefore, in the long term, unsustainable communities destined for collapse.

THE K REGION OF SHIGA AND KYOTO PREFECTURES

The K region of Kyoto and Shiga Prefectures represents both the gradual but steady shrinkage of a comparatively rural, inaccessible region and an industrial restructuring and natural resources–based depopulation scenario. The region also bears a strong link to a distant past. Katsurakawa and Kutsuki are located in Shiga Prefecture, on the west side of Lake Biwa. Kuta is a former township (*kyūshichōson*) located in Kyoto Prefecture, adjacent to the boundary with Shiga Prefecture. It maintains its rural character, but is now incorporated within Sakyō-ku, in Kyoto City. As such, it is the northernmost settlement within the City boundary. Although this region is divided by different municipal borders, its communities are historically and culturally close (Kuta jikkō iinkai, 1977). From the first letter of each town's name (Katsurakawa, Kutsuki, Kuta), we have dubbed this area and will refer to it as the *K region*. It is located about 35–45 km northeast of Kyoto City, approximately one hour by car, and many parts of the region are difficult to access because they are located upstream on the Adogawa River, which flows into the western part of Lake Biwa. Kutsuki (approximately 2,500 inhabitants) is on the so-called *saba kaidō*, a mackerel route along which seafood was transported in times past to the ancient capital, Kyoto, from the Japan Sea coast of Fukui Prefecture. The upland areas are known for narrow winding roads, awe-inspiring gorges, undulating rock strata, and steep mountains and are rich in numerous broadleaf trees and evergreens. Deeper in the uplands, the forests become ominously monotone, thicker and darker because of the densely planted Japanese cedars, an effect that accentuates the gloom of severe depopulation.

In contrast to the dynamic, urbanised, and materially developed Kyoto City, the K region is depopulated, and its living standards are generally low. The region has sparsely scattered houses, most with kitchen gardens and many with abandoned rice paddies. Many of the communities in the K region are *genkai shūraku*, meaning that they are under threat of collapse. The defining characteristic of such communities is a population of predominantly older people. Without demographic and economic revitalisation, these communities—lacking adequate operating budgets and civic momentum—face certain extinction (Ohno, 2005, pp. 22–23).

Within the K region, the most badly affected areas are the uplands—specifically, Harihata (Kutsuki's upland district) and Kuta, where forestry was a major economic activity until the mid-20th century. Many households in these mountainous communities made a sustainable living from their land and forestry, and they also produced charcoal as a way to generate additional income because forestry requires 30 to 40 years for the trees to grow and generate profits (Kuta jikkō iinkai, 1977, p. 61). According to older local people, besides participating in charcoal manufacturing, those who were not landlords worked in multiple occupations to augment their incomes, performing day labour for neighbouring farmers, piecework, silkworm rearing, and domestic service. The dominance of forestry in the area makes the communal depopulation and contemporary economic circumstance of the K region highly representative of Ohno's (2005) empirical description of the transformation of the timber industry, a transformation that has had a severe impact on the large number of communities in Japan's mountainous and forested areas.

In the wake of World War II, Japan lost colonial forests in Sakhalin, Korea, and Taiwan, areas that had supplied 30 percent of the nation's timber (Ohno, 2005, p. 263). Driven by rising demand for building uses and firewood in the postwar reconstruction boom, domestic forests were heavily logged and consequently quickly devastated. In response, the central government began to promote afforestation, predominantly with Japanese cedar and cypress, so as to achieve self-sufficiency in timber production (Ohno, 2005). In 1956 the national government adopted the aggressive reforestation policy referred to as *kakudai-zorin*, subsidising the replacement of what were considered commercially useless natural forests (mostly beech, maple, oak, and other broadleaf or deciduous trees) with more economically productive trees. For the most part, this extraordinary experiment in environmental engineering has involved planting a single species, the Japanese cedar, because of the usefulness of its wood and the speed of its growth (Sterngold, 1995). Though there seemed to be little doubt that the afforestation was economically motivated, this policy would affect the lives of area residents in many ways later on.

In the 1950s, timber prices rose quickly because of increased demand. Because forestry was upland communities' main economic activity, its timber industry peaked, and the rural economy expanded owing to the good quality of the timber. Mr Matsuda (pseudonym; S. Mizohata, interview, 11 March 2009), a native of the area, remarked on the spirit of prosperity and competition for planting more trees in the pursuit of profit, relating how people bragged about planting thousands of trees at community gatherings. Since the number of jobs in forestry significantly increased with afforestation, a labour shortage resulted, and forest owners recruited seasonal workers from other prefectures such as Tochigi, Miyazaki, and the Tōhoku region. At this time, forests were rapidly replaced by artificial plantation of conifers, though the country still had a low dependency on imported timber, rising to just 5.1 percent in 1955 (from 0.3% in 1950) and to 13.3 percent in 1960 (Ohno, 2005, p. 263). Supplying raw materials to urban areas, many rural areas like K region played an important role in the broad growth of the national postwar economy. At the same time, local agricultural output increased due to the development of agricultural lots, mechanisation, and chemical fertilisers' replacing human manure (Ohno, 2005; Partner, 2000). Rural households invested the supplementary agricultural income that this produced in forestry and established agro-forestry households (Ohno, 2005). In the uplands of the K region, some families also invested in new business. One interview respondent, Ms Shimizu, stated:

> It was around 1966 or '67. Shortly after Ojii-san [her father in-law] died, we sold the timber, which yielded about 8 million yen. With that money, we built an apartment in Kyoto.... You know, in the old days we could lead a humble life for a year on the sum of money if we sold a single truck of lumber. (S. Mizohata, interview, 5 June 2007.)

In this way, some forest owners in K region took advantage of the bubble economy and built student apartment buildings in the area around Kyoto University in the northeast of the city. Some families also started real estate companies. Two former mayors and older residents of Kutsuki could count, mentioning by name, at least 20 families from Harihata and 6 to 7 families from Kuta that had constructed apartment buildings in Kyoto City using locally available timber, demonstrating that family wealth was closely tied to private forest ownership.

After the Liberalisation of Trade and Exchange in 1960 brought lower tariff barriers amid continuing economic growth, Japan sharply increased timber imports (Ohno, 2005, p. 263). Because inexpensive lumber was available from overseas (from Southeast Asia and the Americas, in particular), Japanese cedar and cypress lost much of their market competitiveness and imported foreign lumber eventually accounted for 28.6 percent of the Japanese lumber market in 1965, and then jumped to 55 percent by 1970 and 64.1 percent by 1973 (Ohno, 2005, pp. 264–265). Whereas imported lumber came to dominate the domestic market, depressing the price of domestic lumber and leading to the stagnation of cedar production, timber prices continued to increase until 1970 due to overall inflation and higher commodity prices triggered by the oil shocks. Older residents of K region confirm this, describing how the real income from local timber steadily declined after 1965. Mr Hayashi (92 years old, pseudonym; S. Mizohata, interview, 5 June 2007), who worked for an afforestation project at the Shiga prefectural office, said:

> I talked to many people and successfully convinced them to plant the trees, [using his handmade graphs of projected business profits]. Later on, when the timber prices dropped, I felt really bad for them.

Hayashi also referred to another man in his eighties who worked for the Forestry Association (*Shinrin kumiai*), who remarked that, looking back at the heyday of timber industry, he never thought that there would be a day like today when the trees do not make money (S. Mizohata, interview, 7 March 2009).

Moreover, the energy revolution, which took place nationwide starting in the 1960s, severely decreased the importance of firewood and charcoal in daily life. These two fuels, once indispensable for cooking, heating, washing, and bathing, came to be replaced by electricity and propane gas (Kuta kinomi kai, 1993). Domestic timber and all domestic forest-associated products hence underwent dramatic devaluation as lumber suppliers were replaced and modern substitute materials were introduced.

During the period of high-speed economic growth, rural communities saw massive out-migration and population loss. 'Farmers had traditionally devoted much of their efforts to non-cash activities, as they worked to grow food for their own families. [Although] hard work without pay was a fact of life for farmers' (Partner, 2000, p. 772), they soon became aware that they needed gainful employments because of the decline of the traditional economic systems of rural self-sufficiency and self-help. The 65-year-old Katsurakawa native Mr Okamoto said, half-jokingly: 'Why did we leave? The answer is simple. There were no jobs' (S. Mizohata, interview, 1 March 2009).

His remark reflects the reality that the timber industry had gone into decline, which complicated matters for farm successors (*atotsugi*) and other sons maintaining their livelihoods in forestry villages. One interview respondent, Mr Tanaka (age 72), had worked for a timber company before he left Kutsuki in about 1971 or 1972. As the eldest son with an obligation to maintain the household (*ie*), he could not tell his parents that he needed to emigrate to find work and look after the family. The boss of the timber company where he worked persuaded his father to allow him to leave the village, telling him that it was better for his family to ask his son to work somewhere else and send the money home. The father accepted the arrangement, and Tanaka first moved to Nishinomiya City, near Kobe, to work on the development of a golf course, and then moved to work in manufacturing in an industrial conglomerate (*keiretsu*).

With the decline of the timber industry, then, younger people sought alternative labour in nonfarm jobs. In other words, the crisis made more attractive the new, predominantly industrial opportunities that were opening up in urban areas for rural youth to provide financial support for their families. These changes also helped to shift the occupational interests of younger people from insecure and physically demanding primary sector employment to more secure employments in manufacturing and (later) services. Meanwhile, traditional and underdeveloped rural economies were slowly being transformed from an extractive agriculture-forestry base into a cash economy. Although forest owners faced poor prospects because they could not make a profit selling their timber, they hoped prices would recover in the future.

After the first oil shock of 1973, the forestry industry in K region was marked by two significant phenomena. One was a local economy mired in a prolonged economic decline and stagnation, a condition which has continued ever since. The other was the limited maintenance of existing forests, which itself is related to the prolonged decline (see Ohno, 2005, pp. 265–266). Large portions of private forests comprised young trees, planted in the 1950s and early 1960s—trees with a life span of 40–70 years that required regular care and management including weeding, pruning, thinning, and coppicing. However, according to older forest owners, with timber prices too low to pay for the labour of planting and logging, private forests were left without appropriate care. Moreover, forest maintenance has become difficult for the ageing forest owners (S. Mizohata, interview, 30 May 2008).

In sum, natural resource extraction in forestry had long provided a primary means of income in the uplands of the K region. But its importance has declined significantly as the policy shift from afforestation and reforestation to increased imported timbers has negatively affected the upland forestry villages—particularly once the Japanese yen increased in value relative to other currencies (Ota, 2002) and the country's raw-materials needs changed with the rapid industrial and societal transformations of the postwar period. Hence, many people were forced to emigrate in order to make a living in nearby urban areas once their primary sources of income disappeared. Consequently, the outflow of the working population has significantly contributed to demographic ageing and seriously eroded the foundations of rural life.

The next section examines in detail how these processes have manifested themselves in the decisions of individuals and families resident in the rural Kanbayashi River valley of northern Kyoto Prefecture and how these decisions combined have resulted in sustained depopulation and decline—to a point where the very existence of communities and settlements is now under serious threat.

The Microprocesses of Rural Shrinkage and Isolation in the Kanbayashi River Valley

In considerations of community shrinkage at the local level in Japan, attention has tended to fall on the municipality: the *shi* (cities), *chō* (towns), and *son* (villages), which make up the bulk of the administrative framework in the country. Decisions concerning the processes of population decline are made at the level of the individual, however, and affect primarily each family unit. The decisions of whether to move house, when and where to move, and whether to have children or not (and how many) all affect the quality of family life but are unlikely to influence the fundamental issue of family sustainability in the short term. Rather, the immediate community of neighbouring families and households actually experiences the shrinkage and the threat of decline and abandonment through the processes of declining fertility, age-selective migration, and the consequent ageing of the local population. This section highlights the village community of Kusakabe, alongside 50 similar communities located along the Kanbayashi valley. Labelled for administrative purposes as part of the municipality of Ayabe City, Kyoto Prefecture, Kusakabe is situated deep in the Tamba uplands, about two hours by car to the north-west of Kyoto City.

Kusakabe presents a charming picture of rural Japan (photo 5.1). It is a village of about 25 households settled on both flanks of the shallow valley that bears the village's name. It is not a particularly noticeable or special community—in the sense that there are no historic monuments or social traditions to attract the attention of casual passers-by—but the forests, fields, and streams there are pure, and the giant salamander that inhabits this landscape can do so because modern development has not adversely affected the area or polluted its waters. The people of Kanbayashi are always glad to see the salamander (*ōsanshowo*) because its presence traditionally suggests that all is well and that the balance between human activity—rice farming, forest management, and river fishing—and the natural

Photo 5.1. Kusakabe village in the distance, with Torigaki and Ariyasu in the foreground.

Photo by Richard Irving (October 2010).

order of things in this upland environment is as it should be. This is a false reflection, however. The *ōsanshowo* may be thriving, but the environmental caretakers, who have inherited their farmsteads in Kusakabe as a result of long-standing Japanese family tradition, are extremely concerned that the future of the village cannot be guaranteed. There are very few to no sons or daughters who are prepared to stay in the village to ensure the continuity of each household. In sum, the carefully nurtured balance between the inhabitants of Kusakabe (and all neighbouring communities, too) and the surrounding countryside may no longer be sustainable.

The Kusakabe River flows into the larger Kanbayashi River, an important line of communication since time immemorial. The two converge at a point about a 10–15 minutes' walk from the village. From its source near the border with Fukui Prefecture to its confluence with the larger Yura River, the Kanbayashi River cuts a relatively straight southwesterly course 30 km through the hills (map 5.1). Within this wider system, Kusakabe is but one of 51 village communities, all of which feel the threat, to some degree, of impending demise. The Kanbayashi valley is broad enough to allow rice paddy cultivation along most of its length, and its well-defined character, connecting the ancient Kinai Province surrounding Kyoto with Hokuriku Province along the Japan Sea coast, made it a strategically important route in the past. A castle once dominated the central section of the valley and even today this is where the highest concentration of rural settlement is found. The importance of the route the castle once protected is reflected in the fact it is designated Prefectural Highway Route 1 (map 5.1: P1).

In the immediate postwar years, the present Ayabe City comprised 13 autonomous administrative districts, seven of which were

MAP 5.1. Ayabe City, showing the Kanbayashi River Valley and Kusakabe.

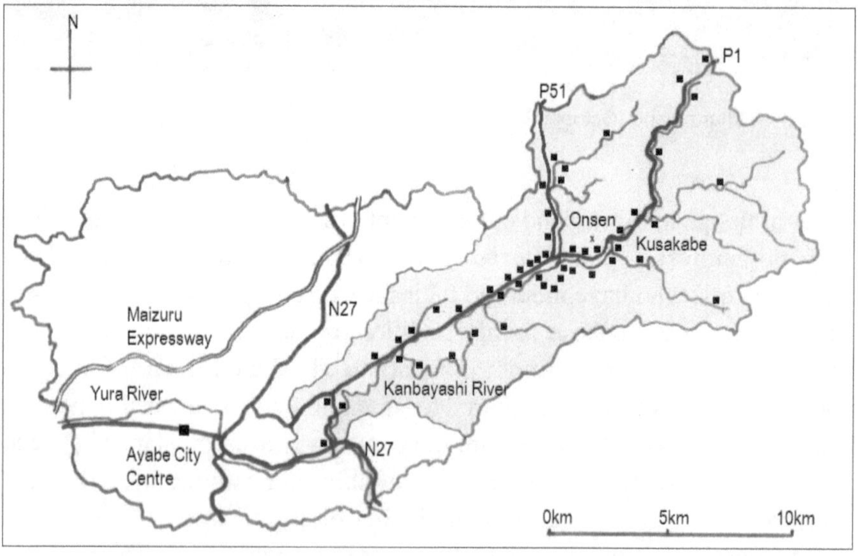

Source. Map by Richard Irving.

amalgamated in 1950 to create the nascent Ayabe City. A second round of amalgamation took place in 1955, bringing five more administrative villages under the umbrella of Ayabe, with the sixth and final village joining the group in 1956. No further amalgamation is planned at present. The Kanbayashi valley is divided into three former village administrations and includes part of a fourth. Farthest from Ayabe City centre is Oku-Kanbayashi (which includes Kusakabe and 14 other settlements), then Naka-Kanbayashi (25 settlements), and Kuchi-Kanbayashi (8 settlements). Three settlements close to the confluence with the Yura River (closest to Ayabe centre) form part of the district called Yamaga. To be clear, each of these former village administrative units is made up of a number of morphologically independent settlements that in English are also normally referred to as villages or hamlets. This is the meaning of the word *village*, or *village community*, as it is used in this case study.

Developing an Index of Isolation

Population data for the Kanbayashi villages are taken from the monthly population summaries issued by the city office, based on information contained in the Basic Residential Register (*Kihon jūmin daicho*). End-of-September figures are chosen as the most suitably representative for each year, for this is the month when population in Japan is considered most stable. When dealing with small populations in village communities such as these, where change rates can fluctuate wildly with the births, deaths, or migration of just a handful of people, the scattered population totals for each year between 1987 and 2009 should be averaged by overlaying a *line of best fit* (figure 5.1). Average annual population change rates are then calculated on the basis of figures indicated by this line. Here, data for the village of Shimizu (Naka Kanbayashi) are illustrated.

Average population change rate per year

$$= (((A - B)/A)/\text{no. of years}) \times 100$$
$$= (((98.5 - 46.5)/98.5)/22) \times 100$$
$$= -2.4 \text{ (N.B.: Population change is negative)}$$
$$R^2 = 0.9.$$

FIGURE 5.1. Population of Shimizu Village (Naka Kanbayashi), and the Line of Best Fit.

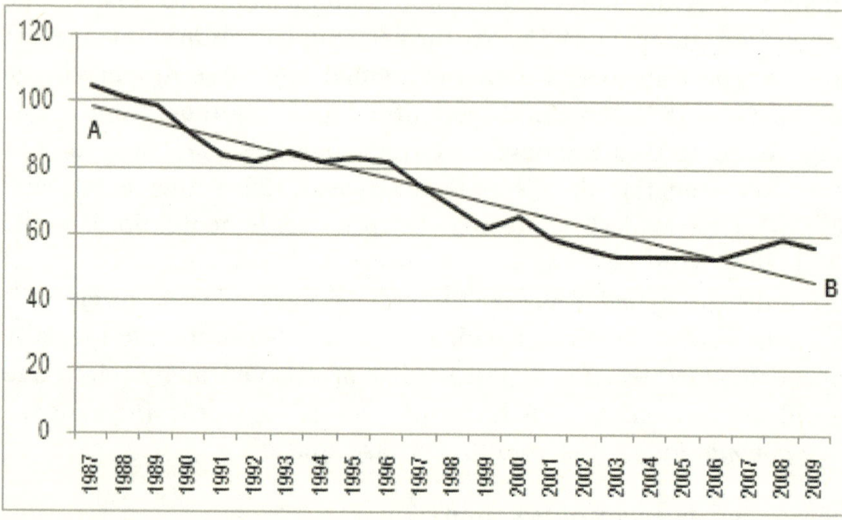

Sources. Ayabe shi (various years) and Richard Irving's fieldwork.
Note. A–B represents the line of best fit used to calculate average annual rates of population change.

Although the actual population of Shimizu village fell from 105 to 57 over the period, application of the line of best fit suggests an average annual decline of 2.4 percent. The degree to which this line reflects actual changes of population is suggested by the R^2 value. If R^2 equals 1.00 there would be a perfect fit between actual and averaged data. A low score of zero suggests a completely random association. In this case the value is 0.9, reflecting not just a high degree of correlation but, more important, that the rate of population change has remained stable—even relentless—over the last two decades or so. Rates of population change and R^2 values for all 51 village communities are shown in table 5.1. The most significant findings are that all but two communities have experienced population decline since 1987 and that in 40 of these settlements R^2 values were 0.8 or higher, suggesting a high degree of consistency in this decline.

The order of listing of settlements in table 5.1 is based on the listings of population totals provided by the city office. Settlements are grouped into *kyūshichōson*—former cities, towns, and villages—with the group farthest from Ayabe City Office listed first. Oddly, the city office listings of communities within each group are ordered in a reverse pattern, reflecting perhaps the sequence of head-counting adopted by census enumerators. Here, this discrepancy is corrected not only by reversing the ordering of communities but also by noting the actual distance from the city office. In general, therefore, the list of settlements in table 5.1 is ordered in terms of remoteness from Ayabe City Office, although the integrity of each *kyūshichōson* grouping has been preserved. Average annual population change rates are shown graphically in figure 5.2, where this same order of listing is preserved.

The most startling revelation in figure 5.2 is how widespread the phenomenon of depopulation is in the Kanbayashi valley. All but two communities have suffered sustained population decline since 1987, with the highest rate (Ichikaya) at a rate of -2.6 percent per annum. A rate of decline of 2 percent or more each year is officially considered of *kaso* proportions—that is, a rate of severe rural depopulation. Eighteen villages suffered a higher rate of decline or one equal to that of Kusakabe (- 1.93%), and as many as 42 villages (82%) experienced sustained decline of 1 percent or more annually. In addition, villages towards the left-hand side of the chart—geographically farthest, in general terms, from Ayabe City centre—seem to experience the highest rates of depopulation. The consideration of distance is a significant one because access to urban functions—or properly, lack of access—has long been recognised as a major factor explaining variations in the severity of rural population decline (Adachi, 1973; Irving, 1984). The notion of a place's remoteness does not only involve simple map measurements to the nearest central place, however. Location along a main road that provides easy access to public transportation, for example, may help reduce feelings of remoteness even though the actual distance to the local city centre may be farther than that from other communities. Conversely, some village communities that are relatively close to the central place but that are isolated from the main road

TABLE 5.1. Household and Population Change and Index of Isolation for 51 Village Communities in the Kanbayashi River Valley.

	1987 Total h'holds	2009 Total h'holds	1987 Pop.	2009 Pop.	Ave. annual Rate of Pop. Change 1987-2009*	R-squared**	Index of Isolation
Oku-Kanbayashi							
Ichikaya	10	7	28	18	-2.6	**0.68**	4
Ogarachi	19	18	49	28	-2.13	0.85	4
Tochi	13	12	42	19	**-2.35**	0.98	3
Kowagi	55	40	131	66	-2.43	0.96	5
Mitsuno	31	22	75	38	-2.06	0.93	3
Koya	8	6	13	7	**-2.27**	0.84	6
Yajiro	23	19	77	34	**-2.58**	0.99	3
Konaka	35	31	110	79	**-1.03**	0.91	2
Kawara	17	15	45	39	-0.9	**0.76**	2
Ariyasu	55	48	151	83	-1.93	0.99	2
Kusakabe	32	25	87	52	-1.93	0.95	3
Torigaki	23	24	76	66	**0.25**	**0.05**	2
Shikoda	18	16	42	31	-1.28	**0.79**	3
Yamauchi	23	19	58	45	-1.18	**0.53**	1
Nagano	22	18	66	35	-2.43	0.95	1
Naka-Kanbayashi							
Ichishi	19	14	42	22	**-2.33**	0.96	5
Mizunashi	17	15	63	34	-2.48	0.94	4
Ichinose	31	24	91	50	**-0.81**	0.96	4
Nushi	23	22	81	57	**-1.38**	0.85	3
Tsuji	17	17	58	42	-1.26	0.94	2
Shimizu	36	29	105	57	-2.4	0.9	2
Yuri	42	38	141	99	**-1.54**	0.94	2
Yuge	27	26	83	60	-1.3	0.88	3

(*continued on the next page*)

TABLE 5.1. (*Continued*)

Oomachi	49	45	136	88	**-1.52**	0.92	1
Shiodani	11	6	24	11	-2.32	0.9	3
Yamada	13	14	42	27	-1.75	0.82	3
Takehara	17	16	69	37	**-2.04**	0.89	3
Katayama	23	27	89	67	**-0.92**	**0.69**	1
Tono	20	16	59	39	-1.6	0.88	1
Baba	21	19	66	34	-2.26	0.98	2
Ishibashi	27	24	91	62	-1.21	0.87	2
Hikidani	28	25	97	64	**-1.33**	0.87	1
Teramachi	26	21	66	36	-2.1	0.96	1
Azura	21	20	65	33	-2.52	0.93	3
Kodani	16	15	48	28	**-1.77**	0.89	1
Nishiya	23	22	70	65	-0.45	**0.18**	1
Hikiji	34	34	88	68	-1.44	0.85	1
Oda	24	26	86	51	-1.89	0.89	1
Mano	27	31	103	76	**-1.15**	0.88	1
Daiichiku	64	60	202	137	**-1.49**	0.94	1
Kuchi-Kanbayashi							
Tadacho	40	41	152	107	-1.24	0.88	3
Tsukudacho	56	43	173	104	**-1.78**	0.99	4
Takeyoshicho	60	59	181	131	**-1.4**	0.89	3
Inecho	32	30	102	59	**-1.66**	0.88	3
Tokura Nabatacho	48	60	165	145	**-0.59**	**0.64**	2
Tokura Mukocho	26	28	86	70	**-0.93**	**0.69**	1
Tokura Nakacho	32	32	74	87	0.26	**0.09**	1
Tokura Shimocho	41	39	114	88	**-0.61**	**0.33**	1
Yamaga							
Asahicho	40	37	129	79	**-1.82**	0.98	1
Hashiuecho	23	20	77	49	-1.94	0.91	2
Higashiyamacho	104	101	336	266	-0.77	0.9	1

Sources. Ayabe shi (various years) and Richard Irving's fieldwork.
Note. *Derived from the line of best fit (see figure 5.1). Bold figures show where decline has worsened in the previous four years. **Also refers to the line of best fit. Bold figures show values less than 0.8.

FIGURE 5.2. Average Annual Population Change Rates (percentages) in the Villages of the Kanbayashi River Valley (1987–2009; Kusakabe highlighted).

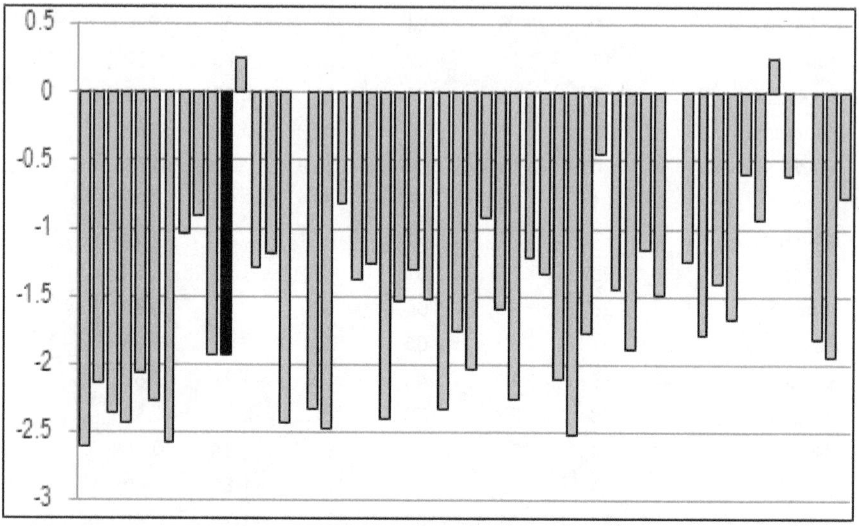

Sources. Ayabe shi (various years) and Richard Irving's fieldwork.

because of their locations near the end of a small tributary valley may have an enhanced sense of remoteness. This is particularly so if, as is common, there are no local, permanent shops or other service facilities and if the main valley cannot even be seen from the village settlement.

Of the 51 village communities, Koya (photo 5.2) probably experiences the greatest isolation. Koya is located in the same tributary valley as Kusakabe, deep in the surrounding hills where the valley sides are so steep as to make rice unrealistic. The village is a 30–45 minute walk from Kusakabe along a narrow road frequently cut by landslides. There is no public transportation service, although, like all 51 communities, Koya is served by a weekly mobile shop delivery operated by the local agricultural co-operative. The real problem of isolation was revealed several years ago, however, when a fire broke out in one of the households and the local volunteer fire service was unable to arrive in time to save the house. The elderly occupants were safe, but

Photo 5.2. Koya—the most isolated settlement in the Kanbayashi River valley.

Photo by Richard Irving (October 2010).

decided to take the opportunity to leave the village for good. By September 2009 only seven people were left in the village, the youngest aged in his late 50s.

In order to provide a sense of the relative isolation felt in each village community, an *index of isolation* has been devised, represented on a scale of 1 to 6. Koya, the village just described, is given the maximum score of 6, reflecting the greatest degree of isolation (table 5.1). Two other communities, Kowagi and Ichishi, are in similarly remote locations, but in both cases their valley environments are sufficiently broad and sunny, allowing rice cultivation. There is not the sense of being hidden away in Kowagi or Ichishi, therefore, as there is in Koya, and so both score 5 on the index. Five villages have an index score of 4, reflecting the fact that they are also located at or near the outermost points of the dendritic Kanbayashi River network (and are thus among the most isolated from Ayabe), but they are no more than a short walk (within 10 minutes) from the main road. Fourteen villages have a score of 3, including Kusakabe. This value indicates that though one or more neighbouring villages may be in sight, the distance to the main road requires a walk of between 10 and 30 minutes. Though not entirely isolated, these villages are still near the periphery of the network. The 11 villages with a value of 2 are either on the main road but beyond the area served by the public transportation network or are within a 10-minute walk from the nearest bus stop.

The 18 villages with an index value of 1 are all on the main road and are served by the fairly frequent bus service that runs between Ayabe JR station and Ayabe Onsen. No distinction is made according to distance from Ayabe station, although in reality the bus journey time is about 20–25 minutes longer for residents of Yamauchi, nearest the *onsen* (hot-spring resort), than for those of Higashiyanaga, nearest to the confluence of the Kanbayashi and Yura Rivers—though both places score 1 on the scale.

The index is clearly prone to a degree of subjectivity, but as far as possible, objective considerations are taken into account. It is, after all, a descriptive device, and the scale is nominal rather than ratio. It cannot be inferred, therefore, that Koya (6) is twice as isolated as Kusakabe (3). It can be said, nevertheless, that Koya evokes a considerably greater feeling of isolation than its nearest neighbour, Kusakabe, which in turn has a greater feel of isolation than its near neighbours Ariyasu (2), Torigaki (2), and Yamauchi (1). It is with this understanding that Figure 5.3 should be viewed; it attempts to demonstrate the relationship between sustained annual population change rates and remoteness, or degree of

FIGURE 5.3. Index of Isolation for Villages in the Kanbayashi River Valley and Population Change, 1987–2009.

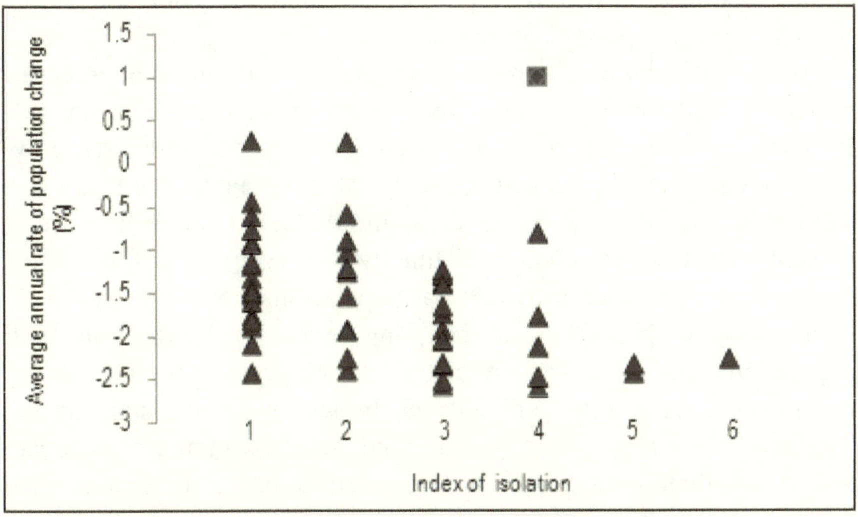

Sources. Ayabe shi (various years) and Richard Irving's fieldwork.

isolation. The graph confirms that the more isolated settlements tend to suffer higher rates of depopulation, but it also demonstrates that some village communities with a relatively high degree of access to central places may also be prone to the dangers of severe depopulation and even village abandonment.

Towards an Understanding of the Dynamics of Rural Shrinkage

Although it is employed as a descriptive rather than predictive device, the linear line of best fit for population change shown in figure 5.1 indicates in most villages an apparently inexorable plunge towards complete abandonment. In the case of Shimizu, extrapolation of the line places termination at zero population in approximately 2009 plus 23 or 24 years—around 2033. For Ichikaya, the village community with the greatest rate of decline, a similar calculation suggests complete abandonment—village extinction—in 2018. Intuitively, such an assertion appears ridiculous, for the whims of human activity rarely conform to statistical projections. That said, R^2 values for the lines of best fit for the Kanbayashi villages suggest a remarkably high degree of consistency in the pace of decline.

Population decline is apparently relentless, and unless an agent of change is forthcoming, future existence for most villages in the valley does indeed appear to be finite. The laws of exponentiality, however, suggest that if sustained, a decline of 1 percent would result in a halving of population every 72 years and that a decline of just over 2 percent would see population decline by half every 35 years or so. It is important to realise, however, that population change rates are most unlikely to remain stable over such long periods, particularly in small populations, because exponential decline suggests continual halving that never reaches zero. Not only do biological factors stand in the way of this, but also after a certain point, surely community members realise that their settlement is no longer sustainable, and demise then follows quickly. This is especially true in areas whose populations are ageing and where few children remain to provide a sense of balance and the potential for continuity. Complete abandonment of settlements in the Kanbayashi River valley has not yet been witnessed, at least not in recent times, but if the demographic structure of these villages is not favourable and if there is no future influx of individuals, then demise may occur in some settlements even sooner than projected by the lines of best fit.

Since 2005 Ayabe City Office has collected population data for all village communities, broken down by age. As an indicator of the ageing of population, the numbers of very old—aged 80 years or more—can now be identified at this level. For all the villages in the valley, the average proportion of people aged over 80 years in 2005 was 16.7 percent. By 2008 this figure had risen to 21.3 percent, or just over one in five of the total population of Kanbayashi. In fact, 42 of the 51 villages experienced an increase in the proportion of the very old during these years. The highest rate, 42.9 percent in 2008, was experienced in two communities, Koya and Ichishi. In other words, two in five inhabitants of these villages are just about to reach or have already exceeded the average life expectancy for the nation as a whole, which in 2005 was 78.11 years for males and 85.20 years for females (National Institute of Population and Social Security Research, 2006). However fit and healthy many of this group may feel, most will concede that death cannot be far away and that the annual death rate for the village as a whole will increase dramatically over the coming years.

An alternative measure, this one in terms of future village continuity, is the number of children (0–14 years) per 10 households. How many of these now raise giant carp streamers each year or celebrate Children's Day in other ways? Whereas in the past an average of 15 or even 20 children for every 10 households would not have been uncommon, in 2005 the average for Kanbayashi as a whole was 1.7, and in 2008 this had fallen to 1.3. In 12 villages there were no children at all, and the highest figure among all 51 communities came from Tsuji, which had 5 children per 10 households. Furthermore, two villages had no people aged 15 to 64 as well as no children present (Irving, 2010). Unless there is a substantial inflow of younger generations, an apparently unlikely prospect, these figures speak for themselves; disappearing villages are not only inevitable but will become reality *soon*.

The Changing Population Structure of Kusakabe Village

In 2008 the proportion of very old (aged over 80 years) to total population in the village of Kusakabe was 32 percent. This is high for Kanbayashi as a whole, but fairly typical for the neighbouring settlements in Oku-Kanbayashi. There were 1.2 children for every 10 households, a somewhat low figure, but not so unusual as to suggest that Kusakabe is in any way untypical among the 51 settlements in the Kanbayashi valley. This observation is confirmed by the comparative data in table 5.1 and the graph in figure 5.2. Kusakabe has a somewhat high annual rate of depopulation, and falls mid-table in terms of the index of isolation. The one thing that does set it apart from the other villages, however, is that detailed population data are available for most years from as early as 1961 (figure 5.4).

Kusakabe village is not only typical of the local area but also could be considered representative of many such settlements found in upland areas throughout Japan (Irving, 2005). The branch valley in which it is situated is broad enough for rice cultivation, and all farms in the past had access to some of this land. Most also held some forest land that provided a small supplementary income in the years before the energy revolution of the mid-1960s. Indeed, forest activity here shared all the characteristics described in the previous section for the K Region of Kyoto and Shiga Prefectures. Silk worm cultivation was the most notable commercial enterprise in Kanbayashi, however; cocoons were sent to Ayabe, where Gunze K. K., a major manufacturer of underwear, is still located. Like other silk producers elsewhere in Japan, cultivators in Kusakabe experienced the rapid demise of this traditionally rural activity with the restoration of trade links with China in the early 1970s.

The data in figure 5.4 have two sources. From 1961 to 1978, population figures were taken directly from the ledgers that contained

FIGURE 5.4. Population of Kusakabe Village (left-hand scale), 1961–2009.

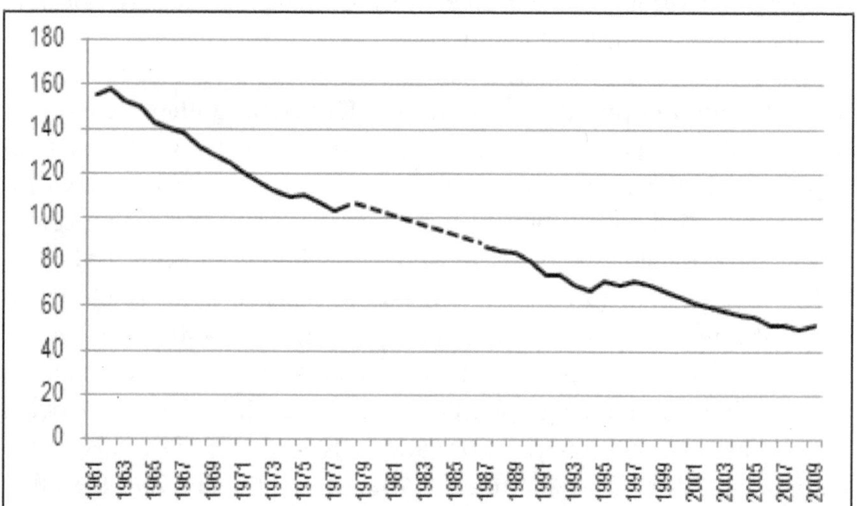

Sources. Ayabe shi (various years) and Richard Irving's fieldwork.

the Basic Residential Register (*Kihon jūmin daicho*). These ledgers are now lost, but since 1987, population totals have been made available through monthly summaries maintained in the city office. Data for the gap years are somewhat conjectural, but interviews with village representatives confirm there was no serious deviation in total population from the path estimated during that period. More important, the graph displays how the pace of depopulation has remained consistent since the early 1960s. Kusakabe seems destined for complete abandonment within the next few decades. How has this state of affairs come about?

Table 5.2 shows changes in vital demographic data in Kusakabe after 1961. Information on births, deaths, and migrations to or from each household was obtained directly from the Basic Residential Register before 1979 and supplemented by interviews. Since then data have been obtained solely through interviews, using the 1979 demographic profile as a base that is updated periodically. Dates of events cannot always be determined to an exact month, but the overall summary picture can be considered accurate. During the 1960s in Kusakabe there were 14 deaths offset by 11 births. The number of deaths can be considered normal, amounting to a crude mortality rate of 9 per 1,000 population per annum. The number of births, however, was already somewhat low (Crude Birth Rate = 7.1 per 1,000) compared to the figure that might

TABLE 5.2. Vital Demographic Data in Kusakabe From 1961.

	Births	Deaths	In-migrants	Out-migrants
1961-1970	11	14	15	42
1971-1978	6	9	17	33
1979-1990	4	14	6	27
1991-2000	2	16	9	13
2001-2005	0	4	1	6

Sources. 1961–1978 Basic Residential Register for Kusakabe, Ayabe City; 1979–2005 fieldwork in Kusakabe.

have been expected based on prefectural population structures (Irving, 1984, pp. 449–462). This is not to say that families were necessarily having fewer children but rather that a break was already beginning to emerge in patterns of household continuity to the extent that fewer households in the village were welcoming a new birth. This trend can be explained by looking at the population structure of Kusakabe for 1965 (figure 5.5).

At the end of 1965, there were 146 people in Kusakabe living in 32 households. The population structure seems normal, except there is a noticeable dip in the number for those aged 20–24 years, both male and female. This by itself is not unusual because young people had for many decades been allowed, even encouraged, to leave the village for a few years prior to marriage in order to earn wages in urban areas. Males at this time tended to move to the larger cities, especially Osaka and Kyoto, whereas the destination for females tended to be closer to home—for example, to what was then Ayabe Town—to find work in the Gunze factory (Irving, 1984). Under the prewar system of inheritance according to primogeniture, second and third sons and daughters were not normally expected to return permanently. That some eldest sons (*atotsugi*) were not returning home for marriage, however, is indicated by the lower-than-expected numbers in the 25–34 years age group and also by the number of young children, especially in the 0–4 years group. The prefecture average for 1965 suggests that 12 children aged 0–4 might have been expected, twice the number that was actually present. Indeed, *atotsugi* had married and did have children in 1965, but already a number had decided to make their homes outside the village and thus break with the established tradition.

As table 5.2 shows, migration was in fact the main determinant of population change in the 1960s. Although a total of six people entered the village for the first time (mostly young brides) and there were nine return migrants (who stayed only temporarily, leaving again to marry into a neighbouring community or to seek new work in the city), as many as 42 people left. This yielded a net migration loss of 27 and an

FIGURES 5.5, 5.6, AND 5.7. Population Structure of Kusakabe Village, 1965, 1987, and 2005.

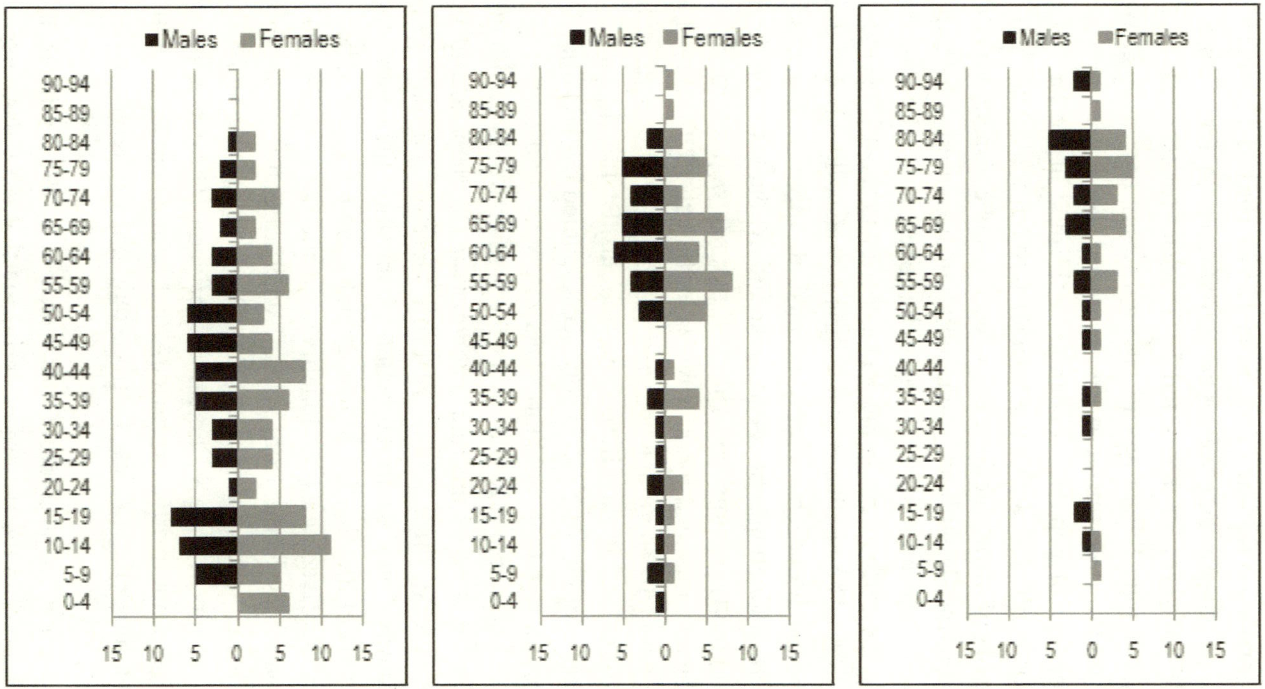

Sources. Ayabe shi (various years) and Richard Irving's fieldwork.

overall population decline of 30, from 155 in 1961 to 125 in 1970. The majority of out-migrants were young first-time leavers, with a median age of 19–20 years for males and 16–19 years for females. Five eldest sons were among this group, in addition to the five *atotsugi* who had already left the village prior to 1961.

The pattern of population change established in the late 1950s and the 1960s continued with little change through the 1970s and 1980s. The number of births declined each decade, and consequently, the number of households without young children increased. The number of deaths remained more or less stable, but because total population was declining, the crude mortality rate had increased to about 1.9 percent annually by 1990. The number of out-migrants was still high, but declining somewhat each decade—simply because the pool of young adults in the village graduating school each year and available to join the exodus was also greatly diminished. Although two *atotsugi* returned to live in Kusakabe accompanied by their wives in the late 1970s, the number of *atotsugi* who left the village between 1971 and 1990 was 15, representing almost half of all the village's households. By this time a new tradition was emerging—the eldest son, accompanied by wife and children, would return regularly on short visits in order to observe major festivals and holiday periods. No doubt the farmer would complain about the declining state of the rural economy and perhaps affirm that, for the time at least, there was no real role there for the *atotsugi* and his young family. They would be better off pursuing their more lucrative career paths in the city. Of course, socially there may have been problems: an increased sense of loneliness in the countryside, perhaps; a lack of vibrancy in the local school, where pressures were mounting to combine cohorts of different years in a single class; and a shortage of new recruits for the volunteer fire brigade. There was no doubt a hope felt—if not overtly expressed—that in due course, when the time was right, the young nuclear family would one day return to live in the village.

The population structure for Kusakabe in 1987 reflects a major transition point in the pattern of shrinkage that the village experienced after 1961 (figure 5.6). The total population had already fallen by almost 45 percent in this period, the most significant losses suffered by the younger age groups. Below the age of 45, all age cohorts were represented in 1987, but in most cases only one, two, or three people were in each group. Together they accounted for just under one third of all villagers, and they lived in only 9 of the 31 households then composing Kusakabe. After 1991 there were two more births in the village, and with almost all young people continuing to leave after graduating from high school, there were only eight people (15% of total population) aged less than 45 years by 2005 (figure 5.7). Not only had the actual volume of out-migration declined after 1990, but the majority of those leaving were now elderly people who, alone and infirm, moved into local care facilities for the aged or relocated farther afield to live with their children in the city. Moreover, the number of deaths after 1990 began to exceed the number of out-migrants for the first time. Kusakabe was truly beginning to feel the negative impact of a rapidly ageing population.

Decline in the number of households in Kusakabe inevitably accelerated, and in 2005 only 23 were still occupied. Seven of these had only a single resident, and 11 households had two occupants. One of the original 32 farmhouses was completely destroyed by fire, and all trace of it has now disappeared from the landscape. Eight farms stood completely or partially abandoned, shuttered against the elements most of the time, including one that is used as an occasional weekend base for the family's Kyoto-based eldest son to continue farming the family plot and maintain links with village affairs.

In 1996 the local and prefectural authorities completed construction of an *onsen* in an effort to stem the tide of depopulation. The facility is a popular one, and in its first three years of operation it enjoyed an average 15,000 visitors per month (Ayabe shi, n.d.). The *onsen* is within sight of Kusakabe, situated on a hillside overlooking the Kanbayashi valley. A number of local people have found employment at the complex, which includes a hotel, hostel, and putter-golf course, but there is no clear evidence that this new opportunity for work has discouraged potential emigrants from leaving the area. Indeed, in the case of Kusakabe, as already noted, most potential emigrants seeking work had already left by the time construction began. The key to restoring demographic viability, at least as far as maintaining traditional family and household—as well as community continuity—is concerned, is the return of *atotsugi* and their families. After 1995, in fact, of the 10 people who entered the village, most were eldest sons. One was the ideal case—an eldest son returning with his wife and young child. A second child was born to this family shortly after, and she remains the youngest person in the village, aged 13 years in 2010. In another case, an *atotsugi* and his wife returned, but their children remained in the city. Two other young adults returned, but only temporarily—prior to marriage and a move to a new home outside the village. One of these was an eldest son, and the episode reflects the difficulty of attracting young brides to permanent residence in rural areas; but this reluctance is not restricted to young females.

Two of the returnees in this period were eldest sons who had divorced or separated and had come back to the village alone. In one of these cases, the son returned aged 60 years, after his retirement from full-time professional employment. This move coincided with the transfer of his mother to a nearby care home. His father would have been left alone, but even in his 90s, he is sprightly and wishes to continue farming. As far as the son was concerned, it was his duty to return, and he wishes to continue living in Kusakabe. The problem is that his wife does not wish to forego the many advantages of living in the metropolitan area (much of their life together having been spent in Tokyo) and so has not come with him to live in the village. Such separations, whether permanent or for a few years only, have occurred in neighbouring villages, too, and are a major topic of local conversation. It is reported that the weekend farmer, who is also retired, would like to return to the village full-time but that his wife does not wish to. These instances may be explained in part by the fact that marriages took place after the eldest son had left the village and that the wives thus have no immediate connection with the rural area. At the age of 60 or so, the women feel unable to uproot themselves and join a quiet village community where most of the people are older and share a different set of traditions. The additional explanation is that the status of women has changed considerably in Japan over the last 50 years and that mature wives now feel sufficiently independent to make their own views felt on where they should or should not live.

The reality for most farms in Kusakabe now is that the older inhabitants continue farming and other familiar pursuits while their children and their families live separate lives in the cities. The bubble economy of the late 1980s allowed little time for reflection on rural woes. Instead, the thoughts of those who had left the countryside centred on securing a more comfortable home, on seeing the children safely through their school years, and on ensuring that retirement from salaried employment came with a decent pension provision. This latter consideration required, of course, a lifetime commitment to the employer. The farmers of Kusakabe were aware that such a commitment would determine the earliest opportunity for *atotsugi* to return, even if they still wished to. Could farmers continue working their land until their own children reached retirement age? This was not the pattern of farm succession they themselves had experienced or perhaps envisaged. Farmers who remained in the village also fear that their grandchildren, occasional and perhaps unwilling visitors to the home village (*furusato*), are becoming increasingly distanced from the rural lifestyle. The *atotsugi* of the 21st century are not yet entirely divorced from their feelings of responsibility to the old *ie* (family) system, however. For some, their moral obligation to the prewar system is paramount, but for others the postwar changes to the constitution of Japan relate not only to rights of inheritance but also to the shared duty of siblings to care for their parents. Indeed, some eldest sons, entrenched in family arguments, insist on their right *not* to return to the countryside.

In 2005 a village representative replied to a question concerning the likelihood of *atotsugi* returning, household by household, in the future. The method was to measure on a scale of 1 to 5, with 1 representing near certainty of return in the future (and therefore continuation of the household) and 5 representing near certainty that the *atotsugi* would not return.

Of the 28 households that could be considered in this way, only one scored 1 on the scale, and five scored 2. Seven scored 3, indicating households about which there is still a degree of uncertainty, and five scored 4. The representative suggested that as many as 11 families would eventually or had already quit Kusakabe for good, awarding them a score of 5 (Irving, 2006).

This perspective, coupled with careful consideration of changes in the village population structure in recent decades, show that the process of shrinkage is largely resistant to developments (such as the opening of the hot-spring resort nearby) that are intended to reverse the trend of severe depopulation. Indeed, it is hard to come to any conclusion except that Kusakabe, as a village community, is in terminal decline. Indeed, this is true not only of Kusakabe but also, it seems, of most other villages in the Kanbayashi valley. Most of the very, very old are still extremely active, and there are still children in the villages. From now it is only a short period of time, however, before these young people are no longer children; after a few more years, they will be considering whether to leave or stay. No new arrivals are expected. The shrill voices of youngsters still echo around the valley from time to time, but these are primarily day-trippers on school visits who have come from the city to study the wonders of the natural environment and seek the elusive giant salamander. The older people in the village, notably the heads of households, are happy to hear the sound of the children. Deep down, however, they are concerned about the legacies they will leave their successors. One of the most important duties of a family member is to honour the ancestors by regularly sweeping and maintaining the grave plots associated with each household. In the last year or so, there has been a sudden appearance of newly built grave plots with ancient headstones assembled together with newer ones, surrounded by a fine marble wall and, placed in the centre of all this, a new marble headstone deeply incised with the characters representing the household name (photo 5.3). These older residents know that as the village disappears, these memorials will be their only tangible memorial to the future.

Photo 5.3. Rebuilding a family grave plot.

Photo by Richard Irving (October 2010).

Industrial Restructuring and Population Shrinkage in Yūbari City, Hokkaidō

Yūbari City made national headlines in June 2006, when it became the first municipality since 1992 to declare financial collapse (Akaike, a former coal-mining town in Kyūshū had done so earlier). The city was built on and had long been sustained by coal (see Culter, 1999). The population peaked in 1960 at 116,908. However, the shift in national energy policy from coal to oil beginning in 1959 condemned the coal industry to a slow but inevitable death (Garside, 2005, p. 190; Allen, 1994, chapter 4) and a once-thriving industrial town on Japan's periphery went into decline. It is a familiar story, and there (as elsewhere) the local coal lobby and labour unions fiercely resisted pit closures. It ultimately took four decades for the industry to be shut down. But as the industry upon which Yūbari had depended gradually disappeared, so too did the miners, their families, and their contributions to the local economy and society.

In the 1980s, Yūbari City tried desperately to stem the tide by propping up the ailing mining company Hokutan (Hokkaidō Coal Mine Steamship Company; Aono, 1987, pp. 92–94, 107–109). The company was a major contributor to local tax receipts and had supported much of the local infrastructure. Its withdrawal from Yūbari following the closure of its last mine in 1987 was a double blow to the area, removing a vital source of local revenue; the city spent JPY 58.3 billion to take over company facilities (such as housing and the hospital) and to clean up abandoned mines. Many in Yūbari felt betrayed by the way the company had withdrawn from the town (Hobo, Kawai, Sasaki, & Hiraoka, 2007, p. 15).

Figure 5.8 illustrates the dramatic rise and fall in Yūbari's population. The population grew in the 1920s as the fledgling local coal industry expanded. Yūbari's population reached a plateau before rising again in the second half of the 1930s as coal became central first to Japan's war effort and then to economic recovery after Japan's defeat. After peaking in 1960, the population plummeted as Japan's industrial structure shifted and the mines closed. This trend of population decline continued after Yūbari City announced financial collapse in June 2006, reaching 11,089 persons in 2010, representing a decline of more than 90.5 percent from its 1960 peak (table 5.3)—a collapse by any standard of measurement.

The loss of the coal industry was the primary cause of depopulation up to the early 1990s, but depopulation has continued in the post-coal era. Yūbari's depopulation in the years just before financial collapse was the now familiar result of two concurrent social processes: first, net out-migration, mainly to Hokkaidō's larger cities (particularly the greater Sapporo area) or out of Hokkaidō altogether; and second, natural population shrinkage precipitated by higher mortality rates than fertility rates. Figure 5.9 illustrates these processes over the period

Figure 5.8. Population of Yūbari City, 1891–2009.

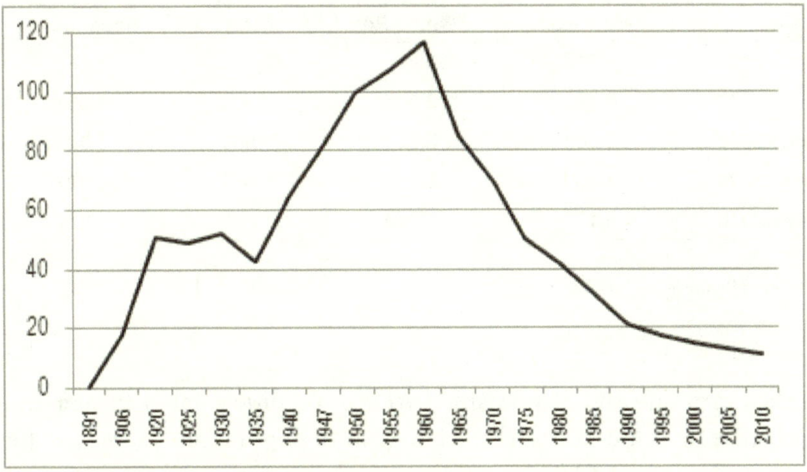

Source. Yūbari shi (2010). Figures based on National Census data.

2000–2008; Yūbari's population had 3.8 deaths for every birth (annual average net mortality, 157 people), and for each person who left Yūbari to live elsewhere, 0.57 people migrated into the city (annual average net out-migration, 292 people).

Yūbari's plight epitomizes the relentless spiral of economic depression and depopulation that occurs under industrial restructuring and that is characteristic of many of Japan's shrinking regions. The greater than 5 percent drop in the population from 13,189 to 12,494 in the single year following financial collapse was partly due to the layoffs of 152 public employees in April 2007, leaving only 165 public employees based at the city office (Yokoi, 2007). These layoffs, though necessary to balance the budget, reduced the working and taxpaying population and contributed to Yūbari's ageing population because many of the laid-off employees moved (with their families) out of the city. Furthermore, the plan to eradicate Yūbari's debt—through raising revenues (e.g., by charging fees for rubbish collection) and cutting expenditures (e.g.,

TABLE 5.3. Population in Yūbari Since the Announcement of Financial Collapse.

Date	Male Pop.	Female Pop.	Total	Households
June 2006	6,212	6,977	13,189	6,783
June 2007	5,888	6,606	12,494	6,507
June 2008	5,609	6,331	11,940	6,302
June 2009	5,399	6,133	11,532	6,202
June 2010	5,170	5,919	11,089	6,039

Source. Yūbari shi (2010).

by downgrading the city hospital to a day clinic)—also further intermingled economic and social factors in depopulation. Increased local taxation for reduced local services encourages citizens, if they are willing and able to do so, to move. Those most likely to leave are those with employment prospects elsewhere. Those most unable or unwilling to move are the economically disadvantaged and older adults, who require the most welfare and health-care assistance—again contributing to the cycle of economic contraction, population shrinkage, and social decline.

Yūbari's demography, therefore, is characterised not only by depopulation but also by poverty and ageing. In 2005 Hokkaidō had the highest rates of public assistance for the poor (*seikatsu hogo*) of any prefecture, at 21.7 per thousand, compared to the national average of 11.6 per thousand, and levels were even higher in Yūbari, at 25.9 per thousand (Seaton, 2010, p. 229). Yūbari also had the highest percentage in Hokkaidō of residents aged 65 and over (39.7 percent) in the 2005 census (Hobo et al., 2007, p. 34), in contrast to the national figure of approximately 20 percent in 2006 (*Japan Times*, 2006). These demographics illustrate the magnitude of the problem Yūbari faces in providing welfare and health-care services to its citizens.

Yūbari is not the only coalmining town in Hokkaidō or in Japan to have suffered population collapse.

FIGURE 5.9. Reasons for Population Change in Yūbari, 2000–2008.

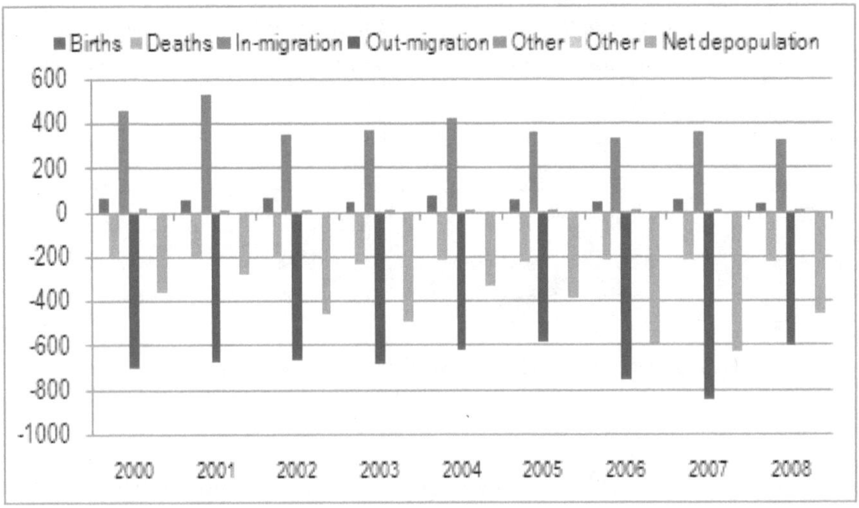

Source. Yūbari shi (2010).

> The Sorachi coalmining region had 103 coalmines that produced 15 million tons of coal in 1960, when the industry peaked. After that year, the mines were closed one after another with the last one ceasing operation in 1995. The total population of the Sorachi region, meanwhile, decreased drastically, from 824,000 in 1960 to 387,000 in 2000. The decrease was particularly significant in the coalmining area of Sorachi region (from 501,000 to 126,000), while the population of the other area within the region has been constant at about 300,000. (Yoshioka, 2003, p. 317).

Table 5.4 shows six former coal-mining towns in the Sorachi region of Hokkaidō whose populations had plummeted to between 10 and 30 percent of their peak populations by 2010. Having been given city status during their peak years, the region now contains some of Japan's smallest 'cities.' Utashinai City has experienced population collapse similar in magnitude to that of Yūbari, and at the 2005 national census, Utashinai was officially Japan's smallest city. Furthermore, its population

TABLE 5.4. Population Decline in the Sorachi Region.

City	Peak Population		Population in August/September 2010	
	Population	Year	Population	As a % of Peak
Yūbari	116,908	1960	11,042	9.45%
Bibai	91,424	1958	26,439	28.92%
Ashibetsu	75,652	1958	17,089	22.59%
Akabira	59,430	1960	12,757	21.47%
Mikasa	62,939	1959	10,531	16.73%
Utashinai	46,171	1948	4,524	9.8%

Sources. Hokkaidō Shinbunsha (1999, p. 80); various city websites.

decline of 12.1 percent since the previous census in 2000 constituted the largest single decline of any city in Japan over that period (Hokkaidō Shinbunsha, 2007, p. 68).

Other areas of Hokkaidō face depopulation problems, too. Sorachi is one of 14 prefectural subdivisions in Hokkaidō. Following the Heisei municipal mergers of 1999–2006, there were 180 municipalities (Hokkaidō Shinbunsha, 2007, p. 215). Figure 5.10 shows the population in 2007 of Hokkaidō's 180 municipalities as a percentage of their population in 1997. The most representative experience for municipalities in Hokkaidō was a 5 to 15 percent drop in population over the decade 1997–2007 (130 out of 180).

By contrast, only 20 out of 180 municipalities have experienced population growth. As table 5.5 shows, 6 of those municipalities with growing populations are in the Ishikari prefectural subdivision, in which Sapporo is located: Sapporo, Ebetsu, Chitose, Eniwa, Kitahiroshima, and Ishikari. That 41.1 percent of Hokkaidō's population is concentrated in 3,520 (4.2 percent) of Hokkaidō's 83,456 km^2 illustrates the heavy concentration of the population in the greater Sapporo area.

Away from Sapporo, some towns have managed to grow. The highest growth was by 24.6 percent in Higashikagura Town, which—along with

FIGURE 5.10. Population of Municipalities in Hokkaidō in 2007 as a Percentage of the Population in 1997.

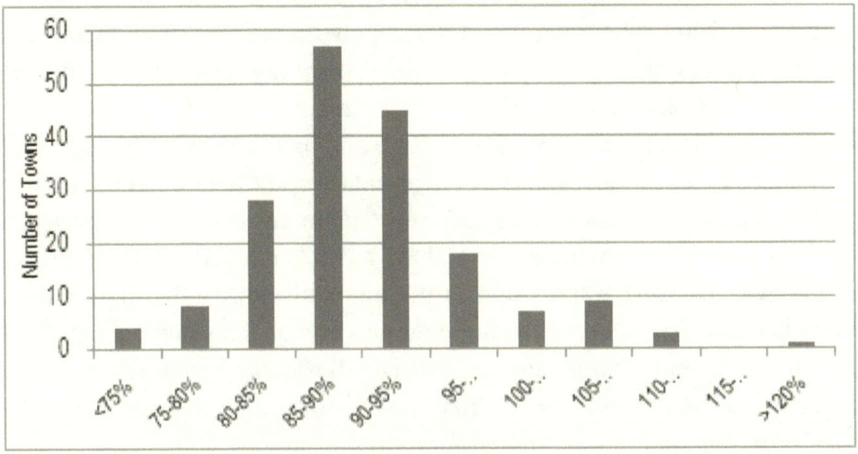

Source. Data compiled from Hokkaidō Shinbunsha (2007).

Takasu Town (5.2 percent growth) and Higashikawa Town (7.9 percent growth)—has grown as a commuter town for Asahikawa, Hokkaidō's second city. Meanwhile, Niseko (2.1 percent growth) enjoys a growing reputation as a world-class ski resort, and Memuro's successful *machi-zukuri* (town development) programme has resulted in new private sector investment and a population increase of 10.4 percent in the period 1997–2007.

Such growth stories, however, remain the exception. Apart from the Sapporo area (Ishikari prefectural subdivision), all other prefectural subdivisions in Hokkaidō are experiencing depopulation. Table 5.5 also indicates that in 6 of the 14 prefectural subdivisions, every municipality regardless of size experienced depopulation. In Sorachi, which contains Yūbari, all 25 municipalities saw depopulation in the period 1997–2007.

In sum, Yūbari's population collapse between 1960 and 1990 was extreme, but it was not atypical when compared to other former coal-mining towns in the Sorachi region. Rates of depopulation since the last mine closed in 1990 are comparable to rates in other towns in the region of Hokkaidō. Such population trends, accompanied by ageing and economic depression, were the underlying cause of Yūbari's financial collapse in 2006. The town could not cope with the loss of younger taxpayers, and many of those who remained were the economically disadvantaged and older adults—that is, individuals with comparatively low incomes and increased needs for welfare and health-care provision.

Yūbari represents an example of near-catastrophic depopulation similar to that occurring in many of Japan's regional towns and cities experiencing industrial transformations. In Yūbari, as in Kamaishi City (introduced in the next section), a transition in the national industrial structure of a town heavily dependent on a single employer was the principal cause of depopulation and ultimate collapse. It is still too early to draw any definite conclusions, but whereas Yūbari has continued to decline, Kamaishi may be experiencing something of a return to stability.

INDUSTRIAL TRANSFORMATION IN KAMAISHI CITY, IWATE PREFECTURE

Kamaishi City represents a case of a single settlement's shrinkage tied to the demise of a local industry that itself is based on proximity to natural resources. The city is located in the southeastern area of Iwate Prefecture, at the centre of the Sanriku coastline in northeastern Honshū. Mountainous terrain runs all the way to the coast, and there is relatively little flat land. The central portion of Kamaishi is situated in the Unosumai and Kasshi River basins near the mouths of the two rivers. Taking advantage of the natural harbours along this coastline, the fishing industry played a significant role in the early development of the area.

Kamaishi City's area is 441 km^2 and its population in 2008 was 41,806 (Statistics Bureau, 2010b). The resident population had been over 90,000 at the beginning of 1960s, during the peak of the local steel industry's operations. As a result of the contraction of steel making that took place in the 1980s, however, Kamaishi City's resident population declined by more than 1,000 people per year, from 65,250

Table 5.5. Shrinking and Growing Municipalities in Hokkaidō's 14 Prefectural Subdivisions.

Subprefectural divisions		Shrinking Municipailities / Total Towns					Towns with Population Growth
Name	Office (Largest city)	Population	Cities	Towns	Villages	Total	
Ishikari	Sapporo	2,303,327	0/6	1/1	1/1	2/8	Sapporo, Ebetsu, Chitose, Eniwa, Kitahiroshima, Ishikari
Oshima	Hakodate	446,977	1/2	8/9	-	9/11	Hokuto, Nanae
Hiyama	Esashi	46,669	-	7/7	-	7/7	
Shiribeshi	Kutchan (Otaru)	246,217	1/1	12/13	6/6	19/20	Niseko
Sorachi	Iwamizawa	358,920	10/10	15/15	-	25/25	
Kamikawa	Asahikawa	535,468	4/4	13/16	2/2	19/22	Takasu, Higashikagura, Higashikawa
Rumoi	Rumoi	60,307	1/1	7/7	1/1	9/9	
Sōya	Wakkanai	73,972	1/1	7/7	1/1	9/9	
Abashiri	Abashiri (Kitami)	319,528	3/3	15/15	1/1	19/19	
Iburi	Muroran (Tomakomai)	425,846	2/4	7/7	-	9/11	Tomakomai, Date
Hidaka	Urakawa	79,931	-	7/7	-	7/7	
Tokachi	Obihiro	357,007	1/1	13/16	1/2	15/19	Otofuke, Memuro, Nakasatsunai, Makubetsu
Kushiro	Kushiro	262,365	1/1	6/6	0/1	7/8	Tsurui
Nemuro	Nemuro	84,171	1/1	3/4	-	4/5	Nakashibetsu
	Totals	5,600,705	26/35	121/130	13/15	160/180	

Source. Data compiled from Hokkaidō Shinbunsha (2007).

in 1980 to 54,339 by 1990 (the year after the first local blast furnace ceased operations), representing a decline of more than 10,000 for the decade (table 5.6). Thereafter, the population decrease continued and was 42,987 in 2005. Demographic data show that the main reason for the population decline was a decrease among the young (14 years and younger), in which age group the population fell from 12,390 in 1985 to 5,229 in 2005, a decline of 57.5 percent over 20 years. Concurrently, the ratio of older people (65 years or older) has continued to rise as a percentage of the total population, reaching 31.2 percent in 2005 (table 5.6). Nearly one in three people in Kamaishi City now belong to this group.

Kamaishi City is famous as the birthplace of Japan's modern steel industry, thanks to the magnetite mine in the nearby Ohashi area. From the late 19th to mid-20th centuries, Kamaishi was one of the centres of heavy industry in Japan. Beginning with the construction of the first Western-style blast furnace in 1857 by Oshima Takato, a prominent iron engineer of Tokugawa Japan, and continuing until the middle of the 20th century, Kamaishi as a region led the industry. In 1950 Kamaishi Steel Works merged with Fuji Steel Works, which had been established after the split of Nippon Steel, and was instrumental in Japan's remarkable postwar reconstruction. In 1960, during the golden age of Kamaishi Steel Works, the expansive operations employed over 12,400 workers and accounted for 36 percent of employment in the city (table 5.6). Due to the prosperity of the steel works, the population grew rapidly, exceeding 90,000 in the early 1960s.

With the restructuring of the steel industry that began in the 1960s, the steel works were buffeted by waves of industrial and corporate rationalisation. As a result of large-scale reorganisations in 1963 and 1968 leading to the relocation of 1,678 workers from the Kamaishi Steel Works to Tōkai Steel Works near Nagoya, and as a result of the rationalisation of large-scale production facilities beginning in 1978, the workforce began to decline rapidly (Kamaishi Steel Works, 1986). By the time of the closure of the large-size section steel factory in 1980, the total number of workers had fallen to about 3,300. When the last blast furnace was shut

Table 5.6. Population Trends and Number of Employees in Kamaishi City, 1955–2005.

Year	1955	1960	1965	1970	1975	1980	1985	1990	1995	2000	2005
Population of Kamaishi City											
Current population	81,006	87,511	82,104	72,923	68,981	65,250	60,005	52,484	49,447	46,521	42,987
Younger generation (under 13 years old)	30,812	30,514	25,102	18,868	16,751	14,797	12,290	9,085	7,298	6,111	5,229
Ratio of younger generation (percent)	38.0	34.9	30.6	25.9	24.3	22.7	20.5	17.3	14.8	13.1	12.2
Older generation (over 64 years old)	2,684	3,012	3,505	4,087	5,077	6,354	7,569	8,729	10,568	12,297	13,411
Ratio of older generation (percent)	3.3	3.4	4.3	5.6	7.4	9.7	12.6	16.6	21.4	26.4	31.2
Working population	30,251	34,546	32,920	32,394	30,621	29,354	26,690	23,850	23,605	21,422	18,954
Employees of manufacturing and mining	10,952	11,448	10,039	8,931	7,489	6,533	5,913	4,934	5,067	4,670	3,942
Number of employees in Kamaishi Steel Works (Total)	7,945	12,438	10,540	9,818	8,831	6,693	5,163	1,350	1,058	618	147
Direct employment	7,945	8,372	6,692	5,176	4,299	3,361	2,592	1,350	1,058	217	147
Indirect employment	-	4,066	3,848	4,642	4,532	3,332	2,571	-	-	-	-
Employees loaned to related businesses										401	-

Source. Matsuishi (2003); Tanozaki (1985); Tokii (2007); Kamaishi shi (2005, 2007); Kamaishi Steel Works (1986); and Shin-Nippon Seitestu (2005).

down in 1989, leaving only a wire-rolling mill still working, there were 1,350 workers; this number had fallen to about 150 as of 2005. Consequently, Kamaishi Steel Works, which once accounted for 36 percent of the total working population of Kamaishi City, now represents a mere 0.8 percent.

In addition to iron and steel, fishing has since the early modern period been a thriving industry in Kamaishi, supported by the numerous natural harbours of the Sanriku coastline. This mainstay industry, however, also experienced decline, specifically in deep-sea and offshore fishing, in the wake of the 1970s oil shock, the establishment of the 200-nautical-mile resource rights agreement, the consolidation and reorganisation of coastal fisheries, and the 1980s rise in fish farming. The number of workers in the Kamaishi area's fishing industries as of 2000 was 1,169, accounting for 5.5 percent of total employment and 29.7 percent of self-employment. What is notable is that the ratio of workers in the fishing industry to the total number of workers is relatively small; however, the fishing industry provides important income-earning opportunities in the form of self-employment (Kase, 2007, p. 89).

From 1971 to 1990, despite the overall growth of such industries in the industrial areas of Kantō and Kansai, the output of the manufacturing industries of Kamaishi City declined (table 5.7). However, this trend reversed in 1995, with manufacturing experiencing a gradual recovery. At the same time, the value of steel shipments, which at one time accounted for no less than 90 percent of the shipment value of the manufacturing industries of Kamaishi City, lost its top position to the machinery industry in 2000 (see table 5.6). Since that time, the city's industrial production has steadily risen; in 2005 it was approaching the peak production achieved in 1971.

What has allowed this change in Kamaishi City's economic fortunes? How was this turnaround in manufacturing (albeit small at this stage) achieved, and what impacts has it had on the city and its population? In part II of this volume, we explore the responses of Kamaishi and of other communities throughout Japan to the processes and problems of shrinkage.

TABLE 5.7. Output of Manufacturing Industries in Kamaishi City, 1960–2005 (JPY millions).

Year		Foods	Iron & steel	Metal goods	Machi-nery	Others	Total
1960	value	1,533	27,643	25	58	706	29,941
	Ratio (percent)	5.1	92.3	0.1	0.2	2.4	100.0
1974	value	8,861	73,128	495	482	7,308	90,275
	ratio (percent)	9.8	81.0	0.5	0.5	8.1	100.0
1981	value	15,668	77,143	708	277	15,075	108,870
	ratio (percent)	14.4	70.9	0.7	0.3	13.8	100.0
1990	value	15,706	37,267	1,803	874	16,979	72,629
	ratio (percent)	21.6	51.3	2.5	1.2	23.4	100.0
1995	value	14,710	29,438	4,229	22,481	21,037	91,895
	ratio (percent)	16.0	32.0	4.6	24.5	22.9	100.0
2000	value	9,349	24,348	5,273	33,780	20,769	93,519
	ratio (percent)	10.0	26.0	5.6	36.1	22.2	100.0
2003	value	7,032	30,408	8,532	27,126	14,207	87,305
	ratio (percent)	8.1	34.8	9.8	31.1	16.3	100.0
2005	value	7,739	47,422	244	30,620	13,731	99,757
	ratio (percent)	7.8	47.5	0.2	30.7	13.8	100.0

Sources: Kamaishi shi (2005, 2007); Matsuishi (2003).
Note. Manufacturers with fewer than 3 employees excluded.

CONCLUSION

In both the K region of Kyoto and Shiga Prefectures and the Kanbayashi River valley of northern Kyoto Prefecture, topographical isolation and changes in external demand have more or less condemned many villages to a slow but inevitable death as the decline of the silk-weaving industry and then agriculture and forestry contributed to out-migration, ageing, and population loss. The data show that microlevel decisions—ranging from those made by individual household members and by families to those made by the village community, the valley, and the municipality—amalgamate at each higher level of data aggregation to demonstrate just how deep and widespread is the problem of rural decline.

The two regional cities examined here, Yūbari City and Kamaishi City, have experienced the effects of industrial restructuring occurring within and beyond Japan, as the country's economic base has changed over the course of the postwar decades. In Yūbari City the loss of economic leverage has exacerbated the area's peripheral character and its isolation, leading to a relentless and, it seems, catastrophic decline in its fortunes. In Kamaishi City a similar process has ensued, but recently the area has been experiencing a turnaround in economic output that is not yet reflected in a growing population. The impacts of the Great East Japan Earthquake and tsunami of 11 March 2011 have, however, put this fledgling recovery in doubt for the time being (see the epilogue to this volume for a fuller account of this event and its significance).

It is difficult to avoid the conclusion that the initial development in a region of an extractive economy serving the centrally coordinated development of the national economic regime initially provides the region with sustenance in the form of externally derived income and employment. However, long-term changes in the structure of the national economy, due in no small measure to the internationalisation and globalisation of the industrial base, have led to sustained and sudden contractions in demand, even though the extractive structure of the international-national-regional economic relationship has remained in place. The loss of the regional economy's sustenance has left it dependent on maintenance activities, a circumstance that has decreased community resilience and that will likely lead to collapse.

Do peripherality and isolation inevitably condemn a place to out-migration and depopulation that, when exacerbated by external economic change, create devastating conditions? Or is a revival of fortunes possible even in the context of a national decline in population? In part II we examine the local, regional, and national responses to depopulation in Japan with a view to exploring their relative success in resolving the difficulties faced in Japan's shrinking regions.

Part II

Responses

CHAPTER 6

REDEVELOPING JAPAN'S REGIONS*

INTRODUCTION

In part I of this volume, we examine the characteristics, impacts, and implications of shrinkage in Japan's regions. The second part describes and analyses some of the ways that regional communities in Japan have responded to the problems encountered as a consequence of shrinkage. We have grouped the chapters around four concepts that emerged from our research: *redeveloping*, *repopulating*, *recovering*, and *reinventing* the region or community. Each regional settlement presented has, in its own way, adopted one or more of these responses to its particular circumstances in the pursuit of community revitalisation. To a great extent, the overall response of community leaders and citizens has been attempts to renew a sense of spatial rootedness, even in the midst of worsening

*The principal contributing authors to this chapter are Thomas Feldhoff, Sachie Mizohata, and Philip Seaton.

circumstances. Responses to shrinkage have met with varying levels of success, and the dominant trend towards further shrinkage has continued as the effects of national depopulation are felt more severely and as strong agglomeration tendencies remain centred on the Tokyo metropolis. This chapter shows that for some settlements, the very structure of the postwar political economy has contributed to the downward spiral of depopulation and economic decline—even as central and local governments have worked hard to reverse the process of regional shrinkage.

The construction industry has been heavily involved in the political economy and society of Japan's regions throughout the postwar period, from the development of public infrastructure, the provision of employment, the channelling of political funds and influence, to being implicated as a major contributor to environmental degradation. The huge—some would say baleful (see Kerr, 2002; McCormack, 2001; van Wolferen, 1990)—influence that this industry has had is such that we would be remiss not to analyse its role in Japan's regional development. Accordingly, we begin part II with an examination of the role of public infrastructure provision in the shaping of Japan's regions. We do this in order to examine central government policy responses and their implementation, and in order to explore the interaction of these responses with regional communities in the postwar era.

We begin, therefore, with a detailed critical analysis of the relationships among government, the construction industry, and localities in the postwar era, arguing that, for its part, the central government has initiated an ultimately corrosive policy of providing fiscal transfers to Japan's regions in the form of often massive infrastructure developments. Although infrastructure provided the regions with necessary facilities for supporting basic needs in the decades immediately after World War II, in recent years a nefarious system of competition and collusion in political and economic circles at the national and regional levels has enabled the development of an 'iron triangle' of political, business, and bureaucratic self-interest that has become separated from the needs and wants of local residents. The system that emerged in the early postwar decades has, we argue, wasted huge amounts of money on public-works projects of questionable value and has further damaged the already fragile socioeconomic and environmental sustainability of Japan's regional communities—thereby accelerating the downward spiral of depopulation and decline. Although recent policy changes signal that government leaders are aware of the serious problem that has emerged in the structure of Japan's political economy, no substantive change of direction has yet occurred.

Next we provide an overview of government responses to regional shrinkage, focusing on the relationship between the central government and rural municipalities in the grip of the negative spiral of depopulation and economic decline. Central government policy has mostly consisted of repeated attempts at economic revitalisation through a series of special laws and fiscal equalisation measures, often in the form of infrastructure developments. We therefore briefly describe the postwar system of financial subsidies for rural municipalities, showing how a complex system of subsidies and loans introduced beginning in the 1970s became entrenched. Many depopulating communities that receive financial assistance to reverse decline have been drawn into an addictive relationship of codependency on central government fiscal transfers, even to the extent that government subsidies have become something of an incentive for communities to maintain their status as depopulating locales.

This leads into the chapter's third section, in which we explore the way the forces just described have collided to devastating effect in Yūbari City in Hokkaidō, where local and national politicians and bureaucrats have attempted—and failed—to revitalise the city through the development of tourism infrastructure. This most extreme and most 'celebrated' example of municipal collapse in Japan's recent history shows how the response to shrinkage was mishandled, such that Yūbari has little prospect, at present, of achieving a turnaround in its fortunes. This process and its outcomes are as pertinent to urban industrial communities (such as Yūbari) as they are to rural agricultural settlements. Though the effects are often more apparent in the former, where the decline is frequently dramatic and sudden, the eventual consequences are no less devastating in the latter. Hence, the story of Yūbari, though extreme, provides a clear example of how difficult community revitalisation is once the recursive trend of regional depopulation and economic decline takes hold.

Accordingly, this chapter questions and critiques the appropriateness of maintaining a rigid growth-first developmentalist policy regime—a policy that commissions progressively more and larger public infrastructure projects, apparently without coordinating these within a sound strategy focused on local potentials and, indeed, needs. Past failures have contributed to the current crisis, and although there are some requirements for new types of infrastructure in Japan's regions due to the severe ageing and societal changes occurring there, current policies are driven by multiple and often competing actors whose only wish appears to be delaying the inevitable rather than seriously moving towards viable and realistic alternatives for genuine community sustainability. The result has been economically and environmentally unsustainable outcomes that over the long term have merely contributed to the further decline and peripheralisation of Japan's regions.

The Construction State in Japan's Shrinking Regions

In the postwar period, the Japanese state has developed its spatial and infrastructural planning policies under the assumption of ever-improving socioeconomic conditions. Today's reality, however, is altogether different. Demographic decline is leading to both rural and, more recently, urban shrinkage and issues of community vitality loss are becoming more evident (Flüchter, 2005; Lützeler, 2008). Shrinking regional settlements thus present considerable challenges for infrastructural planning and require innovative ways of building, managing, and using public facilities. Although current circumstances and future projections are stimulating the consideration of new integrated planning and development approaches, they run contrary to the vested interests of powerful lobbying groups.

Traditional Framework of Infrastructural Planning Policies

Since the 1950s, comprehensive plans for the development of the country (*zenkoku sōgō kaihatsu keikaku*) and strategic infrastructure investment plans characterised by very high levels of central government control have been implemented. Based on these plans, infrastructure development made a major contribution to economic growth, social welfare improvement, and regional development through the decades of Japan's long postwar expansion. By the 1990s the construction and public-works sector had become Japan's largest industry as the government continued to spend vast sums on infrastructure development, even though it was by then of questionable public utility, in order to stimulate Japan's lacklustre economy. Much of this development was devoted to public works in Japan's low-income and depopulating peripheral areas. From the standpoint of social and regional policies, the government justified the investment as a contribution to a more equitable distribution of wealth among the Japanese people and across the country's regions. In consequence, the level of public investment per capita in remote rural areas far exceeded that for metropolitan areas (Kajita, 2001). Since 1998, however, due to greater economic and fiscal restraints, public construction investment has declined—though, as a proportion of GDP, Japan's level of investment is still higher than in any other Organisation for Economic Co-operation and Development (OECD) country. Correspondingly, the Japanese construction industry also constitutes a vast public employment system, composed of nearly 513,000 companies that in 2009 directly employed about 5.17 million people, or 8.2 percent of the total working population (Japan Federation of Construction Contractors, 2010). It is especially in remote rural areas in Hokkaidō and in northeastern and southwestern Japan that construction employment ratios of more than 20 percent of total employment are the norm (Feldhoff, 2005, pp. 102–104).

Despite the government's aim of balanced regional development—supplying hard infrastructure in the form of highways, railways, airports, and large dams in structurally weak regions—the intended regional economic growth has failed to materialize, and public works have not succeeded in reducing spatial disparities. On the contrary, one outcome of regional planning has been the unprecedented concentration of wealth and power in metropolitan areas and the unipolar concentration in Tokyo. Since 2000 especially, so-called wasteful public works have been subject to mounting public criticism that they are little more than a costly large-scale advancement and employment programme for the construction industry (Bowen, 2003; Feldhoff, 2002a, 2002b, 2005, 2007; Er, 2005). Deep concerns have been raised about the following:

1. Dam and barrage projects—for example, the Nagara river barrage in Mie Prefecture and the planned barrage construction across the Yoshino River in Tokushima Prefecture (Jain, 2000).
2. Land reclamation projects, including the Isahaya Bay land reclamation project in Nagasaki Prefecture (Miyairi, 2003) and the Nakaumi estuary farmland reclamation project in Shimane Prefecture (see photos 6.1 and 6.2).
3. Road construction projects for unnecessary and unprofitable roads under the auspices of Japan's public highway corporations, financed mainly through the national toll-pooling system (Feldhoff, 2007).
4. The large number of regional airport projects, in many cases without realistic needs assessments—for instance, Kita-Kyūshū, Kumamoto, and Saga Airports in southwestern Japan (Kyūshū region), Fukushima and Hanamaki Airports in northeastern Japan (Tōhoku region), and New Kobe Airport in central Japan (Kansai region; Feldhoff, 2002b).

From the standpoint of socioeconomic and environmental sustainability—that is, managing the interplay between nature, society, and the economy in accordance with ecological criteria—three main problems are associated with Japan's traditional infrastructure planning policies (McCormack, 2001, 2002; Feldhoff, 2002a, 2005). First, the fiscal crisis is a major issue of concern. The debt-financed model for the allocation of funds for public-works projects to stimulate the economic cycle has incurred massive public debts, inviting an enormous misallocation of resources. Japan's fiscal condition is among the worst in the industrialised world, with an estimated public debt in 2009 of 189.3 percent of nominal GDP (Central Intelligence Agency,

Photo 6.1. The tidal barrier at Isahaya Bay, Nagasaki Prefecture.

Photo by Ryōji Tokitsu (May 2002). Reproduced with permission.

2010). Environmental devastation is a second negative outcome of the so-called *construction state* (*doken kokka*; McCormack 2001); it is the result of intense industrialization and urbanisation processes induced by strong agglomeration economies, especially during the rapid-growth period, and of wasteful public works that contributed to the construction boom of the post-bubble era. In particular, large-scale dams have had especially harmful effects. Third, in recent years local protest movements and referenda against large-scale public-works projects have become more numerous (Jain, 2000; Er, 2005), symbolising the growing opposition of potentially affected local residents to public-works policies. These protests and referenda also reflect a growing indignation among urban citizens at the use of taxpayers' money on projects in rural areas that provide questionable benefits;

PHOTO 6.2. Kumamoto Airport Terminal, Kyūshū.

Photo by Thomas Feldhoff (January 2003).

they also point to concern for future infrastructure needs in socially essential sectors such as health and welfare, care for older people, education, or housing (Kabashima, 2000; McCormack, 2002, p. 20).

One reason for these negative outcomes is the institutional arrangements of the construction state (McCormack, 2001, 2002). According to regional development theory, infrastructure has a positive effect on the regional economy by producing accessibility. On the surface, therefore, its significance for regional development served as grounds for investing billions of yen. In reality, this was but a disguise for robust power politics. According to Broadbent, a construction state can be defined as a government that invests more public funds in the construction of public works than can be realistically justified by public need (2002, p. 43). At its heart, a system of collusion between politicians, ministerial bureaucrats—especially from the Ministry of Land, Infrastructure, Transport, and Tourism (MLIT), which is in charge of infrastructural and regional planning—and construction-related businessmen can be identified. Under the long-term single-party rule of the Liberal Democratic Party (LDP), these actors became linked by an extensive network of formal and informal ties and bound in a so-called iron triangle of benefit and influence (Woodall, 1996; Feldhoff, 2002a; McCormack, 2002; figure 6.1).

For many decades, this iron triangle of major actors was considered a symbol of the country's economic prosperity. However, with revelations

FIGURE 6.1. The Iron Triangle in Japan's Construction State.

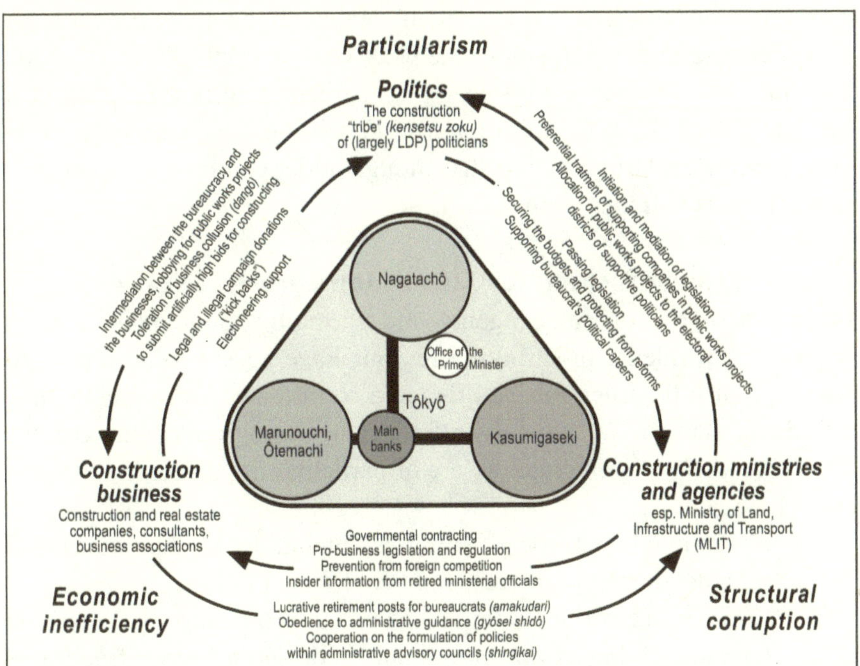

Source. Feldhoff (2005, p. 121).

of illegal practices and abuse, the system of mutual give-and-take connections threw Japan's democracy into crisis. As Bowen pointed out, 'Japan's democracy … suffers from personalism, graft, cronyism, favoritism, bribery, money politics, factionalism and collusion' (2003, p. 3). The resulting severe public criticism bolstered those wishing to initiate a structural reformation of Japan's political system and to reduce construction investment. The advent of nongovernmental organisations, local referenda, and governors who rely on grassroots, nonpartisan support is now challenging the traditional top-down approach of Japanese planning practices (Er, 2005; Feldhoff, 2005), and with the unprecedented demographic changes, the bottom-up pressure to overcome traditional framework-based development will become even more severe.

For the construction business, the recent decline in construction investment has resulted in a 15 percent decline in the number of companies operating in the sector since the peak-year of 1999 (2009: 513,000), and employment declined by nearly 25 percent between the peak-year 1997 and 2009 (from 6.85 million to 5.17 million) (JFCC, 2010). However, Japan's construction industry, though under continuous pressure to restructure, is still very active.

Challenges and Prospects for Japan's Infrastructure Policy

In an era of demographic ageing and shrinking, policymakers must ensure that residents in shrinking regions have access to an appropriate range of infrastructural facilities in a coordinated, accountable, and affordable manner. With special reference to demographic changes, the following kinds of infrastructure are of particular importance:

1. Educational and social facilities, including kindergartens and schools, medical services, and health-care systems.
2. Public transport, including measures to promote social inclusion for those living in rural areas and to design a barrier-free travel environment for older people.

3. The supply of commercial and other services, including recreational facilities and specialised social services for older people.
4. Urban landscape design, including the planning of housing and public spaces, the contraction of urban spaces, and the revitalisation of urban centres.

Facing these challenges, MLIT decided to revise its planning policies and instruments. The new strategy includes plans for road improvement and management, airports, ports, traffic-safety facilities, city parks, sewerage, flood control, collapse of steep slopes and coastal defences (MLIT, 2003). In 2003, the Priority Plan for Social Infrastructure Development (*Shakai shihon seibi jūten keikaku*) replaced nine special infrastructure development and investment plans. In operation since the 1950s, these plans had translated the abstract policy goals of the comprehensive plans for the development of the country (*Zenkoku sōgō kaihatsu keikaku*) into concrete expenditures on a five-to-seven-year-plan basis. Based on the comprehensive development plans defining the public good in accordance with the Comprehensive National Land Development Act (*Kokudo sōgō kaihatsu hō*), efforts were made to improve the transportation and communications infrastructure and the infrastructure for natural-disaster prevention.

Like the centrally planned economies of the old Soviet era, Japan's traditional framework-based planning was growth-orientated, focused on quantitative development of hard infrastructure, and intended to implement monolithic standards nationwide (Mori, 2005). Although the power of the centre to generate economic growth anywhere in the country eventually failed, it successfully sustained the maintenance and expansion of the construction state. However, the concomitant corruption, maladministration, and substantial waste of public money have now seriously undermined the Japanese public's faith in the country's elites (McCormack, 2001, 2002, 2005). It is in this context that the Koizumi government (2001–2006) developed its decentralisation policies and the new integrated Priority Plan, with the intention of shifting regional and infrastructural planning policies from an emphasis on exogenous investments and transfers to endogenous assets and knowledge, and from an emphasis on quantitative to qualitative development. This will translate into improvements of the existing infrastructure stock while putting more emphasis on cost reductions, environmental preservation, the avoidance of social conflicts, and 'soft' infrastructure development that meets the needs of an ageing and shrinking society. In the past, continuous financial assistance for depressed industries and regions generated debt for many cities because the money was used to construct infrastructure that could not generate an operating profit. In the long-run, the heavy maintenance burden served to boost local bond issuance and led to the further deterioration of local authorities' balance sheets.

To facilitate the process of policy reorientation, in 2005 the central government abolished the old Comprehensive National Land Development Act and enacted the National Land Sustainability Plan Act (*Kokudo keisei keikaku hō*; Hayashi, 2006; Matsubara, 2006; MLIT, 2006; Mori, 2005). Based on the new law, National Land Sustainability Plans consisting of a new national plan and wide-area regional plans are to be drafted. In July 2008 the cabinet approved the national plan (*Zenkoku keisei keikaku*) after drawn-out discussions among the principal actors in the ministerial advisory committee for national land development (*Kokudo shingikai*). In order to 'cement' subsequent wide-area regional plans (*Kōiki chihō keikaku*), the government in late 2008 started to convene regional conferences involving all relevant bodies. The new system should be different from that of the past in terms of both planning processes and content because it sets out to create a national and regional planning vision through co-operation between the national and local governments, to analyse regionally and locally specific pressures that require flexible and creative problem-solving strategies, and to foster the participation of a variety of public bodies as well as private sector organisations in planning processes. Wide-Area Regional Planning Councils have been set up for this purpose and in order to discuss the drafting of the plans and their implementation over a period of 10 years.

In vague bureaucratic prose, the overall aim is to establish an integrated national and regional spatial planning system based on horizontally and vertically integrated networks of actors (MLIT, 2006, 2007; Mori, 2005, pp. 321–322). The government has thus responded to a long-standing critique of conventional planning policies that were state-centred, spatially uniform, and led by vested interests. The central element of the new strategy is the establishment of the region (*chihō*) as a territorial unit in spatial planning policies in order to open up new pathways for supraprefectural coordination. This strategy is consistent with the introduction of decentralisation policies and the Trinity Reforms (*sanmi ittai kaikaku*) of Japan's local taxation system in 2003, meant to make local authorities more accountable. At the social level, one important element in all the activities is public involvement, and—indirectly, at least—the evolution of new forms of governance (Hayashi, 2006, pp. 25–26; Matsubara, 2006, pp. 12–14).

Instead of top-down approaches in Japan's planning system, bottom-up involvement and citizen participation in policy shaping and implementation better serve economic, ecological, and sociopolitical interests. In other words, planning processes could be carried out at the community level by providing opportunities for citizens, community reference groups, nonprofit organisations (NPOs), relevant funding agencies, or local authorities to be heard. Indeed, the research evidence presented in this book suggests that there is a great appetite among local citizens' groups for participation the policy-making and regional development processes. Sorensen and Funck (2007a) also referred to the great variety of processes for citizen engagement in place management at the local level as *machizukuri* (literally translated *town making*). *Machizukuri* promotes more flexible bottom-up involvement and citizen participation in policy shaping and implementation instead of conventional top-down approaches that often lack insight, tacit knowledge, and commitment. Moreover, MLIT claims to be increasing its commitment to achieving more bottom-up input in regional level place management processes by adopting the concept of *chiikizukuri* (*making regions*; MLIT, 2007). According to a decision of the minister for MLIT dated 2 August 2009, the wide-area regional plans were finally approved (MLIT, 2009). The plans define key concepts or future *chiikizukuri* visions, strategic goals, and major policies. It remains to be seen if the plans are fit for purpose and adaptable to local circumstances—and whether the people, particularly those in rural areas, will benefit from the new planning scheme.

Remaking Japan's Regions

Public infrastructure and services, as one important aspect of spatial planning, must respond to residents' needs and be designed to offer safe and convenient access to users. However, there are two major obstacles to an integrated, coordinated, and consistent policy approach: systemic power relations deeply embedded in the tradition of central state authoritarianism, and a lively intersectionalism among rival ministries and agencies.

Because of recurring high public debt combined with rising financial obligations resulting from the changing demographic structure of the nation, policy reforms attempt to reduce the capital and running costs of infrastructural facilities while increasing their accessibility and utilisation. With regard to the economic and social revitalisation of shrinking regions, public-works projects based on traditional predictions of growth ignore the problems in Japan's shrinking regions and are, practically speaking, meaningless. Criticism of public-works funding resulted in the new Priority Plan for Social Infrastructure Development and in reduced overall public investment. Nevertheless, even today, money is often spent to the intended benefit of construction-state actors. Active lobbying at the regional and local levels and a lack of a political conception are among the top reasons (McCormack, 2005). Since 1999 the LDP-led coalition government pursued an official policy of reviewing public works, but this was mainly a face-saving exercise. There are considerable hopes that the stranglehold of the construction state on regional development policy may be changed now that Japan has a centre-left government under the Democratic Party of Japan (DPJ). However, the necessity of public-works projects is in many cases still not critically evaluated. Due to the fiscal restraints of government reforms, project realisation and completion times are simply prolonged, indicating that the politicised system of top-down public works has not substantially changed (Sorensen & Funck, 2007b, p. 274).

Lowndes has highlighted the fact that the 'bedding-down of new institutions' is often obstructed by old practices that are not yet deinstitutionalised (2001, p. 1965). Power relations in local and regional institutional contexts prove to be quite stable because actors have vested interests in maintaining the status quo. Efforts to reform formal institutions are subverted because informal institutional relations are deeply embedded in formal structures. This is especially true for the large number of networks based on university cliques (*gakubatsu*); informal prenegotiations among decision makers (*nemawashi*); private or public company management posts for retired bureaucrats (*amakudari*); the powerful role of national administrative advisory committees (*shingikai*); family ties based on marriage and adoption policies; the high proportion of hereditary politicians (*seshū giin*); and unwritten rules regarding political payback (Feldhoff, 2007, pp. 102–103). As a consequence of these internal networks, a holistic understanding of sustainable development around the key areas of society, economy, politics, and environment is not thoroughly argued in the Japanese spatial planning context.

As Japan's spatial planning policy system evolved within Japan's modern nation-state building process after the Meiji Restoration (1868), the authoritarian government also used planning to demonstrate the power of the national elite (Shibata, 2008). This has left a lasting legacy on state–society relations. Officially, the involvement of local stakeholders and citizens in public affairs has been a major tool for dealing with regional and urban development processes since the enactment of a Nonprofit Organisation Law (*Tokutei hieiri katsudō sokushinhō*) in 1998. Sorensen and Funck (2007b) asserted that NPOs and other local organisations are the visible outcome of alternative institutional frameworks of local organising (pp. 275–276). They have played a major role in the growth and strengthening of civil society in recent decades. The establishment of regional decision-making entities, currently under discussion, would provide effective coordination among neighbouring municipalities and prefectures. However, public involvement is still more of an alibi strategy to incorporate divergent interests into governmental planning structures. In the end, the changes taking place are about legitimising state authority instead of substantive bottom-up policy making or local self-governance. A consultation mechanism empowering citizens to influence the planning process is still lacking and, of course, is an ideal that is difficult to attain within an authoritarian political culture (Bothwell, 2003, p. 147).

Nevertheless, there have been changes concerning the roles of citizens and the state in place management (Sorensen & Funck, 2007a, 2007b). But *true governance*, defined as a process in which public and private actors co-operate, is still lacking because administrative reforms have failed to weaken the power of the ministerial bureaucracy in policy making and in the centralism of the state administration. In particular, the highly centralised nature of the public-finance system has remained virtually uncontested. In fact, the new Priority Plan for Social Infrastructure Development is still very much subject to bureaucratic discretion. It contains neither project details nor concrete investment expenditures but only broad, long-term objectives. Moreover, the possible establishment of the region as a new territorial unit in spatial planning policies should not be expected to change central-local relationships radically. It is not yet foreseeable if the region will ever become a political entity with new discretionary powers, though the *dōshūsei* reorganisation vision appears to be gaining strength. Its aim is to reorganise Japan's 47 prefectures into broader regional bodies with strong political and administrative powers (Johnston, 2008; Mutai, 2008; Rausch, 2010).

There is little doubt that the new governmental strategies are an improvement in addressing key issues faced by Japan's shrinking regions. However, the interplay of actors in the process of urban and regional shrinkage is changing only slowly. State authorities facing severe financial problems and unable to solve pressing issues have come to realise that a new balance between state and citizens may be a good thing (Hayashi, 2006; Taira, 2006). This implies an adjustment of planning rationality that replaces the absolute rationality of scientifically and politically legitimated planners with the qualified rationality of open planning discourses (Blotevogel, 2000, p. 124). Whether such spatial management will emerge from the ongoing changes in society in Japan is, however, another question. On the regional level, rivalries between cities and prefectures due to increased locational competition are hindering the shaping of common policies. Kanai (2007) asserted that the Heisei mergers will 'debilitate functions and services essential to regional vitality and quality of life. The cessation of fiscal support from the national government would oblige Japan's local governments to fend for themselves' (p. 5).

The spatial consequences of Japan's ageing society constitute a challenge that needs to be addressed (Usui, 2003, p. 20; Matsubara, 2006). Growing regional and social disparities will ultimately create winners and losers among municipalities (Tamura, 2007) and aggravate wider issues of equality, access, and inclusion. Recognising the everyday concerns of the people could help improve the evidence base required to develop effective policies, promote an ongoing dialogue between government and local stakeholders, and foster engagement in networking processes in policy that counterbalance the power of the prevailing elite-dominated policy networks. However, the panacea implied in this vision is not without its political costs. The DPJ-led government is facing severe criticism regarding its scrutiny of public-works projects through the budget-screening (*jigyō shiwake*) process. It is not easy to cut back or cancel long-planned large-scale construction projects, because local areas depend on public-works spending and there may be claims for compensation. The situation became even more complicated with the DPJ's July 2010 Upper House Election defeat. The DPJ lost in more sparsely populated prefectures—the traditional base of the Liberal Democratic Party (LDP), with high construction-employment rates—where spending cuts have fostered voter disenchantment with the DPJ. In the next section we examine regional policy development and implementation in Japan with greater emphasis on the perspective of municipal authorities.

Entrenching Regional Shrinkage: Policies and Subsidies for *Kaso* Areas

Starting in the 1970s, in response to increased lobbying and demands by local authorities, the Japanese government has enacted a series of laws that have specifically recognised and addressed regional depopulation, beginning with the 1970 Depopulated Areas Emergency Measures Law (*Kaso chiiki taisaku kinkyū sochihō*), which remained valid for 10 years. The law had five principal objectives:

1. to support the independence of depopulated areas,
2. to improve the welfare of residents,
3. to increase employment opportunities,
4. to limit or reduce regional wealth gaps, and
5. to support the continuing existence, or formation, of a beautiful countryside. (Mutai, 2008)

In order to reduce regional disparities and improve social conditions in depopulated areas, special measures within the law covered both political and fiscal policies in the form of subsidies to fund improvements in infrastructure for transportation and communication. Since the initial law was passed, the government has regularly renewed and updated the legislation, targeting depopulated areas every 10 years in response to various initiatives by concerned rural groups. In 1980 the government enacted the Depopulated Areas Special Promotion Law (*kaso chiiki shinkō tokubetsu sochihō*), also with a 10-year time limit, the objective of which was to improve the conditions of rural life and to address the problem of rural ageing. In total, these laws—passed between 1971 and 1989—directed JPY 25 billion at improving transportation infrastructure. In 1990 the 1980 *shinkōhō* was again modified and updated as a special revitalisation law (*Kaso chiiki kasseika tokubetsu hō*), once more with a 10-year time limit. More than the earlier laws, this version emphasised communal autonomy through the creation of local income and the promotion of comprehensive communal development, a form of soft development, to accompany such hard development as infrastructure and public institutions.

The central government has also tried to restructure and revitalise the economies of local areas. In 1989 the administration of prime minister Noboru Takeshita implemented the so-called hometown revitalisation movement (*Furusato sōsei undo*), which allocated block grants of JPY 100 million to villages throughout Japan, allowing them to invest in hard developments that might aid in revitalising local economies and halt the ongoing population losses. The national government also saw the service sector as a potential growth industry suited to rural areas and therefore promoted rural tourism development and the cultivation of specialty agricultural products as a means of local economic revitalisation. These actions were taken during a period when the central government was initiating decentralisation as the guiding principle in relations between the central government and local administration. The reality, however, was that these *furusato* grants were 'a symbolic acknowledgement' that the national government was in a quandary over how to address the persistent depopulation and demographic ageing of rural villages (Thompson, 2003, p. 94). Unfortunately, many of these tourist developments, which included hot-spring resorts and Western-style theme parks, ended up financial debacles, and the ensuing debt remained with the municipalities. Nonetheless, though many rural villages have failed to regain social and economic vibrancy, village survival might not have been seriously doubted so long as the national government provided special subsidies and protections.

Advantages of Being a Designated *Kaso* Area

One form of subsidy for depopulated (*kaso*) areas is *Kaso taisaku jigyō sai*, or *kasosai* (*sai* signifies *debt*). *Kasosai* is a special deficit bond issued by and restricted to local governments that are designated as *kaso* municipalities. In 2000 the central government precisely identified *kaso* areas as those (1) undergoing a greater than 25 percent depopulation between 1960 and 1995, (2) with a 24 percent or greater proportion of people over 65 and a 15 percent or smaller proportion of young adults (ages 15–30), and (3) with an index of financial potential (ratio of local income to expenditure) lower than 0.42 (Lützeler, 2008, p. 63). According to these definitions, 51.7 percent of Japan's land area was officially designated as under- or depopulated (Lützeler, 2008, p. 63). Under the subsidy programme for these areas, 80 percent of *kasosai* (both the principal and annual interest) were to be paid off or have been paid off by the central government. Technically, this *kaso* subsidy is for hard projects, but these have come to be called *hakomono—empty gestures* or *white elephants*—signifying the fact that many such projects are neither necessary nor useful for capacity building and improving the long-term prosperity of the area. The word *hakomono* aptly evokes the hollowness of this type of infrastructural development, reflecting a partial or complete irrelevance to the immediate needs of local people. In other words, these expensive *hakomono* projects have compromised the potential for useful infrastructure development in *kaso* villages and deprived the villagers of opportunities for improving public amenities and living conditions. In addition to such *kasosai*, depopulated rural municipalities receive from the central government the *chihō kōfuzei* (now consisting of income tax, corporate tax, and consumption tax), which can also be used to pay up to 80 percent of *kasosai*, with the *kaso* municipalities owning the remaining 20 percent themselves (Katayama, 2008).

Katayama (2008) asserted that *kasosai,* which was originally issued with the intention of reversing continuing population decline, has ironically yielded the reverse result. Most local government heads have taken advantage of this subsidy, which provides several tens of millions of yen to applying municipalities. However, in order to win these subsidies, municipalities must be designated as *kaso* areas. Katayama argued that local leaders benefit from maintaining the status quo, keeping their villages designated as *kaso* areas and retaining *kasosai* in order to receive financial benefits from the central government meant to protect the village from collapse. Consequently, *kasosai* has given local leadership little incentive to address the underlying causes of rural depopulation. In this way, Katayama also asserted, the lack of long-term vision on the part of the central government, together with financial mismanagement by local elected officials, is partly to blame for the accumulated *kaso* deficits. For example, in 1995 the total accumulated *kaso* debt of Kutsuki in K region was JPY 3.556 billion, and had increased to JPY 5.865 billion by 1998 (Kutsuki mura, 2006). Nevertheless, Katayama most pointedly blamed the system that has resulted in depopulated rural areas' dependency on subsidies, thereby undermining endogenous community capacities and opportunities. This explains how the *kaso* laws, emphasising the independence of depopulated areas, have ironically contributed to dependence on subsidies.

Katayama's argument is persuasive, but should be balanced by an understanding of the pervasive problems of depopulated communities. In interviews, three previous mayors of Kutsuki attested that *kasosai* greatly helped to create potent financial advantages and incentives for economic development (S. Mizohata, interviews, 2 March 2009). They stated that their basic objective had been to escape depopulation, and they recalled facing decreased development prospects and being forced to manage municipal affairs on limited resources; but *kasosai* alone was not enough to revitalise the municipality. Municipal administrations, then, have not been able to reverse depopulation trends, and *kaso* communities cannot find ways to combat the burdens of demographic change and persistently poor employment prospects for local residents. Katayama's explanation of the impacts of the subsidies is consistent with our critical analytical approach to processes of government spending for public-works projects, particularly in rural areas. Although the collusive system based on public works sustained by self-interest is becoming more widely known, it is difficult to prove such occurrences in small communities. What is clear is that *kaso* communities without economic power have suffered under weak tax-raising capabilities and have consequently felt compelled to receive revenue transfers in order to maintain community services.

Despite the generally accepted fact of the government's special treatment of rural areas, residents in many of these communities have benefited little. In the K region of Shiga and Kyoto Prefectures, for example, the proportion of the population engaged in the primary sector shrank from 71.7 percent in 1960 to 14.3 percent in 1995 (Kutsuki mura, 2006). Despite the decline in the importance of rice cultivation and forestry, farm roads and roads between forests were extended from 3.9 m/ha to 11.2 m/ha between 1970 and 1998. At the same time, by 1998 the sewage treatment rate had only reached 42.0 percent of households, and even in 2009 the area had no hospitalisation facility.

In another example, parts of the mackerel route have been improved, including widening the roads and building bridges, over a period lasting 30 years. Construction of the new Harihata Bridge (223 m; photo 6.3), located on a branch road of the mackerel route in Katsurakawa, cost JPY 1.3 billion, whereas the previous 90-minute drive from Kyoto City to Kuta has been reduced to 50 minutes (Kuta jikkō iinkai, 1977). Although the road improvements have met the needs and expectations of some of the villagers, there has been little significant contribution from these projects to the overall standard of living of the K region's residents; many older people in these mountainous villages, for example, still rely on humble outdoor squat toilets and septic tanks.

In the years after 2000, the Koizumi administration attempted to change direction by promoting its policy of decentralisation and structural reform

PHOTO 6.3. Hirahata Bridge and the old road winding around the mountain.

Source. Shiga ken (2007). Photo reproduced with permission.

in order to enhance fiscal efficiency while better serving local residents. The ostensible objective was to provide local governments with more autonomy to govern in a manner that matched their particular circumstances. However, the central government simultaneously slashed subsidies, grants, and tax redistribution to local authorities while allowing them latitude to compensate by collecting taxes directly, knowing that local governments already had weak tax-raising capacities. The consequence has been hundreds of local authorities across Japan in dire financial condition. According to an April 2006 survey by the Hokkaidō prefectural government, there were 53 municipalities in Hokkaidō 'in danger of undergoing financial reconstruction' in a manner similar to Yūbari (discussed more fully later). An *NHK* (*Nippon Hōsō Kyōkai*, Japan Broadcasting Corporation) *Special* documentary in April 2008 declared that Japan was in the *daihensai jidai*, or the *era of great repayment*, and that Japan's cities, towns, and villages had a combined debt of JPY 200 trillion. Based on results of a questionnaire sent to over 1,800 municipalities with a 98 percent response rate, NHK discovered that 287 were in immediate danger of bankruptcy and that 524 needed action to stabilise their finances. Some 29 percent of the authorities expressed unease about their financial situation and 56 percent said increased payments by citizens for local services and cutbacks in those services would be necessary (NHK, 2008).

But it is not only local authorities that are in debt. The national debt in Japan is one of the highest, if not the highest, in the OECD. The government's decentralisation rhetoric since the 1980s, therefore, may not be primarily about concern for increased local autonomy, and Hein and Pelletier (2006) noted that decentralisation can also be interpreted as a way of shifting the responsibility for central government expenditure and debt onto local authorities. The transfer of social and welfare services to local control in 1990, for example, was not accompanied by an equivalent transfer of revenues (Schebath, 2006). 'Decentralization is thus first and foremost a function of national government needs, underscored by government's heavy investment in public works in the provinces' (Hein &Pelletier, 2006, pp. 166–167).

The so-called Trinity Reforms (*sanmi ittai*) of 2003 were part of the government's decentralisation policy; they radically shook up Japan's local taxation system and targeted regional fiscal redistributions as part of Prime Minister Koizumi's attempts to rein in Japan's national debt. But this was also part of Koizumi's political 'passion' to '[gut] the network of finances that sustains porkbarrel politicians and their supporters' (DeWit and Yamazaki, n.d.). The three components of the Trinity Reforms were (1) cuts in conditional transfers (or national treasury disbursements), (2) cuts in unconditional transfers (the local allocation tax), and (3) transfers of tax-raising authority from central to local government (Shirai, 2005, p. 215). Figure 6.2 shows the increase in municipal debts in Japan and is broken down by sources of funding. What is noticeable is that central government funds showed a decrease in 2004, immediately

FIGURE 6.2. Municipal Debt in Japan by Source of Funds, 1993–2004 (JPY trillions).

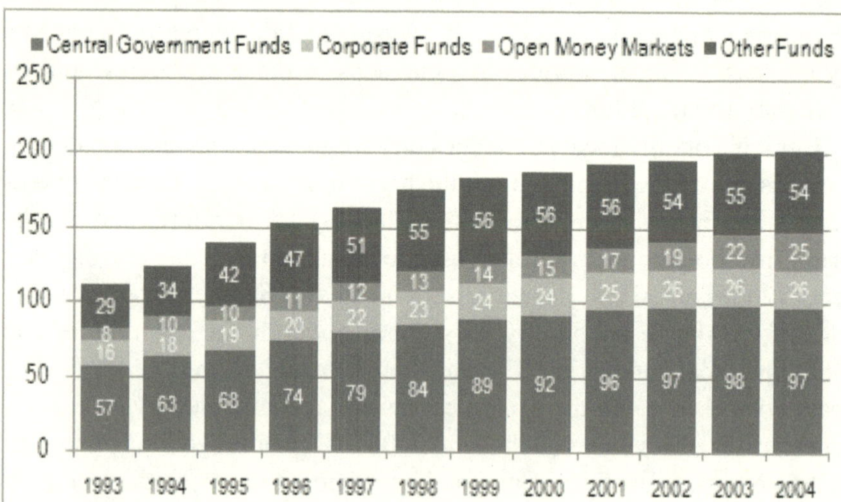

Source. MIC (2006, p. 3).

after the Trinity Reforms were passed and that municipal authorities sought to borrow from elsewhere, such as money markets and corporate sources. Moreover, in terms of the country's capacity to maintain debt, Japan's accumulated municipal debts amounted to 42.5 percent of GDP in 2008, nearly 10 times the OECD average of 4.9 percent. Debt interest payments for municipalities across Japan have risen to more than 17 percent of annual revenue (Ministry of Internal Affairs and Communications, 2010).

Along with this budgetary crunch, there was a nationwide push to merge municipalities—particularly rural and financially constrained municipalities—in the Heisei Great Merger of 1999–2006 (Mutai, 2008). Moreover, the government, emphasising the positive stimulation of competition, adopted some market-based forms of service delivery, including long-term care insurance and public transportation services. However, privatisation has negatively affected transportation services in rural areas, for example, because buses and trains lack the capacity to compete and eventually have to cut service provision. In this way, under the guise of structural reform, the national administration has transferred responsibility to vulnerable localities without providing them with the power, the resources, or the economic means to deliver basic provision. The following section focuses on how this iron triangle of politics, business, and the bureaucracy has shaped attempts at revitalisation through tourism infrastructure development in Yūbari, Hokkaidō.

Industrial Heritage Tourism in Yūbari, Hokkaidō

In part I of this volume, we discussed Yūbari City in Hokkaidō, which rose and eventually fell with its dependence on the local coal industry, providing an example of an economy that necessarily underwent complete restructuring as its primary industry collapsed. Yūbari's policy response was dubbed *tankō kara kankō e* (*from mines to tourism*) and comprised an attempt to revitalise the city's fortunes as a tourist town by remaking the defunct coal industry as the town's industrial heritage.

Yūbari's tourism strategy emerged against the backdrop of Japan's domestic tourism boom in the 1960s and 1970s, a boom that resulted when the country's economic expansion reached ordinary people during the period of high-speed economic growth. Higher incomes led to higher discretionary spending, a part of which was tourism. Hokkaidō was a beneficiary of this new economic reality, and visitors to Hokkaidō increased through the 1970s such that in March 1981 the Hokkaidō prefectural government announced plans for the prefecture-wide development of recreation facilities as a foundation for the development of local tourism (Satō, 2008, pp. 60–66). As a former coal-mining town, Yūbari received subsidies and assistance from both the prefectural and central governments to offset the effects of mine closures, and this money was poured into improving Yūbari's infrastructure. Culter wrote,

> Between [my] first visit to Yūbari in 1985 and my last stay there in 1992, the degree to which the city's physical structure changed was phenomenal. During those seven years the bridges had been rebuilt and painted a bright welcoming red. The numerous rows of old wooden housing had been torn down and replaced with new tourist attractions. The highways had been widened and the storefronts repaired. (1999, p. 55)

The development of tourist sites was rooted in the notion of taking advantage of what Yūbari already had to offer visitors, based on four active themes: *miru* (seeing: the great outdoors), *manabu* (learning: Yūbari's industrial heritage), *asobu* (having fun: leisure facilities), and *taberu* (eating: the local specialty, the Yūbari melon; Yūbari City History Editorial Board, 1991, p. 126). Initially, the transition seemed to be succeeding. In 1985, at the zenith of Japan's 'economic miracle,' the number of visitors to Yūbari's tourist attractions was 1.85 million, placing it 15th on the list of Hokkaidō's tourist destinations (Aono, 1987, p. 71). By 1987 the success of Yūbari's tourism policy was reflected in national policy: the government passed the Law for Development of Comprehensive Resort Areas 'to revive peripheral regions while at the same time boosting domestic tourism demand' (Funck,

1999, p. 333). Yūbari was heralded as a model for other towns experiencing economic downturn and depopulation. Following the launch of the Yūbari International Fantastic Film Festival, the city won the Minister for Local Authorities Prize for its attempts at revitalisation through tourism (Washida, 2007, p. 26; Yomiuri Shimbun Hokkaidō Shisha, 2008, p. 137).

Yūbari appeared to have succeeded in its economic regeneration strategy through implementing prefectural and national policy in a growth sector. In doing so it had won many plaudits. But with local resort initiatives souring after the 1980s economic bubble burst and cheap holidays abroad becoming more readily available (Funck, 1999, p. 341), Yūbari's attraction faded. As figure 6.3 illustrates, following a peak of about 2.3 million visitors in 1991, visitor numbers declined to 1.5 million in 2006. Financial collapse in 2006 then forced the closure of many of Yūbari's

FIGURE 6.3. Tourist Visitor Numbers to Yūbari City, Rekishi no Mura, and Mount Racey.

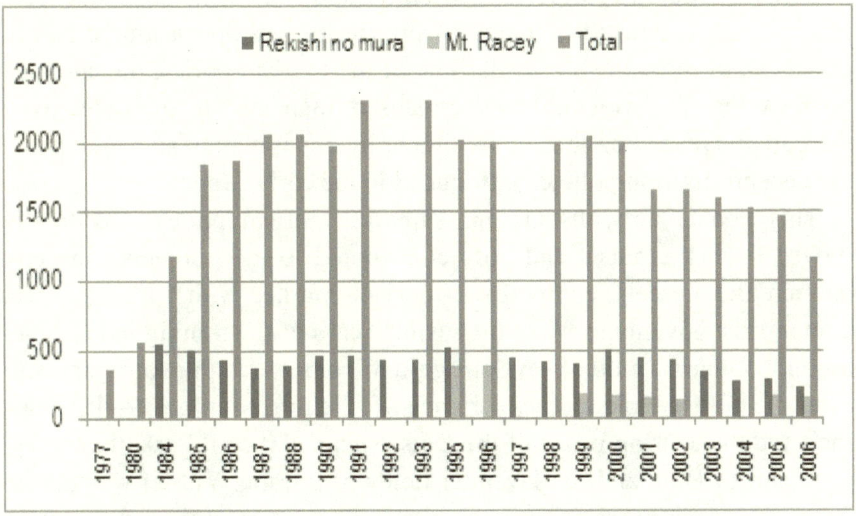

Source. Yūbari shi (2007).

tourist attractions, some temporarily, others permanently. The 'from mines to tourism' policy had ended in disaster.

The city's Draft Reconstruction Plan revealed that 53 percent (JPY 18.6 billion) of the JPY 35.3 billion of debt that had to be repaid had been accumulated by the tourist sector alone (Yūbari shi, 2007). However, the precise significance of tourism spending in Yūbari's financial meltdown is a matter of debate. Hobo, Kawai, Sasaki, and Hiraoka (2007, pp. 51–52) and Hisada (2007, p. 22), for example, have downplayed it. They stated that out of JPY 58.3 billion spent over the period 1979–1994 as part of the Yūbari City Policy to Counteract the Effects of Mine Closures (of which JPY 18.5 billion came from central and prefectural government grants and JPY 33.2 billion was raised by local bonds, *chihōsai*), only 7 percent was spent on tourism. However, this ignores three important factors: (1) profligate spending post-1994, in the final decade before financial collapse when the warning signs were clearest; (2) the construction of leisure facilities and parks, arguably integral to the tourism policy and which if included in the reckoning would make tourism's share of the expenditures under the policy 20 percent; and (3) other public-works projects, including bridge reconstruction and road widening, that were essential for creating the image of prosperity befitting a tourist resort. However, even taking a critical view of the tourism policy, the case can be made that Yūbari would have collapsed financially in any case, given the burdens placed on local government by depopulation and ageing and the decentralisation policies introduced in the early 21st century.

This debate notwithstanding, Yūbari's tourism policy was fatally flawed from the outset and only contributed to its problems. The city entered the fiercely competitive tourism market with little apparent competitive advantage. With the visible scars of the mining industry all around, Yūbari would always struggle to compete with nearby areas to offer the classic Hokkaidō experience of 'the great outdoors'—its rivals included the soaring peaks of the Daisetsuzan National Park, the rolling farmland of Biei, and the lavender fields of Furano. Yūbari was not an *onsen* (hot-spring) resort town, so overnight visitors preferred to stay in one of Hokkaidō's many *onsen* resorts or to base themselves in Sapporo, with its vibrant night life. Yūbari also faced geographical disadvantages. Situated at the end of the road in the mountains, it could not easily attract visitors en route to another site, thereby cashing in on the pivotal bus-tour industry. Remoteness may be part of a tourist site's appeal if visitors want wilderness, but Yūbari's museums and theme parks needed accessibility. Furthermore, heavy winter snowfalls make access difficult from November to April, so attractions such as the theme park Adventure Play Land had only a limited season. Yūbari has a ski resort for winter tourism, but it is small compared to the Hokkaidō venues with growing international reputations, such as Niseko, Rusutsu, and Furano.

Whenever Yūbari did manage to gain a competitive advantage, it could not keep it for long. The Adventure Family Play Land referred to earlier opened in 1983 and at the time was the largest in Hokkaidō. But it faced competition almost immediately from Hokkaidō Greenland, which opened in 1986 in neighbouring Iwamizawa. With newer rides, a picturesque location in lush Iwamizawa Park, and easy access (only five minutes from the Iwamizawa interchange on the expressway linking Sapporo and Asahikawa), Hokkaidō Greenland started attracting Adventure Play Land's customers. Other theme parks opened at about the same time (in Rusutsu, for example), further eroding Yūbari's market. The deserted rides in Yūbari quickly became a symbol of the failure of the city's tourism policy.

Yūbari did have a sustainable competitive edge, however, in industrial heritage tourism. There is certainly a niche for industrial heritage tourism, and the Coal-Mining Museum is a fine example of its genre. But despite the museum's value as a record of the town's coal-mining heritage, it was always unlikely to contribute significantly to economic regeneration. The tourism industry in Yūbari attracted primarily day and local visitors rather than overnight visitors from afar. This is a characteristic of industrial heritage tourism, as Cole pointed out in an examination of coal-mining–related tourism in the United Kingdom, where 'the direct economic benefits of industrial heritage tourism may … be overstated' because it 'tends to attract day visitors, rather than overnight stays' (2004, p. 485). In 1988, just before tourism peaked (in 1991), some 68,476 people stayed overnight (188 people per night), compared to 1.95 million day visitors (5,342 per day)—indicating that only 3.5 percent of tourists stay overnight—and 95 percent of visitors were from Hokkaidō (YCHED, 1991, p. 128). This pattern constrained the commercial potential of Yūbari's tourism sector in two ways: tourists staying overnight spend more on food and accommodation than day visitors do, and day-trippers are not bound by the Japanese custom of giving *omiyage* (usually a box of local cakes or sweets purchased in the placed visited) to family, friends, and work colleagues after a trip.

A characteristic of Yūbari's tourism strategy was the construction of museums. At the best of times, museums struggle to make a profit. The economics of the Coal-Mining Museum illustrate why. It was constructed between 1978 and 1980 using JPY 1.49 billion of public money, much of it in the form of grants from prefectural and regional government (YCHED, 1991, p. 131). To put this figure in perspective, the museum would need to attract 1.5 million visitors paying an average admission fee of JPY 1,000 in order to recoup construction costs alone (in 2009 entry cost JPY 1,200). In an interview (P. Seaton, interview, 18 September 2007), the former director of the Yūbari Coal-Mining Museum said that the museum had initially attracted about half a million visitors per year, but this figure dropped to under 300,000 by 2004. Of these, 30 to 40 percent were children on school trips (*shūgaku ryokō*) and thereby on group or reduced rates (Aoki, 2007). Although the cost to Yūbari proper was considerably less than the museum's JPY 1.49 billion price tag, the point is that public money, wherever it originated from, was being poured into projects with little potential of providing a stable long-term financial return.

The high capital and operating costs of museums easily push the institutions into the red. Even with large numbers of visitors paying high admission charges, many museums require alternative revenue sources from gift shops, cafeterias, donations, corporate backing, or public money. Again, an informed planning process could have prevented this shortage in Yūbari. Cole noted precisely the same problems in UK mining heritage sites, where only 1 in 27 large mine heritage sites in her survey made a 'comfortable profit.' The rest broke even or relied on grants. 'Clearly, the mines that attract the most visitors do not necessarily make the biggest profits, or avoid dependency on grants,' she commented (Cole, 2004, p. 488). It took three years for Yubari's Historical Village complex (centred on the Coal-Mining Museum) to register an operating profit, let alone start repaying construction costs. By 1984 plans for redemption of long-term borrowing to finance construction had been deferred from 10 to 25 years. Even Aono (1987), a vocal supporter of the tourism project and its architect, mayor Tetsuji Nakada, acknowledged that the road ahead would not be easy.

To make things worse, the political importance of the mines to tourism policy meant that the city effectively underwrote the risk assumed by private tourism companies. In a manner echoing the abandonment of Yūbari by the Hokutan mining company (described in chapter 5), Matsushita Resort Development, which had joined Yūbari's resort development project in 1988, pulled out in 2002. By buying out Matsushita's Yūbari investments (the city had no alternative if it wanted its main hotel and ski resort to remain operational), the city once again took on financial responsibility for a private sector company that simply left Yūbari when business became tough (Hobo et al., 2007, p. 15; Washida, 2007, p. 77).

Despite all these indications highlighting the difficulty of making a profit through tourism, Yūbari borrowed money and, for over two decades, poured it into constructing a tourism industry. A fossil museum opened in 2000, and a cinema museum opened in 2003. Ultimately, of 47 tourism and leisure projects constructed between 1980 and 2005, costing in total over JPY 17 billion, 38 were buildings (Yomiuri Shimbun Hokkaidō Shisha, 2008, p. 149). When Yūbari declared financial collapse, only 4 of the 28 tourist attractions for which the city was trying to find private owners were running at even a small profit: the ski resort Mount Racey, two hotels (Shūparo and Mount Racey) and the hot spring Yūparo no Yu (Washida, 2007, p. 42). The loss-making Robot Museum was torn down in 2008, and the Hill of Nostalgia Centre House (Yūbari Plaza, a rest area only opened in 2003 and possessing no obvious money-making potential) was shut for the 2009 summer season.

In addition to all these miscalculations regarding the economic potential of tourism, the tourism policy failed to address broader issues relating to Yūbari's depopulation and economic regeneration. The tourism policy aimed to attract tourists rather than permanent residents and therefore did little to combat depopulation. Yūbari needed to create permanent jobs so as to encourage people to settle there. but the contractors building the tourist sites brought in labourers from outside the city, who then left again once the work was completed. Then, when tourist sites opened, the employment created was seasonal. This, too, did little to encourage an influx of permanent residents (Culter, 1999, p. 98).

Overall, there had been catastrophic delusions regarding the economic potential of tourism in Yūbari. Sustainable tourism is usually a component of an otherwise sound and diversified local economy, whereas a local economy centred on tourism usually requires a site of national and international significance. Yūbari had neither. A number of mining areas worldwide have developed tourist industries, but Yūbari did not have the benefits of operational mines and UNESCO World Heritage status, as do Bolivia's Potosi silver mines, for example. Yūbari had neither the backing of a mining giant (such as de Beers) nor a spectacular landmark such as the Big Hole of South Africa's Kimberley diamond mines. Its current population was not greater than that during its mining boom (compare Australia's Ballarat gold-rush museum; see Pretes, 2002), and Yūbari mined coal, which does not have the tourist-attracting lustre of gold, silver, and diamonds.

Yūbari was receiving large sums from the government as assistance for depressed industries and regions, so the city shouldered only part of the total cost of these failed developments. Nevertheless, in the long run these handouts generated only deficits for Yūbari because they were used to construct buildings that could not generate sustainable operating profits. There is also a substantial opportunity cost to consider: for example, how government subsidies might have been better spent on other forms of economic regeneration, such as efforts to attract other types of business.

But egged on by central and prefectural government and the Resort Development policy, Yūbari (along with other towns in Hokkaidō) invested in tourism. As Culter (1999) noted, in the late 1980s, there were more resort-development plans (mostly ski resorts, golf courses, and lodges) than municipalities in Hokkaidō: 250 development plans versus 220 municipalities (p. 182). The resorts were developed at great cost during the period of bubble optimism, but intense competition and overcapacity meant some bankruptcies were inevitable (Schebath, 2006, p. 90). The constant need to keep ahead of the competition encouraged a reckless propensity to use deficit financing in addition to government handouts. Yūbari also raised billions of yen through local bonds (*chihōsai*). Into the 1990s, as tourist numbers and the population declined, Yūbari's predicament worsened. Ultimately, the JPY 2 billion annual interest payments on bonds amounted to double the city's entire local tax revenue (Hobo et al., 2007, p. 53).

This damning critique of Yūbari's reckless expenditure on tourism is not presented merely with the benefit of hindsight. These critiques were voiced within Yūbari at the time (Culter, 1999, p. 96). But to understand the city's march towards bankruptcy, one must consider the architect of the mines to tourism policy: Tetsuji Nakada.

Yūbari and the Politics of Regional Revitalisation

Tetsuji Nakada joined Yūbari City Hall after the Second World War and became involved in union activism; his campaigns resulted in some of the highest public sector salaries in the nation for civil servants in Yūbari. After a term on the Board of Education, he became involved in town development. Nakada realised early on that coal would not sustain Yūbari, so after becoming assistant to the mayor in 1971, he put forward a plan for what would ultimately be the centrepiece of his tourism policy: the Yūbari Coal-Mining Museum. The plan met resistance at first, but following the sudden closure of the Hokutan Yūbari Number Two Mine in 1977 (which marked the closure of all the mines in the northern sector of Yūbari), Nakada gained enough support to turn the recently closed mine into a museum. Construction started in 1978, and the museum was opened in 1980. In 1979 Nakada was being heralded in some quarters as the saviour of Yūbari. Amid demands that he be given the town's top job, he was elected uncontested as mayor. He held the post for 24 years until April 2003, just a few months before his death in September 2003 (Aono, 1987, pp. 14–74; Washida, 2007, pp. 76–77; YCHED, 1991, pp. 25–55).

A colourful figure, Nakada engaged in several publicity stunts to promote Yūbari—he released a record and appeared in a television drama, for example—that were too much for some residents. His leadership style also caused resentment. Culter's interviews with Yūbari residents are revealing:

> While the mayor had his followers and supporters in the city who cheered him on, his zeal had also given rise to a silent rebellion of those who objected to what he was doing but would not speak against him.... [T]he mayor made the decisions for the city and ... others followed his lead.... It was not uncommon to hear someone say that even if anyone disagreed with the mayor's plans, he or she would not protest. Some said they would not protest because they feared the consequences and cited stories that made their apprehensions seem well-founded. (Culter, 1999, p. 97)

Culter did not elaborate on what the 'consequences' could have been, but mining towns in Japan had a reputation for being rough places with strong traditions of loyalty via the *oyabun-kobun* (senior-junior) system. Another possible explanation is tied to the role of Kichitaro Hagiwara, a former director of Hokutan, who worked closely with Nakada when he was mayor (Washida, 2007, pp. 71–78). Hagiwara had been head of recruitment for Hokutan during World War II, when forced labourers toiled in Yūbari's mines, and had led the fight against union activists in the postwar period.

To his supporters, however, particularly in the 1980s, Nakada was a saviour. Many asserted that his critics simply did not understand him (Aono, 1987). Ultimately, Nakada grew rich as Yūbari slid toward bankruptcy, and his reputation is now in tatters. During his talk to participants on the Yūbari Documentary Tour (17–18 July 2007), city councillor Masayuki Denri commented ruefully but more charitably than many, 'I think Nakada was a great mayor, until his third term.'

In many ways, Nakada was an archetypal late Shōwa-era regional politician. Brash, self-confident, and persistent, his was the politics of 'regeneration through concrete,' similar to the politics of Kakuei Tanaka and other regional politicians of Japan's construction state. He was driven by the goal of securing as much funding as possible from central government for public works, and his connections and charisma made him good at it. Writing in the 1980s, Bunsaku Aono declared that Nakada had secured money from prefectural and central government for 90 percent of Yūbari's applications (Aono, 1987, p. 101). Unfortunately for himself and his town, Nakada was the architect of his own downfall. Like Tanaka and other construction-obsessed politicians who have collectively pushed Japan toward hazardous levels of national debt, often enriching themselves in the process, Nakada overextended Yūbari's finances.

For Yūbari, the decentralisation policies of the Koizumi administration (discussed earlier in the chapter) were a blow. They led to a massive drop in revenue from central government with little hope of replacing the income though local taxation given the city's dwindling and ageing population. Furthermore, the reforms came on the heels of the 2001 termination of financial assistance from the Temporary Law for Promotion of Coal Producing Areas, which had been in place since 1961 (Culter, 1999, p. 34). Central and regional governments' role in Yūbari's collapse did not end with the Trinity Reforms. In a 2005 paper that was prescient about the problems Yūbari would manifest the following year, Shirai (2005) stated that 'local governments are able to issue bonds that are legally guaranteed by the central government without engaging in any serious structural reforms. These arrangements have weakened fiscal discipline among bond-issuing local governments' (p. 182). The levels of bond debt incurred by Yūbari indicate a lack of supervision on the part of prefectural government. It also emerged in 2006 that, with the knowledge and involvement of the Hokkaidō prefectural government, Yūbari and five other municipalities in the Sorachi region had engaged in the practice of *yami kisai* (illegal bond issues; Seaton, 2010, p. 11). For the critics of the national and Hokkaidō governments' roles in Yūbari's financial collapse, therefore, both governments were complicit and negligent in allowing Yūbari's finances to spiral out of control.

Creating Winners and Losers out of Policy Reform

In this context, one might view with some cynicism the Law to Restore Health to Local Finances (*Jichitai zaisei kenzenka hō*), passed on 15 June 2007 (Japan Research Institute, 2007). Drafted in the aftermath of the 'Yūbari shock,' the legislation required local authorities to reveal the accounts of their public corporations and the third sector (i.e., semi-governmental organisations and government-related NGOs). Had this law been in place earlier, Yūbari would not have been able to conceal for so long the losses incurred by tourist sites within its third sector. Although the law introduced much-needed accountability into local finances, it was effectively a tacit admission that the former accounting practices had been deficient and had allowed many local authorities to conceal the extent of their troubled financial conditions.

For Yūbari, this law came too late. But there are hundreds of other depressed, depopulating local authorities saddled with debt for ill-advised construction projects. In neighbouring Ashibetsu, another former coal-mining town that had hoped tourism could save it, the forlorn, dilapidated theme park Canadian World remains open only because Ashibetsu, like Yūbari, took on its operation and cannot afford to liquidate the site until the JPY 5.2 billion construction costs are repaid (Hornyak, 2004).

The same *NHK Special* (2008) mentioned earlier also featured the town of Nagase, in Kumamoto prefecture, which was on the brink of financial collapse after investing heavily in a state-of-the-art sewage system and goldfish museum (closed at the time of programme's broadcast). The pattern is similar. Loss-making construction projects were undertaken with the government's blessing and in the belief that borrowing was underwritten by the central government. But then the national government changed the accounting rules and thrust the local authority into hazardous levels of fiscal deficit. The consequent need for local authorities to reduce their deficits by charging people more for local services then exacerbates depopulation; NHK's documentary included the story of a woman who had moved to Tottori in order to escape rising health-care costs for her infirm husband in Shimane, only to find after moving that Tottori had raised its charges, too.

The hard reality of decentralisation policies for Japan's local authorities is that the risk and responsibility increasingly lies with the municipality rather than with the central government; but it is the municipality that is the most vulnerable to financial pressures over the long term as the problems associated with depopulation and ageing mount. Some municipalities with strong local and corporate tax bases are able to cope financially, but others like Yūbari have spiralled into debt. There is a growing wealth divide (*kakusa mondai*) not only among individuals but also among municipalities. In his book about municipal wealth inequalities, Tamura (2007) used the terms 'winner' (*kachigumi*) and 'loser' (*makegumi*) municipalities (pp. 76–89). Yūbari was the first case among his sample of losers.

Neoliberal economic theory since 2000 has underpinned decentralisation policy. The new blueprint for Japan's regions is almost that of municipalities as businesses in competition with each other to attract Japan's dwindling working-age population, new business ventures, and visitors who will bring money into the region. There will inevitably be losers, just as there will be winners, and Yūbari is only one of many debt-ridden 'loser' municipalities. The odds are clearly stacked in favour of heavily-populated business and industrial centres, such as Tokyo-Yokohama, Kyoto-Osaka-Kobe, Nagoya, Sapporo, and Fukuoka.

Nevertheless, though municipalities are like companies in that they can go bankrupt, settlements cannot be liquidated. Life in Yūbari must continue, and care in old age for the 40 percent of its population over 65 must somehow be maintained. Among the advanced industrial nations, Japan is second only to the United States in terms of the percentage of people classified as living in relative poverty (Asahi Shimbun, 2008). There are, therefore, significant dangers of ghettoization of poorer areas and of the entrenchment of social inequality, with all the implications for crime and social order that such inequalities bring. The balance among accountability, autonomy, and social equality is always delicate, but the pain of the neoliberal revolution in public finances in the early 2000s has been felt throughout Japan; Yūbari is merely its most public face. Given Japan's decentralisation and national fiscal policy in the 21st century and the financial problems of many municipalities that did not face the complete collapse of their primary industry and a 90 percent drop in population, the case can certainly be made that Yūbari's financial collapse would have occurred even without the disastrous tourism venture. Wherever the blame for collapse lies, however, Yūbari's financial woes have only exacerbated its depopulation problems; those who can do so seek places to live where their tax money buys them local services rather than debt servicing.

CONCLUSION

The central government's regional policy has played a crucial role in Japan's shrinking regions, fostering an addictive relationship of municipal dependence on the central government for fiscal transfers and expensive but questionable infrastructure developments. These relationships have had devastating results, particularly with respect to tourism development policy and its implementation, in Yūbari City in Hokkaidō. Domestic tourism has been a major part of regional policy across Japan throughout the postwar years (Kelly, 1986; Knight, 1996; Tamaki, 1996) and has often been integrated with the regional redevelopment strategies of the national and prefectural governments that have involved huge sums of money funnelled into the construction industry for the ostensible purpose of building regional tourism and transportation infrastructure. This strategy has delivered mixed results, and much work remains to be done if tourism development is to meet the expectations of local planners and community leaders in stabilising and revitalising regional communities.

The economies and societies of Japan's regions are changing, and with change comes the requirement to act differently—to develop new policy orientations and strategic objectives and to implement these to suit emergent circumstances. Until very recently the construction industry was one of the mainstays of regional economic stability and employment, and its position was boosted by the flow of funding from central government to the regions. However, this strategy is in need of renewal, not only because the vested political interests involved often have little concern for the needs of local communities but also because of the evident waste of resources that has taken place. In the following chapters we enquire into the potential for regional revitalisation through policies that build upon the existing needs and attributes of specific locales.

CHAPTER 7

REPOPULATING THE REGION*

INTRODUCTION

One expected response to shrinkage in developed countries comprises attempts to reverse the depopulation trend through a policy of replacement immigration either from elsewhere within the national space or from overseas. As discussed in chapter 2 with respect to Scotland, some European countries and regions have already adopted this response, and various commentators have made similar suggestions for Japan (see Japan Forum on International Relations, 2010).

Japan's national population is now decreasing, and if present trends persist, it will continue to do so for some decades. Attempts by the national and local governments to reverse that trend by providing incentives for adults to have more children have largely failed, for the total fertility rate (TFR) among women remains low. It is therefore a mathematical certainty that, in the absence of immigration from overseas, any population

*The principal contributing authors to this chapter are Peter Matanle and Yoko Sellek.

gain by one region (e.g., the capital region) necessarily means a proportionately larger decrease in another (non-metropolitan cities, towns, and villages). Moreover, this process is likely to exacerbate ageing processes in rural communities as they lose their economically active residents to emigration, thus dealing a double blow to revitalisation attempts in regional economies. As discussed towards the end of this chapter, some of the residents of Japan's more remote rural areas are already aware that, under such circumstances, their regions will most probably be subject to shrinkage; that with continued growth in the nation's capital region, their own communities will continue to age and shrink; and that these phenomena may accelerate as older people grow older still and in increasing numbers pass away. With these things in mind, this chapter looks to the future and discusses the potential for immigration from overseas to mitigate population decline in Japan's peripheral regions.

Chapter 2 presents evidence and analysis from the Highlands and Islands of Scotland, a region that bears a close resemblance to Hokkaidō and Tōhoku in Japan in terms of its physical and human geography and its experience of depopulation. Immigration into this region from the newest eastern members of the EU has not been straightforward. Like Scotland, Japan already has some experience of overseas immigration and settlement. However, also like Scotland, Japan has not yet deployed inward migration in the construction of its national foundational principles and myths, and in both countries there remain considerable political challenges to establishing and maintaining a positive immigration policy. Indeed, despite frequent waves of immigration into Japan throughout the country's history, the development of modern society around the notion of an ethnically homogenous and isolated island nation (see Oguma, 2002; Weiner, 2009) is arguably even more pronounced in Japan than it is in Scotland. On a more pragmatic note, until now most immigrants to Japan have tended to settle and work in metropolitan areas, with few venturing into the more peripheral and remote rural areas. Thus although immigration to Japan from overseas will undoubtedly continue and will feature as part of an overall policy mix of responses to shrinkage, the evidence indicates that such a policy on its own cannot realistically bring dramatic results or reverse the dynamics of shrinkage to produce a numerically stable outcome for regional—especially rural—communities.

Ethnographic evidence from Sado Island demonstrates that at least some of the residents of Japan's more rural areas already accept the future inevitability of continued depopulation; how some are initiating innovative solutions based not on redeveloping or regrowing the community and region but on coping with shrinkage and remaking their communities as comfortable places in which people can live decent and dignified lives. In this way, many residents of Japan's rural regions are already ahead of national policy makers, who in general adhere to unattainable, spatially unbalanced growth-first solutions.

Repopulating Regional Japan?

Immigration policy in Japan, as in other industrialised countries, is considered not only a means of controlling the entry of foreigners but also a part of the country's overall labour and economic policies. In the case of Japan, the ageing and shrinking of the population has serious implications for the maintenance of the size of the country's workforce, the shrinkage of which itself has implications for the government's ability to finance the future pension and care arrangements of Japan's growing proportion of older people.

The United Nations Population Division (UNPD, 2001) report entitled *Replacement Migration: Is it a Solution to Declining and Ageing Populations?* offers six scenarios for considering the international migration streams needed to achieve specific population objectives or outcomes in Japan. Using its 2000 medium variant projection, which in Japan's case is one of the least pessimistic of recent population projections, the scenarios are as follows.

Scenario I is based on 1998 projections by the UN and assumes no net immigration to Japan from 1995–2050. After reaching its peak the population would decline to 104.9 million, with 57.1 million of working age (15–65) and 33.3 million over 65.

Scenario II is based on revisions to the 1998 projections, but as it also assumes no net immigration to Japan for the same period, the results are the same as Scenario I.

Scenario III is based on the 1998 revisions and assumes that Japan will keep its population at its peak of 127.5 million achieved in 2005. The country would need 17 million net immigrants to 2050 (381,000 per year 2005-2050), and by 2050 the immigrants and their descendants would make up 17.7 percent of the nation's population.

Scenario IV assumes that Japan will maintain its 2005 population and the working age population of 87.2 million achieved in 1995. Japan would need 33.5 million net immigrants in the period 1995-2050 and the population of the country would expand to 150.7 million, with 46 million (30 percent) being immigrants and their descendants.

Scenario V requires the support ratio to be maintained at 3.0 working people per non-working person through to 2050. In this scenario 94.8 million immigrants would be needed in the period 2005-2050 (2.1 million per year). By 2050, out of a population of 229 million, 124 million (54 percent) would be immigrants and their descendants.

Scenario VI keeps the 1995 support ratio of 4.8. Under this the country would need 553 million immigrants and the national population will expand to 818 million, with 87 percent of these being immigrants and their descendants. (UNPD, 2001, pp. 53–54)

In addition, the UNPD calculated that in the absence of increased immigration, it would be necessary to raise either or both the labour-force participation rate of Japan's adult population by 15 percent and the customary retirement age to 77 in order to maintain the 1995 support ratio through 2050 (UNPD, 2001, p. 53), with the former measure providing only a partial palliative to the decline in the support ratio due to ageing.

Rural areas have been hit the hardest by ageing and depopulation, pushing many communities to the brink of collapse; therefore this section focuses on the question of whether immigration into Japan's rural areas represents a part of a realistic policy solution to the shrinking population and decline of those regions.

Overview of Immigration in Japan

Currently, Japan has an immigration policy that combines encouragement of immigration by selected groups with prosecution of illegal immigration. On the one hand, Japan tries to attract foreigners with advanced professional skills and knowledge on the premise that such individuals will enhance Japan's total factor productivity. On the other hand, Japan is officially a closed country for ordinary manual workers because of the perceived potential risks they pose. Although Japan has allowed its number of long-term foreign residents to increase, the country has long maintained strict controls on foreign labour. However, since the late 1980s Japan has been experiencing an expansion in the number of foreign manual workers—among these, illegal workers—into the country. The principal factor has been the acute demand for labour, stemming from a shortage of domestic labour in so-called 3K or 3D industries (*kitanai, kitsui, kiken*: dirty, difficult, and dangerous)—that began with the bubble economy in the second half of the 1980s. Although there was a formal prohibition on the importation of foreign manual workers, various legal channels appeared to allow them entry to Japan through 'side-door mechanisms' (Cornelius, 1994, p. 395)—for example, under the long-term resident and foreign trainee visas, made possible by amendments to immigration law in 1991. These changes allowed an unlimited scope of activities, thereby granting holders of these visas special economic importance within the Japanese domestic labour force. The majority of foreigners who fall into the long-term resident category are Japanese Brazilians and Peruvians, called *Nikkeijin*, whose ancestors had settled in Latin America in the early years of the 20th century, a period when Japan was one of the major sources of migrants from Asia to the Americas. Many additional foreign trainees are from China and other neighbouring countries in East and Southeast Asia.

Since the late 1990s, the formal acceptance of unskilled workers in Japan has been the subject of active discussion among political and economic commentators, focusing on two issues: possible legal means of using foreign workers to counter the population decline, and decreasing the number of unlawful immigrant workers. Although government policy has focused on domestic labour through measures relating to (1) increasing the birth rate, (2) creating greater employment opportunities for females and the aged, (3) encouraging younger generations to participate in regular employment, and (4) improving labour productivity by technological innovation and increases in efficiency, immigration control policy has gradually come to influence the country's overall labour policy as well. In that sense, though Japan is keen on attracting skilled and professional foreigners ('high-quality human resources') in order to maintain and increase the country's global competitiveness (Japan competes with other industrialised countries in Europe, North America, and Australia to attract such qualified foreigners), the government has relaxed employment restrictions for certain categories of skilled-knowledge workers in sectors with serious labour shortages. For manual workers, however, although the ministries involved have agreed concerning the necessity for the formal introduction of manual workers, they have not yet reached a consensus on the treatment of existing foreign workers, such as foreign trainees and the Brazilians who entered the unskilled-labour market through the side door. Finally, regarding illegal immigrants, dramatic tightening of immigration policy in recent years reflects a growing public concern that foreign unskilled workers (particularly illegal workers) are involved in criminal activities and thus represent a risk to the public.

The registry of foreign nationals residing in Japan shows how many foreign nationals live in Japan for a relatively long time as well as their purposes for doing so. Japan has the lowest proportion of foreigners of any major industrialised country, at 1.71 percent of total population, or 2.186 million among a population of 127.51 million in 2009 (Ministry of Justice, 2010a). Of the current 2 million plus, some 681,518 are Chinese; 578,495 Koreans; 267,456 Brazilians; 211,716 Filipinos; 57,464 Peruvians; and 52,149 Americans; the rest are distributed across a range of other nationalities. Until the late 1980s, most foreign residents in Japan were North and South Koreans and Chinese special permanent residents and their descendants, who had been absorbed into Japanese society after the first half of the 20th century, when both Korea and parts of China had been colonised by Japan. Since that time the number of special permanent residents has been declining because many have decided to naturalise as Japanese under ongoing changes to rules governing the status of this group. However, there has been a significant increase in the Chinese population in Japan, which exceeded that of Koreans for the first time at the end of 2007. This increase is related to significant labour demand by Japanese technology and trading companies for employees who know the Chinese business culture as well as the language and to the large number of Chinese students who have stayed on in Japan after graduating from Japanese institutions. Chinese accounted for 31.1 percent of the total number of foreign residents in 2009. The majority of Brazilians and Peruvians are *Nikkeijin* whose residence status is *ordinary permanent resident*, *spouse of a Japanese national*, or *long-term resident*. The majority of Filipinos are female; many work in the entertainment industry and others have married Japanese men who had not, for any number of reasons, married Japanese women. The Immigration Bureau of the Ministry of Justice recently estimated that in addition to the population of registered foreigners, about 91,778 overstaying foreigners, or illegal immigrants, live in Japan, mostly employed as manual labourers (MOJ, 2010b, p. 16).

Whereas the numbers of registered foreign nationals residing in Japan show the state of the population, the statistics on foreign nationals' entries and departures show the flow of foreign nationals in and out of the country. Based on statistics for legal entry provided by Japan's Ministry of Justice (Statistics Bureau, 2009), the net flow of people into Japan is now running at a small positive balance (figure 7.1). Entry into Japan for 2005, 2006, and 2007 shows a positive net inflow of 17,122 people, 26,186 people, and 15,186 people respectively. The majority of entrants into Japan in those years came from greater China (53,190 people, 48,374 people, and 51,241 people respectively). The number arriving from Brazil and Peru, however, appears to have peaked and turned downward, with 21,906 arriving in 2000, some 6,681 arriving in 2006, and just 1,831 in 2007. Probably owing to the declining economic conditions in Japan for this group, smaller numbers are arriving from South America, and the number departing has been consistent since 2000, leading to a fall in net immigration. However, the number of Brazilians and Peruvians who have successfully changed their status from either *spouse or child of Japanese national* or *long-term resident* to *permanent resident* has been consistently increasing, suggesting that many are also settling into Japanese society. An aggregate of figures for legal entry and departure between 1950 and 2005 shows a small positive overall balance of 1.172 million over that 55-year period (Statistics Bureau, 2008).

The figures reveal three important lessons for Japan's potential immigration policy. First, if migration is to be an effective tool for mitigating the effects of ageing and depopulation, then Japan is not yet welcoming enough people into the country for the policy to have a major impact. Second, immigration is an unstable and unpredictable phenomenon and it is extremely difficult for policy makers to achieve a desirable balance; immigrants may decide to leave in large numbers if conditions appear unfavourable, and the government has limited options if too few 'desirable' and too many 'undesirable' people immigrate. Third, in terms of maintaining the population, the numbers of Japanese leaving the country are concerning, with net losses for 2005, 2006, and 2007 of 77,416 people, 77,279 people, and 95,625 people, respectively (see figure 7.1).

Foreign Workers Residing in Peripheral Areas

Figure 7.2 shows the geographical distribution of legally registered foreign residents in Japan by prefectural distribution (all nationalities and those with Asian nationalities).The geographic distribution of foreign workers in Japan reveals a concentration in and around the metropolitan areas of Tokyo, Osaka, and Nagoya. However, a growing number are also distributed in some regional and occasionally peripheral and rural areas suffering from labour shortages. In peripheral regions, nonetheless, the number is still small, and most foreign workers reside in urban locales.

Brazilians

Brazilians have settled mainly into manufacturing cities in regional areas and are most often employed as a flexible labour force through the

FIGURE 7.1. Entry Into and Departure From Japan by Continent and Selected Nationalities (selected years, in thousands).

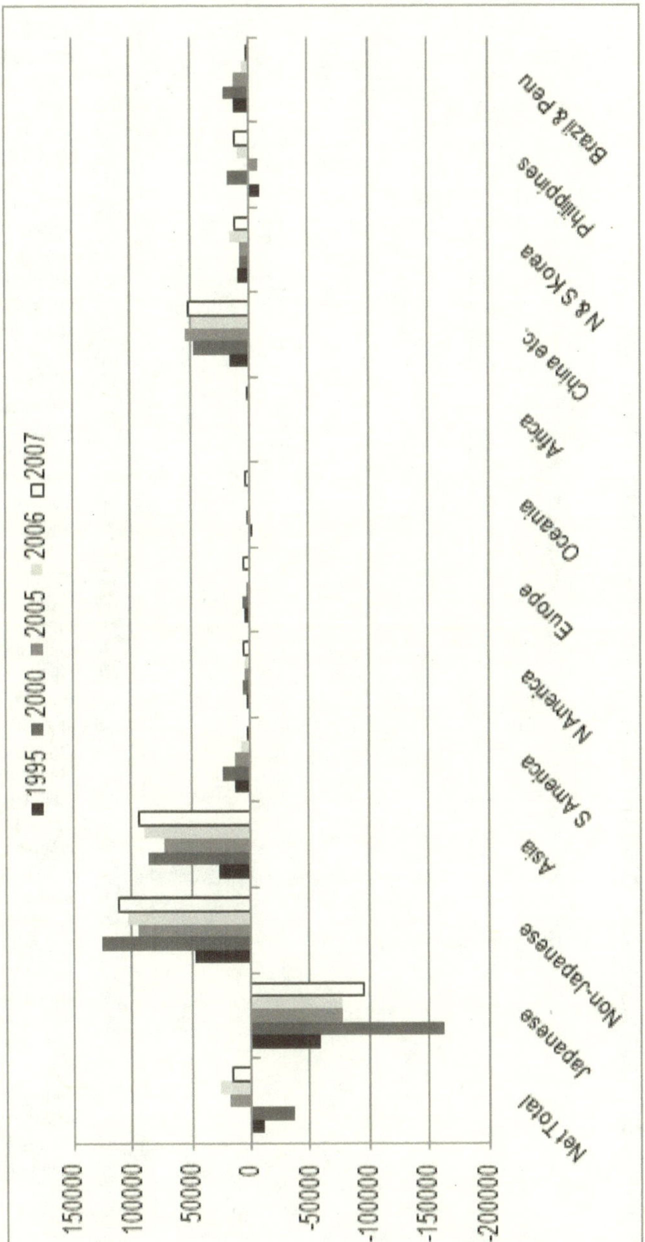

Source. Statistics Bureau (2009).

FIGURE 7.2. Legally Registered Foreign Residents in Japan by Prefectural Distribution.

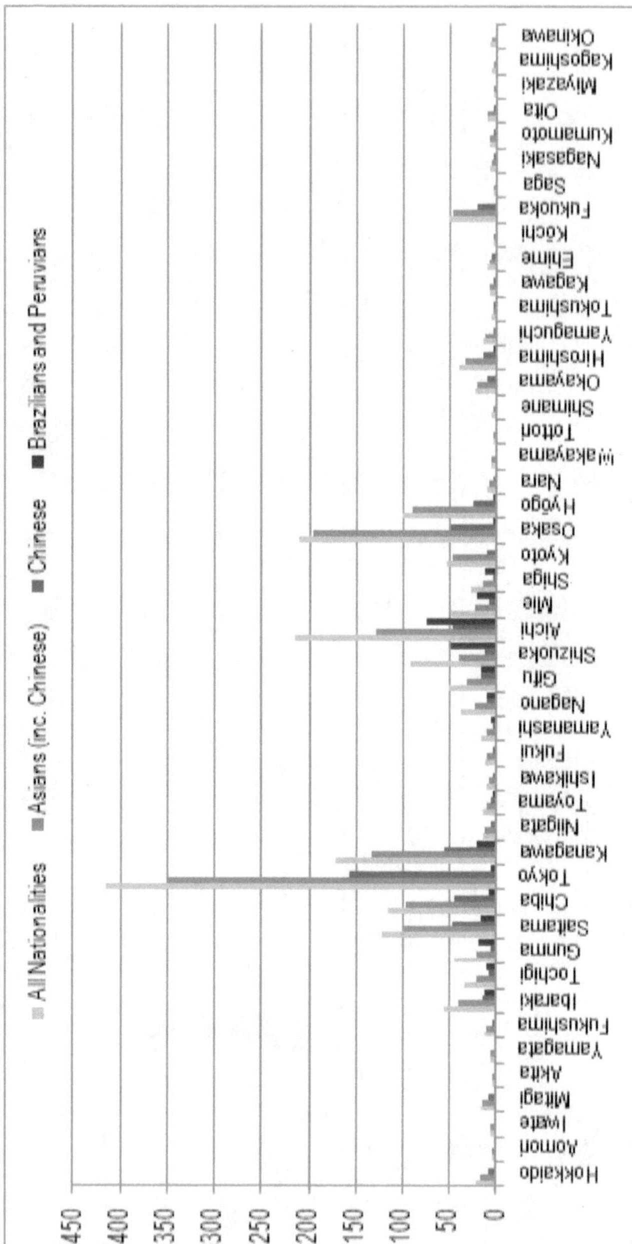

Source. Statistics Bureau (2010h).

labour-contracting system. More than 90 percent of Brazilians are contract workers recruited and employed by Japanese labour contractors or brokers and are made available to subcontractors and sub-subcontractors of large manufacturing firms, auto and auto-component makers, and to a variety of other types of jobs in, for example, the food-processing and metal-manufacturing sectors (Higuchi, 2006). A considerable number of Brazilians are concentrated in Shizuoka and Aichi Prefectures in central Japan, as well as in the Kantō prefectures of Kanagawa, Gunma, Ibaraki, and Saitama. During the recent period of economic stagnation, Brazilian immigrants have increasingly moved to semiperipheral areas in the central Chūbu region, such as Nagano, Gifu, and Mie Prefectures (Tanno, 2010, p. 123).

Chinese

Chinese from the People's Republic of China (PRC) form the largest minority in Japan, and they are by far the most numerous arrivals since the end of the 1970s. The community of Chinese new arrivals has been augmented by large numbers of Chinese students who have arrived since the 1980s. The influx of Chinese has become substantial since 1983, following a proposal made by former Prime Minister Nakasone to accept 100,000 foreign students by the beginning of the 21st century as part of a campaign to internationalise Japan (this goal has now been increased to 300,000). In a sense, the proposal opened up a privileged migration route for Chinese people. Between 1984 and 1989, the government significantly simplified the procedure for the issuance of pre-university student visas. Since the early 1990s, the influx of Chinese students (those entering education courses in Japan in preparation for entry into universities and colleges) on these visas as well as on university student visas has been increasing. Foreigners registered as pre-university students in 2008 numbered 41,313, and 25,043 of those were Chinese—accounting for 60.6 percent of the total (MOJ, 2009a, p. 26). Significantly, those registered as pre-university and university students are allowed to work—four hours per day and 28 hours per week, respectively, and up to 8 hours per day during long vacations; these students contribute foreign labour in part-time employment, usually in service industries (Ministry of Health, Labour, and Welfare, 2009).

Many students from China aspire to become long-term or permanent residents of Japan and try to find employment there after completing their studies. Many decide to stay on in Japan to work for Japanese companies, using their educational backgrounds and enjoying Japan's high standard of living and high wage levels. Furthermore, faced with economic globalisation, Japanese firms have become increasingly conscious of the competitive threat represented not only by China itself but also by Chinese entrepreneurs in various Southeast Asian countries. This has produced an increased demand for those with Chinese-language skills and an understanding of Chinese business culture. In particular, Chinese graduates who have received MA and PhD degrees from Japanese schools in engineering-related fields have been in high demand in Japanese firms. With the revised Immigration Control Act of 2009, university graduates may now engage in employment-search activities for up to one year, and in addition, the residence statuses of *university student* and *pre-university student* will be integrated into the single university student status in order to achieve the target of 300,000 foreign students by the year 2020 (MOJ, 2009b, p. 72).

Foreign Trainees

Foreign trainees have spread throughout Japan, employed in small- and medium-sized manufacturing, food-processing and textile plants, and in the tourism, agricultural, and fishery sectors. The foreign trainee system is problematic in that it is sometimes used as a side-door mechanism to address labour shortages, often in rural areas. The Industrial Training Programme (ITP) was organised by the Japan International Training Cooperation Organisation (JITCO), a semi-governmental organisation with a shared jurisdiction among five ministries (Justice; Foreign Affairs; Health, Labour, and Welfare; Economy, Trade, and Industry; and Land, Infrastructure, and Transportation), with a main function to assist the Technical Internship Programme (TIP). TIP was set up in September 1991, with the objectives of developing human capital and technology transfer. The *foreign trainee* residence status is based on the assumption that individuals complete their training in Japan and return to their home countries to utilise their newly learnt skills. Permitted by law to stay in Japan for a limited period and not allowed to bring their families, trainees in this programme are not protected by Japanese labour laws. Thus the trainee system, by its very nature, has functioned as a convenient mechanism for the legal and constant supply of workers to companies with labour shortages; foreign trainees provide unskilled labour under the guise of on-the-job training.

In April 1993 the government launched a new TIP, also under the direction of JITCO, which permits trainees to engage in employment, including manual labour. The TIP programme allows interns who have entered Japan on a trainee visa to participate in an industrial training programme for one year. After successfully completing their one-year training, which includes Japanese language lessons, participants move on to the TIP, and their residence status is changed from *foreign trainee* to a category called *designated activities*. These trainees are allowed to remain in Japan as interns at firms for up to two years (for a total of three years, including the initial one-year training period). TIP trainees are allowed to work in semigovernmental bodies, private corporations, and co-operative associations; in fields such as agriculture, fishery, construction, food production, textile and clothing manufacturing; and in the machinery- and steel-manufacturing industries. Of the 50,064 trainees accepted as foreign trainees with support from JITCO in 2009, fully 91 percent were accepted by co-operative associations, including the National Federation of Agricultural Co-operative Associations, reflecting a dramatic increase in the numbers of trainees moving to rural areas (JITCO, 2010).

TIP gives trainees many rights as workers. During the period of internship, the trainees have an employment contract, are covered by all labour-related laws, and also receive wages under the Minimum Wages Act, as do Japanese employees (during the first year of training, the monthly allowance is limited to JPY 60,000; the monthly pay rises to about JPY 120,000 during the internship period). However, they are not allowed to leave the firms providing their training and employment, and they are subject to the rotation principle. TIP trainees are mainly from China, Indonesia, and other Association of Southeast Asian Nations (ASEAN) member countries.

Some municipalities designated by the government as *Special Zones for Structural Reform* incorporate foreign trainees into their revitalisation plans. The special zones reform is an attempt to promote regeneration of regional economies by allowing regulatory exceptions in specific regions based on proposals drawn up voluntarily by local governments (M. Ito, 2008, pp. 90–91). One example of such regulatory exceptions is a firm of fewer than 50 employees in a special zone that is permitted to accept six foreign trainees, twice the number normally allowed. In many rural areas, the number of foreign trainees involved in the agricultural and fishing industries—a sector in which labour needs can no longer be met solely by Japanese nationals—has been increasing dramatically: 7,496 foreign trainees were accepted in the agricultural sector in 2006 (M. Ito, 2008, pp. 90–91).

Kawakami Village in Nagano Prefecture has a population of 4,800 people and is a good example of the use of TIP trainees in agriculture. Located in a plateau area surrounded by high mountains, the key industry in the village is the cultivation of highland vegetables; Kawakami is the largest producer of lettuce in Japan, with an 80 percent share in the country's production. However, the village has been suffering from serious depopulation and a labour shortage; 26 percent of the village's population is over 65 years of age (Sankei Shimbun, 2008). Since 2004 the village has relied on foreign trainees from China. The 200 farmers in the village have jointly launched a co-operative association that is certified to accept trainees; the farmers have been allowed to accept up to two trainees per household. In 2008 some 702 Chinese trainees (who had initially studied Japanese language and who then began working in the fields) arrived in the village. The trainees were paid JPY 85,000 (about GBP 400) a month, or about JPY 530 (about GBP 2.50) an hour as an allowance. The level of allowance is lower than the minimum wage set in the prefecture of JPY 669 an hour, but it is not against the Minimum

Wage Law because the law does not apply to the Chinese trainees in ITP who return to China within seven months (Sankei Shimbun, 2008).

Although the original aim of the foreign trainee system was to achieve skills transfer overseas, the actual function of the system is to secure labour that could not otherwise be obtained. Numerous cases have been reported in which ITP and TIP are not carried out properly and instead fuel demand for exploitative cheap labour under conditions that involve human rights violations (Scott, 2010). In 2008, more than 450 companies and other organisations that accepted foreign trainees were involved in illegal practices, and about 60 percent of them involved violations of labour-related laws, including withholding wages and overtime allowances (MOJ, 2009b, p. 78).

The amendment to the Immigration Control and Refugee Recognition Law was passed in July 2009 in order to deal with this situation. It was enforced beginning on 1 July 2010 and ensures that labour laws, which had applied to foreign trainees from their second year, now also apply to those in their first year of training. This means that foreign trainees have proper employment contracts, just as Japanese workers do. The government is also poised to revise its regulations to mandate monthly inspections (as a minimum) of companies and organizations that accept foreign trainees, in order to ensure that their working conditions are legal and that stiffer penalties are levied against those involved in illegal labour practices (MOJ, 2009b, p. 71; Watanabe, 2010).

Foreign Brides

The importance of so-called foreign brides, foreign women married to rural Japanese farmers, in relation to immigration and as a means to address the shrinking rural populations cannot be ignored. Such a marriage is meaningful for the rural Japanese community, and for many of the brides it means not only a secure residence status but also the ability to remit financial assistance to relatives in her home country. In rural marriages, the foreign spouse is usually a woman, primarily from China, the Philippines, and South Korea; some of these marriages are mediated by international marriage brokers and some through noncommercial and personal introductions.

International marriage in rural farming areas as an outcome of depopulation has gained media attention. Brides have been introduced into farming families not only by profit-making international marriage brokers, but also with the support and organised intervention of some local governments in mountainous depopulating areas, particularly in the 1980s. Initially, women from the Philippines, Thailand, and Sri Lanka made up the majority, and later South Korean and Chinese women surpassed them; these have been accompanied more recently by women from the Pacific maritime provinces of eastern Russia. The difficulty of finding Japanese brides in rural agricultural areas stems both from the reality of depopulation of these areas and from the undesirability of farming as a lifestyle for many young Japanese women, who enjoy more freedom and opportunity (H. Nakamura, 1989, p. 231). Although the reality of rural life and intergenerational transfers is changing rapidly in Japan, a few urban dwellers still assume that it is ingrained in the eldest sons from rural areas that their life's work is to till the ancestral fields, to ensure the prosperous continuation of the household, and to look after their ageing parents. Many modern Japanese women, particularly those from urban areas, are reluctant to marry into rural families because life as a farmer's wife is believed to be arduous not only in terms of physical labour but also in terms of the concomitant social responsibilities of village life. Although the wife of an eldest son does not have much authority regarding household management, she is expected to participate actively in running the household, to live with her husband's family and look after her in-laws, to act as supplementary labour by performing menial tasks in the fields, and to perpetuate the family (and produce a future work force) by bearing and rearing children. If one of the major roles of women is the reproduction of human resources—childbirth and manual labour—the negative attitude of Japanese women towards traditional norms and practices in farming families has brought this reproduction system into crisis. As a consequence, and in order to ease this strain, marriage with non-Japanese women has become a means of preserving farming families as both economic and social units. The introduction of Asian brides in this way illustrates the reproduction of human resources transferred internationally (R. Ito, 1996, p. 257); a similar pattern can be perceived in other industrialised countries and has created a 'commercial trade in brides,' manifest in the system of mail-order brides (Sellek, 2001).

Yamagata Prefecture, located in the northeast region of Honshū, has attracted attention for its foreign brides because local governments there have actively promoted this type of marriage. The result is that 78 percent of Yamagata's foreign residents are female, of which 80 percent are from China, South Korea, and the Philippines and whose residence status is either *permanent resident* or *spouse of a Japanese national*. The demography of Yamagata indicates that the phenomenon of rural depopulation is a factor behind its rapidly ageing population, and in 2004 one in four residents in the prefecture was over 64 years of age (Burgess, 2007). The fertility rate is low, and one of the main factors contributing to the declining fertility rate is the falling marriage rate. Of men who are 50 years old and over, more than 1 in 10 have never been married (1960: 1.10 percent; 2005: 11.4 percent). The prefecture is also known to have the highest percentage of three-generation households in Japan. With these trends as a background, some local governments became concerned at the increasing number of unmarried eldest sons and encouraged local men to marry foreign brides as part of the implementation of measures to retain heirs in the traditional household system.

The local government in the town of Asahi in Yamagata Prefecture was the first to accept Filipino brides, in 1985. The Asahi Town office organised group tours to the Philippines, arranged face-to-face meetings between Japanese men and Filipino women, and managed to match up nine local men with Filipino women in 1985 and 1986. The Asahi case was considered a success, and the town of Okura in Yamagata adopted the same approach, resulting in the introduction of 10 Filipino women aged between 18 and 25 years (H. Nakamura, 1989, p. 233).

By 1992 about 100 local governments in rural areas had started to recruit women from other countries (including South Korea, China, Sri Lanka, and Brazil) who were willing to marry Japanese men living in rural communities. Yasuzuka Town and Yūzawa Town in Niigata

Prefecture, Higashiiyayama Village in Tokushima, Masuda Town in Akita, and Sawauchi Village in Akita are some of the local governments that have accepted brides from Asia as a part of their revitalisation measures. Some of these local governments, including those in Kanagi Town in Aomori Prefecture and Kurobane Town in Tochigi Prefecture, decided to use taxpayer money from a rural revitalisation fund, 'the *furusato* [hometown] program,' which prime minister Noboru Takeshita had set up offering JPY 100 million to each of 3,050 towns and villages in Japan in order to revitalise their communities (*Japan Economic Journal*, 1986).

However, this intervention by the local governments has ceased in the wake of criticism that it amounted to participating in the commercialisation and exploitation of the financial plight of poor families from developing countries (H. Nakamura, 1989, p. 233). The practice of sponsoring Japanese-foreign marriages is also criticised because it usually involves substantial personal adjustments on the woman's side, with little reciprocation by the man. Furthermore, the success of such a union is often measured by whether the marriage produces children for the Japanese man and his family and not necessarily in terms of the mutual happiness of the adult participants. Therefore many claim that an unequal relationship exists between the parties: Each subject on the Japanese side (the Japanese husband, his family, and the mediator) is in an advantageous position with respect to the bride in terms of economic and informational power. This unbalanced relationship has substantially reduced the level of individual choice in marriages. The notion that marriage is a matter for each individual has justified and supported 'the commercial trade of brides' in this context (R. Ito, 1996, p. 258). In response to such criticism, many of these governments no longer actively participate in encouraging women from other Asian countries to marry Japanese men in their jurisdictions, keeping the marriage brokers at arms' length; local authorities now work instead to provide follow-up services for foreign wives, hoping that good circumstances will provide incentive for more foreign women to marry into rural Japanese families.

The Potential of International Migration for Repopulating Japan's Regions

The national population decline is a reason for Japan as a whole to seriously consider adopting immigration as a policy tool for maintaining the current growth-oriented economic regime, unless higher-than-trend increases in productivity can be achieved. Theoretically speaking, overseas immigration into rural areas may potentially ease regional decline and prevent collapse in the future, at least in terms of the actual numbers of economically and biologically reproductive community members. However, as already discussed, this potential solution is not straightforward, and realistically speaking the available evidence suggests only limited potential for Japan's regional areas to positively alter their current and future population disequilibria through overseas immigration.

First, it is perhaps a truism to suggest that foreign immigrant workers are subject to market forces, but they are also, quite naturally, utilising a comparatively open market system to gain advantages for themselves. Although the Japanese government has prohibited the formal importation of manual labour and has not offered amnesties to illegal immigrants or to those who overstay their visas, the government has unofficially introduced foreign workers as countermeasures to mitigate the shortage of indigenous workers in the market. As a result, some industries (e.g., automobile and electronics manufacturing) employ a few hundred thousand foreigners, mostly Brazilians, and other industries (e.g., textiles and food processing) currently engage more than 40,000 foreign trainees of various nationalities. However these foreigners are categorised, they function as foreign manual labourers, and a huge gap exists between the political intention of the government and the reality of these immigrants' living and working conditions. Most significantly, although foreigners such as Brazilians and trainees have been making a significant contribution to Japan's regions, their contribution is mainly economic and the movement of such workers is determined most of all by labour-market mechanisms. Even if the government introduces a new residence status in order to import immigrants with the specific intention of preventing community collapse, attractive employment opportunities must exist in those geographic areas to prevent workers' understandable tendency to move away from the periphery towards the more numerous and better-paid opportunities in the industrial agglomerations of Japan's metropolitan regions, as has occurred hitherto (see figure 7.2).

Second, regarding the current political assumption that long-term settlement of migrant labourers should be prevented, a comprehensive immigration policy has yet to be established at the national level (Kajita, Tanno, and Higuchi, 2005). This contradicts the proposed use of immigration as a potential policy tool for boosting the long-term economic and biological reproduction of Japan's regional communities. Not only are different political circles (the Ministry of Justice; the Ministry of Health, Labour, and Welfare; the Ministry of Economy, Trade, and Industry; and Japan International Training Cooperation Organisation, amongst others) pursuing their own, often conflicting, policies regarding the treatment of foreign workers, but existing immigration policy does not have a long-term perspective. Yet such a perspective, one that encourages immigrants to settle and naturalize, is precisely what is needed if immigration is to contribute to Japan's population shortfall. Consequently, the policy regarding the control over the entry and departure of foreigners to and from Japan does not yet operate in tandem with integration measures. For example, it is the Immigration Bureau that deals with entries and departures of foreign nationals and their applications for permanent residence, but it is the Civil Affairs Bureau that deals with the process of naturalisation.

To address this situation, two bills were submitted to the Ordinary Session of the Diet in 2009 and approved: a bill to amend the Immigration Control Act, including the introduction of a new system of residence management; and a bill to amend the Basic Residents' Registration Act, making foreign residents subject to the residential basic books. Both acts are to be enforced within three years. Under the new system, foreign nationals residing lawfully in Japan for longer than three months will be issued a residence card accompanying the permit for landing permission, and they will be obligated to file a notification with the Minister of Justice of any changes in circumstances that occur during their stay.

The current alien registration system will be abolished with the introduction of a new system of residence management, and foreigners residing in Japan for the medium or long term will become subject to the Basic Residents' Register System set up by the municipalities, as Japanese nationals are (MOJ, 2010b, pp. 34–36). The intention of the government is to establish a systematic and integrated policy that will encourage future immigration and also assist in providing solutions for specific labour shortages and regional decline. Without such measures, it is most likely that immigrants will be seen as subordinate and therefore expendable over the long-term and that they will not become integrated members of Japanese society.

It is important to note that immigrants to one country are emigrants from another. Thus international migration should be viewed as a part of the globalisation process, influencing the economic, political, and cultural character of both sending and receiving countries. Immigration has provided Japan with much-needed human resources, but it has also given rise to a variety of social problems in both Japan and the home countries. Although international migration can provide countries of origin with remittances and occasionally facilitate the transfer of skills and technology, it may also entail the loss of substantial investments in social and human capital formation in the sending countries. This may arise either in terms of overall declines in the quality of social and human capital in sending countries, caused (or at least exacerbated) by the act of emigration itself, or in terms of sending countries' not receiving adequate returns on their educational and training investments. In this way, developed receiving countries like Japan benefit from the investments made by developing countries, taking advantage of reduced education and training costs by importing trained labour from overseas. For example, poor educational attainment among Brazilians and high rates of non-attendance at school for second-generation immigrants to Japan will limit long-term occupational and wealth-accumulation opportunities for these groups not only in Japan but also in Brazil, should they or their parents return. The early 20th-century descendants of the original wave of Japanese immigrants to Brazil stood out for their strong performance in education. However, among their descendants who have immigrated to Japan and their children, the sometimes limited acquisition of both the Japanese language and their native tongue—coupled with the lack of social and occupational mobility faced by all foreign immigrants to Japan—may contribute to their remaining disadvantaged, as many long-term Korean immigrants have. Moreover, in the case of the foreign trainee system, very little investigation has been carried out to determine whether foreign trainees who have returned to their home countries after training in Japan have managed to utilise their skills in their home countries in positions other than those available in Japanese subsidiaries or in joint-venture plants established by the Japanese firms that trained the workers in Japan.

As already discussed, introducing foreign brides is one response to what might be termed a crisis of the human reproduction system in rural areas; these newcomers can look after ageing parents and help sustain the agricultural basis of rural life. This issue needs, however, to be discussed not only in the context of a human reproductive crisis but also in the context of the changing environment with respect to marriage since the 1970s—changes that have supported the expansion of international marriage in urban areas. Japanese society has become more affluent, and the tendency to avoid undesirable marriage conditions has grown in parallel with the tendency of Japanese workers to seek to avoid 3D types of work (dirty, difficult, dangerous). In fact, the living, working, and marriage conditions in Japan's rural regions are more reflective of the situation across Japan's population than is commonly assumed. In the case of male–female relationships, rural conditions simply represent a more extreme form of many factors that have deterred some urban women from marrying urban men, eventually contributing to a low level of human reproduction throughout Japan (having children outside of wedlock remains very uncommon in Japan due to the heavy social stigma that remains associated with it). In this context, marriage involving brides from Asia carries three major inequalities. First, gender-based inequalities exist between Japanese men and foreign women, with Japanese men possessing the economic power to marry Asian women.

Second, structured inequalities between Japan and developing countries serve to maintain a relationship of international codependency and subordination among Asian countries, with Japan remaining at the apex; and third, domestic discrepancies continue between industrialised areas in Japan that are growing (for now) and rural regions that are declining (Kumagai, 2007).

In the context of international migration, more women from Asia's developing countries are moving abroad for marriage; Japan, as well as South Korea and Taiwan, is experiencing an increase in international marriages, mostly involving foreign women and local men. The general factor behind this trend is continuing urbanisation in high-income economies coupled with impending depopulation due to low fertility and ageing populations (Economic and Social Survey of Asia and the Pacific, 2008). The trend has also been facilitated by the expanding network of international marriage brokers. These brokers are not always the same as 'job brokers,' who target foreign women for work in the entertainment and sex industries, but their networks are similar to those that have been used to support the importation of Asian women for these purposes. The evidence discussed earlier clearly indicates that if Japan accepts a large number of immigrants from neighbouring countries, this will further deepen an already complicated relationship of codependency.

Moreover, under the increasing accessibility of long-distance travel for people in developing countries, itself both a cause and a consequence of globalisation, labour migration between developing and developed countries is on the increase worldwide. Thus far Japan has benefited greatly from the economic opportunities opened up by this process. However, following previous waves of migration, when immigrants have become dissatisfied with their new circumstances in Japan, the return journey has been either impossible due to lack of resources or undesirable due to the strong likelihood of returning to a life of poverty. There were also few possibilities available for moving to a third country in order to take advantage of any opportunities that might exist there. Consequently, international migrants in the past tended to remain rooted in their first new country of residence, regardless of whether their actual working and living conditions met their expectations. These circumstances have now changed: Return migration is both possible and increasingly common among South American and Southeast Asian migrants to Japan, and the data are beginning to demonstrate this. There are now opportunities for advancement appearing in the home countries as these regions develop their economies and societies, and these are proving attractive enough for migrants to Japan to make the journey home, particularly when conditions in Japan have not met the expectations of many who moved there in the 1980s and 1990s. Many migrants will have gained useful work experience, skills, and knowledge in Japan. In addition, it is also becoming more feasible for migrants to move on to third countries and to take advantage of their experiences in Japan—Filipino nurses trained in Japan, for example, are able to make a jump to employment in Western Europe and North America. And Japan's development and globalisation facilitates still another factor: Larger numbers of Japanese, at least as compared with numbers in the later decades of the 20th century, are taking advantage of increased international mobility and are moving away from Japan. Many of these emigrants are younger women who have decided to abandon the traditional patterns of marriage and employment in Japan, especially in rural areas, and seek greater opportunity for personal development in other areas of the world. This factor, too, has significant consequences for immigration as a meaningful contributor in repopulating Japan's regions.

Finally, as established in chapter 2, other developed countries have their own shrinking regions, ageing populations, and declining labour forces. The average total fertility rate (TFR) for more developed regions of the world is currently 1.64 children per woman in her lifetime, whereas that of less developed regions—from which Japan receives most of its immigrants—continues to decline, standing at 2.7 children per woman in 2009 (UNFPA, 2009, p. 91). The TFR for East Asia including China is 1.73, and the average for all of South America is 2.12. Much of Europe is already experiencing real population declines, and these circumstances will only become more common across the world in the coming decades. Over the long term, the probable scenario is one of increasing demand among developed countries for immigrant labour from less developed areas of the world and of a dwindling supply of labour from these countries as they, too, develop their economies and their rate of population increase slows; Japan will therefore find it increasingly difficult to utilise immigration as a policy tool for boosting its regional populations. Japan is not the destination of choice for many of the highest quality immigrant workers from the less developed world; for various reasons, most prefer to settle in North America, Australia, New Zealand, and the larger economies of Western Europe. As already explained, migrant labourers who go to Japan will also find it easier to move on to North America and Europe because opportunities there have the potential to increase in scope and number.

It has always been the case in industrialised countries that the introduction of foreign workers in order to mitigate labour shortages creates a variety of new socioeconomic questions. Although the government and private agents pursue solution-oriented policies and actions, new problems are constantly created as 'latent side-effects in modern societies' (Beck, 1992, p. 13). So far, this chapter has considered the general issue of immigration to Japan as a possible solution to the country's demographic shrinkage and the issue of maintaining Japan's economic strength. This approach to the problems of demographic decline and uneven spatial development assumes the continued pursuit of a growth-oriented political economy. However, repopulating Japan via a programme of mass immigration from overseas would be both numerically and politically difficult, if not impossible, and as an enterprise it does not ensure the continued expansion of either the national or regional economies. The policy would also produce unexpected consequences, some of which may result in its ultimate failure to produce the desired outcome. Moreover, such a policy is unrealistic given the known effects of mass immigration on both the receiving and sending countries. Therefore international migration is only ever likely to be implemented as a part solution to regional shrinkage, and even then, realistically speaking, it will play only a minor part in a much broader policy mix. The next section takes this notion forward, exploring how residents in a particular locale understand demographic shrinkage and its economic and social consequences in their own lives and neighbourhoods—and how they acknowledge their own roles and functions within these processes.

ACKNOWLEDGING AND EMBRACING SHRINKAGE ON SADO ISLAND

The previous section explores the subject of repopulating Japan's shrinking regions from a macrolevel policy orientation; in this section, we adopt a microlevel ethnographic approach that focuses on independent local agents and the activities that they have initiated as responses to rural shrinkage. What follows is a qualitative investigation of local attitudes to demographic and economic shrinkage among residents of Sado Island, Niigata Prefecture.

Evidence was gathered via guided conversations with local residents on repeated visits to the island over a period of five years between 2004 and 2009. We interviewed local businesspeople, craftspeople, public sector workers, and retirees, as well as residents who had moved back to Sado after a sojourn living and working in urban locales. Overall, the data indicate that many residents of Sado acknowledge that despite hitherto substantial efforts to reverse the trend, the island's population will continue to shrink and age—and that it seems unlikely to begin growing again in the foreseeable future. When questioned, most respondents assumed that the population would not fall to zero but stabilise at a level considerably lower than its current size. This premise appears to indicate that some residents are reorienting their thinking from a growth-first perspective towards reducing the rate of shrinkage and eventually establishing stability in the island's economy and society. Such a reorientation would create a regional community that is foremost a comfortable and attractive place to live, one that, in the words of the mayor of Sado City, is a '*sumiyasui tokoro*' (Sado Shichō-shitsu, 2008). Residents have differing views as to what *comfortable* and *attractive* mean and about how to achieve that objective. Nevertheless, there is an expanding awareness around the notions of accepting and acknowledging the inevitability of future shrinkage, creating interdependent and co-operative relations among community members and, most significantly, countering the gravitational power of Tokyo in favour of establishing long-term local socioeconomic stability and sustainability.

Like residents in other remote rural regions of Japan, many residents of Sado are, in their own ways, working independently and interdependently simultaneously both to support themselves and their families and to positively influence the broader social, economic, cultural, and environmental quality of life on the island. Following conventions in the growing body of research on this subject, we term these individuals *social and environmental entrepreneurs* (see Mort, Weerawardena, & Carnegie, 2003; Leadbeater, 1997, p. 53; Schaper, 2002). To contextualize these entrepreneurs' activities, we begin this section by discussing current business and employment conditions on the island.

Economic and Employment Conditions on Sado Island

Despite a labour participation rate of 61.2 percent (the prefectural and national rates are 58.5 and 56 percent, respectively) and an unemployment rate in 2005 of only 1.9 percent (Sado shi, 2009; Niigata ken, 2009), common laments among Sado residents are that economic conditions are continuously difficult and that employment opportunities are few, particularly for younger people. Locals state almost unanimously that the jobs available are unattractive to younger people because they provide a low income, require physical labour in poor conditions, or because they offer poor long-term security and stability. This is the principal reason why adolescents and younger adults have tended to move away to urban areas in search of higher and more stable incomes, better working and living conditions, and a perceived greater range of opportunities for personal development. This process has been a major contributor to a long-term negative and recursive spiral of ageing and depopulation, declining fertility, economic contraction, and further ageing and depopulation in Sado.

More than half of all employment in Sado is in the primary and secondary industries (55.6%): agriculture, construction, and transportation. Tertiary employment is predominantly in retail premises and tourism sites, with some growth in care and services for older people. Income and employment in all industries except financial services and insurance and government services has steadily fallen since the 1990s; and despite a temporary uptick in the national economy in the 2000s, the number of small businesses has been on a long-term negative slide, falling 12.8 percent from 1,701 to 1,483 businesses between 2004 and 2008 (Sado shi, 2009).

All our informants were aware that Sado Island's society and economy face some difficult challenges stemming from ageing and depopulation, though they had differing and sometimes conflicting views on whether and how the island's society could secure a stable and sustainable population. Interviews with local residents on their general impressions of business and employment conditions present a rather gloomy portrait; key issues that emerged were (1) difficulties with demand for local goods and services, (2) increasing competition with businesses based outside the island, and (3) the reluctance of younger people to engage in the island's industries (P. Matanle, interviews, 2004–2009).

Younger people also encounter structural difficulties when trying to secure well-paid employment in more comfortable occupations. Thus employment combines with government rationalisation measures and the intensification of globalisation processes, contributing to the downward spiral of regional shrinkage. Traditional routes into work are being progressively closed to new entrants, particularly in public sector employment in education and town administration; agriculture and forestry co-operatives; and family craft, retail, hospitality, and service businesses. For example, the common route into stable public sector employment for eldest sons who are expected to take over household farms and businesses is becoming more difficult under state rationalisation measures driven primarily by the central government in Tokyo, itself a response to larger-scale national pressures, among which ageing and national population decline feature prominently. Due to the recent municipal merger of the island's 10 village and town municipal administrations into a single city, Sado's local municipal administration has been downsizing and has not been recruiting new high school and university graduates. In 2008 approximately 80 employees retired from the municipal authority and were replaced by—at most—a couple of new recruits (P. Matanle, interview, April 2008). The island's elementary and junior high school systems face similar circumstances; school mergers because of the rapid fall in the number of children born on the island have reduced the requirement for teachers and support workers. In agriculture, fishing, and crafts production—once a prominent route into stable work for eldest sons inheriting family assets—employment is shrinking rapidly; fewer children are being born, and fewer of these when they are grown seek to inherit their parents' lifestyles. Moreover, as the traditional *ie* system of inheritance collapses under a pattern of very small and geographically dispersed families, the education system is not taking on the responsibility of transmitting local specialist knowledge in many of these areas of work, and the island's artistic and culinary cultures, as well as its economic heritage, are eroded (Matanle 2006, 2008). Residents are also fearful of the consequences of being employed on irregular contracts at chain stores and of losing their economic autonomy. Many opine that branches of national retail, tourism, and hospitality chains are forcing local establishments out of business through aggressive (some say predatory) competition; the national chains either hire fewer locals or reduce their pay and security through increasing part-time, temporary, and contract employment. Local people criticise corporate employment patterns in which store and restaurant manager positions—regular employment—are often filled by so-called *tanshin funin*, who are sent to Sado from the headquarters in Niigata, Tokyo, or Osaka on limited-term experience and on-the-job training sojourns to establish and manage the operation and report to base, and who have little stake in the long-term overall prosperity of the wider community. The remaining positions—made up of low-paid and insecure employment, such as clerical, warehousing, delivery, waitressing, and customer-relations jobs—are then offered to local hires, usually middle-aged married women needing to supplement the family income in order to help pay for their children's education (which will involve leaving the island and releasing rural savings investments into distant urban economies) (P. Matanle, interviews, 2004–2009).

Deserted and shuttered shopping arcades are both the consequence and cause of low demand and ageing proprietors who have not been able to maintain their businesses (photo 7.1). Branches of national chains based in metropolitan areas attract customers with ample car parking and brightly coloured storefronts (photo 7.2). Processes like this have negative consequences for the quality of employment and economic autonomy in rural regions.

In order to get a qualitative snapshot of general business conditions in Sado, we researched independent retailers in Ryōtsu Port, once Sado's economic hub. Between 11.00 a.m. and 3.00 p.m. on Saturday 29 March 2008 (prime shopping time), we counted all the stores along the main shopping street. We asked neighbouring shopkeepers about the status of those shops that appeared closed. We also asked shopkeepers for their interpretations of business conditions along the shopping arcade. Of the 144 shops we counted, 47 (33%) had closed for good, the status of 8 was uncertain, and 89 (62%) were open for business, though some of the latter barely had any stock. The reasons shopkeepers gave for poor conditions were, in order of importance (using retailers' comments):

1. There are few convenient parking spaces … so customers go to the big [chain] stores in Sawata … especially in winter when there is a lot of snow.
2. Competition from big stores. It is expensive to import items from Niigata and the mainland, and big stores can always get things cheaper.… They [big stores] can provide more choice and longer opening hours.
3. Death and ageing. Most shopkeepers are older people who don't have the money or energy to reform their shops … [and] when they get too old or die there is no one to take over.
4. Economic conditions. Incomes in Sado are decreasing, and there are fewer tourists.

Independent retailing can sometimes usefully be employed as a qualitative barometer of local economic conditions and opportunities because

PHOTO 7.1. A shuttered and deserted shopping arcade in Ryōtsu port, Sado Island.

Photo by Peter Matanle (June 2009).

PHOTO 7.2. A zone of large warehouse chain stores with ample car parking is being developed in the Sawata district.

Photo by Peter Matanle (June 2009).

the industry provides the functional interface between producers and consumers. The situation in Sado is quite typical of what is occurring in Japan's more remote rural regions as the traditional heart of Japanese retailing—rows of family-run, independent stores arranged along covered arcades called *shōten gai*—gives way to out-of-town mega-sized chain stores grouped in large warehouse-like buildings around vast car parks. Previously thriving arcades suffer from much-reduced traffic, which decreases sales; eventually shops begin to pull down their shutters—giving rise to the increasingly used dark pun '*shata gai.*'

Education

Educational advancement is a significant contributor to out-migration from non-metropolitan regions and, in particular, from remote rural locales. This has both national and local structural causes. In 2005 the nationwide entry rate into higher educational institutions reached 76.2 percent of all 18 year olds, with 51.5 percent of the cohort progressing to universities and junior colleges (Ministry of Education, Culture, Sports, Science and Technology, 2006, p. 11). For Sado Island, the proportion was 76.3 percent for 2008 (Niigata ken, 2009). Until April 2008 Sado had no post-secondary educational institutions, requiring all younger people with expectations of progressing in their education to emigrate, usually either to Tokyo or to Niigata City. Locals complain that there are few good employment opportunities for younger people on the island, and thus education is a means to seek better opportunities in urban areas and to avoid employment in industries and occupations that are declining due to the progression of globalisation and changes in government support mechanisms. However, informants also suggested that the education system itself must bear some responsibility for rural decline by simultaneously preparing students for urban educational and employment advancement opportunities and even on occasion restricting access to knowledge and infrastructures that favour stable employment in rural enterprises and occupations particular to the region. Although many informants are critical of the system of progression to post-secondary education because younger people feel compelled to move away and rarely return to settle, some agree that spending time away in education is a form of escape from a sometimes closed and restrictive rural society where privacy and social networking opportunities are scarce. However, once established in urban locales, people from rural origins can find it immensely difficult to return home if and when they feel the desire to do so (P. Matanle, iinterview, June 2009).

Despite these difficulties, one of the most significant recent developments in Sado is the opening of the island's first post-secondary educational institution, and many informants expressed either hope or expectation that it would initiate some change in the education–migration dynamic. In April 2008, Niigata Sōgō Gakuin (NSG), the largest provider of post-secondary vocational education in Niigata Prefecture, opened its Sado Campus. The college teaches nursing care for older adults, environmental management, traditional architecture, and traditional crafts. Located in the central populated agricultural plain of the island, the college began with the acquisition of a previously vacated public girls' senior high school, and a JPY 150 million (USD 1.25 million) subsidy from Sado City government for the renovation of the buildings, purchase of equipment, and other start-up costs. Of the first cohort of 27 students, 26 have progressed to the second year, and 15 of these came from homes outside the island. In 2009 the college recruited 37 students, bringing the total to 63. The college has ambitious plans to accept two entry cohorts of 200 students each and to recruit students from all ages, backgrounds, and regions.

Although it is unlikely to reach its recruitment targets soon, the college has important consequences for the sustainability of society in Sado. It provides opportunities never before available for some young adults to remain in Sado instead of moving away, and it attracts others from beyond the island to settle in Sado either temporarily or permanently. Moreover, the college teaches skills that are applicable to living and working in rural locales; to establishing independent businesses; to reproducing the island's cultural, social, and economic assets; and to conserving its environmental heritage. NSG has researched local concerns and designed its courses with these new markets in mind, and in interviews, senior managers insisted that the college is a viable venture founded on sound business principles as well as a contribution to local social and environmental sustainability. The crafts-based course, for example, which teaches ceramic arts and bamboo design, is aimed at regenerating crafts indigenous to Sado, on the one hand, but that have wider currency in Japan and beyond, on the other—crafts that, as already alluded to, have until recently declined because of inattention in the formal education system. Moreover, the nursing course has a ready market among younger people and adults with family-care responsibilities in Sado. The environmental management course is designed for those who aim to work in agriculture, tourism, and public administration and who have environmental interests associated with employment in these sectors.

Towards Stability and Sustainability

This section builds on the theme of working to establish stability and sustainability, as NSG has done by establishing a post-secondary educational institution, and presents what some of Sado's residents and community leaders told us about what they are doing in their local communities. Many efforts are yet in their infancy, tend not to be coordinated, have varying degrees of success, and at times face indifference or even opposition. Nevertheless, constructive action is being taken at varying levels of intervention by official bodies, business leaders, volunteers, and social and environmental entrepreneurs.

We concentrated some of our research on the local saké-brewing industry, which is both a mainstay of the local economy and a business in precipitous decline due to intensifying global competition from other alcoholic beverages, such as beer and wine. However, this business sector has potential both for developing value-added activities rooted in local attributes and for developing more complex operations that employ larger workforces in complex tasks. According to informants, the remoteness of Sado's geography can be either a handicap or an attractive branding tool if marketing is able to connect with the right categories of consumers. Moreover, these local saké brewers are passionate about generating hitherto unexplored opportunities as a method both of expanding their businesses and of broadening and deepening their social and environmental influence, as the following interview extracts reveal.

> A big handicap is our geography. It is difficult to set up business here and you can't grow the business unless you export from the island.... By chance I got the opportunity to sell saké to Nobu's restaurant in New York. One reason for this success is, strangely, our geography. For many foreigners, Sado is a remote and mysterious place. When they come here they quickly discover its charms and want to take that back with them. So, when we started to sell our saké in Nobu's we had a party in New York and I invited Robert De Niro to come here to see for himself. He came by helicopter and we got a little drunk on our saké, but he is now a fan of Sado and our business is doing well over there. He calls Sado 'Saké Island'! (P. Matanle, interview with saké brewer in Akadomari, April 2008).

> I inherited the business from my father, but I quickly decided when I came back from Tokyo that I would take a different route. Saké sales are declining in Japan, and many brewers nationwide are going out of business. But we have been able to expand and employ more people. We provide saké to the first class cabin on Air France, and we export to the USA, Europe, and Asia. The whole world is an opportunity for us, so why stop at Tokyo? ... I want to do something to promote Sado overseas, to attract people here and show them what a wonderful place it is.... We have a project in development to export Sado culture to the world. If it works we will be able to bring in a lot of creativity and energy. Our aim is the sustainability of society, culture, and the environment here by cooperating in technology and tourism and in education. For example, I am working with a local environmental entrepreneur who is developing new waste-disposal technologies and we are starting some bio-ecology internships for local senior high school graduates to try to generate high quality employment.... We hope eventually to make Sado into an 'eco-island' and an example for others to follow. (P. Matanle, interview with saké brewer in Mano, May 2009).

> We are now producing organic saké. It is a little more expensive to buy the organic rice from our employees and local people, so we sell it at a slightly higher price. We have been doing it for 4 or 5 years now and sales are slowly increasing. We sell it in Niigata and Tokyo, for example. There is no difference in taste and quality between this and the normal saké, but we wanted to do more for the environment, especially for the Toki [crested ibis] and their food. (P. Matanle interview with saké brewer in Sakata, April 2008).

As in so many rural areas in Japan, tourism in Sado is another business sector in which entrepreneurs are becoming involved. Sado is currently

PHOTO 7.3. Saké is being produced in Sado and exported for consumption in restaurants in Western countries.

Photo by Peter Matanle (April 2008).

experiencing a decline in the number of visitors. Informants state that visitors often stay for short periods of one or perhaps two nights and their spending does not percolate into the local economy; instead, it is recycled back to Niigata City and Tokyo because consumption takes place in premises and activities that are owned by large tourist conglomerates headquartered outside of the island (P. Matanle, interviews, 2004–2009). Consequently, the municipality, in conjunction with the tourist association, has recently begun a new campaign to attract visitors from heretofore unrecognized tourist groups in the hope that they will stay longer and that their consumption patterns will shift to benefit the local economy more. However, tourism suffers from a poor reputation among locals seeking good quality permanent employment because many feel that it has a tendency to pay low wages on a seasonal and part-time basis. Again, new branding opportunities and new business models may offer a route out of this cycle for some people. For example, the tourist association has a new policy not to concentrate

Photo 7.4. Temperate rain forest on Sado Island.

Photo by Peter Matanle (June 2009).

on attracting higher numbers of tourists but to focus on improving the quality of visitors' experiences so that they will stay longer or return. The association is creating various day programmes of activities—for instance, two ecotourism day trips to the original-growth temperate rain forest in the north. However, numbers are restricted because human pressures could potentially damage the sensitive ecosystem there. The association is also trying to attract foreign visitors, who tend to stay longer than many Japanese tourists. A director of the association told us that foreign tourists like to rent bicycles, take buses, and so on, and the association is promoting these modes of local transportation as a means of providing more face-to-face contact between tourists and local businesses so that these tourists will be more likely to purchase local products through locally owned businesses, rather than the more traditional bus tours that have a tendency to stop at souvenir stores and restaurants that are owned by the tourism conglomerates based in Tokyo.

Conflict and Disagreement

Beneath the surface of society in Sado, conflict and disagreement are, predictably, present. Activists and entrepreneurs—who are often returnees and migrants who have spent time in urban areas—talked about locals who refuse to change, and some farmers and fishermen refer to outsiders' having a poor understanding of local concerns. In their different ways, informants described the potential for cognitive separation between residents of the island and the outside world, due mainly to the island's remoteness from mainstream Japanese life. Some pointed to the lack of a sense of urgency, a lack of consensus on what to do, and a lack of coordination in implementing strategies for stability, and others identified rifts between the local population and incomers in terms of their expectations of rural life, as one informant described:

> People from urban areas who come here have this image that rural life is slow-paced and comfortable and they think it would be nice to live here. Actually, it is really hard and city folk find that out quickly if they come. When they see these fields bursting with

rice they think that 'nature is so beautiful.' But that is not real nature. These terraces were built out of the sweat of generations of farmers over hundreds of years.... It is cold in the winter, with snow blowing around. Tending persimmon orchards or repairing windbreaks is not easy work. City folk that come [I-turn, meaning people who were born in a metropolitan region and who later migrated to a rural area] are often surprised at how hard it is. One can't go hiking at the weekend, as the tourists do. There is work to be done! Although things like hiking are practiced in the countryside, they are urban hobbies. City folk have a very poor understanding of rural life. They want to come here and lead an urban lifestyle. But that is not really possible in a place like Sado. (P. Matanle, interview with volunteer guide in Kanai, May 2009)

PHOTO 7.5. Rice terraces tumble down the side of an isolated valley in Sado Island.

Photo by Peter Matanle (June 2009).

One approach to rural shrinkage to which some residents of Sado appear to be turning is acknowledging and accepting depopulation as inevitable for the foreseeable future and deciding how the remaining community members might make the best of their circumstances, lead a comfortable life, and build an attractive community. For some, depopulation is even a desirable outcome that might facilitate the caring roles that are necessary in an ageing society, whereas others use an acknowledgement of shrinkage as a starting point for questioning how people will live under such circumstances and perhaps even how they can build a new type of society. Many informants who expressed such perspectives are rural returnees who had moved back to Sado after retirement or who had grown dissatisfied with urban living.

> I am a typical U-turner [person born and raised in a rural area who moved to an urban locale and returned later to his or her birthplace]. I was born here and spent 40 years working in Tokyo.... I came here two years ago to look after my mother.... At that time I heard a lot of rumours, but the local newspaper had been discontinued. I also felt that the government was abandoning rural areas with its reforms. So I decided to set up a newspaper. It is only a monthly town-sheet, and there is little real news, as it is just me collecting everything.... The content is on history, people, culture, events, and sometimes social issues, and local people submit articles on various topics. I don't earn an income, but we don't have any labour costs. Little by little we are increasing sales by word of mouth. We even send 160 outside of the island ... I want to contribute to the island's society with the newspaper, and I think that is happening slowly.... I get the printing done in Sado, even if it is more expensive, and that helps the local printer to keep going. I think it is very important to keep money and resources here.... The future is not bright. Soon there will be just 20–30 thousand people. Of course, the population will not fall to zero, but we are all talking now about how we will live in that atmosphere and what kind of a society we should build. I hope that my newspaper will contribute to that. (P. Matanle, interview with social entrepreneur in Sawata, April 2008)

Finally, the following informant, a ceramic artist and Living National Treasure, cited contradictions between the sustainability of rural life in

Sado, the unipolar centralisation around the Tokyo metropolis and the orientation towards continuous expansion. For him, the idea of urban Japanese migrating in sufficient numbers to areas such as Sado is currently a fanciful one, for such is the strength of Tokyo's gravitational pull that he believes the island's population will continue to decline. He acknowledged the potential for the island's inhabitants to pull themselves out of their current difficulties by embracing globalisation and the opportunities that this brings, but expressed doubts that they have the capability and resources to do so (see Matanle, 2006).

> As you know, Sado is declining now. In my lifetime the population has halved and people are now talking about it dropping below 50,000.... Yes, I agree with you that many people want to live in the countryside, and that would be a good thing in theory, but in reality they can't. They can't separate themselves from Tokyo. Centralization is good for growth and prosperity but the effect has been to open up a gap between Tokyo and the countryside. Tokyo is where everything is judged, but that is not a good thing. It draws everyone into itself.... But the character of one's own region is important as the long accumulation of tradition, knowledge, technique, and so on brings forth new ideas.... Tradition should not be fixed. We should keep its basic elements and develop that. Fixing shape and technique prevents the artist from thinking and so we need to keep tradition flexible.... One's own humanity is important too. Ingredients, place, history, people, essence are all mixed up and I can't easily explain what goes into [making pottery]. What I do is made up of a complex mixture of technique, brand, and blood. These are not new techniques [that I use] but just the first time [I have employed them] using Mumyoi clay.... Happiness is not an individual thing. You cannot be happy without other people. You ask if I have achieved self-realization. I don't know. If I had, there would be nothing left for me to do and then I wouldn't be happy. There is always something more. I want to continue to make more beautiful pottery for now.... You talk about bringing globalisation to Sado. That is a good idea in theory, and we are trying. But we lack the know-how to do it in practice. (P. Matanle, interview with ceramic artist and Living National Treasure in Aikawa, May 2005)

CONCLUSION

Under the current circumstances of national depopulation and a centralised growth-oriented national political economy, it is inevitable that areas in Japan will continue to experience ageing and depopulation. Most residents of the more remote rural locales already understand and have accepted this fact for themselves and their communities, even if the inhabitants of regional towns and cities on the cusp of depopulation are as yet in the process of digesting it. Moreover, immigration from outside of Japan does not present realistic potential for mitigating the impacts of shrinkage and providing a return to expansion. Hence, many discussions that are now taking place in communities like Sado Island focus not on how to achieve growth but on how to live well and comfortably in a shrinking region and on how to achieve personal, familial, and community stability in the face of the intensifying pressures of globalisation and the continued pull of the Tokyo metropolis.

Building on this discussion, we turn to exploring ways in which other communities in Japan are currently dealing with the problems of shrinkage. The next chapter examines ways some regional communities are attempting to recover their economies and break the downward cycle of depopulation and economic decline.

CHAPTER 8

RECOVERING THE REGION*

INTRODUCTION

The two preceding chapters critically examine redevelopment and repopulation as past and possible future responses to regional shrinkage in Japan and conclude that for differing reasons, both provide little potential for revitalisation in Japan's regions in the 21st century. Chapter 6 describes how local communities may have been unwittingly led by the Japanese government to maintain their official status as depopulating communities in order to continue receiving subsidies, mainly in the form of the construction of physical infrastructure. These circumstances, as one might expect, have served to entrench the status quo and over time have contributed to the threat—or in a few cases, the reality—of complete community collapse. With the deepening crisis brought about by the now-established fact of national depopulation and the reforms initiated by the Koizumi

*The principal contributing authors to this chapter are Andrew David, John Knight and Naofumi Nakamura.

administration in the early years of the 21st century, many communities feel a renewed sense of urgency to devise new ways of dealing with shrinkage. These we attempt to capture in the remaining three chapters.

Shrinkage presents communities and people with the requirement to act. In this sense, community recovery and revitalisation does not simply happen; it has to be achieved—hence the active voice implied in the gerund that forms this and other chapters' titles. In this chapter, we move away from presenting the reasons some municipalities have relied on pre-established and addictive patterns of codependency with the central government in order to discuss communities that have begun recovering a sense of their own place in response to the impacts of shrinkage. In these communities, the responses can be interpreted as beginning with an appreciation and an acknowledgement of current circumstances, which have motivated a desire to defend, restore, preserve, and reinvigorate their places—geographical and metaphorical—by building on local attributes. We have arranged this chapter around case studies at the village, regional city, and prefectural levels—studies from Hongū Town in Wakayama Prefecture's Kii Peninsula, Kamaishi City in Iwate Prefecture, and Kōchi Prefecture—because we believe that only through a multilevel and multi–case study approach can one appreciate the depth and breadth of the crisis and opportunity that currently exist in Japan.

The principles and practices of restoration implied in this chapter's theme of recovery are evident at their most basic level in the remote forested mountain villages of the Kii peninsula, where efforts are directed at better managing the natural surroundings so that the village can remain a place where its ageing inhabitants may live in relative comfort, security, and dignity, without feeling that they are being pushed out by the natural succession around them—a process that is itself a consequence of depopulation and ageing's changing the relational dynamics between the region's human society and natural environment. In Kōchi and Kamaishi, recovery efforts can be seen through attempts to recover local economies through endogenous mechanisms. An examination of the approaches that each community and region has taken makes apparent that in these cases local actors are coming to appreciate effective coordination and management by key agents of socioeconomic change as essential to successful recovery. But beyond this lie also the transformative consequences of the intangible and immeasurable human qualities of hope, creativity, and imagination.

Restoring the Village: Struggling to Preserve a Shrinking Community in the Kii Peninsula

Nationally directed policies and subsidies, though important attempts by the central government to provide remedial assistance to specific areas, are also subject to the vicissitudes of changing political and economic priorities within the establishment in Tokyo and sometimes fail to provide precisely what is required in response to idiosyncratic local changes. The physical deterioration of the rural village and its environment is one outcome of depopulation that is not evident in national statistics and that is often not addressed by government interventions. Yet this gradual erosion of residents' sense of the village as 'their' place represents the real experience of hundreds, if not thousands, of rural communities today. This is shown in the examples of abandoned houses, encroaching forests, and aggressive wildlife in the mountain villages of the Kii Peninsula, our first case of a regional community struggling to recover its sense of place within circumstances of shrinkage. The Kii Peninsula offers examples of attempts to manage the impacts of natural succession on the sustainability of rural mountain villages through the conservation of a community's spatial configuration and, consequently, its way of life.

Depopulation has turned mountain villages into spaces of environmental disorder. Reduced human presence in upland areas leads to unwanted plant growth and to unwanted animal trespassing. Village-edge timber plantations, farmland afforestation, and secondary forest growth combine to change the character of the outer reaches of village space, turning it into forest, as already discussed. The term *shrinking cities* has acquired widespread currency in recent years, though this is used metaphorically of cities undergoing population decline. In the case of depopulating villages, however, human space is experienced as *literally* shrinking—that is, as contracting. The disappearance of arable land and the reduction of open space that occurs as the forest expands become disturbing signs of community decline. This impression—that part of the village is no longer truly the village—is only reinforced by the appearance of forest animals in places once frequented by people.

There are many approaches to countering village deterioration and loss. One response to the problem of tree encroachment, for instance, which is usually an outcome of untended plantation growth, is to cut down the offending trees. Complaints about the issue of plantation tree-shading of residential areas have been raised in the Hongū Town council a number of times. One councillor went so far as to call the problem of tree shade a *kōgai* issue, a *pollution* issue, one that infringes the residential rights of Hongū citizens. The same councillor has called on the mayor to provide public funds so that the worst cases of light-blocking trees can be cut down and the residential environment improved (Hongū-chō, 2003).

All over rural Japan, municipalities have sought to counter the timber plantations' darkening effect on the village environment by passing ordinances permitting the felling of trees by municipal decree. In 1992 the municipality of Oguni in Kumamoto Prefecture launched an initiative called *kagekiri* (*shade cutting*), in which roadside trees and trees near houses were cut down to increase the amount of natural light in the area (Miyazaki, 1994, pp. 158–159). An example on the Kii Peninsula can be found in Totsukawa-mura, the vast mountainous municipality that borders Hongū to the north. In 1995 the new mayor Tadamasa Nojiri launched a policy initiative known as the Village Environment Maintenance Project (*Shūraku kankyō seibi jigyō*), the aim of which was to improve the residents' living environment by subsidising the felling of cedar and cypress trees within 50 m of houses or fields. The mayor argued that by creating clearings between residences and the forest, the measure would increase the amount of sunshine received by houses. In the course of the following five years, intrusive conifers were cut down in 480 separate sites in the Totsukawa area.

Remote rural residents have also responded to the problem of tree damage to graves. One response is to cut away the offending growth by pruning overhanging branches. Conifer stands may also be felled. For example, in Kiwa, to the east of Hongū, villagers whose graveyard had become enclosed by a cedar plantation cut down a 10 m belt of the plantation trees from around the graveyard's perimeter to brighten up the graves. But such actions first require the permission of the forest landowner. In Kiwa, the local Buddhist temple owned the land and duly agreed to the request.

An alternative to removing the trees is to move the graves. In recent decades there has been a trend in rural Japan towards consolidating and relocating family graves, the purpose of which is usually to create more space in the plot for future burials. Individual sets of bones are collected and put into separate pots that are placed together in an alcove beneath the new collective gravestone occupying one part of the plot. Relocation (which often entails consolidation) generally involves moving the grave to a more accessible or auspicious site—for example, moving the graves down from an elevated mountainside area to sites closer to the settlement. This makes the graves easier to visit for the older adult village population. Grave relocations have occurred in a number of Hongū villages. In 1981 one third of the households in a village moved their family graves to a new site about 20 m farther down the mountainside. In this new location, it was clear of the forest and close to the settlement.

Efforts have also been made to address the problem of intruding animals. One traditional response to this problem is to physically guard the fields. In the past, farmers guarded their fields from monkeys in what were known as *sarunoban* (*monkey watches*), which were practiced to protect vulnerable fields close to the forest (Knight, 2003, pp. 107–109). Because the macaque is a diurnal animal and active during daylight hours, *sarunoban* is in principle a day-long, dawn-to-dusk undertaking, especially in the late summer and fall as harvest time approaches. But it is labour intensive, a prohibitive factor in the depopulated and ageing upland villages of contemporary Japan where fewer and fewer people are capable of the required physical exertion. One such municipality in Akita Prefecture under siege from crop-raiding monkeys has resorted to pleas in the national media for help defending its fields—and has successfully attracted urban volunteers to come and guard its crops (Kahoku Shinpō, 1998).

Another response, increasingly common as the numbers of residents in villages decrease, is to establish physical fortifications. Barriers are erected around individual fields, around a wider area of farmland, or around the village as a whole. Since the 1960s electric fencing with voltages as high as 10,000 volts has been introduced to protect crops from wild boars and has even been hailed as a *kindai heiki* (a *modern weapon*) in the war with the boar (Shinano Mainichi Shinbunsha, 1969, p. 24). Electric fencing has also been of particular importance in relation to intrusions of monkeys; it is increasingly viewed as the only reliable means of reducing monkey damage in rural Japan. In one central settlement in Hongū, an antimonkey electric fence 1.6 m high and 720 m long runs along the boundary between rice fields and forest.

Another response is directed at villagers themselves: encouraging village residents to be more assertive, even threatening, when they spot animals in or around the village. It is clear that a key factor in the increase in wildlife damage and trespassing is the animals' loss of their fear of humans. It follows, then, that a restoration of this fear would be a vital part of any solution, for it would increase animals' tendency to avoid humans and human spaces. Many initiatives aimed at achieving this have been launched across the regions of Japan. Village residents are encouraged to frighten away intruding monkeys by shouting loudly or throwing firecrackers or stones at them, so that the monkeys learn that 'humans are the enemy' (Inoue, 2002, p. 2). In 1994 Kanagawa Prefecture introduced an emergency measure, known as the *oiharai oiage jigyō* (drive-away-and-send-back initiative), in which localities were encouraged to form 'drive-away squads' to chase monkeys all the way back to the forest. Similar to the action taken in Akita, the Kanagawa initiative also had the explicit aim of 'planting fear of humans' in the monkeys (Hirotani, 2000, p. 30). This same principle—making humans an object of fear and avoidance—informs recent efforts to keep deer away from mountain villages (Inoue & Kanamori, 2006, pp. 116–118).

How effective is this strategy? The obvious problem is that depopulated villages tend to lack the manpower required for the chase-away strategy. The overall number of village residents is much smaller, and those who remain are primarily older people. Although some of these residents may be willing to participate, others are likely to be reluctant or unable to do so. Moreover, there is a lack of financial and other resources for putting up and maintaining fencing, chopping down trees, pruning, and clearing undergrowth. Residents may also find it difficult to maintain their own homes and land, and defending and restoring empty neighbouring homes and farms is an added burden. They are likely to feel uncomfortable about venturing into and tampering with another family's property, even if it appears to have been abandoned. In addition, small remote hamlets and villages are normally unable to muster the institutional resources and mechanisms required to lobby successfully for assistance and to coordinate its effective implementation should it be granted. Finally, news reports of older people in rural areas being injured or killed by bears protecting 'their' fruit orchards and of bears and monkeys becoming bold enough to venture into urban locales, are on the rise. However, public attitudes towards mammals are changing in Japan, though slowly, and some urban dwellers are less inclined to agree with the pleas hunters. This may suggest a growing acceptance that natural succession and village disappearance may be unavoidable. Under such circumstances, it is hard to avoid the conclusion that many remote and comparatively inaccessible rural villages—especially those hamlets located in forested mountainous areas—are destined to disappear in the decades ahead.

Reinvigorating the City: Local Consciousness and Engineering Hope in Kamaishi City

Kamaishi's experience from the high-speed economic growth period of the 1960s to the beginning of the 2000s was characterised by steady economic decline and population loss. Efforts to address the economic issues include green-tourism development (see chapter 9), such that Kamaishi is today finally seeing signs of returning stability. The research presented in this section was written immediately prior to the Great East Japan Earthquake and tsunami of 11 March 2011[6], which badly affected Kamaishi. It is framed by the after-effects of a long period of industrial decline and economic malaise and aims to identify the mechanism by which local communities that have experienced such setbacks can initiate economic recovery in their once prosperous regions. The principal focus is how the city government, industries, and people of Kamaishi have co-operated and coordinated efforts to regenerate their community in contemporary Japan's dramatically changing economic environment. We aim to identify what the local people have thought and felt, as well as how they have behaved during the process of recovery. Ultimately, the research attempts to identify the often elusive character of hope that is present in Kamaishi.

Hope Studies Research in Kamaishi

The present Kamaishi research was not envisioned as a simple area study but as a study with the final aim of formulating a hypothesis concerning the *social phases of hope* through a coordinated multiproject research design based at the University of Tokyo's Institute of Social Science. The project began in November 2005 as a general regional research project from an interdisciplinary social science perspective. The following two research objectives were prioritised:

1. The inquiry would be into *changes in hope* among various socioeconomic strata due to the long-term process of restructuring of the core industry (i.e., Kamaishi Steel Works, Nippon Steel Corporation).
2. The project would be a multidisciplinary examination of *the rebirth of hope* in a company town (Kamaishi) where the local society and economy are undergoing change.

Based on these objectives, research was undertaken in July and September of 2006, and three themes have emerged: the role of networks, a common sense of hope, and a reorganisation of local identity.

The Role of Networks

Historically, though the Kamaishi region had the appearance of a unidirectional company town dominated by the steel industry, it also displayed a long-term relationship of interdependency and opposition between the core company and the local community. In particular, in the process of the contraction of Kamaishi Steel Works beginning in the latter half of the 1960s, there was significant tension between the municipal government and the company. However, since the shutdown of the blast furnaces during the rapid contraction of the steel works, Kamaishi City and Nippon Steel Corporation have co-operated by working to diversify the city's companies and offices and by setting up new enterprises. Since 1973 they have succeeded in bringing 26 companies to Kamaishi, 13 of which were still operating as of August 2006. The number of employees at these companies at that time was about 2,000, which corresponds to the number employed at the Nippon Steel Corporation's Kamaishi Steel Works in 1988, immediately before the shutdown of the last operative blast furnaces. In that sense, the mutual co-operative efforts of industry and city to attract firms and maintain employment has succeeded to some degree.

However, it is impossible to ignore the fact that half of the companies brought in through this effort withdrew a decade or so later. Thus it appears that for Kamaishi, the invitation and withdrawal cycle for new industries and companies continues. Another emerging problem is that, because individual companies were invited to Kamaishi independent of one another and solely for the purpose of providing employment in whatever industry the company was working in, the interindustry relations among these companies and between them and existing local companies are weak, leading to weak regional networks. The industrial categories of the 25 companies invited since the 1980s represent a wide variety—textiles (one company), foodstuffs (one), electronic parts (seven companies), general machinery (two), tool and die (three), metals (seven), and chemicals (four)—with no pre-existing or co-operative relationships between them except for those in the metals industry invited at the initiative of Nippon Steel. This lack of interindustry linkages and coordination was undeniably one cause for the low survival rate of the invited companies (Tsujita, 2007a).

Since 1996, however, when the direct involvement of the Steel Works in the invitation of companies decreased and Kamaishi City's government came to dominate the invitation activities, the local longevity rate of the companies locating in Kamaishi has increased. It seems that based on the lessons it learnt in the first half of 1990s, the city government began to gather information carefully on its own before sending out invitations. Furthermore, full-fledged efforts are now being made towards the formation of networks either between companies and research institutions or among companies, based on the premise of a clear future vision for an eco-town initiative, creating some hopeful future prospects (K. Nakamura, 2007).

It is also notable that many of the invited companies have cited as their reason for locating in Kamaishi 'the high-quality workforce that does not mind a three-shift work system or time-and-energy intensive manufacturing' and the existence of 'industrial infrastructure' centred on a 24-hour port (K. Nakamura, 2007). In terms of industrial management and efficiency, these are resources that were accumulated during Kamaishi's long history as a steel town, and they can be seen as a gift from Nippon Steel to the future prospects of Kamaishi as a site attractive to industry.

Based on the rediscovery of this industrial labour and port infrastructure, a transformation of sorts has been occurring since the beginning of the 21st century; Kamaishi's industrial structure as a 'steel town' has been transformed to that of a 'town for steel and machinery.' Now, with a new industrial structure based on the machinery industry as a key to its future, there is a need for Kamaishi to expand its area of networking to the midlands area of Iwate Prefecture (the Kitakami region), where the machinery industry is currently flourishing. A widening of such industrial networking is also crucial in order to vitalise not just the manufacturing sector but also services, including tourism and commerce (Kikkawa, 2006). Since the beginning of the 21st century, entrepreneurs who initiate their own corporate activities have emerged in Kamaishi (K. Nakamura, 2007). Many, however, have little contact with one another in the region and operate in networks that are outside the area (Tsujita 2007b; Kikkawa, 2007). In this sense as well, connections between networks inside and outside the region, along with the formation and expansion of networks within the region, will be a challenge for industrial promotion in Kamaishi.

As with the relationships between companies, there are challenges for the formation of an autonomous network of social relationships and relationships among community organisations in Kamaishi, and in this respect, the city government has an important role to play. During the heyday of the steel works, there were disparities between steel industry employees and other local residents in terms of their standards of living and lifestyles, to the extent that some came to use the term *segregation*. This local reality, typical of company towns, disappeared rapidly with the industry's decline and the closure of the steel works. However, for most of the post-closure history of Kamaishi, no new, clearly evident organising structure for local social relationships has emerged to replace this segregation (H. Kato, 2007). According to a survey of residents, people living in Kamaishi have less involvement in voluntary organisations than do those in other cities of the same scale, and in cases where conflict resolution is necessary, there is a tendency to rely on families and the city government rather than on specialist organisations or legal experts (Sato, 2008). For the Kamaishi community, which had built and organised social relationships around the nexus of a huge entity—namely, the steel industry and the Kamaishi Steel Works—the rapid decline of its influence has diluted local social relationships nearly to the point of nonexistence.

Recently, however, the formation and solidification of various resident networks has been an integral factor in community revitalisation, particularly in terms of encouraging local residents to take charge of area development. In a situation where individuals and companies eager to perform social and corporate activities are isolated from each other (Kikkawa, 2007), the city government is taking great pains to organise them. This is perhaps one of the most important roles of the city government that has been brought to light by this research.

A Common Sense of Hope

Where individuals and organisations are isolated from one another, even though they share the same community, it is difficult for them to form a mutually agreed and understood future vision. This common vision is the basis of a sense of hope for the city, the people, and for the future in general. Unfortunately, when a city has lost its past and cannot define its future, it is common for multiple, distinct, and contradictory city images, along with different future visions, to coexist. In Kamaishi, for example, conflicting visions have emerged: one group promotes a vision of a 'town of factories,' with a future secured by attracting new industry; the other group envisions a 'town of nature and the environment,' with its future in tourism. It is common not only for images to exist independently of one another among residents of the same town but also for very little interaction to exist between the groups holding these images and visions. Given the nature of these two visions for Kamaishi, it is clear that fostering such interaction, integrating these two images, and creating a new Kamaishi culture will be a major challenge (Ohori, 2007).

Kikkawa's (2006) notion of 'wide-area tourism development' is noteworthy in that it incorporates both industry and nature. Kikkawa's idea is to define Kamaishi as a tourist locale by rediscovering, recombining, and reconfiguring (1) the marine resources of its coastal areas and harbours, represented by the Sanriku Coast brand, and (2) the industrial resources of the Hashino furnace remains, namely, the Iron Historical Museum and the Kamaishi mine. These two images, together with the Kamaishi wide-area wind farm, Tōnō-area folklore, and the JR Kamaishi line from Hanamaki to Tōnō to Kamaishi (which was the model for Kenji Miyazawa's novel *Ginga Tetsudo no Yoru* [Night on the Milky Way train]), provide the basis of a broad-area regional tourism development. Creating a narrative and a brand name for the tourism resources centring on the Kamaishi line (*Ginga Tetsudo*) and establishing a Ginga Tetsudo brand could make a significant contribution to the development of tertiary industries in Kamaishi (Kikkawa, 2006).

However, realising the full potential of even one element of this multidimensional vision and fulfilling this sense of hope—the marine products of the Sanriku Coast brand, for example—will require meeting the challenge not only of bringing together the local fishing industry to tailor its own approach to the broader industry-tourism vision but also of bringing the fishing population together with that of the industrial sector under the banner of tourism. Particularly among the fishing population, clear differences in their city image and particular visions of hope exist, depending on the person's age and type of fishing operation, meaning that it will be difficult to create a shared sense of hope even among the members of the working community (Kase, 2007). The problem seems even more daunting considering the deep antagonism that has long split the fishing sector from the industrial sector regarding notions of coastline development. In contrast, various points of agreement have recently been found between the fishing population and those involved in tourism, as full-fledged efforts to develop eco- and green tourism have begun. These activities will be able to play an important role in developing the Ginga Tetsudo brand by incorporating co-operation with Tōnō, one of the national bases of ecotourism, into the plan. In that sense, people involved in the tourism industry must become intermediaries between the fishermen and manufacturers in the pursuit of a future vision and a shared sense of hope.

It is noteworthy that Takayoshi Uekami, who carried out a questionnaire and interview surveys of Kamaishi City council members, found that for the most part, city assembly members share a common consciousness on issues concerning policy challenges (Uekami, 2007). In the Kamaishi City Assembly, he found that 'securing employment' and 'industrial promotion' were seen as the most important issues for Kamaishi, regardless of assembly members' political affiliations or pre-political backgrounds. It is interesting to note that the blow to the local economy and society from the contraction of the core company led to the formation of a nonpartisan position in support of community recovery and revival, resulting in a softening of political confrontation. Thus in Kamaishi today, at least the final goal of area reinvigoration is shared by various social organisations. However, a consensus has yet to emerge on the measures necessary to achieve it or on the concrete features of any future vision.

Reorganisation of Local Identity

Hope is a reflection of one's future vision. However, in defining this vision, it is also necessary to understand identity; in Kamaishi's case, identity is understood in local residents' views of their town's past. In the present research, one can identify the potential for a shared hope among residents of the Kamaishi area in this appreciation and acknowledgement of the past. Two approaches were taken to examine the history of Nippon Steel's Kamaishi Steel Works, which was once the core company in Kamaishi: a survey on job changes and hopes of former workers and managers using the oral history method, and a survey on the transmission of technical skills at a wire factory. In the first survey, the focus was on the issues of transfers to Tōkai (Nagoya) in the 1960s and of rationalisation based on medium-term production structure plans since the end of 1970s, through which the state of hope among workers and managers in the period of Kamaishi Steel Works' decline could be discerned. As a result, we have developed the hypothesis that the workers who had maintained a consciousness of their membership in the Kamaishi Steel Works (a form of local community) since before World War II recognised anew during the processes of reorganisation and rationalisation that they were members of the common corporate society of Fuji Steel or Nippon Steel, and went on to reconstruct their hopes accordingly. Although Aoki (2007) noted that the rapid contraction of the Kamaishi Steel Works was carried out without much disorder thanks to a sharing of 'organisational hope' by both labour and management, for the local community what developed was a crisis of identity.

The history and culture survey group researched the formation of local identity in Kamaishi itself through an examination of how Kamaishi's residents have come to understand, or even not understand, their town's past. The research was conducted at Kamaishi Commercial High School and found that with the memories of Kamaishi's past prosperity fading—memories that had sustained older residents—many high school students held views concerning the future that could not be classified as positive. It appears that although Kamaishi has a historically unique culture as a successful industrial city where residents associated with the steel industry led comfortable lives, this culture is neither apparent at present for young people nor connected to the town's future development in a form that is readily familiar. For a community like Kamaishi, a positive local identity and a shared hope and vision of the future provide the impetus to integrate and activate the various networks that are dormant in the area. Currently, however, in Kamaishi these elements—identity, vision, and hope—are vague and scattered. Kamaishi's future seems to lie in a rediscovery of its own history as the way to create a new local identity, a clear future vision, and a shared sense of hope.

Revitalising the Prefecture? Assessing the Potential for Sustainable Employment Creation in Kōchi

Beyond infrastructure development and tourism, which have provided Japan's regions with mixed results in terms of social and economic stability, are there additional opportunities for local entrepreneurs and municipal administrations to develop businesses that provide long-term stable employment to local residents and thus contribute to sustainable regional economic recovery in Japan? In this section we examine economic recovery efforts at the prefectural level with an investigation of Kōchi Prefecture.

As noted in chapter 3, the long-term demographic and economic trends in Kōchi are generally negative, even without considering the impacts of the most recent downturn in the Japanese economy as a result of the worldwide financial crisis and economic recession that began in 2007. Nevertheless, Kōchi does have some industries that may provide foundation for employment; many of these represent sectors that have potential throughout regional Japan. First, the primary sector makes only a small contribution to Kōchi's economy when considered in isolation, but when related industries are taken into account, agriculture becomes more significant. Second, the ageing of Kōchi's population creates significant employment opportunities in the medical, health-care, and welfare sectors.

Kōchi's experience also indicates other avenues that prefectures can pursue to promote economic development based on their particular circumstances and cultural and natural assets. For example, Kōchi was the first prefecture to commercialise deep seawater, and businesses now realise approximately JPY 15 billion annually in sales of deep-seawater products. Second, the recently founded Kōchi University of Technology has generated a number of spinoff companies as a consequence of the work of entrepreneurs and technologists associated with the university. Finally, local high-tech manufacturing enterprises represent some individual success stories, though overall this sector has been declining in Kōchi over the long term, especially since the onset of the most recent financial crisis and recession led to significant declines in Japanese manufacturing as a whole.

Agriculture, Fishing, and Related Industries

Although agriculture and fishing account for only a small proportion of Kōchi's prefectural output, when related sectors are included, the agricultural sector makes a much larger contribution to employment and the prefecture's economy. In 2005 employment in agriculture and fishing stood at 39,766 and 5,193 persons respectively (Statistics Bureau, 2010b). Another 5,282 people were employed in agricultural, forestry, and fishery co-operative associations in 2004 (Statistics Bureau, 2010i). Moreover, in 2005 some 1,234 people were employed in manufacturing agricultural machinery; 714 in manufacturing beverages, tobacco, and feed; and 5,759 in manufacturing food (Ministry of Economy, Trade, and Industry, 2010). In aggregate these figures amounted to approximately 16 percent of employment in Kōchi Prefecture in 2004–2005 and represented at least 21 percent of manufacturing shipments in 2007 (METI, 2010).

This does not mean that all these sectors in Kōchi are thriving, however. In the manufacturing sector, food shipments increased by 24 percent from 2002 to 2007, and shipments of beverages, tobacco, and feed increased by 6 percent (though value added for the latter decreased)—but shipments of agricultural machinery decreased by 7 percent, and agricultural machinery value added decreased by 28 percent (METI, 2010).

In addition, the farming population is ageing rapidly, with 60 percent of farmers at least 60 years old in 2005 and 80 percent of farmers at least 50 years old (Statistics Bureau, 2005). Nevertheless it is clear that agriculture remains an important part of Kōchi's economy, and future economic development strategies need to take into account the importance of this sector. Future economies of scale, for example, could be generated in agriculture through land consolidation as the farming population ages and decreases still further; this has yet to take place.

Medical Services and Health Care

Medical services, health care, and welfare represent one of the fastest growing areas of employment in Kōchi with employment reaching 47,000 persons in 2005 (Statistics Bureau, 2005). As Japan's population, especially in rural regions, is ageing rapidly, the number of employment opportunities for workers in health- and welfare-related services is increasing, particularly for younger workers; and Kōchi is no exception. In 2005 some 21 percent of people employed in this sector in Kōchi were under the age of 30, and 45 percent were under the age of 40, exceeding the prefectural average of 35 percent and 16 percent, respectively (Statistics Bureau, 2005). In 2004 wages per employee were 28 percent higher than wages in the service sector in Kōchi overall (Statistics Bureau, 2004).

There have been significant increases in the number of pharmacists and in the number of physicians in Kōchi, but the largest increase has been in the number of nurses, which rose from 2,985 in 1984 to 7,426 in 2006 (Statistics Bureau, 2010d; Statistics Bureau, 2010i). The majority of medical-care personnel in Kōchi are nurses and assistant nurses; nurses account for 40 percent of medical personnel and assistant nurses for 25 percent (figure 8.1; Statistics Bureau, 2010i).

Given Kōchi's expected demographic trajectory for the coming years, it is fair to say that most aspects of medical, health, and welfare services have the potential to be important for the retention of younger workers in Kōchi and may be a source of good-quality stable employment for younger people. It is, however, difficult to imagine how Kōchi could build beyond providing services, for there is little in the way of

FIGURE 8.1. Numbers of Nurses, Pharmacists, and Physicians in Kōchi Prefecture, 1984–2006.

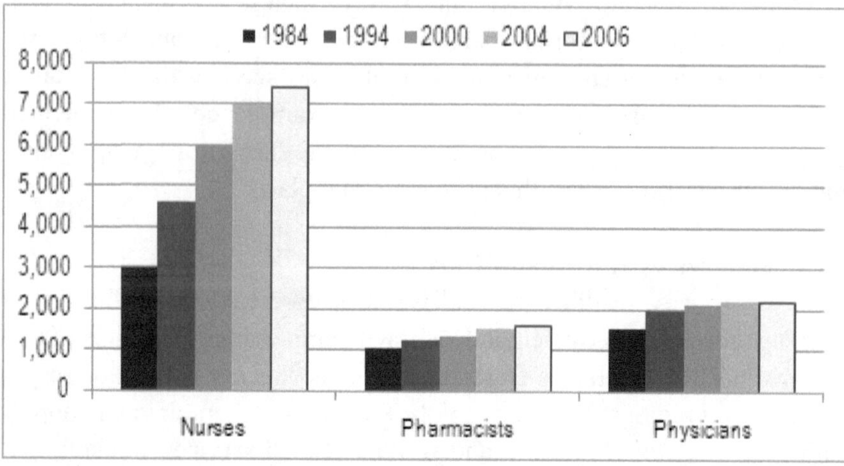

Source. Statistics Bureau (2010i; 2010d).

an institutional or research base on which the prefecture might develop advanced knowledge-intensive industries in these areas.

Deep Seawater

One area in which Kōchi has developed early advantages is the commercialisation of deep seawater. In 1995 companies began pumping seawater off the prefecture's Pacific coast from a depth of more than 200 meters. The water is believed to provide many health benefits, coming as it does from an area of ocean rich in minerals. Kōchi's proximity to both the Nankai undersea subduction zone (the meeting of the Philippine and Eurasian tectonic plates) and the warm Kuroshio ocean current, as well as the perceived absence of harmful bacteria at such depths, makes this water a valuable resource. The deep seawater is bottled and sold as drinking water and used in food and cosmetics. Over 100 companies mar-

FIGURE 8.2. Proportions of Medical Care Personnel in Kōchi Prefecture, 2006.

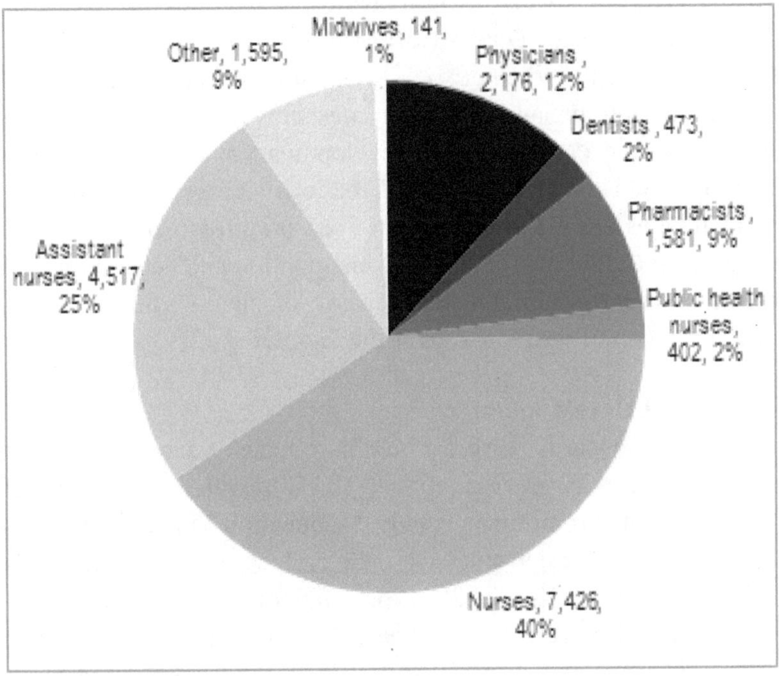

Source. Statistics Bureau (2010i).

ket products with deep seawater from Kōchi, and sales increased from JPY 800 million in 1996 to JPY 10 billion in 2000 and again to JPY 15.5 billion in 2004. However, sales have levelled off and there is increasing competition from other prefectures in Japan and from imported deep seawater, especially from Hawaii, which is generally considered higher quality than water from Japan. Sales of deep seawater–related products totalled JPY 13 billion in 2005 and JPY 15 billion in 2007 (Kōchi Shimbun, 2006; Kōchi Prefecture Deep Seawater Laboratory, 2010; *Nikkei Weekly*, 1999, 2000; Daily Yomiuri, 2002; *Japan Economic Newswire*, 2003; Hao, 2006; Wiles, 2008; Hsieh & Li, 2009, p. 288).

Other uses for deep seawater have been identified by recent research, particularly through work at universities, sometimes in co-operation with the private sector (Japan Corporate News Network, 2006; Hsieh & Li, 2009, p. 291). Whether such research and changes in approaches will result in a significant increase in sales, however, remains to be seen. Nevertheless, the establishment, development, and commercialisation of this new industry have benefitted the local economy, demonstrating that advantages can be developed in even the most peripheral prefectures, given the right combination of imagination and dedication among a region's entrepreneurs and the presence of natural endowments that can be commercially exploited over the long term.

Research and Development

One consistent success story for Kōchi in recent years is the creation of Kōchi University of Technology (KUT), which was established as a means of promoting technical education, industry–university collaboration, and local businesses in the prefecture (Development Bank of Japan, 2001, p. 33; Kondo, 2001, p. 14). Some of the faculty members Kōchi hired had private sector experience, such as Hiroyuki Mizuno, a former vice president at Matsushita Electric, who was hired to oversee research (Kondo, 2001, p. 14; *Nikkei Weekly*, 2002). KUT also integrated into its curriculum small-business classes on business formation and management (Crooker, 2007, pp. 67–68).

KUT has been very successful in fostering research that can be commercialised. According to two 2005 surveys of spinoffs of academic institutions, such as research centres and collaborative projects, KUT ranked in the top 20 among all universities in Japan, with 23 or 27 spinoffs, depending on the survey. Not all spinoffs are located in the prefecture, but even so Kōchi ranked fairly high for its academic spinoffs among prefectures. According to the same surveys, there were 18 or 20 academic spinoffs located in Kōchi. Kōchi was 16th or 18th of 47 in terms of the number of university-initiated spinoffs per prefecture (Harada & Mitsuhashi, 2008, pp. 27, 30).

High-Tech Manufacturing

Kōchi has also had some success in developing high-tech manufacturing industries (table 8.1). Some of these have grown by utilising Kōchi's traditional strengths in papermaking, now put to use manufacturing components for the electronics industry. For example, Kōchi-based Hirose Paper Manufacturing Company makes wet-laid nonwovens for a variety of applications (e.g., beverage filtration and battery separators) using a process that is related to papermaking, and in 1943 Nippon Kodoshi started making paper for use as separators in capacitors (table 8.1). Other Japanese companies have established manufacturing plants in Kōchi (in Casio's case, this was in part because the company's founder is originally from the prefecture; Casio, 2010a).

Overall, Kōchi's record in high-tech manufacturing industry has been mixed. There are individual success stories, as noted earlier, because of the establishment of manufacturing plants by companies based outside of Kōchi, or because the development of a local industry based on Kōchi's strengths (e.g., papermaking), or because the plant's founder had particular personal associations with Kōchi. Up till now, however, these individual successes have not been widespread enough to significantly increase manufacturing in the prefecture. Not only has manufacturing overall declined in Kōchi, but shipments and value added for electronic parts and devices, which increased from 2002 to 2004, were significantly lower in 2007 than in 2004. Shipments and value added for electronic parts and devices declined by 15 and 38 percent, respectively, from 2004 to 2007 (METI, 2010). The global recession likely had a further impact on this sector as it did across manufacturing throughout Japan. For example, Nippon Kodoshi's sales dropped from JPY 17.1 billion in the fiscal year ending in 2008 to JPY 12.6 billion in 2009, then recovered slightly in 2010 to JPY 13.4 billion (Nippon Kodoshi Corporation, 2010). Despite the declines, all of these companies continue to produce in Kōchi, and M. Setek actually added a plant in 2009 (M. Setek, 2009).

Furthermore, although attracting manufacturing companies is an important part of economic recovery efforts, there are several limitations. First, manufacturing in industrialised countries today tends to be highly

TABLE 8.1. Selected High-Tech Manufacturing Companies With Production Facilities in Kōchi.

Company	Headquarters	Product	Notes
Hirose Paper Manufacturing Co., Ltd.	Kōchi	Wet-laid nonwovens for a variety of applications such as filtration and battery separators	Three plants in Kōchi.
M.Setek Co., Ltd.	Tokyo	Ingots for solar industry	Two plants in Kōchi, one opened in 2004 and one in 2009.
Ortus Technology Co., Ltd.	Tokyo	Displays	Plant originally part of a wholly owned subsidiary of Casio called Kōchi Casio. Kōchi Casio was transferred to a new display manufacturing joint venture with Toppan Printing Co., Ltd. in 2010. Under Kōchi Casio this plant produced thin-film transistor (TFT) liquid crystal display (LCD) panels.
Nippon Kodoshi Corp.	Kōchi	Capacitor separators	Three plants in Kōchi. 70 percent global market share for capacity separators.
Renesas Electronics Corp.	Tokyo	Semiconductors	Formerly a Mitsubishi Electric plant, then part of Renesas Technology, now part of Renesas Electronics Corp. In 2009, second floor production was eliminated and combined with first floor production due to the decline in semiconductor demand resulting from the recession.
Tosa Denshi	Kōchi	Electronic components	Multiple plants in Kōchi.

Sources. Websites of individual companies and former companies; Jiji Press (1986); Casio (2010b).

Figure 8.3. Electronic Parts and Devices, Shipments and Value Added, Kōchi Prefecture, 2002–2007 (JPY billions).

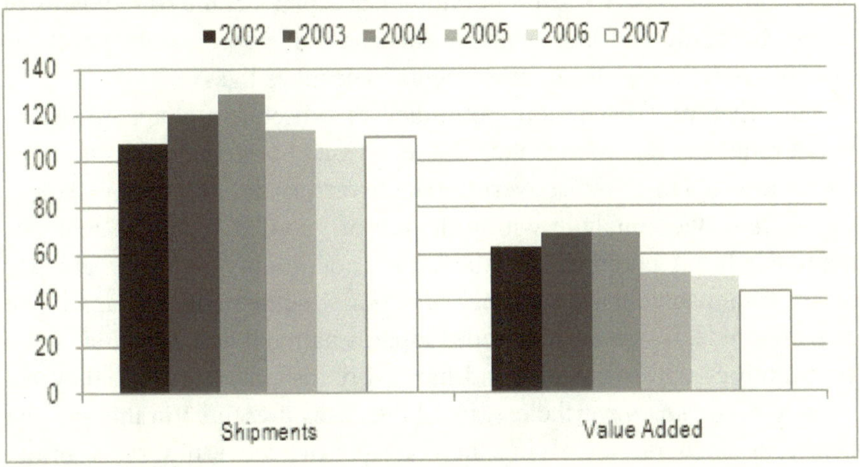

Source. METI (2010).

automated; therefore job creation at new plants may be limited. Second, most of the companies discussed here are clustered in the areas around the comparatively urban Kōchi City, with outlying rural locales less likely to benefit from new manufacturing plants. Thus primary industries will likely remain important in any economic-development strategy developed by prefectural and municipal authorities.

Conclusion

Achieving economic growth in Japan's shrinking regions will necessarily depend upon establishing a rate of productivity growth that is higher than the rate of shrinkage of the regional labour force. This will be exceptionally difficult to attain in ageing and depopulating communities, located for the most part also in Japan's periphery and possessing few competitive advantages over core metropolitan areas. Consequently, the most likely scenario over the long term is that regional economies will gradually shrink along with their populations. This is not to say, however, that such decline will necessarily result in falling per capita income or standards of living. Carefully and imaginatively managed, therefore, could shrinkage present opportunities for improvements in people's lives?

This chapter's discussion (continued in subsequent chapters) examines a range of responses at the village, city, and prefectural levels, all of which are rooted in rediscovering the characteristics and circumstances of a locale. We conclude with a degree of guarded optimism that this approach bears potential for successful community recovery and for the re-establishment of sustainable regional settlements in Japan. We also conclude, however, that under Japan's national depopulation, some communities will eventually and inevitably disappear; indeed, they are already doing so. Nevertheless, in all the cases presented in this and the next two chapters, underlying the concepts of recovering, reinventing, and reimagining is the notion of a rediscovery by community members of some aspect of themselves and their place—and the notion of their intentional redeployment in the service of endogenous restoration, reinvigoration, and revitalisation of regional community life.

The national economy possesses tremendous wells of competitive advantage and vigour, and spill-over effects from metropolitan regions will most probably continue. However, there are dangers in too much regional reliance on the performance of the national economy. Expansion in metropolitan regions is likely to encourage out-migration from regional communities, and recession often hits the peripheries more severely than it does the centres. For economic stability to be achieved despite ageing and depopulation, non-metropolitan communities should perhaps develop a greater level of economic independence from the centre of Japan's political economy. Endogenous development of inherent cultural assets and natural endowments, therefore, represent a possible way forward for Japan's regional economies.

It is a truism that one's own circumstances are inescapable, and it is essential to consider the underlying contexts that have brought each community to its present circumstances; this realisation allows for an evolving approach based on the motivation to recover a region's vitality. Recovery will necessarily incorporate a sometimes odd marriage of *both* acceptance of shrinkage and community loss *and* optimism for the future that may subsequently yield sustainable outcomes. However, this approach is significant not because it is predicated on the absolute requirement to regrow, either demographically or economically, but rather because it is rooted in the solid foundations of what is already present; it simultaneously reconnects the community with its past and offers the potential to break with the recurring failures of established practices.

Japan's regional cities, towns, and villages will inevitably experience depopulation—as indeed many already are—and some will succumb to collapse and disappear altogether. The patterns that once provided an established way of life are becoming outdated, and geographical peripherality and inter- and intraregional competition present obstacles to successful revitalisation. Though maintaining the face of a community may not lead either to its repopulation or its redevelopment—at least not directly and not in the short term—it can lead to the rediscovery of what the community means for its inhabitants, who can subsequently create a sense of meaning that may encourage residents to remain and outsiders to visit or even settle.

In the next chapter, we expand on these conclusions to examine tourism as the dominant emerging industry in regional Japan. Like any other industry, tourism is competitive and necessarily produces winners and losers, and, as already discussed, the isolation and small size of peripheral places puts many at a disadvantage in such scenarios. Nevertheless, the very act of competing can often bring hope of a chance to continue—an outcome not necessarily enviable, but real. And the future for Japan's regions will also likely include space, if not an expanding space, for the type of industry with which tourism can coexist and upon which it can capitalise.

Chapter 9

Reinventing the Region I

Current Practice in Tourism*

Introduction

In this fourth chapter of Part II, we build on the theme of recovery by analysing attempts to forge innovative paths for tackling regional shrinkage based on rediscovering and then reinventing a region's inherent attributes for the purposes of developing regional tourism. The three regions presented here—the Oga Peninsula in Akita Prefecture, the remote islands of Okinawa Prefecture, and Kamaishi City in Iwate Prefecture—present contrasting cases of tourism development under circumstances of shrinkage. In rural Akita, attempts to open up the remote Oga Peninsula reveal the competing priorities of different actors involved in the various projects and the need for tighter coordination to ensure that tourism facilities remain economically sustainable. In Okinawa, which has had a thriving tourism industry for some decades due to its location,

---

*The principal contributing authors to this chapter are Ken Ohori, Richard Siddle, and Donald C. Wood.

authorities are increasingly turning to ecotourism as a method of maintaining viable economies in the small and remote islands that make up the archipelago. And in Kamaishi, famous as an industrial town and the birthplace of Japan's steel industry, efforts to develop a green-tourism[7] identity remain as yet in their infancy.

With the steady and continuous attenuation of agriculture and forestry as the principle sustenance activities for rural locales and with the transformations in the global economy that make extraction, process, and manufacturing industries unviable in areas outside the country's industrial agglomeration, communities are turning to tourism in order to maintain their increasingly fragile economies. The problem with this approach is that non-metropolitan communities already face one negative-sum game as they compete against each other to maintain stable populations, but they are now entering another, competing against each other for tourist income. The consequence, as in any competitive enterprise, is that there will be winners and losers. Okinawa, owing to its natural heritage, is likely to be among the former, whereas Akita and Kamaishi risk being among the latter. Although Kamaishi is geographically distant from Tokyo, it has good transportation links to the capital region and has a deep industrial heritage from which it can draw to develop a broad-based economy in heavy industry, services, and tourism; Kamaishi is already succeeding somewhat in this endeavour. Remote rural locales such as the Oga peninsula, by contrast—with roots in agriculture, forestry, and fishing and home to an inhospitable winter climate—are likely to feel the cold winds of competition more keenly.

Beyond competition, the significance of these three cases lies in the potential of image, culture, environment, and local consciousness to be realised in the reinvention of a local identity, and in the potential for a renewed sense of optimism for some of the communities in Japan's shrinking regions. This response of invention contrasts with those in chapters 6 and 7 in that it is not delivered by the central government or big business in a top-down, dirigiste manner but is instead rooted in a community's rediscovery of its own place. As a consequence, this response provides opportunities to diverge from entrenched policies and practices with a sense of self-confidence and self-renewal. As the following discussion shows, although the development of a tourism industry may also require new infrastructure, the process of reinvention need not be based upon a growth-first approach, and for this reason we contend that the experimental process of rediscovery and reinvention has a greater chance than traditional approaches of providing communities with socioeconomic stability and sustainability in the face of continued depopulation.

Tourism Development on the Oga Peninsula, Akita Prefecture

Tourism is now big business in Japan. It is also closely connected to regional development. This has been so especially during the postwar years, as the country's regions became progressively interconnected economically and became increasingly tied to the national and global political economies, as well. As Japan's economy has grown and its infrastructure developed, the number of foreigners entering Japan has dramatically increased, from 18,046 foreign visitors in 1950 to 7,450,103 in 2005 (Ministry of Justice, 2008). In 2008 this figure topped the 9 million mark, only to fall back to the 2005 level the following year (MOJ, 2010c). Coupled with a parallel long-term increase in domestic tourism, the general trend has provided unprecedented opportunities to capitalise on tourism across the greater part of the archipelago. Even relatively isolated Akita Prefecture saw its total tourist visit numbers rise from 18.6 million in 1970 to just over 45 million in 2007 (Akita ken, 2010, p. 3). Consequently, prefectural and municipal authorities and private organisations across Japan have been working hard to reinvent themselves as tourist destinations in order to take advantage of the boom in domestic and international tourism in Japan. However, there are some clouds on the horizon: Domestic overnight stays appear to have peaked in the mid-1990s and stagnated or even decreased since then (figure 9.1).

Despite the long expansion in domestic and international tourism in Japan, residents in rural prefectures such as Akita have often been left out of the boom, and this is reflected in the story of the development of

FIGURE 9.1. Numbers of Japanese Tourists Travelling Overseas and Foreign Visitors to Japan (left-hand scale, ten thousands) and Number of Domestic Overnight Stays in Japan (right-hand scale, hundred millions).

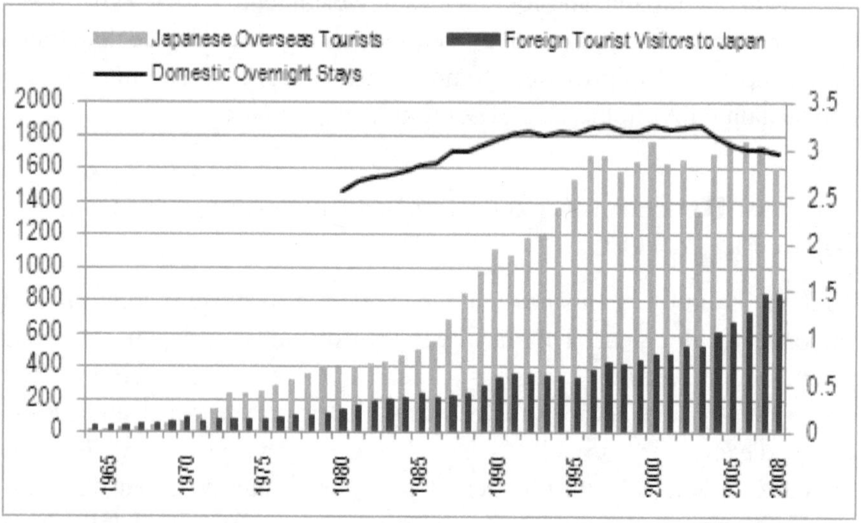

Source. Japan Association of Travel Agents (2009).

a tourism industry on the Oga Peninsula. Two points become clear from an analysis of this case. First, regional tourism development in Japan is a complicated process involving numerous actors with a variety of objectives but exhibiting little overall coordination (see Bailey, 1991; Moon, 1989). Second, the sources of capital behind the construction and management of a tourist facility can have strong effects on the function of that facility and on the way it assists in local development objectives. This latter point is important because local support for the development of tourism infrastructure has been shown to contribute to its continued existence and success (Lankford, 1994; Murphy, 1985; Whittaker, 1997). These points lead to questions regarding public versus private—and local versus nonlocal—investment in and management of regional tourism development. In this section, we first present an overview of tourism infrastructure development in the Oga Peninsula and then provide examples of tourism development projects with a view to analysing their impacts.

Akita is one of six prefectures composing Japan's northeastern Tōhoku region. In 2008 its population stood at 1,108,000, a number that has been on the decline since 1945 (Statistics Bureau, 2010e). More important for area development, though, is the troubling fact that the number of younger people (aged 0–14 years) has been falling steeply: from 189,000 in 1995 to 163,000 in 2000 and then 143,000 in 2005. Even in the prefectural capital city, the number of children is decreasing (Wood, 2009). This is typical of most of Tōhoku, and has contributed to societal ageing, requiring much social adjustment (Traphagan, 2000; Traphagan & Knight, 2003). Situated just to the northwest of the capital city, the Oga Peninsula (map 9.1) is in a good position for attracting visitors. As a result of the Heisei municipal mergers (see Rausch, 2005a), the 200 km^2 landmass now falls entirely under the auspices of Oga City, currently home to about 32,000 people. The peninsula contains a 8,156 ha quasinational park (*kokutei kōen*). The area has economic roots in fishing, but the number of fishing households is declining, and the industry now involves a disproportionate number of older people (Ministry of Agriculture, Forestry, and Fisheries, 2010). Oga has a few centres of fairly dense population, but by and large it is a collection of small villages with relatively loose connections to one another and a large proportion of so-called *genkai-shūraku*, villages that have reached the limits of their depopulation.

Access to the Oga Peninsula has long been troublesome for outsiders. When Funagawa Station (now Oga Station) opened in 1916, the mayors of the peninsula's 11 towns and villages petitioned the prefectural governor to fund road construction that would allow easier access to the western coast, arguing that this would benefit both the peninsula and the rest of the prefecture (Isomura, 2000, pp. 104–105). Construction has been very important in the development of Oga since then. Postwar tourism growth on the peninsula received its first big boost with the building of toll roads by the Akita prefectural government, the first of which was finished in 1961 and ran to the top of Mount Kanpū. The following year,

MAP 9.1. The Oga Peninsula.

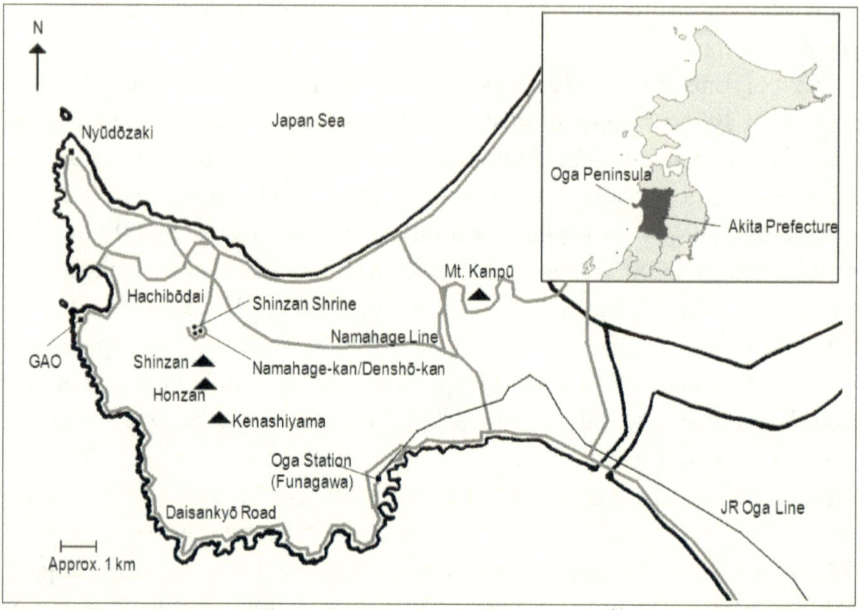

Source. Map by Donald Wood.

the Akita Business Enterprise Department (BED) took over the management of the Kanpū road and embarked on a project to develop Oga further, starting with the construction of more toll roads. Next was the Nyūdōzaki Hachibōdai Road in 1964, a 12 km stretch allowing access to Hachibōdai, a scenic overlook above Toga Bay. Other roads also appeared, and the last major one built by the BED was the magnificent 13 km Daisankyō Toll Road in 1970, which successfully opened the western coast. Each was operated on a toll basis until paid for; the Kanpū Road was paid for in 1986, the Nyūdōzaki Hachibōdai Road in 1989, and the Daisankyō Road in 1991. At its own expense, Oga City completed the newest major artery on the peninsula, the Namahage Line, in 1999; this eased access to the far end of the peninsula.

Like the improved transport in Yūbari in Hokkaidō, these roads represent a paradox of progress, for the increased accessibility generated by the investment in transportation has resulted in a decreased need for visitors to stay overnight, thereby eroding the long-term earning potentials of some local businesses, especially those in the hospitality sector. With easy access, tourists can now get out to the area quickly, have a hot spring bath and a meal of fresh local food, and get back home fairly early. The paradox of transportation in this scenario holds that increasing the cost or difficulty of access to the tourist, whether by charging tolls or by limiting road improvement, will make visitors more likely to spend more time, and more money, once they are in the area. This view was also expressed by a civil servant in a community centre:

> People don't have to necessarily stay a night if they come out to Oga anymore. Years ago I visited the Nōtō Peninsula (Ishikawa Prefecture) and I'll tell you—if you go all the way out to the end, it's unlikely that you'll make it back home that same day. Hotel owners out there can easily get those visitors for the night. They're lucky. (Donald C. Wood, interview with employee of Oga City, June 2005)

Regardless of whether toll roads or free roads are better for Oga, new roads have contributed more than any other factor to the development of tourism there, but visitations to parks like Oga's are now on the decline. According to local government data, there were 16.16 million visits in 2002, compared with just under 12 million in 2008 (Akita ken, 2010, p. 167)—though care must be taken with these data because tourism-facility visitor numbers are often subject to problems of double counting.

The Oga Aquarium (Old and New)

Akita Prefecture built its first aquarium on the rocky western shore of Oga, at the entrance to Toga Bay, in 1967. Although designed by the Tokyo-based Daiken Sekkei Corporation, the planning, building, and management of the facility was overseen by the BED. Visitor numbers remained fairly high throughout the facility's first 15 years but then steadily declined from 442,477 visits in 1968, to 114,717 visits in 2001, the last year of operation. In 1991, the year the Daisankyō road became toll free, there were 20,000 more visits than the previous year.

In the autumn of 2002, construction began on a new facility. Daiken Sekkei was again awarded the building contract, which totalled about JPY 7 billion—roughly 10 times the cost of the former facility. Commonly known as GAO, which stands for 'Globe, Aqua, and Ocean,' the words arranged to constitute a new brand identity, the new aquarium opened in July 2004 with three floors and at about twice the internal area of the original (photo 9.1).

There were immediate complaints about the new facility. Many claimed that it was difficult to feel close to the animals and that it lacked

PHOTO 9.1. The new aquarium, GAO.

Photo by Donald C. Wood (June 2005).

the distinctive sea scent of the old aquarium. Local residents complained that the aquarium was set too far from the area's villages—a problem of distance often overlooked by politicians and bureaucrats—and that they were not allowed to operate food stands or sell local products outside the new facility, something they had done when the old building was in operation.

The changes are in part a result of the aquarium's current management structure. The original aquarium was operated under a third-sector arrangement. First appearing in 1973 under a plan originally drafted by the cabinet of Prime Minister Ikeda (Imamura, 1991, p. 16), *third sector* basically describes a union between a public body and a private enterprise in the form of a small-scale joint-stock corporation owned by both. It was really a private enterprise with strong government connections, operating like a commercial subsidiary of a governmental body. A large number of hotels, hospitals, and other facilities have been run in this manner since the mid-1970s; often located in rural areas, most probably could not have existed otherwise. Through third-sector companies, Tokyo wanted to stimulate economic and infrastructure development—essentially to help improve lifestyles and conditions in outlying regional areas, with some notable successes (Bailey, 1991, p. 200). However, in practice many such facilities became somewhat distanced from local residents, who were often unable to get through the complicated bureaucracy of the management systems in order to obtain jobs. More important, third-sector undertakings developed a reputation for wasteful and unprofitable business practices, and became targets for much criticism (Ikuma, 2002). The publically subsidised third-sector facilities were also usually able to continue operation despite running at a loss.

In 2003 the national government mandated that by September 2006, public facilities not directly managed by a government body (as the original aquarium had been) would be operated under a new designated-operator (*shitei kanrisha*) system (Idei, 2005). Local governments would have to conduct a public search for a legal entity to operate a facility, and this entity would contract with the local government to manage a facility for a set period, at the conclusion of which either another open bidding process would take place or operations would continue under the original contract (if changing operators would likely have demonstrably negative effects). In addition to allowing local governments to reduce and control their budgets, this system was expected to improve services. However, the system's complexity and limited flexibility have proven to be major drawbacks (Idei, 2005, p. 34).

Since it opened, GAO has been managed by the Oga Aquarium Corporation (OAC), which was created by Akita's prefectural government and which brought in the Saitama-based Kokudo Corporation for its management expertise. The breakdown of stock ownership for the OAC is as follows: Akita Prefecture, 51 percent; Oga City, 31 percent; Kokudo Corporation, 10 percent; and 2 percent each for Akita Bank, Hokuto Bank, Akita Central Transportation, and the Oga Tourism Association (OTA). Kokudo's share entitles it to place one of its own employees in the general manager position. All others working at GAO are employed by the OAC itself. Many are Oga natives, because commuting from major cities off the peninsula is impractical, but there are now no Toga residents on the payroll. Some locals have donated live specimens for the open 'touching pool,' and some have volunteered as guides inside the facility and also as attendants in the parking lots, especially on weekends and during busy periods. But no locals operate food stands or other kinds of shops outside the facility, as they once did. In this case, the original third-sector arrangement was better for integrating the aquarium into local community life.

The Namahage-kan and the Denshō-kan

The Shinzan Shrine, high in the central mountains of Oga, is the focus of Namahage lore and activity. The Namahage are supernatural creatures that, according to folk custom, pay visits to Oga households every New Year's Eve in order to scare children and their young mothers into behaving themselves during the coming year (see Y. Yamamoto, 1978). A Namahage visit is also believed to chase away any malevolent spirits that might be lingering about and thus to bring good luck to the household. The roles are played by young men of the area who wear masks and straw coats (*kede*) and stomp and roar loudly for effect. Namahage are

Photo 9.2. The Namahage-kan.

Photo by Donald C. Wood (June 2005).

not the only kind of *ko-shōgatsu* (New Year) visitors in Akita, or even in the country, for that matter, but they are probably the most famous today. Located a short walk from the shrine is the Namahage-kan, a modest museum celebrating the history and local cultural value of the creatures (photo 9.2). The main attractions of the museum are a theatre that shows short films and a large room with a variety of life-sized Namahage, each with a different mask, illustrating that every hamlet in Oga originally had its own mask style.

The Oga Shinzan Denshō-kan is an old farmhouse standing between the museum and the shrine and was brought in from another location. At the Denshō-kan, visitors can experience a re-enacted Namahage house

PHOTO 9.3. A Namahage harassing visitors inside the Densho-kan.

Photo by Donald C. Wood (June 2005).

visit, complete with brief explanations and two noisy Namahage that freely harass the guests (photo 9.3). They can watch the creatures search in vain for children and the young mother of the house, and see the grandfather placate them with food and cups of saké and then send them on their way with promises to make sure his grandchildren and daughter-in-law work hard the following year.

The Namahage-kan was built by Oga City but is managed by the small joint-stock corporation Oga Shinkō Kōsha. Of the facility's 250 shares, 200 are owned by Oga City, 12 by Akita Prefecture, 10 by Akita Chūō Kōtsū (Akita Central Transportation), 10 by the Akita Prefecture Fishing Co-operative, 8 by Hokuto Bank, 5 by the South Akita Agricultural

Co-operative, and 5 by Akita Shinkin Bank. The Oga Shinkō Kōsha originated under a third-sector arrangement but has now been contracted as a designated operator, creating closer ties to area residents. These ties are reflected in a local volunteer group selling handmade postcards in the gift shop and in the presence of volunteer guides in the museum. Having older men serve as guides in the museum capitalizes not only on their understanding of the Namahage but on also their experience in performing Namahage in their youth. The museum's close ties with the community as a whole are also reflected in its relationship with the Denshō-kan, which is owned by the shrine and operated entirely by volunteers. Visitors to the museum can buy a ticket for the museum alone or for both the museum and the Denshō-kan.

Nyūdōzaki and the Onsen Area

One of the first lighthouses built in Japan was at Nyūdōzaki—the northernmost tip of the Oga peninsula—in 1898, and there has been one in operation there ever since. Nyūdōzaki is one of the region's most scenic points, making it an excellent site for tourism development, which began with the US Army's building a radar base in the area and a small airstrip on the point in 1946. As many as 200 military men (many with families) were posted there at one time, prompting nearby residents to open temporary shops and bars. The Americans left Oga in 1955, but by that time buses had started bringing Akita residents out onto the peninsula, and a local tourism industry was born. Then, to prepare for hosting the *kokutai* national athletic competition in 1961, the Akita government rearranged the shops in a straight line on the inner edge of a grassy field facing the lighthouse and the sea beyond, and prepared a parking lot. Today there are seven large souvenir shops and restaurants forming a neat row, there is a locally owned boat-ride business on the beach, and the lighthouse is open to visitors during certain times of the year.

Just to the east of Nyūdōzaki is Yumoto, the *onsen* area, where people have been enjoying the waters since at least the early Edo period. Today there are 10 hotels of different sizes clustered there. Local residents' homes and small bars are scattered among the smaller hotels. The hotels, although in competition with one another, are also united by membership in the Oga Hot Spring Co-operative Association, which uses the membership dues to distribute advertising materials and operate a website with links to each hotel. The co-operative also provides buses between the *onsen* area and Oga Station, as well as a 'sunset bus' that takes visitors to Nyūdōzaki to watch the sunset over the Japan Sea.

The co-operative has also helped organise Namahage drumming shows. The group Namahage Sato Kagura performs an embellished form of *taiko* drumming while dressed as Namahage, and its performances have attracted much attention across the country. Originally there was no central place for the group to perform, so they moved from hotel to hotel, but in 2007 the city, in tandem with the local tourism association, built a new hall in the hot-spring area where the drummers now perform regularly. This new facility has become a major selling-point for the *onsen* area and is an example of the local government's improving tourism conditions on the peninsula. With control of public funds, it can create new facilities for the benefit of a particular spot. However, data indicate that visits to the *onsen* area are on the decline: 195,000 visits were reported for 2003, but this had dropped to 153,000 in 2008 (Akita ken, 2010, p. 168).

Hotel Kiraraka (Sakurajima-sō)

In 1979 the BED opened the doors of Sakurajima-sō Hotel (photo 9.4), which remained a popular stop for drivers on the Daisankyō Road for years. The hotel offers hot-spring baths, and the dining room has a fine view of the sea and a variety of fresh fish on the menu. Despite the hotel's amenities and scenic location, however, it consistently operated at a loss. In the wake of the national government's drive to eliminate the third sector, the BED eventually let go of Sakurajima-sō, and its doors closed in autumn 2003.

Akita Prefecture soon put the facility up for sale, and the highest bid came from the Warabi-za, a theatre group based south of Lake Tazawa, 75 km away. Warabi-za was founded in February 1951 by a handful of performers living in a commune-like setting, but it has changed dramatically since then; it became a joint-stock corporation in 1971. Its headquarters are at the Tazawako Art Village, which includes a hotel (complete with an *onsen*), art galleries, a brewery that produces Tazawako Beer, and the Warabi-za Theatre. The corporation has over JPY 750 million in capital and has numerous satellite business offices across the country, including in Tokyo and Osaka. The company's website explains:

> Warabiza uses Japanese traditions to shed light on various aspects of modern humanity. Through its activities, Warabiza focuses on positive potential in humans and presents this image of happiness and cooperation to as many people as possible. Modern society is filled with violence that seems to deny the humanity in people. Nevertheless, Warabiza is committed to its love for humanity and

Photo 9.4. Sakurajima-sō, reborn as Hotel Kiraraka.

Photo by Donald C. Wood (June 2005).

> for each and every human being. Warabiza's purpose is to depict human dignity and love and to give people vital energy through its artistic activities. (Warabi-za, 2005)

Under the management of Warabi-za, the coastal facility reopened as Hotel Kiraraka in 2004. Its original appearance was maintained, and most of the current employees live in Oga. Locals handle the day-to-day management, and the general manager is an Akita native who has experience managing facilities in the Tazawako Art Village. Although business is generally good on warm weekends, the winter season is problematic. Warabi-za performs small-scale shows on weekends, but the place is too small for larger shows, and the company does not have the resources to put on full-scale shows there. As with the aquarium, the original third-sector arrangement was actually better for most casual travellers—Sakurajima-sō was special primarily because of its view, but it also had a range of low-cost dishes on the menu. It was cheap and easy to feed children there, so families and younger people would often stop for lunch on weekends. Kiraraka's menu is tailored more for adults, so it is less attractive as a stopping point for people looking to keep their food expenses down. Nevertheless, the regional shrinkage that doomed Sakurajima-sō provided an opportunity for the Warabi-za to expand and do more for Akita. Perhaps the group can turn Kiraraka around in the future.

The Oga Tourism Association (OTA)

In most parts of Japan, layers of entities tie together different tourism elements. This is the same for Oga, where the city tourism division and the Oga Tourism Association (OTA) operate simultaneously. The city office is, of course, a public entity staffed by city employees. It has an annually fluctuating budget, and it must consider all of Oga (which grew in 2005 by merging with the town of Wakami), not only the peninsula itself. This consideration, together with the inherent separation between government and the various individual actors on the peninsula's tourism scene, limits the speed, versatility, and precision with which the division can act to stimulate local growth. One of the things it can do, however, is initiate large-scale development with public funds—like the Namahage performance facility in the *onsen* area, for example.

In contrast to the city office, the OTA has a more stable but much smaller budget. It is fairly flexible, it can reach different local actors quickly, and it is the main source of direct information for tourists. The association was founded in 1954 as a nonprofit operation, and it is still located in a small building next to Oga Station in Funagawa. The OTA collects dues from the various districts on the peninsula, and facilities and proprietors pay according to their level of involvement and ability to pay. Each area selects a representative to report to the association and vote on proposals. In Nyūdōzaki, the shop owners (all relatively equal) pool their money to pay dues and take turns serving as representative. At Toga Bay, however, the aquarium can pay much more than the local inn operators, so its proportion of the area dues is greater.

Contradictions in Strategic Tourism Development Planning in Oga

It should come as no surprise that the development of a tourism industry on the Oga Peninsula has been a somewhat fragmented and disjointed affair from the beginning. After all, the landmass did not originally fall under the control of a single municipal entity, and its hamlets and villages were quite independent during the early postwar years, when Oga's tourism industry was born. Moreover, the peninsula is geographically very rough and varied. Before the main roads were built and cars became commonplace, individual settlements were more isolated from one another than they are today; even with the roads in place, geographical distance remains a problem in matters of unity. Additionally, in the 1950s the people of Oga were not very concerned with luring visitors—most got by on fishing and farming and off-season work in other locales (*dekasegi*). This is not to say that residents enjoyed an idyllic and quaint rural life. It was a difficult existence, but there were many more people (including children) than there are today, and the outlook for future development was good.

To start with, it was important for the prefectural (and national) government to help build up Oga as a specific place for living in and visiting in Akita. As in the case explained by Bailey (1991), an 'Oga identity' was established through municipal mergers, the most recent one in 2005. These mergers were imposed upon the people of Oga from the top and orchestrated locally, but money also flowed in from Tokyo in return (Rausch, 2005a; Samuels, 1983). Today only one municipal body handles all matters of life on the landmass. It was also crucial for the prefectural government to build up the peninsula's infrastructure (mainly roads) and establish most of the earliest tourism attractions, including the aquarium and Sakurajima-sō. This trend also generally conforms to that described by Bailey (1991). However, whereas Bailey presented a case in which one individual was largely responsible for luring public money to the community for development and for organising everything, in Oga no such single leader has emerged, although local mayors were instrumental in the prefecture's early start on road-building. This basic framework set Oga on its current path.

More recently, the Akita prefectural government has been able to largely back away from funding and operating tourist facilities on the peninsula because Oga has achieved some level of independence, and most of the necessary infrastructure is now in place. Public funding for local projects is now harder to obtain because there is simply less funding available and the competition to obtain it has increased. Consequently, money for tourism endeavours now has to be gathered locally (Thompson, 2006). The tourist spots and facilities covered here have largely moved toward local funding. The Namahage-kan and Denshō-kan are almost entirely locally funded, although Akita Prefecture and a few other external entities own stock in the former. The shops at Nyūdōzaki have always been privately owned, and the *onsen* area hotels and other businesses have always been owned by a combination of both local and external interests. But the Oga City government took a significant step in building the Namahage drumming venue—a public initiative but also a local one, with high levels of resident participation in its operation. The prefectural government-run Sakurajima-sō has re-emerged as the privately owned Hotel Kiraraka.

Like the hotels in the *onsen* area, it employs mostly local people. It is, however, struggling as a private entity.

But Akita Prefecture's financial stepping away from Oga can also be seen as a redistribution of resources in its overall investment in Oga—cutting off noticeably wasteful spending on unprofitable ventures and increasing spending on the aquarium, which is arguably the key piece of the Oga tourism package. This position is witnessed in the frequency with which the aquarium is featured on the evening news programmes of various national television networks—a reflection of the prefectural government's influence. However, the aquarium's ownership and management structure (not to mention its design) have made it more socially distant from the local population than its predecessor was. Given this tension, it seems fair to question the priorities of Akita Prefecture: Is the government more concerned to have an aquarium that provides a connection to the people of Oga (not to mention Toga Bay) or to have one that can be held up as evidence that Akita can build an aquarium that not only resembles Okinawa's Churaumi facility but that also has a polar bear (it has one)? And the aquarium is not the only facility that was closer to the public in its earlier, third-sector form. Sakurajima-sō has also changed in a similar way, with a similar result. The main difference between the two is that the prefecture still owns the aquarium and will not let it sink—for now. Notably, Feng (2008) reported on a situation in rural Hunan Province, China, that mirrors the plight of Oga (and many other parts of regional Japan) in the wake of the massive, sudden privatisation of the county's cultural resources for tourism development—a shift that has brought benefits to only a limited few while effectively barring most residents from accessing those resources and forcing them to pay the costs of the new system. In other words, the new public–private partnership, much touted by the local government, has basically failed the local people. Japan's situation is not as drastic, but the lessons are not so very different.

As for Oga's facilities and their ownership and operation, a look at the gift shops of different tourism facilities on the peninsula is telling. Many items sold in these shops offer little contribution to the local economy beyond the profits of the gift shop itself, such as cookies or crackers in the shape of a locally famous image or bearing the area's name or symbol—but these items are manufactured elsewhere. Although Oga shops generally sell these mass-produced treats—items of unknown origin suggesting local products, landmarks, or traditions (e.g., Chinese-made ball-point pens with Namahage characters on them)—mixed in with locally grown and made items (e.g., Oga seaweed, dried strips of squid, Namahage masks carved by area artisans), once again, the aquarium gift shop provides the exception. Stocked with plastic sharks and stuffed polar bear dolls, cookies in metal cans and paper boxes, each with the GAO insignia and cartoon-like fish on them, the shop sells virtually nothing of local origin or manufacture.

The Namahage-kan, however, is different. Its gift shop carries a number of original, locally made items, such as postcards, bookmarks, carvings, and foods. Local volunteer guides are crucial to the museum's operation, and the Denshō-kan is run on an entirely volunteer basis and is locally owned and managed. Though debates over the authenticity of the performances might confirm that such staged authenticity (MacCannell, 1999) reflects Boorstin's (1992) assertion that tourists seek 'pseudo-events' for their diversion, perhaps the most effective way to analyse what the Denshō-kan offers is in terms of Taylor's (2000) notion of *sincerity in tourism*. In this case, sincerity is what comes of honest interactions between outsiders and locals, or the bearers and actual practitioners of tradition (Wood, 2004, 2005). It is not about convincing anyone that what they are seeing with their own eyes is 'the real thing,' but rather it is meant to convey a certain sense of what happens or happened, among local inhabitants and when the performer is not constrained by the act of producing culture for the purpose of tourist consumption. At the Denshō-kan, local volunteers are sharing their tradition with the public, mainly on their own terms.

As mentioned, the fragmented nature of Oga's tourism industry is not only due to its history; geography also poses a problem. Moon (1989) found in a village in Gunma Prefecture that the building of a ski resort resulted in friction between those who were able to benefit from its presence and those who were not. In Oga, the peninsula residents are scattered over a large area, and those who are concerned about tourism and in a position to benefit from it can look to the city's tourism division and, more important, to the OTA for help. The latter especially unites participants, although it has a very limited budget and has some imperfections (of which the dues arrangement stands out). But the Namahage drumming facility in the Yumoto *onsen* area is an example of effective coordination between the OTA and relevant local parties and of the city's strong connection with the peninsula's tourism package.

The Namahage tradition also unites the people of Oga. As Thompson (2006) argued, such traditional folk (*minzoku*) practices have enjoyed a comeback in recent years 'because as a countermeasure to contemporary societal changes, they link the past meaningfully to the future by helping those associated with its practice to transcend the outmoded boundaries of hometown folk performance in the present' (p. 127). The Namahage tradition, although it has faded somewhat as a ritual (Smith, 1978), has recently burst out across the entire prefecture as a tourist attraction, and the Oga Namahage (not the only such New Year's Eve visitors in the area) have become the mascots and symbols of Akita Prefecture itself. Likenesses of them appear at every tourist spot on the peninsula, including the aquarium. They are unhindered by geographical barriers. The Namahage is a—perhaps *the*—prime tourism resource for Oga. It fits in well with the peninsula's cultural tourism assemblage and contrasts with the more glamorous and expensive prefecture-owned aquarium. Related to Feng's (2008) findings in China, Chambers (1997) has warned of the dangers inherent to 'the appropriation of cultural resources in ways that bear little relationship to local knowledge or vitality' (p. 13). This warning comes specifically in reference to Whittaker's (1997) conclusion that even massive and locally directed tourism ventures can fail if they do not relate much to—or at least feed the interests of—the local population. Similarly, in the village of Ogata-mura, near Oga, locally initiated projects proved to be largely unsustainable because they failed in their appeal to the host population, resulting in greater social fragmentation (Wood, 1999, 2003).

The situation of the Namahage of Oga is different; it is better than that of the local traditional dance described by Thompson (2006) in Iwate

Prefecture. Even though the aquarium and the Namahage-kan were both built and are owned by government entities and are now run by designated operators, the latter is closer to the people of Oga as a whole than the former. This is partly because the local government built it but also because its message appeals to local sentiment and its mission is deeply embedded in local culture. This is the best recipe for successful local development, including that of tourism (Itō, 2000). In other words, considering the aquarium in opposition to the Namahage-kan/Denshō-kan combination suggests that this cultural factor has the power to transcend the institutional arrangements of public versus private or designated operator versus local volunteers. It was the Namahage drumming (a local grassroots initiative) that recently drew the city to invest in the Yumoto *onsen* area, thus forging a stronger connection between that spot and the centre of Namahage lore and activity high in the mountains above, and providing the potential to boost business at Nyūdōzaki, which is linked to the *onsen* area by local bus. Furthermore, the Oga City government is now leading a drive to obtain UNESCO Intangible Cultural Heritage status for the Namahage tradition. If this initiative succeeds, additional financial support for the tradition—and anything related to the Namahage—will be easier to obtain from Akita City and perhaps also from Tokyo. As a point of local appeal, local control, and local funding, the Namahage can perhaps be Oga's saving grace as the area grapples with the brutal effects of a shrinking population and a stagnating tourism market. At any rate, it is clear that the entrenched 'if we build it, they will come' approach to tourism that disregards local appeal and culture in regional Japan is now at a dead end—a lesson that will probably not go unheeded in Oga.

Resorts or Repeaters in the Remote Islands of Okinawa?

Tourism is massively important to the Okinawan economy. Moreover, the promotion of *ritō* (outlying islands) tourism is seen as vital to sustaining viable communities in the rural peripheral islands by officials at all levels in the Okinawan Prefectural government and by many locals themselves. In 2008 some 5.9 million tourists visited the prefecture, generating JPY 436.5 billion in revenue (Okinawa ken, 2009a). However, the prefectural government appears locked into a policy of ever-increasing reliance on tourism. Despite concerns that overcapacity and decreasing domestic expenditure on tourism will lead to increasing competition between operators and with other regions, the governor's objective is to raise the annual number of tourists to 10 million (Okinawa ken kankō kikaku ka, 2008, pp. 2–3). In 2007 about 754,000 visitors made it down to Ishigaki and 543,000 to the Miyako region. The designation of much of the maritime environment of the Ishigaki islands as Japan's newest national park in August 2007 (extending the original Iriomote National Park) is perceived as a strengthened opportunity for the prefecture to reinvent its tourist image by boosting *ritō* tourism, though rebranding as a national park also brings zoning requirements and restricts development. Moreover, there are clearly limits to the numbers of tourists that small island communities can accommodate—and clean up after.

Just what kind of tourism is appropriate for the *ritō* is therefore subject to debate. Although the resort model of tourist development has made inroads into the outlying islands of the prefecture, these areas have seen relatively little of the large-scale resort development that many believe blights the main island of Okinawa (McCormack, 2003). Miyako has a large Tōkyū operated beach resort and even a struggling German Village theme park, and it has built sports facilities to attract professional baseball teams for winter training camps. Ishigaki hosts All Nippon Airways, Japan Airlines, and Club Med resorts that cater to package-tour groups, and cruise ships from Taiwan call there during the summer. Nevertheless, local officials are increasingly wary of such developments and associated package tours that bring large numbers of tourists for a limited time in a highly controlled fashion, leaving behind considerable rubbish but little income in the hands of locals. These officials are proud of their distinct local identities and keen to promote sustainable tourism in tune with the environment and local culture (R. Siddle, interview at Ishigaki Town Office, 8 April 2008).

So prefectural and municipal tourism officials in Okinawa aim, instead, for *repeaters*: independent tourists who stay for longer, use local lodgings, leave a kinder footprint, and often return. Overall, whereas in the 1980s over 80 percent of tourists were first-time visitors, in 1997 the proportion of repeater tourists to Okinawa Prefecture overtook first-time visitors and has remained slightly higher ever since (Okinawa ken kankō kikaku ka, 2009, pp. 9–10). In the same year, independent tourists became the largest single category (although organised tour groups, including school trips, and package-holiday tourists combined still accounted for 63.5 percent of visitors (Okinawa ken kankō kikaku ka, 2009, p. 7).

One of the aims of the prefecture's Third Tourism Promotion Plan (2008–2011), alongside the inevitable resort development and increasing the numbers of foreign visitors, is to pursue 'the realisation of high quality Okinawa tourism' including repeaters, long-stay and *ritō* tourism (Okinawa ken kankō kikaku ka, 2008, p. 1). Some 14 new styles of tourism have been identified, including ecotourism, heritage tours, nature study, trekking, health, volunteer work, camping, and urban tourism (Okinawa ken kankō kikaku ka, 2009, p. 5). Diving has attracted independent visitors over the years (in addition to its inclusion in packaged tours), and is now one of the major tourist activities throughout the islands. For the *ritō*, these trends can be broadly summarised in two main alternative models of reinventing tourism to the outlying islands, models that have begun to emerge with the aim of encouraging the repeater. One is cultural tourism, perhaps most completely practised in Taketomi, which has almost become a living museum of *ritō* culture. The other is ecotourism, exemplified by the canoe operators and nature tours of Iriomote.

Resorts

One factor hindering the development of large-scale resorts in outlying islands is the lack of transportation infrastructure—in particular, airports capable of handling large jets. Whereas Naha airport in Okinawa sees numerous jumbo jets hourly disgorging tour groups, the outer islands have only a handful of airports large enough for even small passenger-jet aircraft. Miyako airport was upgraded in 1983 and again in 1997 to take medium-sized passenger aircraft, and smaller jets can land at Ishigaki and Yonaguni. One impetus for the new airport planned on Ishigaki was the stimulation of tourism. Initially proposed in 1979, the new facility was successfully opposed for years by citizens' and residents' groups who emphasised its destructive impact on the environment (Tanji, 2003). The final plan has incorporated various environmental safeguards, including a reconstructed habitat for an endangered species of bat. Development of this kind has also been opposed by newcomers, mainly retirees or alternative-lifestyle seekers from urban Japan who settle or spend lengthy periods on Ishigaki and who resent the shattering of their dream of a rural tropical idyll. Often possessing considerable social capital and organisational capabilities, such residents have banded together and antagonised locals who see development as a way of increasing their own incomes and keeping their families together.

The resort mentality is certainly not dead in the *ritō*. The small island of Kohama near Ishigaki, famous in Japan as the location for the popular television series *Churasan*, boasts the exclusive Haimurubushi Resort complex, complete with private beach, pool, ranch, golf course, tennis courts, and conference and wedding facilities (Haimurubushi, 2009). It employs 91 people, about one fifth of the island's population. Developed by the Yamaha Corporation, it was sold to Mitsui Real Estate in 2007 due to poor profits (Yamaha, 2007). Despite the severe operating conditions that plague such resorts, in post-bubble Japan some local authorities still dream of a resort of their own. The tiny isolated island of Hateruma, Japan's southernmost point with an area of less than 13 km^2 (of which half is occupied by sugarcane), is nurturing a plan for a small-scale 60-bed resort on an isolated northern beach to accompany a new airport. There was only one 30-bed hotel along with a few smaller guest houses on the island in 2007. Locals are desperate to revive the local air service and also to keep some of their 30 schoolchildren on the island. But this raises the issue of human resources, and whether the jobs available will match the skills and aspirations of local youth or will be filled by seasonal labour brought in and housed by the resort's management company.

Cultural Tourism

In contrast to resort development, the distinct cultural heritage of the *ritō* is an asset that can be reinvented, commoditised, and packaged for tourists. The islands display considerable variation within the archipelago, but their food, architecture, clothing, music, language, religion, and social organisation are different enough from those on the Japanese mainland for some academics and activists to have classified Okinawans as a separate ethnic group, although this classification usually has more to do with politics than with any objective differences (Siddle, 2003). Prewar folklore scholars, in contrast, saw in Okinawa instead surviving elements of a 'pure' Japanese culture that had been corrupted by modernity in Japan proper, although the masked festivals and gods of some of the smaller islands may well have roots in Southeast Asia. The exposure of local cultural practices to

PHOTO 9.5. Shuri Castle, Okinawa.

Photo by Richard Siddle.

the anthropological and touristic gaze has not been without consequences; in the postwar period the masked Akamata Kuromata festival in the tiny islands of Aragusuku became notorious not only for its secret initiation rites but also for violence directed against intrusive outsiders. Even now, the tiny handful of visitors who do make it to Aragusuku by private charter are strictly warned not to enter any shrines (Ishigaki shi, 2009).

The marketing of local culture has always featured alongside the beaches in Okinawan tourism, especially since the reconstruction of Shuri Castle in the early 1990s and its designation as a UNESCO World Heritage site in 2000. Alongside this 'high' culture of the historic Ryūkyū Kingdom, the prefecture has recently identified previously 'underutilised' aspects of everyday Okinawan lifestyle and culture, popularised by mainland media attention and health fads, that can be turned into tourist resources—including cuisine and health foods, music, and dance (Okinawa ken kankō kikaku ka, 2009, p. 17). Many localities in Japan objectify and market their culture for domestic tourism, appealing to the nostalgic image of the *furusato* as an antidote to the ills of modern urban life. This is *heritage tourism*, based on a local sense of place and in which there is less concern with the preservation of an authentic past than with its idealised representation, the confirmation of a local identity in the face of globalisation. The culture of the *ritō*, however, does not resonate with the imagined *furusato* of the average Japanese visitor; instead, here the exotic, reinvented Other becomes the object of the tourist's gaze. Rides in carts pulled by water buffalo, for instance, feature prominently in Taketomi.

In the *ritō*, Taketomi more than any other island has pursued an agenda of cultural tourism to boost local livelihoods and retain its young people. Taketomi is a small (circumference 9.2 km), flat, circular island off the coast of Ishigaki (see Ishigaki shi, 2009). It consists of a central settlement of traditional Okinawan houses, red-tiled wooden dwellings with guardian lions (*shiisa*) on the roofs, surrounded by coral walls and flowering tropical plants. The narrow streets are covered with dazzlingly white crushed coral sand. Visitors hire bicycles to get around, or take a water buffalo–cart ride. There are few vehicles on the island, mainly minibuses that shuttle the short distance between the village and the ferry terminal and the odd farmer's truck on the tarmac road that circles the island's periphery. It is a pretty and a tranquil place (after the day-trippers have gone), the picture-postcard-perfect vision of an apparently authentic, traditional Okinawa.

Naturally, it is not as authentic as it seems. The 'traditional' houses with their tiled roofs, for instance, are not peasant dwellings. Roof tiles and *shiisa* were the preserve of the nobility during the days of the Ryūkyū Kingdom; the peasant made do with straw. Nevertheless, Taketomi has taken advantage of its heritage, environment, compact size, and convenient location (just 10 minutes from Ishigaki by high-speed passenger boat) to remake itself as a major tourist destination. In 2007 about 513,000 tourists visited this island of only 344 residents, the overwhelming majority on day trips from Ishigaki.

The cultural heart of Taketomi is the newly constructed Yugafukan (Taketomi Visitor Centre), a local museum and resource centre next to the small ferry terminal. It is, in essence, a heritage centre. Heritage objects (buildings, sites, artefacts) are vehicles to bring the past into the present and confer identity. Heritage sites treat the 'inauthentic' (simulations, reconstructions, replicas) as equivalent to the 'authentic' (artefacts). Unlike museums in the traditional sense, heritage centres do not seek to preserve the past but to represent or even reinvent it. In its displays, videos, and performances, the Yugafukan aims to impress on visitors the spirit and culture of the island (R. Siddle, interview in Taketomi, 11 April 2008). The curator of the centre fully recognised that cultural practices and identities are not static but change with the times. One example concerns the island's major festival, the Tanedori, held every November and promoted as an excellent way to see the 'more than 600 years of history that have been passed on through the generations' (Ishigaki shi, 2009). These ritual occasions always used to involve the slaughter of a cow, but the regulatory apparatus of the modern state has made that illegal without a license. The curator himself is a 'returnee' to the island, having actually been born and raised in Tokyo in a family of Taketomi origin. Aware of the conflicts between locals and outsiders on other islands, the elders of Taketomi have attempted to retain local

Photo 9.6. The post office on Taketomi complete with traditional relaid red roof tiles.

Photo by Richard Siddle.

control over tourism to the extent of discouraging outsiders from settling on the island. There is even a Taketomi constitution, though naturally it has no legal force. In such ways, and by presenting its heritage in the Yugafukan, the local community is attempting to retain control over the way it is represented and consumed.

Nevertheless, the experiences of other islands show that there is not necessarily a conflict between outsiders and the preservation of 'authentic' local culture. Indeed, outsiders have often been instrumental in seeking to preserve the cultural heart of the vision of tropical paradise in which they have invested. The involvement of newcomers has actually helped maintain or revive certain local traditions and festivals.

Despite the success of cultural tourism on Taketomi, there is also talk of a resort there. At present few visitors actually stay on the island because transport links with Ishigaki have made Taketomi a convenient stop on a tour group's itinerary. A resort was initially opposed by islanders, but many now believe that if constructed and managed in an appropriate and sensitive way, it could bring financial advantages (R. Siddle, interview in Taketomi, 11 April 2008).

Ecotourism

A third model of tourist development being attempted in the *ritō* is ecotourism. Divers have been coming for years to explore the rich coral reefs, and now efforts are being made to market other natural assets, in particular the unique (for Japan) mangrove swamps, subtropical forests, and wildlife of Iriomote island, home to Japan's only endemic species of cat, the Iriomote wildcat. In Zamami, close to Okinawa itself, whale-watching boat tours are very popular. The prefecture recognises this new trend and seeks to encourage it (Okinawa ken kankō kikaku ka, 2009, p. 4). Ecotourism fits the concept of the repeater, the independent tourist looking for an experience more unique than the package tour. Many of the visitors are wildlife enthusiasts or birdwatchers.

The nature of Iriomote has also been marketed for tour groups, which for years have been day-tripped over from Ishigaki and shuttled up and down the mangrove-lined banks of the Urauchi and Nakama rivers in high-speed boats. But according to the local Eco-Tourism Association (ETA), ecotourism is an attempt to foster quality over quantity—in other words, to entice repeaters, who will stay longer and make a smaller environmental impact (R. Siddle, interview in Iriomote, 10 April 2008). The association's volunteers monitor the environment and the wildlife, and attempt to raise awareness among tour operators. The ecological balance is already delicate; for instance, mangroves are damaged by the high waves caused by tour boats rushing to keep to schedules. The environmentally friendly alternative is to hire a canoe from one of the many small operators and paddle independently or in a small group. Guided nature treks through the jungle are also available.

The efforts of the ETA to promote environmentally friendly tourism are encountering obstacles, however. When the association held an Eco-Tourism Forum on the island in 2007 to raise awareness of the environmental impact of the river trips, only one of the big operators attended (R. Siddle, interview in Iriomote, 10 April 2008). Moreover, the canoe operators are all outsiders and tend to resent attempts to organise them. Here again, conflicts arise between locals and outsiders with respect to resources. Another example is conflict throughout the islands between dive operators, again nearly all outsiders, and local fisherman over dive sites on the coral reefs.

Sustainable Tourism in the *Ritō*

In practise, most of the islands promote a combination of these styles of tourism. Iriomote, for instance, combines ecotourism with a couple of small-scale resorts, one boasting Japan's most southerly *onsen* (hot-spring) resort. Yonaguni, which receives about 40,000 tourists annually, markets its geographical location as Japan's most westerly point. It utilises the environment to promote marlin fishing and has become a famous diving spot since the discovery of massive underwater rock formations that resemble an ancient drowned city. It is also home to a unique breed of small horse that roams wild and a species of Atlas moth that is the largest in the world, celebrated in a local nature centre. With regard to heritage, Yonaguni has a small private museum and an active centre for the production of local hand-woven cloth, once produced as tribute for the Ryūkyū court. Local young women have both a connection to their heritage and a source of employment in the production of this cloth by traditional methods in a special workshop. Tourism has been further encouraged through a recent hit television show that depicted a local doctor and was filmed on location there (the filming itself brought a boost to the local economy when some 120 staff resided on the island for several months).

Some islands promote other images or commoditise other aspects of local life as part of their *machizukuri* or community-revitalisation planning. In Kohama, with its upmarket resort, an alternative form of tourism (boosted, no doubt, by the popularity of the television series

PHOTO 9.7. Tourists enjoy the tranquillity of a sandy beach on Hateruma.

Photo by Richard Siddle.

Churasan) encourages volunteers to stay for one to three months to help harvest sugarcane. Board and lodging is provided, but with no pay for this 'very tough' but 'rewarding' work (Ishigaki shi, 2009). Miyako, in contrast, with its baseball camps and triathlon, promotes itself as a sports island. Kuroshima, a major centre of beef production near Ishigaki where the couple hundred residents are heavily outnumbered by cattle, attracts visitors by hosting a Cow Festival every February that includes a tug-of-war between people and a cow (which usually wins). There is also an ecotourism dimension in Kuroshima, where a research centre is dedicated to preserving sea turtles (Ishigaki shi, 2009). The area's Marine Village resort, though, closed in September 2008.

Alongside more conventional policies to improve life in the outer islands, it seems likely that tourism will increasingly be a key strategy for halting population decline and alleviating its impact. Whether these efforts will be enough to encourage young people to stay or to return after completing higher education away from their home island or after periods of work in urban Japan is open to question. There must also be a limit to the numbers of tourists that the environment and the local infrastructure can sustain. Conflicts between locals and outsiders over resources, exacerbated by different perceptions of development, will continue to be an issue. Then there is the impact of tourism on the local way of life. Cultures are never static, and authenticity is always contested, but the enthusiastic commodification of culture as a tourist resource risks turning the *ritō* into a giant exotic theme park. Nevertheless, this reification of cultural forms and practices may ensure their survival, and their positive evaluation may raise their status as symbolic markers of a reinvigorated local identity.

Green Tourism in Kamaishi, Iwate Prefecture

The postwar history of Yūbari in Hokkaidō—both in its ascent, connected to Japan's industrial development, and in its descent as a shrinking city—mirror the rise and fall of the coal industry in the region; the history of Kamaishi also mirrors this trajectory to some extent, in this case bound up with the fate of the steel industry. Kamaishi is rediscovering its sense of place by combining its potential for tourism with a functioning industrial base within the city. As a part of this strategy, the city has begun the process of reinventing itself as a destination for green tourism based on the region's agricultural and fishery resources.

Reinventing Kamaishi as a Green Tourism Destination

For Kamaishi City to develop tourism in general and develop green tourism in particular, community and business leaders must confront the issue of image. Before turning to the specific case of green tourism in Kamaishi, we consider the place's pre-existing image and its potential image, specifically, the image of Kamaishi held by outsiders—both ordinary people from other areas and, perhaps more important, workers in the tourism industry nationwide.

Outsiders have long viewed Kamaishi as an industrial town in general terms and as a steel town in direct reference to its economic base. As such, Kamaishi does not have a base on which to build a strong image as a tourist area. Endo (2005) asserted that for 'tourism to exist ... the destination should be given significance as a tourist area and its image as a tourist area must be formed systematically' (pp. 94–95). Kamaishi's association as an industrial town does not advantage an image related to green tourism, either. Generally speaking, few tourists would want to experience nature, agriculture, and fishery in an industrial town. A participant of the Green Tourism Monitor Tour, an exploratory green tourism program organised by Kamaishi City in 2000, stated that 'for us outsiders, steel is associated with terms such as 'cold,' 'hard,' 'industry,' and so on, and it feels rather far from green tourism' (Kamaishi shi, 2000, p. 45). Using Endo's (2005) analysis of the tourist character of Nara City, near Osaka, as a methodological guide, the following evaluation considers the extent to which Kamaishi is viewed as a tourist location.

From July to September of 2007, Japan Railways (JR) East staged a North Tōhoku District Destination Campaign. In promotional materials for the campaign on its webpages, Iwate prefecture was divided into five areas, with Kamaishi included in the Hanamaki-Tōnō-Kamaishi area. Nine tourist spots were introduced in Hanamaki and six in Tōnō. The only information specific to Kamaishi was for a festival called Kamaishi Yoisa. Moreover, the May 2007 issue JR East's free monthly magazine for Shinkansen passengers, *Train Vert*, featured a 23-page section highlighting a 'trip to experience the life of Iwate,' but Kamaishi was not included in this special feature. Clearly, JR East does not consider Kamaishi a strong tourism destination that would attract passengers onto its super-express trains.

Whether a cause or a result of this limited exposure relative to that for other tourist locations in Iwate Prefecture, the aggregate number of visitors to Kamaishi for tourism and recreation purposes is fewer than the number visiting either Tōnō or Miyako, which are both often presented as tourism spots (table 9.1). Furthermore, the number of visitors to Kamaishi has been decreasing since 2000. The number of tourists was relatively stable at about 1.2–1.3 million through the 1990s (although it peaked at 2.32 million in 1992 with the Sanriku Sea Exhibition), but it started to decrease in 2000 and fell to about 1 million in 2009 (figure 9.2).

The weakness of Kamaishi's tourism image is recognised also in Kamaishi itself. In the draft version of the *Kamaishi Tourism Promotion Vision*, developed in 2006 by the city office, the following passages appear: 'Together with the mixed image of Kamaishi as a city of steel and fish, tourism too is stagnating because the city cannot be differentiated

TABLE 9.1. Aggregate Visitor Numbers to Kamaishi and Other Cities in Iwate Prefecture.

	Number of Visitors
Kamaishi	998.221
Tōnō	1,617,782
Miyako	1,591,360
Hanamaki	2,535,162
Hiraizumi	2,076,600

Source. Iwate ken (2010, p. 33).

FIGURE 9.2. Trend in the Aggregate Number of Visitors to Kamaishi (in thousands).

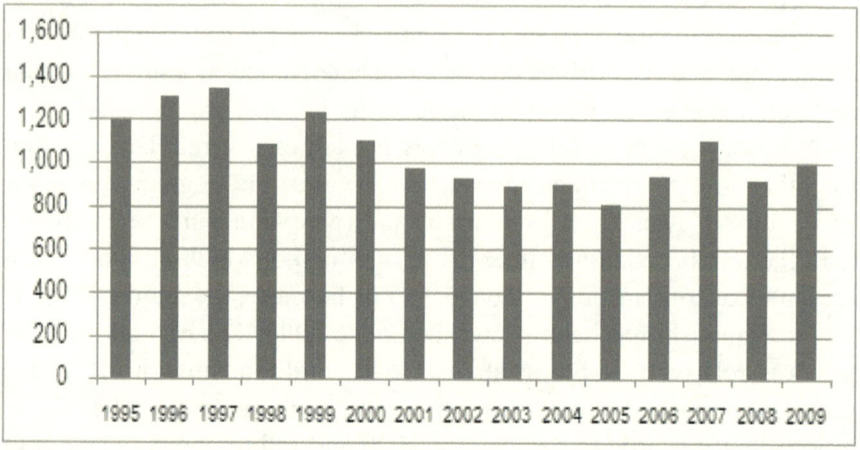

Sources. Iwate ken Kankō Kyōkai (2004, p. 41); Iwate ken (2010, p. 39).

from its neighboring cities'; 'Due to its strong image as an industrial city, Kamaishi lacks the image of a tourist area' (Kamaishi shi, 2006a, p. 27).

Because the image of Kamaishi as a tourist destination is weak, then, unless actors in the tourism industry come to hold an image of the city as a tourist spot, visitor numbers are not likely to increase. This is the background for the present examination of city tourism policies.

The Importance of Policy

In 2001 Kamaishi City drew up its fifth general city plan. One of the three 'basic goals for community building' was identified as creating a 'community with bustling and vigorous industries,' and to this end, a policy for 'building a bustling community' was cited. Specifically, the intention was to 'promote tourism utilizing the characteristics of the area, while promoting events and various exchanges between regions in order to increase the number of tourists' (Kamaishi shi, 2001, p. 17). The plan also established a goal of increasing the number of tourists from the 1.09 million attained in fiscal year 1998 to 1.29 million in fiscal year 2010 (Kamaishi shi, 2001, p. 50). However, in light of the reality of dwindling numbers of tourists, the basic plan for the second half of the fifth general plan, drawn up in 2006, revised the goal for 2010 to 1 million (Kamaishi shi, 2006b, p. 35).

The draft *Kamaishi Tourism Promotion Vision* suggests that an increase in tourism can be attained on the basis of two points. First, the ageing of the Japanese population overall and the increasing number of baby-boom-generation retirees will contribute to an increase in demand. Second, the construction of a new Sanriku expressway and port facilities serving the area will make it more accessible (the port was completed in fiscal year 2006). The vision plan also cites 'viewpoints to push tourism-related policies,' the most important of which is to 'establish tourism as an industry' that 'will be ensured through furthering the development of tourism whose aim has changed from exchange to settlement' (Kamaishi shi, 2006a, p. 35). Given these developments, the question arises whether an effective, comprehensive tourism project can be implemented.

First, the national government–sponsored Sennin Tōge Expressway, to which the Sanriku expressway will connect and which now connects the cities of Tōnō and Kamaishi, is already providing an increase in tourist visitors. With this improved access, numbers visiting Kamaishi during the 'golden week' vacation period in early May increased dramatically, by about 38,200 to approximately 87,600 in 2006–2007 (Yomiuri Shimbun, 2007). It is therefore likely that the Sanriku Expressway, which will connect Sendai and Miyako via Kamaishi, will also contribute to tourism in Kamaishi.

Improved access provided through national government infrastructure projects aside, there remains the question whether the city itself will be able to capitalise fully on its tourism potential, first and foremost because of a lack of proper recognition and utilisation of its present tourism resources and local attributes. Many local sites should be considered tourism resources but are being neither preserved nor upgraded. One example is the *Kyōjō ichiba*, literally, the *market on the bridge*.

This market was established in 1958 on the Oowatari Bridge spanning the Kasshi River that flows though the centre of Kamaishi City. A market building was constructed on the bridge where vendors sell various goods, from local marine products to daily necessities; due to its unique location, the site gained popularity as a local tourist attraction. However, as the Ōwatari Bridge aged, the prefectural government called for the market's relocation. Although the local retail association expressed opposition at first, it eventually agreed to the move in 1995, and the new market location opened in January 2003 (Niibari, 2004).

Another example is the *Kōyō no taki*, the *waterfall of autumn leaves*. The waterfall is situated along a tributary of the Katagishi River, which flows into Tōni Bay in the southern part of the city. It was featured as a tourist spot in a pamphlet published by the city and local residents cite this waterfall as a local resource (see Kamaishi shi, 2003, p. 41). However, by November 2006 the access road had become overrun with bushes, and a bridge across the river that provided an important part of the experience of the area was in a state of disrepair almost to the point of being unusable (photo 9.8). Though local residents may venture into the area, it would be quite difficult for tourists to enjoy the waterfall.

There are financial constraints on Kamaishi's capability to realise tourism goals, too. According to a medium-term financial forecast by the city, expenses are expected to surpass income from 2006 through 2010. The ratio of the balance was 90.9 percent in fiscal year 2006. Financial flexibility is lost with a ratio of over 80 percent, and consequently the level of financial freedom in Kamaishi is now low (Kamaishi shi, 2006c). Thus tourism-related projects have become harder for the city to carry out and so has the objective of building an image of Kamaishi as a tourist destination.

Considering the Views of Kamaishi's Residents

Although the intentions of the city government with regard to tourism are important, so are the views of local residents. In opinion surveys conducted in 1999 and 2004 by the city, residents were asked what kind

Photo 9.8. Remains of the bridge over the Katagaki River, upstream from the Kōyō no Taki.

Photo by Ken Ohori (November 2007).

of business should be given priority in city planning. The 1999 responses revealed a focus on marine products, for which 21.7 percent responded favourably, and the second-highest response was tourism, at 17.6 percent, followed by industry, at 16.6 percent. Responses were similar in the 2004 survey, in which the highest response again went to the marine products industry at 20.0 percent, with the second- and third-highest responses again given to tourism, at 18.6 percent, and industry, at 17.7 percent (figure 9.3).

Although expectations for tourism in Kamaishi City are high, so too are expectations for industry. It would therefore be an overstatement to argue that the citizens of Kamaishi fully desire a transformation from an

FIGURE 9.3. Kamaishi City Residents' Preferences for City Promotion, 1999 and 2004 (percentage of residents' opinions).

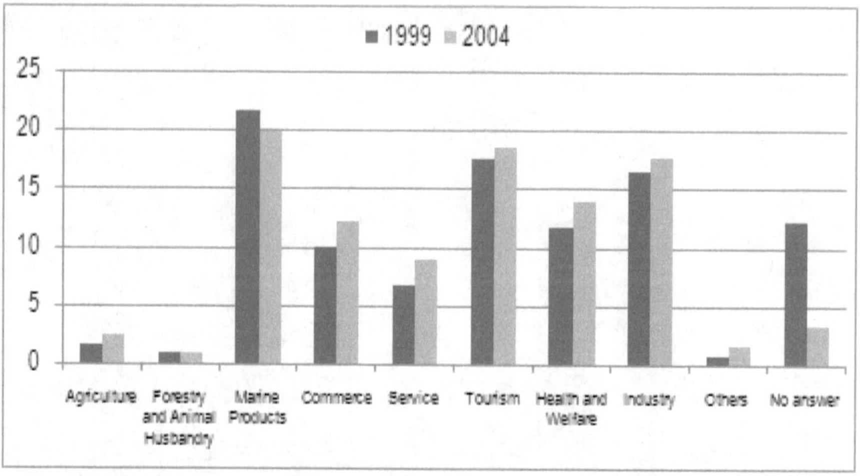

Source. Kamaishi shi sōmu kikaku bu sōgō seisaku ka. (2004, p. 6).

industrial to a tourist town. One reason could be the sense of history and pride that citizens have about Kamaishi's place as an industrial town. Another could be that the ratio of employees in local secondary industries has not changed significantly in the period after the rationalisation of the steel works, from 34.5 percent (10,132 people) in 1980 to 30.3 percent (5,743 people) in 2005. Indeed, as already discussed, efforts toward maintaining Kamaishi as an industrial town have met with some success. For example, in October 2006 both Dowa Forging Corporation (metals) and Japan SMC (pneumatics) decided to build new factories in the city.

Ultimately, however, the choice facing the residents of Kamaishi may be between a future as an industrial town or a future as a tourist town, because there is tension between these two opportunities: the policy orientation and citizen consciousness that sustain an industrial town often run counter to those that are necessary to build and sustain a tourist town, especially when the kind of tourism concerned prioritises conservation of natural resources, as green tourism does. The two possible outcomes are not necessarily mutually exclusive, but some sort of choice will have to be made. As it stands, on the basis of the opinion polls, it cannot be concluded that the citizens of Kamaishi have yet truly chosen for themselves a future as a tourist town.

Kamaishi City and Green Tourism

Green tourism in Kamaishi originated in 1997 and began full operations a year later. The first concrete action related to green tourism was the establishment of the Horaikan Inn, which obtained an official designation as a '*Minshuku* [guest house] Providing First-hand Experiences in Agriculture, Forestry and Fishery' from what was then the Association of First-hand Experiences in Agriculture, Forestry, and Fishery (now the Organisation for Urban-Rural Interchange Revitalisation). Horaikan Inn is located on Nebama Beach, one of the leading tourist spots in the Unosumai district (see map 9.2) in the northeastern part of the city. In July 1998 a steering committee was formed by the officials of the Iwate Prefectural Kamaishi Regional Development Office, the Kamaishi City government office, and the Ōtsuchi Town government office, as well as by management from the Horaikan Inn and other *minshuku* operators and those involved in related activities up to that point. From rather humble beginnings—the number of participants cited by the steering committee for 1998 was nine—participation has been steadily increasing. For 2002 the committee received a high school field trip from Sendai City, after which it received a request from a junior high school in Osaka in 2004. As a result of these efforts, the aggregate number of participants in 2009 reached 2,663 (figure 9.4).

An important element in the success of green tourism is the diversity of the parties involved. For example, groups knowledgeable about direct marketing for tourism sites and farmer-run restaurants are important actors in green tourism. The Kamaishi/Ōtsuchi Local Foods Study Group, established in 2004, is a local group that sponsors the Enjoy Local Dishes event. Formation of the Local Foods Group, though an outcome of the co-operative effort of four organisations, can be attributed

MAP 9.2. Kamaishi City and Its Districts.

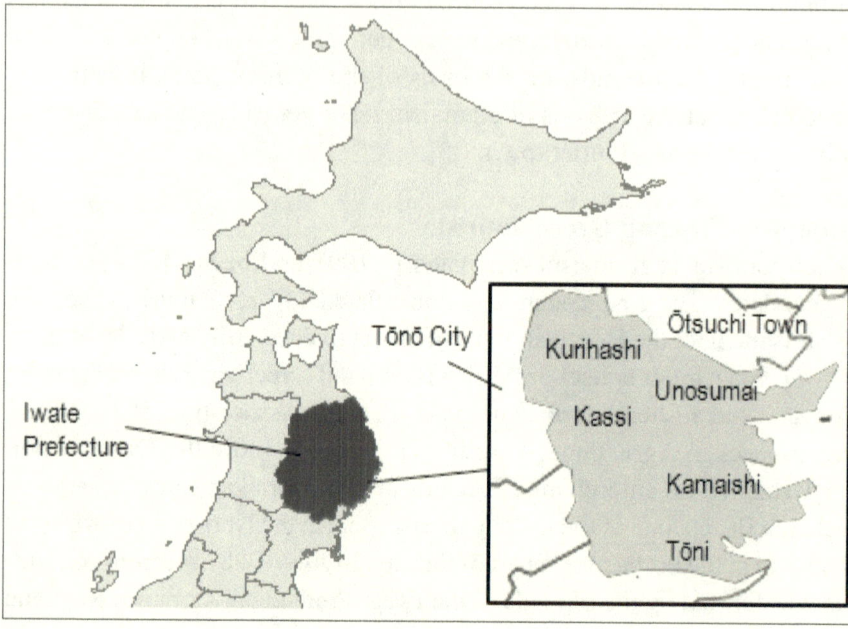

Note. Original source map author: lincun. Map available under Creative Commons License at Wikipedia (http://ja.wikipedia.org/wiki/%E9%87%9C%E7%9F%B3%E5%B8%82).

primarily to the Aonoki Shufu no Kai (Aonoki District Housewives Association), which operates a shop selling local products along with a restaurant in Aonoki, located in the western part of the Kurihashi district, and to the Women's Department of the Kamaishi East Fisheries Co-operative Association of the Unosumai District. The Aonoki Shufu no Kai was established in 1984, and even before the establishment of the tourism steering committee by the Regional Development Office in1998, the Shufu no Kai was developing green tourism–type activities. These included cultivation of a vegetable called *chorogi* (*Stachys sieboldii*), which is used in *osechi ryōri*, a traditional dish in Japanese New Year's cooking, and the development and marketing of a product based

FIGURE 9.4. Aggregate Number of Participants in Green Tourism in Kamaishi City.

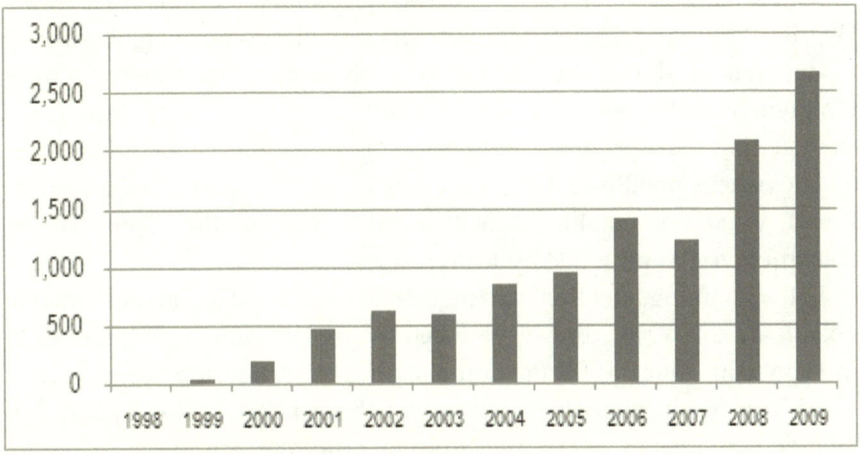

Source. Kamaishi shi (2006d, 2007).

on the vegetable *sennin chorogi* (*longevity joy*). These activities attracted national interest, and in 1995 the group was awarded the National Land Agency Director General Award—the highest prize in the Food Amenity Activity Contest, sponsored by what was then the National Land Agency and by the Rural Development Planning Commission—and the Iki-iki Chūsankan Sho (Lively Upland Area Prize) of Iwate Prefecture in the same year (Iwate Tōkai Shimbun, 1995). The Local Foods Group itself also received the Iwate Omoshiro Chisan-Chisho Taisho (Iwate Interesting Local Production–Local Consumption Grand Prize) in fiscal year 2005 (Iwate Tōkai Shimbun, 2006).

Another case of local actors in green tourism is the Hashino Sanchoku (Hashino District 'Farm-fresh' Produce Co-operative), also known as *Donguri Sanchoku*, which was established by local farmers in the Kurihashi district in May 1996 and started selling agricultural products on Saturdays and Sundays. After the group expanded its sales business to include weekdays 'at the strong request of its customers' from May 1998 (Iwate Tōkai Shimbun, 1998), it also received the Iki-iki Chūsankan Sho, in 1999. The Hashino Shinko Kyōgikai (Hashino District Promotion Society, an umbrella organisation of neighbourhood associations in the Hashino District) received financial assistance from the municipal development office in 2005 and built a water mill at the shop selling local products and providing green tourism activities such as buckwheat noodle-making activities called Donguri Hiroba (Acorn Field). What was notable about this effort was that the labour for the construction was provided by local residents.

In the planning, creation, and maintenance of local green tourism, one notable case is a saké brewery owned by the Hamachidōri Corporation in Kamaishi. Since 1998 the company has been holding what is calls 'saké-brewing participatory events' for the general public, events that include activities on everything from planting the rice to preparing the ingredients for making the saké. In 2004 the brewery received the Iwate Prefecture Chisan-Chisho Taisho (Local Production–Local Consumption Grand Prize). The quality and reputation of the saké produced are high, and the brewery received the Gold Prize of the National New Saké Exhibition for the 2005 and 2006 brewing years. Thus the Hamachidōri Corporation has long been engaged in green tourism–type activities as one way of encouraging participatory tourist activities on local farmers' land (photo 9.9), even well before an employee of Hamachidōri joined the planning committee in March 2007. These activities accentuated the business of a successful brewery and also generated activities that can be considered green tourism, thereby contributing to the local economy.

In addition to these pioneers, other participants have become involved in green tourism more recently. The Mini Sanchoku Cosmos, located in the Kasshi District in the western part of the city, opened a farmer's restaurant in January of 2007. The restaurant received a prize at the Iwate Prefectural Local Food Contest in 2006 for its chocolate-based sweets using Kasshi persimmon, which is a specialty of the Kasshi District. In another case, a local landowner turned a fallow rice field into a cosmos-

Photo 9.9. Rice-planting event held by the Hamachidōri Corporation.

Photo by Ken Ohori (May 2007).

growing field in 2000 with the assistance of a direct-marketing project the following year (Iwate Tōkai Shimbun, 2007).

Nature conservation activities also relate to green tourism in Kamaishi and Ōtsuchi. After aquaculture facilities in the sea were damaged by rivers flooded in a typhoon in July 2002, activities for the comprehensive preservation of the area's mountains, rivers, and sea took on a new seriousness. In March 2003 the Council for Promoting Mountains, Rivers, and Sea Environment Preservation was established. The purpose of this organisation is to promote the preservation of forested mountains and river channels in order to ensure the quality of river water reaching the coast—in order to prevent the deterioration of water quality at the beach and in the near-shore areas—and its main activities include an Environment Forest Creation Project and an Environment School, with lectures by experts in fisheries and agriculture. This council was established at the call of the regional development office, which acts as the secretariat of the council, and it claims 32 participant organisations, including environmental organisations, fisheries co-operative associations, and agricultural co-operative associations in the Kamaishi and Ōtsuchi areas. Another activity of the council was the establishment of an Environment Preservation Society in each district of Kamaishi and Ōtsuchi. In October 2005 the Tōni District Environment Preservation Society was organised in the Tōni District in the southern part of Kamaishi. In March 2006 the Ōtsuchi-Kozuchi District Environment Preservation Society was organised, and in November the same year, the Uno-Kuri Area Environment Preservation Society in the Unosumai and Kurihashi districts, seen as at the centre of green tourism activities, was established to create a link between environmental preservation activities and green tourism.

It needs to be said that, at this stage, the scale of green tourism in Kamaishi City remains small, and its influence cannot justify a claim that it is playing a major role in developing the tourism industry in Kamaishi, let alone that it is making a contribution to the revitalisation of the city as a whole. However, through these activities, the residents of Kamaishi are establishing and experiencing a new multiple identity for their city as both an industrial and a tourist town. And they are proving to themselves—and to others—that peripheral communities can, through a rediscovery of local resources, reinvent themselves for living and working in 21st-century Japan's shrinking regions.

CONCLUSION

The transformations taking place in the national and international economies have brought dramatic consequences for Japan's regions. The loss of a community's economic base prompts people to reach out to secure new opportunities, and all across regional Japan, communities are striving to develop their tourism resources. With this development come the dangers of overexpansion and the failure of many expensive and high-risk projects. It is likely that those communities that face accessibility problems, whose tourism potential is constrained by seasonal factors, and that possess little economic diversity will be the ones most exposed to the risks of oversupply. Tourism is also subject to fads and fashions, and large numbers of repeat visitors are very difficult to achieve; this means that tourism facilities need to generate substantial returns very soon after their completion. Therefore many of Japan's regional communities that are relying on tourism to return them to growth may end up disappointed and saddled with large development debts.

The examples presented in this and the previous chapter demonstrate that specific places and the communities within them have trajectories of experience and that these are based on conscious efforts to rediscover and shape the identity, image, consciousness, and hope of a place as much as they are based on the attributes of the places themselves. In Akita's Oga Peninsula, a desire to capitalise on local cultural resources has stimulated the prefecture to open up this previously inaccessible locale to outside visitors. A desire to persuade visitors to return has prompted the rediscovery and reinvention of the culture and environment of the island communities of Okinawa Prefecture. And a need to diversify and move away from dependence on a single industry has prompted Kamaishi City to consider tourism as an alternative and to begin the long process of reinventing the town's image, though, as already stated, the 11 March 2011 disaster in Tōhoku is likely to have a dramatic impact on the direction of the city's future development. The cases in this chapter show the potential even in a radical reinvention of a place's identity, so long as this is rooted in the commitment of communities and individuals to follow through with pragmatic application. Ultimately, therefore, it is the human imagination—the true realm of a community's membership—that will determine the fate of any place as its inhabitants struggle to understand and then respond to the pressures of contemporary life.

Chapter 10

Reinventing the Region II

Theoretical Potential*

This study has already shown how some communities have embarked on processes of recovering their economies and reinventing their identities. This chapter concludes the main body of this book by tying together the chapters of part II and adopting a bottom-up theoretical approach to the reinvention and revitalisation of the economies and societies of Japan's regions through an examination of the potential for reconfiguring and rebranding local cultural and natural attributes in Japan's regions.

Tsugaru *nuri* lacquerware is just one example of the hundreds, if not thousands, of local goods being produced by entrepreneurs in Japan's regions—products that range from fresh fruits and vegetables and processed sweets and beverages to high value-added arts and crafts, manufactured goods, and hospitality and health services. Various areas have tremendous potential to add value to local products and services through

---

*The principal contributing authors to this chapter are Thomas Jones and Anthony S. Rausch.

innovative production and branding processes that respond to market needs in a way that provides real returns to producer investments. However, our research also demonstrates that producers and retailers as yet do not capitalise on these value-added opportunities as well as they might. For example, we argue here that communities hoping to develop themselves in this direction would gain increased value-added returns through a more thorough bottom-up investigation and operationalising of their indigenous cultural attributes. Furthermore, we argue that natural resources offer potential for the establishment of economic and social stability in Japan's regions through connecting tourism with a rebranding of natural environmental capital and a more effective and better coordinated implementation of brand. Thus we also consider the potential for Japan's 29 national parks to act as a platform for attracting tourists to an area for the purposes of revitalising shrinking regions. Japan's national parks form a major component of the country's natural heritage, and the Japanese government and people are taking important steps to preserve that heritage for the enjoyment of present and future generations. Nevertheless, we ask whether more can be done to coordinate the various groups that make up the national park's management system such that they can both contribute to the revitalisation of rural areas as well as serve as examples of successful brand management for locales outside of the national park system that also wish to capitalise on their natural endowments.

NEGOTIATING THE TRANSITION FROM CONCEPTUAL IMAGE TO OPERATIONAL IDENTITY IN TSUGARU

This section focuses on the Tsugaru District of Aomori Prefecture and the potential of Tsugaru *nuri* lacquerware as a cultural commodity to contribute to the revitalisation of the region. In this case, both the place and the commodity provide the discursive space for theoretical insights into how local cultural resources can be arranged conceptually and then used as a tool in the reconfiguration of regional identity in a manner that also constitutes a revitalisation response.

Accessibility has always been a factor in Aomori's peripheral status. With a population of approximately 1.5 million, Aomori has the seventh-lowest population density of Japan's prefectures (Yano Tsuneda Kinenkai, 2006). Aomori also has a shrinking and ageing population, and it ranks low on virtually every economic indicator—from employment and income to industrial production and small-business sales. Annual per capita income ranks 45th nationally and is currently half that of Tokyo, with monthly real income per working household ranked 37th (Yano Tsuneda Kinenkai, 2006). Fourteen percent of the prefectural labour force works in the primary sector, with another 25 percent in the secondary sector and just under 60 percent in the service sector (Yano Tsuneda Kinenkai, 2006). As for Tsugaru, once a powerful military domain on the northern frontier of Edo Japan centred on the culturally rich Hirosaki Castle, it now fares worse than its historical rival, Nambu, now also part of present-day Aomori Prefecture. Centred on the Pacific coastal city of Hachinohe, Nambu benefits from its deep-water fishing harbour. Tsugaru, in contrast, now languishes; regional administrative functions were moved to Aomori City with the establishment of the prefecture at the Meiji Restoration in the 19th century.

Identity and Image in the Revitalisation of Tsugaru

Identity and image are important for local revitalisation (Roca, 2000). As for what constitutes contemporary Tsugaru identity, responses to a 2004 Tsugaru Cultural Commodities Consumer/Producer Survey—a written mail-return survey, undertaken by A. S. Rausch for the present research, which was distributed at a local products fair among both consumers and producers—showed that local residents prioritised natural resources first, followed by local agricultural and fisheries industries. Moreover, a specific Tsugaru character, followed by Tsugaru history, culture, and commodities, constituted a sociocultural component of respondents' conceptions of Tsugaru identity. The lack of urban infrastructure and industry in Aomori, its expanses of forested mountainous tracts, and the predominance of agriculture there foster an identity that stresses natural resources and agriculture. Encouraging in terms of cultural resources is the recognition of a specific local character in terms of the area's history and culture and cultural commodities that can be brought to local revitalisation.

In terms of operationalising this local identity for revitalisation, agriculture and fisheries constitute the most important factors for Tsugaru as perceived both by the residents and cultural-commodities producers surveyed (table 10.1). Residents followed this primary-industry base with a focus on an innovative and entrepreneurial spirit, cultural-based

TABLE 10.1. Factors of Tsugaru Development: Comprehensive View.

	Resident		Producer	
	Rank	Mean	Rank	Mean
Present agriculture and fisheries	1	1.53	1	1.53
Innovative and entrepreneurial spirit	2	1.83	3	1.88
Cultural-based commodities and events	3	1.94	7	1.97
New industry and enterprise	4	1.96	9	2.06
Local administrative leadership and policy	5	1.96	8	2.06
Citizen education / participation in policy	6	2.04	5	1.97
Expanding external markets	7	2.06	4	1.91
Local consumer support of local enterprise	8	2.17	2	1.86
Financial support to local enterprise	9	2.18	6	1.97
Present small/medium enterprise/ industry	10	2.18	10	2.23
National administrative leadership and policy	11	2.18	11	2.32
Public-private (third sector) projects	12	2.43	12	2.44

Sources: Tsugaru Cultural Commodities Consumer/Producer Survey (2004); N (consumers) = 850; N (producers) = 63.

Note. Likert response with 1 = strongly affirmative to the item as a factor of Tsugaru's development, 2 = affirmative, 3 = negative, and 4 = strongly negative.

commodities and events, new industry and enterprise, and local administrative leadership and policy. The producers, in contrast, viewed local consumer support of local enterprise as the second-most important aspect of Tsugaru's revitalisation, followed by an innovative and entrepreneurial spirit, expanding external markets, citizen education and participation in policy making, financial support for local enterprise and only then cultural-based resources and events. Although a mutual focus by both consumer and producer on innovation and entrepreneurship was apparent, there was clear rejection of joint public-private third-sector projects and a lack of confidence in national administrative leadership and policy, as well as in local small and medium enterprise and industry.

Considering these responses, it appears that both consumers and producers are aware of multiple identity clusters and the combinative nature of tangible and intangible factors in development (Bryden & Munro, 2001). Among local consumers, there was recognition of the natural resource base of the area as well as of the potential of the area's history, culture, and commodities to play a role in local revitalisation. Both groups identified an awareness of the need for a human resource base in the form of an innovative and entrepreneurial spirit. Consumers noted an infrastructural need for new industry and enterprise and an aspect of institutional performance; they highlighted the importance of local administrative leadership. Producers, meanwhile, prioritised community and consumer support. These responses show that both groups have a fairly good understanding of the reality of the multidimensional requirements of local revitalisation, though there are several notable differences in prioritisation.

Focusing specifically on cultural commodities in local revitalisation, the 2004 survey indicated that both producers and consumers prioritise major local festivals and local natural resources first, followed next by the character of local towns and villages, and finally by local traditional commodities and performances (table 10.2).

Considering cultural resources in revitalisation from a creation and management perspective (see Ray, 1998), consumers focused on an innovative-entrepreneurial spirit activating historical and cultural

TABLE 10.2. Tsugaru Cultural Resources in Local Revitalisation.

	Consumer		Producer	
	Rank	Mean	Rank	Mean
Major local festivals	1	1.26	1	1.47
Local natural resources	2	1.39	3	1.64
Character of local towns and villages	3	1.70	5	1.94
Local traditional commodities and performance	4	1.81	4	1.86
Local hist., heritage and cultural characteristics	5	1.99	6	2.06
Local famous persons	6	2.03	2	1.61
Local 'special' tourism and events	7	2.05	7	2.24

Source: Tsugaru Cultural Commodities Consumer/Producer Survey (2004).
Note. Likert scale response with 1 = positive response to prompt and 4 = negative response.

resources first, followed by tourism promotion outside the prefecture and local consciousness regarding cultural commodities, whereas producers prioritised local consciousness regarding cultural commodities and tourism promotion outside the prefecture (table 10.3). Both groups saw local administrative leadership and policy as more important than cultural commodity-based organisational leadership and policy, on the one hand; on the other hand, consciousness and knowledge on the part of local cultural workers and cultural commodities-related small retailers and enterprises were not seen as important factors in creating and managing local cultural commodities in regards to local revitalisation.

Reinventing a Tsugaru Cultural Commodity: Conception, Policy, and Strategy

Looking at the overall conception of Tsugaru's cultural resources, the consciousness of the tourist appeal of cultural commodities is notable, followed by images prioritising the necessity of both local consumers' support and government support (see table 10.4). This conception of

TABLE 10.3. Creation and Management of Tsugaru Cultural Resources in Local Revitalisation.

	Consumer		Producer	
	Rank	Mean	Rank	Mean
innovative/entrepreneurial spirit activating historical/cultural resources	1	1.81	3	1.92
tourism promotion outside the prefecture	2	1.82	2	1.80
local consciousness regarding cultural commodities	3	1.83	1	1.79
local administrative leadership and policy	4	2.06	4	1.97
consciousness / knowledge on behalf of local cultural workers	5	2.07	5	2.03
tourism promotion within the prefecture	6	2.11	6	2.09
tourism promotion internationally	7	2.21	6	2.09
cultural commodity-based organizational leadership / policy	8	2.31	8	2.12
cultural commodities-related small retailers and enterprises	8	2.31	9	2.30

Source: 2004 Tsugaru Cultural Commodities Consumer/Producer Survey.
Note. Likert response with 1 = positive response to the prompt and 4 = negative response.

Tsugaru's cultural commodities also highlighted a focus on the 'place' aspect of Tsugaru's cultural commodities, in a recognition of the specific history and tradition of the cultural commodities, as well as a focus on the characteristics of the commodities themselves, in the appeal of creativity and the appeal of a specific technique.

Though festivals and natural resources clearly constitute highly regarded cultural resources for the Tsugaru District, in the interest of considering a cultural resource that is concretely associated with the area, our research focuses on a high-profile and tangible local cultural commodity, Tsugaru *nuri* lacquerware. Tsugaru *nuri* can be viewed as a legitimate Tsugaru cultural commodity, obviously by virtue of its place

TABLE 10.4. Conception of Tsugaru's Cultural Commodities (Consumers).

Cultural commodities seen as . . .	Rank	Mean
place related based on local character of the area	7	1.99
reflecting resident identity	8	2.03
based on appraisal as a local cultural treasure	11	2.04
commodity related based on a unique history and tradition	3	1.80
based on creativity and innovation	5	1.94
based on a specific technique	6	1.96
based on uniqueness and originality	8	2.03
based on a secretive history and techniques	12	2.33
based on a useful product	13	2.84
culture economy related based on tourism influence and potential	1	1.66
based on resident support	2	1.76
based on government support	4	1.90
influential on local economy	8	2.03

Source: Tsugaru Cultural Commodities Consumer/Producer Survey (2004).
Note. Likert scale, with 1 = positive response to prompt and 4 = negative response.

designation in naming, but also based on its local history and contemporary significance. Like most regional Japanese lacquerware, Tsugaru lacquerware originated during the early Edo period, when it was produced through local patronage of lacquerware artisans, who met the demands of the feudal elites for original and innovative designs for lacquered military items and later for household goods (Mochizuki, 2000). In meeting this demand, innovation was rewarded, many varied lacquering techniques were developed, and a variety of materials were used.

With the end of the patronage of the Edo period, the Tsugaru lacquerware industry was forced to accommodate a market-oriented approach. The term *Tsugaru nuri* was coined in this transitional period and represented the first reference to the lacquerware produced in the Tsugaru district using a regional appellation; the term's appearance signalled the start of a process of standardisation of Tsugaru lacquerware, for representative patterns of what was to be referred to as Tsugaru lacquerware had to be maintained. The postwar era saw the lacquerware designated a Prefectural Small Business Promotion Product in 1949 and a steady increase in the fortunes of Tsugaru lacquerware through the 1970s. With its designation as a Traditional Craft Product by the Ministry of International Trade and Industry in 1975, Tsugaru lacquerware was established as a craft tradition in four representative techniques and patterns (of which, two effectively dominate); the designation in effect legitimised a false tradition, one that ignored the true creativity of the lacquerware's origins. Most contemporary Tsugaru lacquerware is based on wooden forms, although other materials can be used, and the most common

Photo 10.1. Traditional Tsugaru *Nuri (Nanako-nuri).*

Photo courtesy of Hirosaki City Chamber of Commerce.

forms are those of functional items such as food utensils and furniture, but decorative objects and stationary items are also produced.

As with many regional industries designated traditional crafts, Tsugaru lacquerware has received extensive subsidies and promotional support from national, prefectural, and local governments, while experiencing a continuing downturn in sales. From a peak of approximately 200 enterprises and over 700 workers in 1974, the Tsugaru lacquerware industry in 2005 comprised fewer than 100 enterprises and somewhere around 150 workers. Likewise, from a peak production value of JPY 2.124 billion in 1986, the industry had contracted to just over JPY 600 million by 2005 (Zaidan Hōjin Dentōteki Kōgeihin Sangyō Shinkō Kyōkai, 2006, p. 10).

As the dominant Tsugaru cultural commodity, Tsugaru lacquerware provides a detailed example of cultural-commodities policy originating at national, prefectural, and municipal levels. The lacquerware was designated a Japanese Traditional Craft Product under the 1975 Traditional Crafts Production Promotion Law, which brought it national funding under the Traditional Crafts Products Promotion Plan. Analysis of the national funding reveals an initial priority shift from industry reforms, which included establishment of a Tsugaru Lacquerware Production Co-operative Association, to economic objectives related to promotion and sales through exhibitions and public-relations campaigns in major cities throughout Japan. This was followed by another shift to new product development and design (see Rausch, 2005).

Current prefectural and municipal reports reflect how prefectural funding is directed locally toward operation subsidies for the Aomori Prefecture Lacquerware Co-operative Association Federation itself, as are travel subsidies for local lacquerware groups to participate in regional and national exhibitions and funding for two groups undertaking new product development. Materials provided by municipal officials showed that municipal funding by the Hirosaki City Commerce, Industry, and Labour Section supported preparation of Tsugaru lacquerware medals awarded at the Fifth Asian Winter Games 2003 (held in Aomori Prefecture) and also showed participation by Tsugaru Lacquerware Association representatives in the national exhibition events, several of which have led to collaborative development of new Tsugaru Lacquerware designs. Finally, the materials showed artisan participation in an Aomori Prefectural Traditional Crafts Industry Area Promotion Plan, which brings consumers and design specialists together with lacquerware producers for new product development. Hirosaki City also provided a Homepage Subsidy and funding for Tsugaru Lacquerware Technique Preservation Activities, which provided financial support for the establishment of Tsugaru lacquerware as a cultural treasure for the formation of technique-preservation groups, through which seasoned artists pass down techniques to succeeding generations of Tsugaru lacquerware crafters. The Hirosaki City Chamber of Commerce also took the lead in a Japan Tsugaru Brand Project starting in 2005, part of a national effort to establish Japanese brands at national and international levels, with a focus on new product development and realisation of a multilevel global market and sales network.

A 2004 Traditional Craft Products Production Area Investigation Report (ZHDKSSK, 2006) closed with a Tsugaru Lacquerware Local Industry Problem and Promotion Plan, which reflects the policy controversies within the industry as well as in industry responses to policies promoted by the national, prefectural, and municipal governments. Three industry-level proposals focused on information dissemination, subsidy disbursement, and expansion of local demand. Most controversial among these was the question of subsidies: One proposal called for a quality-reward system, in which subsidised financial support would be awarded based on sales success at events supported with subsidy money. This orientation contrasted with proposed revisions in the subsidy-application procedure that would expand the number of subsidy recipients while decreasing the per-case amount. Increasing local demand for Tsugaru lacquerware brought contrasting proposals, as well; one focused on increasing prefectural and municipal public-relations campaigns within the region to stimulate consumption by locals, whereas another focused on government working to redirect local institutional purchases toward Tsugaru lacquerware—for example, for school food-service items and in local government-subsidised facilities. Five proposals were identified at

PHOTO 10.2. New forms of Tsugaru *Nuri* at a Japan Brand exhibition in Paris in 2009.

Photo courtesy of Hirosaki City Chamber of Commerce.

the enterprise level, the most controversial of which called for encouraging variation in the materials as a means of controlling costs, thereby reducing the price of lacquerware. The counterargument cited the need to control the characteristic high quality of Tsugaru lacquerware first and foremost and made price a secondary concern. Brand image proved controversial as well; a proposal to strengthen the overall place association of Tsugaru lacquerware was countered by those who favoured an independent approach, in which a particular craftsman's lacquerware could be fully distinguished from that of rivals. The report concluded with a two-step promotion proposal, with the first step focusing on reforming and strengthening the regional association by identifying a unified purpose, and the second step promoting individual activities by association members.

Cultural Resources in Rural Revitalisation: From Conceptual to Operational

What this examination of the resident conception, government policy, and industry strategy for Tsugaru *nuri* lacquerware shows is the variability of elements that must be recognised, addressed, and managed in bringing culture and cultural resources into play in local revitalisation. First and foremost, cultural resources must have a form that can be organised and managed so as to meet these goals; this necessitates an informed process of reduction to a set of working parameters. It is in identifying these characteristics of a cultural resource—not solely physical, but rather historical, cultural, social, and economic—that the parameters of a conceptual space can be outlined; it is in an understanding of this conceptual space that the broader potential of a cultural commodity can be identified, yielding an operational space. It is in the manipulation of this operational space—through representation and promotion, together with manner of production and patterns of purchase—that an approach to securing the future of the cultural commodity, both in its own realm and in local revitalisation, can be developed. Ultimately, through this process a cultural commodity can be reconfigured and integrated into the local identity and image, thereby contributing to the area's revitalisation.

For Tsugaru lacquerware, this conceptual–operational space can initially be conceived of as based on the six fundamental criteria outlined here, configured as intuitively contrasting criteria (also shown in figure 10.1):

1. Origin and history of techniques prioritising innovative creativity
2. Transition to standardised and representative forms and patterns

3. Priority on high quality–high price resulting in product exclusivity
4. Priority on participation and price accessibility yielding extensivity
5. Focus on economic promotion prioritising exploitation
6. Focus on cultural promotion prioritising appreciation

The criteria used to describe the space should be seen as inclusive, meaning that a cultural commodity can be conceived of as fulfilling each of the criteria. In principle, a cultural commodity can have both a standardised and representative form while also allowing for creativity and innovation; a cultural commodity can accommodate exclusivity by virtue of being costly in some forms while allowing for accessibility to the widest number of consumers in others; a cultural commodity can be regarded as a cultural artefact justifying preservation on the basis of varying degrees of government support in some forms while also recognising economic potential arguing for exploitation through market mechanisms in other forms. In reality, however, most cultural

FIGURE 10.1. Tsugaru Lacquerware Conceptual Space.

commodities reflect a concentration in or across certain areas of this conceptual space, the result of their specific historical trajectories—being, for example, innovative, exclusive, and subject to preservation in one case, or standardised, extensive, and exploited for economic potential in another. Both within the community that controls the destiny of any cultural commodity and within a local economy that attempts to place the commodity in the realm of local revitalisation, there will be tensions between competing objectives—tensions that can be illustrated in an operational-space view of the commodity. In the case of Tsugaru lacquerware, the operational space can be mapped. Tsugaru lacquerware has been standardised to representative forms and patterns, yet it is fairly exclusive because of its price. It is also to a significant degree supported through government subsidies attained on the basis of assumed economic potential (see figure 10.2).

This operational space, however, misses the potential in combinations of innovation–creativity and quality–price exclusivity with cultural

FIGURE 10.2. Tsugaru Lacquerware Operational Space.

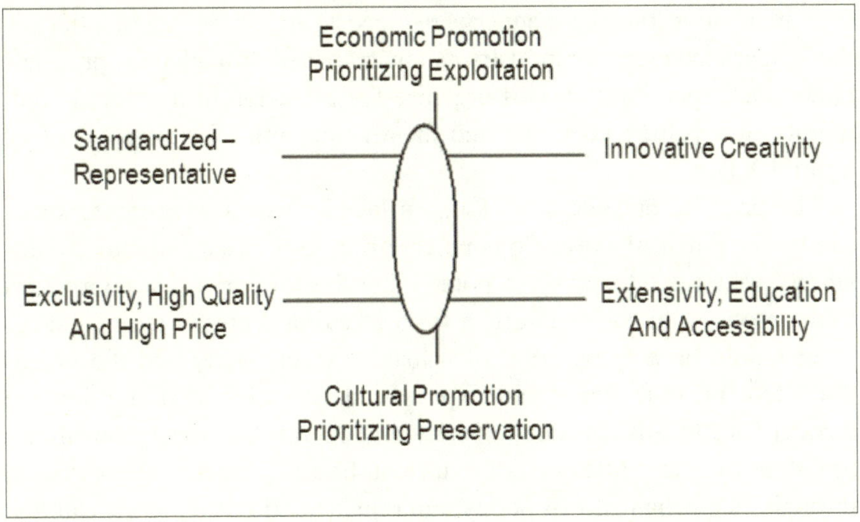

promotion, in the creation of pieces for the connoisseur, or in ensuring the extensivity of the lacquerware by maintaining a reasonable quality and appeal while keeping the product's price accessible. The operational approach of innovation and extensivity highlights combinations of those who see the lacquerware as still constrained by the fundamental notion of craft as solely functional—producing table and tableware items, even jewellery or house furnishings—and those who see Tsugaru lacquerware as art, for sale as an artistic work to a buyer who values the piece itself (or the artist) rather than its association with history or place. These combinations reflect both the priorities of those who would preserve the local market, working to ensure that Tsugaru lacquerware sells in Tsugaru, whether to locals or to tourists, and those who prioritise promotion and expansion into new and highly competitive markets as far away as Europe and North America. Such combinations organise the promotion of a Tsugaru *nuri* consumption consciousness as well; the outcome is that a consumer is motivated by recognition of the lacquerware as an appropriate gift, by a sense of local solidarity with the lacquerware craftsman and the Tsugaru District as a place through a purchase for personal daily use, or by romanticism and connoisseurship that enables an understanding of the lacquerware and prompts the purchase of an expensive and truly innovative Tsugaru lacquerware piece of art. These combinations in the Tsugaru lacquerware industry can be managed through an appropriate operational space, which will organise the inclusion of a cultural commodity in a culture economy and identify potential for expansion (see figure 10.3).

The promise presented by Tsugaru lacquerware's operational space can be seen in *both* innovation and creativity *and* extensivity and accessibility. What is interesting to note is that the former would be a return to the roots of the lacquerware, a form of cultural preservation, and the latter would be a recognition of a local market reality and the potential effect of educational and experiential activities in promoting the lacquerware locally. In terms of how this operational space contributes to cultural commodities in Tsugaru revitalisation, the culture economy, through its mechanisms of policy and representation, can work with the

FIGURE 10.3. Potential Identified in the Operational Space for Tsugaru Lacquerware.

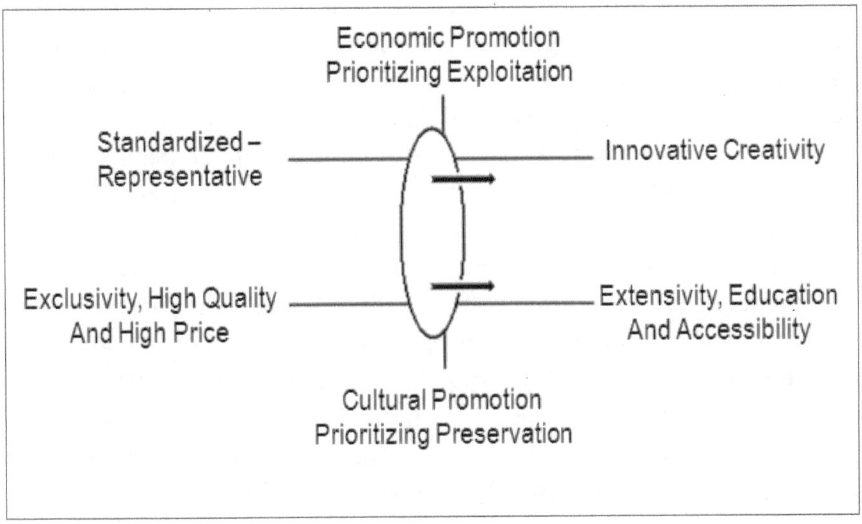

industries and communities to push or pull these cultural commodities to fill the potential identified in the operational space. The degree that the operational space of any one cultural commodity of a place is balanced in combination with the operational spaces of other cultural commodities of that place is indicative on one level of the potential of the place and its cultural resources and is indicative on another level of the efforts by residents, stakeholders, and policy makers in realising a successful culture economy. The cultural commodities of an area, managed in this way, can then be integrated into an overall area brand. This is the theme taken up in the section on branding national parks.

Local Identity in Rural Revitalisation: From Conceptual to Operational

This section concludes by applying these processes of conceptual-space creation and operational-space manipulation for a place-based cultural commodity in a construction of *the operational space of local identity in rural revitalisation*. What the examination of Tsugaru lacquerware has shown is how government policy, media representation, and the industry strategy each creates a specific focus in rural revitalisation, one that can be configured and reconfigured both conceptually and operationally. In the case of local identity, the complexity lies in combining the specific orientations of government (prioritising objectives through budget allocations to create and disseminate a local identity), media (disseminating various representations of this identity locally), and the revitalisation industries (producing and offering a consumable projection of identity, whether as a product, an experience, or an idea for the consumer). It is ultimately in the overall integrative compatibility of the multiple operational parameters that identity as a fully contributing element of rural revitalisation is found.

Following the case for Tsugaru lacquerware as a cultural resource outlined previously, the conceptual–operational space for Aomori as a place can also be conceived initially and in part as based on the six fundamental criteria, configured as intuitively contrasting (also shown in figure 10.4; see Gardenfors, 2000, 2004):

1. Identity in economic objectives that prioritise exploitation of local resources
2. Identity in cultural objectives that prioritise preservation of local resources
3. Identity that reflects standardisation and representative forms of an idealised locale
4. Identity that reflects innovative creativity and entrepreneurship in an evolving locale
5. Identity in an exclusivity that is based in the geographical peripherality of the area
6. Identity in the extensivity based on dissemination and consciousness of the image

Figure 10.4 represents elements of such a conceptual–operational space—namely, objectives that are related to preservation (and experience) rather than exploitation (and consumption), potential in entrepreneurial

FIGURE 10.4. Conceptual-Operational Space for Local Identity in Aomori Revitalisation.

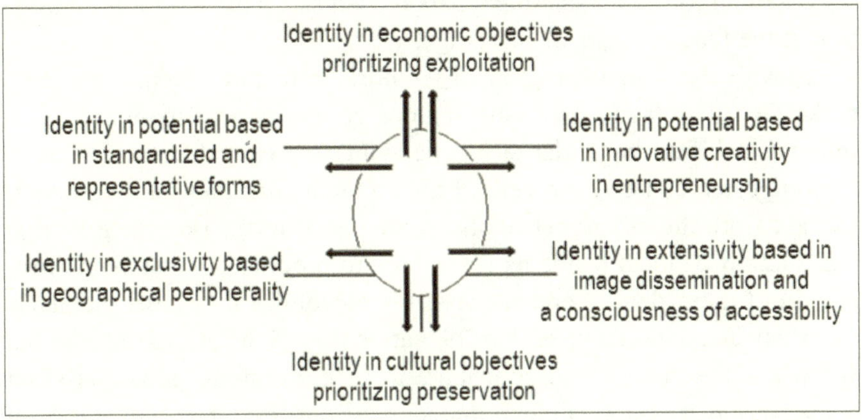

innovation and creativity rather than representative standardisation, fostering extensivity by disseminating an image of Aomori to people in other locations rather than accepting exclusivity by virtue of geography.

This section looks at the case of local identity in the revitalisation of the Tsugaru District of Aomori Prefecture through an examination of Tsugaru *nuri* lacquerware, but obviously the case for any specific locale would be different, a reflection of historical trajectory and contemporary circumstance. That said, the operational space of local identity in the revitalisation of any rural locale can be identified, managed, and maximised in an informed assessment of local cultural resources, guiding government, media, and cultural-commodity producers in the process of identity creation.

Branding Japan's National Parks

In addition to cultural resources, which have potential for operationalising local identity, natural resources also offer potential for the establishment of economic and social stability in Japan's regions through connecting tourism with the natural environment. In this next section we consider the potential for Japan's national parks to act as a platform for revitalisation in the face of regional shrinkage.

As with the Tsugaru region of Aomori Prefecture, Japan's national parks face the classic shrinking regions conundrum of maintaining an internal stability that is largely dependent on external inputs. Though funding often comes from central government subsidies and most visitors are from the urban metropolises, the parks must foster the affection and support of local residents if they are to produce a consumable projection of their identity and successfully reproduce it to meet the needs of urban demand. Each of the 29 national park locations throughout Japan has the potential to contribute to its surrounding area, yet strict conservation regulations mean that such a contribution comes not from direct resource exploitation but rather through a rediscovery of the specific qualities of each park and from a reinvention of the consciousness of particular places that can then begin anew to draw both attention and visitors to the locale through the deployment of a successfully (re)constructed brand image.

Tourism and Regional Revitalisation of Rural Areas

Behind the pressing need for regional revitalisation in rural areas lurks the demise of former stalwart industries such as agriculture, fishery, and forestry. As noted elsewhere, employment in the primary sector has declined drastically, as demonstrated in the forestry industry where the number of full-time workers nationwide dropped from 97,497 in 1970 to a postwar low of 30,960 in 2005 (Tachibana, 2009).

With stagnant rural economies propped up for decades by large-scale public-works projects, the defeat of the Liberal Democratic Party (LDP) in 2009 seemed indicative of a shift away from rural subsidies funnelled into pork-barrel projects towards a long-term tourism strategy. Tourism had been somewhat ignored by the central government as an economic growth pole because of its seasonal employment and unreliability; in 2004, however, under Prime Minister Koizumi, the Tourism Nation strategy was conceived; it was implemented in 2008 after the Basic Act on the Implementation of Tourism Promotion was passed in the National Diet. The Japan Tourism Agency (JTA) was established in 2008, and in addition to a headline target of 10 million foreign visitors to Japan by 2010, the strategy also aimed to 'ignite local economies … building highly distinctive communities that attract visitors … foster[ing] a spirit of regional autonomy and independence' (JTA, 2008). Based on these criteria, Japan's national parks would seem one of the few viable mechanisms of mitigating rural depopulation and decline; yet in reality, they have remained largely overlooked due to a complicated *chiikisei* system.

Japan's *Chiikisei* National Park System

At 5.5 percent of Japan's total land area, the 29 national parks currently so designated cover a substantial area of mostly mountainous and marine environments that have been protected by their remoteness and inaccessibility. Their administration has seen two wholesale changes; first, the new parks were transferred in 1938 from the Cabinet Ministry to the newly formed Ministry of Health and Welfare. In 1971 the Environment Agency was formed, assuming bureaucratic control over the parks until it was upgraded to ministry status and became the Min-

TABLE 10.5. Overview of the National Park System in Japan.

Park Classification	Designation	Management	No. of Parks	Area ('000 ha)	Percentage of Japan's land area
National Park	MOE	MoE	29	2070	5.5
Quasi-National Park	MOE	Prefecture	56	1340	3.6
Prefectural Park	Prefecture	Prefecture	309	1960	5.2
		Total	394	5370000	14.2

Source. National Parks Association of Japan (2004, p. 205).

istry of the Environment (MOE) in 2001. The current legal framework, although subject to frequent amendment, dates back to 1957, when the Natural Parks Law was enacted to define national, quasinational, and prefectural parks.

Within this trio, national parks are the flagship for protection of the nation's finest scenic assets and biodiversity; they are therefore designated, managed, and financially supported directly by the MOE. However, land ownership is dominated by the Forestry Agency, with National Forest accounting for over 60 percent of all national park land, including

FIGURE 10.5. Land Ownership of Japan's National Parks.

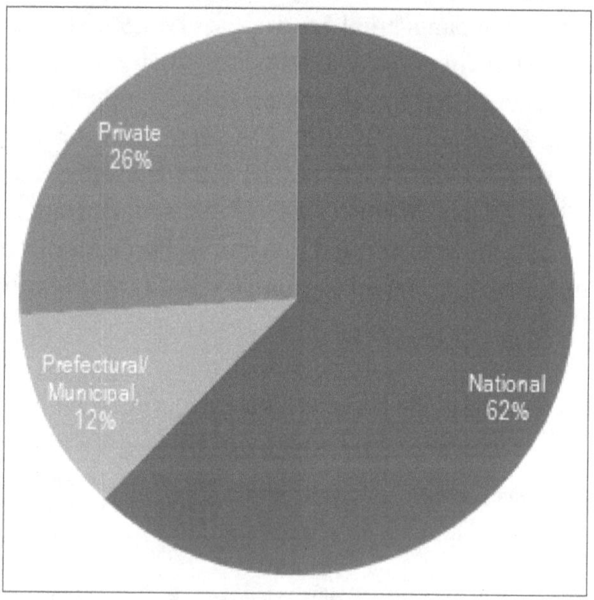

Source. Forestry Agency (2006, p. 120).

TABLE 10.6. Overview of National Park Zoning.

	Area (ha)	Percent	
Special Protection	274724	13.3	
Class I	242864	11.7	
Class II	475457	23.0	58.1
Class III	483562	23.4	
Ordinary	591229	28.6	
Total	2067836	100.0	

Source. NPAJ (2004, p. 86).

78 percent of Special Protection Areas (areas with the strictest level of conservation) and 96 percent of World Heritage areas. A quarter of park land is privately owned, and the remaining 13.5 percent is publicly owned by local governments. Crucially, the MOE, despite being responsible for overall management of the *chiikisei* system and for direct administration of national parks, owns a mere 0.2 percent of the total national park land (M. Kato, 2008, p. 14).

As with the lived-in landscapes of protected areas in Europe, Japan's long history of rural settlement negated a set-aside parks system like that which exists in the United States. Instead, a *chiikisei* framework of 'national park management by zoning and regulation' evolved, resulting in 'multiple-use parks' (Hiwasaki, 2005). In practice, this meant that areas of land could be designated regardless of ownership, with subsequent development regulated through zoning. *Chiikisei* is thus a patchwork management system that accommodates multiple stakeholders with diverse interests.

Under-recognised and Overused? National Park Visitor Trends

Visitation rates to Japan's *chiikisei* national parks are among the highest in the world, with an annual 2.47 visits per capita estimated in a 2008 study (figure 10.6; Pergams & Zaradic, 2008). There was an explosion in visitor numbers in the postwar era, with a 19-fold increase in annual visits from 1950 (22 million) to the recorded peak in 1991 (416 million). However, these data are somewhat unreliable because they are based on a combination of self-registration systems and indicators such as lodge guest books and parking areas (Shoji, Yamaguchi, & Yamaki, 2004). Nonetheless, these trends reflect the prolific rise in visitors that has brought sweeping changes to the parks themselves, the way in which they have captured the affection of the nation, and ultimately the way they are recognised and consumed as a brand.

Why have national parks become so popular? Japan's postwar recreation boom closely traced the economic-miracle years, with the post-Korean War surge steepening during the so-called golden '60s (Johnson, 1982). In addition to providing free time and prosperity, this extended period of rapid economic growth also created a distinct style of mass tourism characterised by group tours, such as *shokuba dantai*, package

FIGURE 10.6. Annual Visitor Numbers to Japan's National Parks (in millions), 1950–2008.

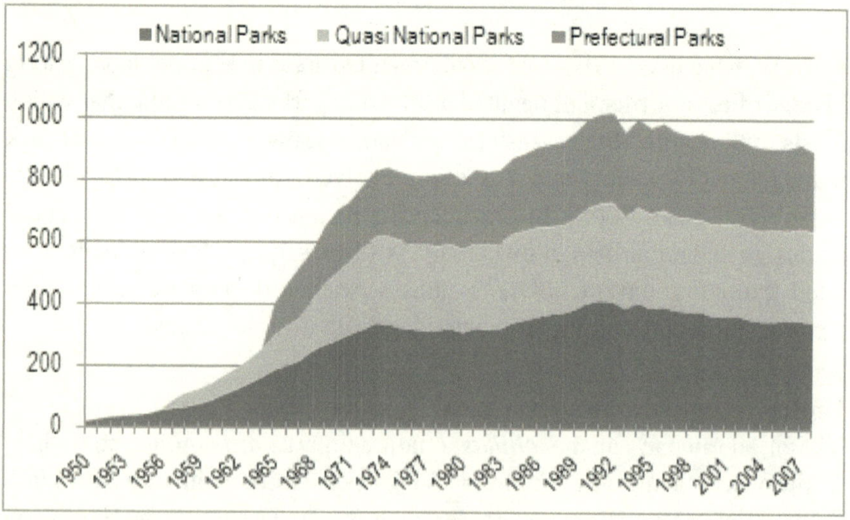

Source. MOE (2010).

travel arranged by companies for their workforces. The short stays of these group trips along a predetermined itinerary of sightseeing spots and accompanied by the de rigueur purchase of local souvenirs became travel characteristics of the era, and the substantial economic impact of such tours was one of the factors behind a wave of new national park designations. Designation—and the stamp of legitimacy that it conferred—saw the national park brand become a highly prized commodity, actively sought after by boosters and conservation factors alike.

The economy-first LDP approach of this period also affected recreation indirectly. For example, the postwar drive for hydroelectric power resulted in new roads, bored into the mountains by dam construction companies and later developed into a nationwide network of new access roads to remote recreation areas. This improved infrastructure, coupled with the affluence to afford private cars, brought these remote recreation spots within a day trip of the urban masses. However, even as the rapid rise in car ownership and convenient bus tours brought ever-greater visitor numbers to popular destinations, the patchwork *chiikisei* governance meant that few visitors were aware that the destinations they were visiting were in fact national parks.

Fewer still perceived the parks in terms of a comprehensive system, and once again following the arc of the national economy, the national parks have posted a steady decline in visitation since the 1990s. In the current post–mass tourism era, the parks thus face a new set of socioeconomic challenges, including decreased visitation and overcapacity in lodgings and service areas where congestion from coachloads of package tourists was once a primary management concern. Rising numbers of foreign visitors have begun to fulfil the goal of international tourism and acquisition of foreign currency, one of the original aims of national park establishment in the 1930s (Murakushi, 2005, pp. 265–274). However, inbound tourists alone cannot compensate for the decline in domestic overnight stays and the demise of core domestic markets like skiing. Meanwhile, visitor consumption trends point to the spread of low-cost accommodation and drive-through or day trips without overnight stays. Younger generations of visitors are said to be declining most rapidly;

many have forsaken outdoor recreation altogether in favour of other pursuits, and the vicious cycle of underfunding and declining use is still undermined by the perennial lack of awareness of national parks.

National Parks and the Potential for Regional Revitalisation

In light of these generally discouraging trends, is it really possible that simply improving the efficiency of national park branding can enhance the parks' role in regional revitalisation? A brief review of place branding in Japan is followed here by some case studies from the national parks.

Global place-branding techniques are by no means a new phenomenon; indeed, the 'conscious attempt of governments to shape a specifically-designed place identity and promote it to identified markets, whether external or internal is almost as old as civic government itself' (Kavaratzis & Ashworth, 2005, p. 506). Definitions vary, but it is widely accepted that corporate branding techniques can be employed reflexively to reinvent the identity of a place (the desired perception of the place) and hence influence its image (or how it is perceived; Kavaratzis, 2005). Thus branding Japan's parks should, in theory, help raise visitor awareness and revitalise local communities.

Talk of place branding is not new in Japan's regions, either. After all, *isson ippin*—the one village, one product movement launched in Oita Prefecture, Kyūshū, in 1980—was the rallying call for a local political campaign 30 years ago, and *mura okoshi*—a generic term to describe independent attempts to revive villages—also dates back to at least the early 1980s, when 'U-turners' began to reject urban life to return to work in their hometowns. The term *chiiki burando* first entered the lexicon in 1982 to describe a local specialty product (e.g., Shinshū Soba), but by the turn of the millennium its meaning had broadened to include the 'added value of the region itself' (Nakajima, 2005, p. 37). This echoed Rainisto's (2003) 'corporate umbrella brand' in its stated intention to combine existing strategies and products from different industries (e.g., tourism and real estate) into an overall blueprint for regional revitalisation. One early example was Aomori Prefecture's Brand Management

Project Team (see Ishii, 2009), which investigated Aomori's perceived image from an internal and external viewpoint based on interviews with local residents and potential consumers from the Kantō area, respectively. The subsequent Aomori Brand management (ABM) strategy aimed to link tourism, agricultural products, regional goods, and lifestyle into a complete package to revitalise the region. However, despite receiving considerable attention in the media as a pioneering attempt to use corporate branding techniques in local government, the ABM project was unhinged by a number of familiar factors, notably longevity and political unity, although not before it had helped spark a national *chiiki burando* boom across Japan.

As the jewels of Japan's natural and cultural heritage, the national parks should be an obvious target for such branding exercises. They already have many of the necessary criteria for a *chiiki burando*, given that a 'brand embodies a whole set of physical and socio-psychological attributes and beliefs which are associated with the product,' (Kavaratzis & Ashworth, 2005, p. 508). With an annual rate of approximately 2.75 visits per capita, the parks contain the resources to host more than just sightseeing; the diverse *chiikisei* system is able to incorporate many of the same products originally targeted by the ABM—including agricultural goods, regional products, and lifestyle services. Japan's parks could thus fulfil a role similar to that of the French Regional Parks, which 'support local economic activities through the promotion of regional produce and products, and the broader revitalisation of local commerce and industry' (McCarthy et al., 2002, p. 667). In this light, better use of corporate branding techniques could be used to boost product placement, as is already the case with a plethora of 'national park goods,' ranging from foodstuffs (Minami Alps Mineral Water and Fuji Melon Pan) to second homes (Hakone and Lake Yamanaka). But by the same token, the breadth of the national parks brand makes it difficult to manage because 'brand equity is formed by the assets and liabilities linked to a brand forming its value' (Aaker, 1991, pp. 39–41). Hence management issues such as congestion and pollution can negatively influence visitor experience, adversely affecting brand loyalty.

If brand management is indeed a logical extension of park management, then the Achilles heel of such a national park brand is surely the inherent weaknesses in the *chiikisei* system. For although the flexibility in designation criteria circumnavigated the need to buy up large tracts of private land or relocate local communities, *chiikisei* has resulted in a complicated power-sharing system that requires the involvement of multiple stakeholders with diverse—and often incompatible—management aims (Kato, 2008). For example, one symbolic conflict came to a head in Hokkaidō in 1987 between the logging objectives of the Forestry Agency, which is the major landowner, and the conservation-based agenda of the MOE, which oversees park management.

Moreover, the MOE is hamstrung by its lack of directly owned land and insufficient funds; despite the 2001 upgrade from agency status, it remains 'the smallest ministry in terms of personnel and budget size' (Imura, 2005, p. 56). Initially conceived as a policy-making think tank, the MOE still lacks clout in the field today despite the recent introduction of Active Rangers to boost staff numbers and visible presence. In 2005, for example, there were only 246 MOE Rangers across the entire country, resulting in an average administrative area of 8,300 ha per person (S. Yamamoto, 2007). Furthermore, as civil servants, the rangers are rotated every few years, undermining efforts to develop long-term partnerships with local organisations or groups.

In short, the MOE's administrative role has been largely limited to rubber-stamping permits, undermining its capacity to coordinate management between different factions and to provide visitor services. Thus the MOE's chief role is to maintain the status quo through top-down regulation of the private sector, and local businesses provide most visitor services such as hotels, mountain huts, camp sites, and ski resorts. *Chiikisei* has ensured that governance acts primarily as a brake on the use of national park resources, but there are signs of a recent shift towards a more proactive form of administration. The following two examples demonstrate how the potential of branding national parks has begun to offer a platform for more holistic park management.

Communicating more effectively with national park visitors

To mark the 50th anniversary of the passage of the Natural Parks Law, the MOE published a pair of pamphlets in 2007 entitled *National Parks of Japan* and *Japan's Nature*. The pamphlets, in Japanese and four foreign languages (English, Korean, mainland Chinese, and Taiwanese Chinese) had a total print run of 120,000. In addition to representing a recognition of the increasing number of foreign visitors to Japan's parks, the undertaking also marked a symbolic turning point in MOE policy, with the tacit admission that the ministry's role was not merely limited to park regulation but also included promoting natural resources as a means of active conservation. Hence in addition to their distribution at Visitor Centres and local Tourist Information Centres, 34,000 pamphlets were sent out via the

Photo 10.3. *National Parks of Japan* pamphlets published by the MOE.

Photo by Thomas Jones.

PHOTOS 10.4. and 10.5. National park brand strengthening being achieved by the standardisation of Fuji trail signage.

Photos by Thomas Jones (August 2009).

Japan National Tourist Organisation under the auspices of the Visit Japan Campaign (T. Jones, interview, 1 February 2009). The publication of the pamphlets also sought to address two other key problems—namely, the low level of national park awareness among domestic visitors, and the lack of recognition of Japan's parks system among international visitors.

Another hugely popular destination for foreign visitors is Mt Fuji, which at 3,776 m is the tallest mountain in Japan and the showpiece of the Fuji-Hakone-Izu National Park. Its brief summer climbing window attracts one of the highest densities of climbers in the world; in 2008 MOE trail counters recorded a total of over 300,000 climbers in the two-month climbing season. Following Fuji's 2007 nomination for designation as a UNESCO World Cultural Heritage site, as well as the opening of a new airport in Shizuoka in 2009, a Fuji climbing boom ensued that included large numbers of young, first-time climbers without guides and increasing numbers of foreign visitors. The situation demanded effective intervention from management in order to communicate key national park rules and channel large numbers of climbers along congested trails in difficult terrain (Jones, Yamamoto, & Aramaki, 2009). In March 2009, an innovative council created a set of guidelines for a new colour-coded trail system, including the following recommendations: (1) standardisation of place names in four languages, (2) creation and distribution of standardised map, (3) removal of unnecessary signs and notices, and (4) standardised design, including night function.

UNESCO and World Heritage Brands

As the case of Mt Fuji shows, the pros and cons of branding protected areas are aptly demonstrated by the example of UNESCO World Heritage. Much like Japan's national park designation in the 1950s and 1960s, UNESCO designation today represents a prestigious label and is actively sought by regional planners for its perceived economic benefits. However, a number of side effects have been observed, including overcrowding, that affect the local community and the natural environment.

Japan's three Natural UNESCO sites, Shirakami, Yakushima, and Shiretoko, are cases in point. The Shirakami Sanchi mountains in the Tōhoku region are now billed as one of the world's largest virgin beech forests. Yet the natural environment has been damaged; the UNESCO designation in 1993 led to a 150 percent increase in visitor numbers (Natural Environment Agency, 2005). A similar situation arose on Yakushima Island, where maintenance costs shot up after the UNESCO designation, increasing 'by 6.5 times from 21.02 million in 1992 to 137.52 million yen in 2002' (Shibasaki, 2007).

The hope is that these hidden costs, which fall on both the natural environment and the (usually municipal) government, can be offset by the added revenue that the extra tourists bring. In Yakushima's case, ecotourism has been promoted as an appropriate interface between its World Heritage brand and its visitors, who come mostly from urban areas. The success of Yakushima's ecotourism brand is demonstrated by its consistent first-place ranking in an annual awareness poll conducted among Kantō residents (Japan Ecotourism Society, 2007). The ecotourism brand, then, is one way to actively communicate the UNESCO—and

FIGURE 10.7. Colour-Coordinated Fuji Trail Signs.

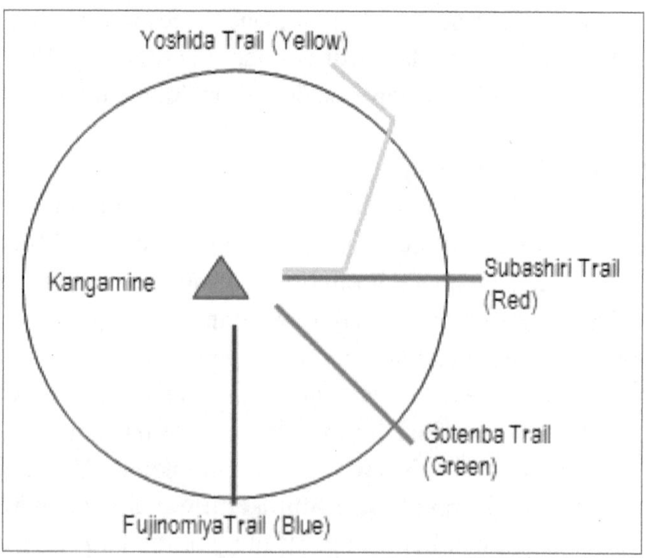

national park—values by guaranteeing to provide an authentic experience in a pristine natural environment.

Another tactic borrowed from corporate branding is the ability to match a product with the needs of growth markets, and here again Yakushima has been successful, attracting an urban client base that includes younger visitors keen on ecotourism as well as the middle-aged and older visitors who are already the dominant market in national park visitor profiles. The current period of the retirement of the baby-boomer generation has ensured a steady supply of visitors with disposable income and leisure time; the 'boomers have a strong interest in both domestic and foreign travel' and are 'inclined towards SITs [Special Interest Tours] in which a small number of people travel to a place of particular interest' (Nitta, 2006). But in the current scenario, in which this generation and other market segments are targeted by large urban-based tour operators, Yakushima's brand management is in a sense being outsourced to the private sector, a circumstance that could undermine its regional economic impact and sustainability in the long term.

Reconfiguring the *Chiikisei* System

Although Japan's national parks were originally modelled loosely on the Yellowstone theme of 'enjoyment in perpetuity' (Roosevelt, 1903), the current limitations of the *chiikisei* model make it difficult in practice to implement the long-term strategies that can comprehensively safeguard and promote the brand. Instead, under de facto load-sharing systems such as that at Yakushima, management and marketing are carried out autonomously by different organisations with broadly different goals.

The UNESCO example therefore demonstrates the potential pitfalls of certification, but also the benefits which could outweigh them. By repackaging the national park brand in a similar way around policies of sustainable development and tourism, the parks could bridge the gap between management and marketing to become growth poles for remote areas of the rural economy—attracting investment and human resources, providing the employment to support rural communities, and encouraging collaboration between diverse stakeholders such as local residents, government agencies, and tourism-related enterprises.

However, in order to fulfil this varied agenda, the *chiikisei* mechanism must be reconfigured and recalibrated to create a more flexible management system that includes transparent platforms for public participation, resulting in a targeted and clearly defined set of short-term goals within a long-term strategy for each individual park. Successful examples of this branding through *chiikisei* management are still few and far between, but the need for such structural reform has been demonstrated by examples such as Akan, one of five national parks in Hokkaidō, which established an innovative regional committee to bring together six surrounding municipalities (Hara, 2007). It is this kind of joint initiative that Kato

FIGURE 10.8. Co-operative Chiikisei Management Needed to Build a National Park Brand.

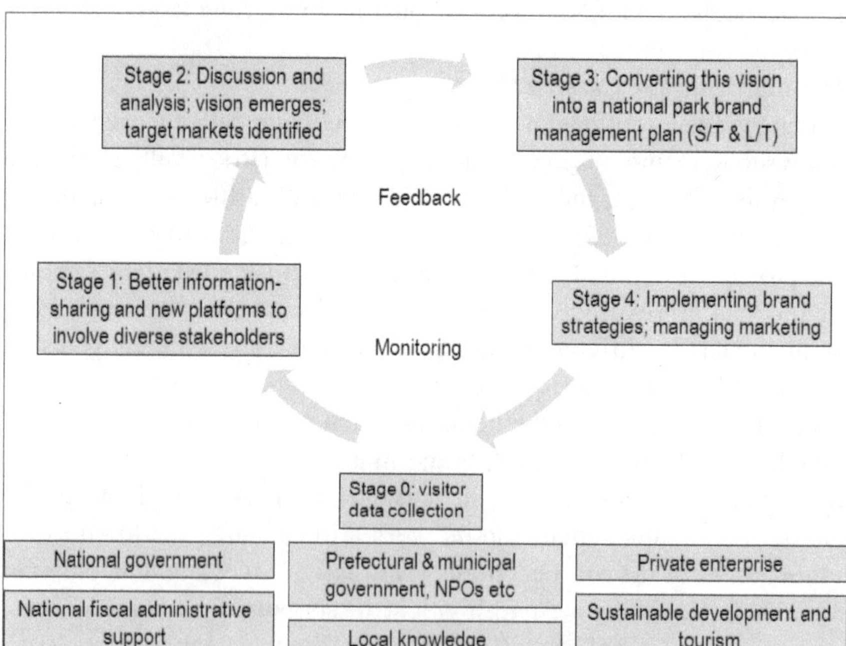

(2007) described as the 'co-operative management' necessary to maximise the potential of the *chiikisei* system.

Despite the clear need for structural reform, many of Japan's *chiikisei* parks are already extremely adept at fulfilling their twin goals of attracting tourist revenue and preserving the natural environment. However, with visitor trends changing at an unprecedented rate, the fragmented nature of the *chiikisei* system can no longer be ignored, underlining the need for a more holistic approach to park management that includes more integrated marketing efforts.

By symbolising the two-way process of communication between identity and image, branding cuts to the heart of the debate on the rural–urban and national–local divides. Located as they are at this crossroads, national parks face the challenge of raising both internal and external brand awareness. Internally, networking among diverse stakeholders can be structured around information-sharing or collaborative projects, such as monitoring, which can encourage community participation and foster a greater sense of identity. Other, seemingly minor internal changes (such as the Fuji park's standardisation of trail signs) can help present external visitors with a more coherent image of the national parks, raising awareness and appreciation of a system of which many visitors are oblivious; uniformity of other park logos and workers' uniforms would be a similarly helpful measure. Also, external support through financial grants or training for targeted industries such as heritage guides ensures that the parks can offer a range of authentic interpretative experiences. This results in a higher rate of repeaters, and over time improved brand awareness leads the general public and local communities to become more actively involved with the national park management process, deepening the sense of stewardship for the natural resources.

Conclusion

Earlier chapters in part II investigate various case studies that present the past and current realities of regional revitalisation attempts through natural and cultural-heritage tourism in Japan. A good deal of the potential for these locales to generate economic stability and sustainability is lost due to poor planning and co-ordination and the poor execution of projects that include too many participants with competing objectives.

This final chapter of part II looks to the future. Its first section investigates how rural revitalisation involves producing and offering added value to local cultural commodities through the consumable projection of identity—in this case Tsugaru *nuri* lacquerware as a product, experience, or idea for the consumer. The chapter's second section shows that national parks in locations with little alternative to natural-resource exploitation face an additional urgent need to actively brand natural and cultural resources and cultivate a more cohesive internal local consciousness that can then be projected to external markets. In both cases, carving out a theoretical understanding of the potential for reinvention and reconfiguration of indigenous resources can be pragmatically negotiated through the conceptualisation of place and its operationalisation via the deployment of cultural commodities and natural heritage resources.

The two cases presented here show how an informed assessment of the indigenous cultural and natural attributes of a place might assist in the reinvention of identity and image, which can then be translated through value-added production and increased income into economic recovery and societal and cultural revitalisation. This need not be predicated on a growth-first orientation; rather, the first priority should be focusing on the attribute itself and concentrating on its conservation and deployment as a local marker. Economic returns will follow. Depopulation will no doubt continue in most regional communities, but their economies need not shrink. Indeed, economic stability within a depopulating region automatically translates into increased per capita prosperity, so long as communities can rediscover and reconnect with their own attributes and go on to reconfigure and reinvent them for the benefit of current and future generations of residents.

Chapter 11

Conclusion

Embracing Depopulation in Japan's Shrinking Regions*

Japan's spectacular postwar economic expansion, together with the manner with which it was achieved, was one of the seminal events in 20th-century history. Japan's success proved beyond any remaining doubt that industrialisation and modernisation are not Western phenomena and that purposive, accelerated economic development in order to lift a people out of poverty and catch up with the world's wealthiest and most industrially advanced countries was possible for a nation that does not possess a European heritage. In this sense, Japan's achievement as the world's first modern and successfully developed developing country is also one of the best 'good news' stories ever to have occurred.

Japan's development into one of the world's most prosperous and technologically advanced countries has therefore excited considerable

*The principal contributing authors to this chapter are Peter Matanle and Anthony S. Rausch.

interest around the world—among scholars and students, businesspeople and policy makers, journalists and ordinary citizens. This is particularly true in the other countries of East and Southeast Asia, where many governments have, consciously or unconsciously, adapted their understanding of the Japanese growth model to their own development strategies. Although some Asian governments may not wish to acknowledge this, Japan can thus be understood as fulfilling Akamatsu's (1962) suggestion that it be the 'lead goose' in Asia, initiating a continent-wide accelerated development process and thereby helping eliminate poverty from large areas of the world and close wealth and opportunity gaps between Asian countries and the advanced industrial economies in the West. It needs to be said, however, that dangers may be lurking in the future for countries that have adopted Japan's approach. Japan's development has not been free of difficulties, and the rapidity of its expansion may have sown the seeds of its own relative decline in the coming decades, especially if the consequences of rapid ageing and depopulation are not well managed.

Perhaps more than any other country, Japan has achieved economic success in part as an outcome of the demographic dividend that high rates of population growth had conferred on the nation, growth which can be regarded as both a cause and a consequence of the country's rapid economic development. That is to say, high birth rates and decreasing mortality in the first half of the 20th century produced a massive, rapid, and long-term expansion in the population in the middle decades of the century (see chapter 3, figure 3.1), whereas the benefits that had accrued from economic growth and decreasing mortality helped to reduce fertility in the second half of the 20th century (Bloom, Canning, & Sevilla, 2003; National Institute of Population and Social Security Research, 2010; Omran, 2005). These factors in combination changed the dependency ratio between the working and nonworking population in two ways. First, the proportion of older people in the population did not increase as rapidly as the proportion of working-age people until comparatively late in the century (the 1970s), and, second, the proportion of children in the population began its long fall as early as the late 1940s. Hence the proportion of working-age people continued to expand all the way through to 1990, reaching 69.5 percent in that year (figure 11.1; NIPSSR, 2010). This demographic window of opportunity provided considerable support for the Japanese government's efforts to initiate and successfully manage a sustained period of high-speed economic growth and improvement in material standards of living, driven by a state-led industrial and modernisation policy (Bloom et al., 2003; Johnson, 1982; Katz, 1998; Tominaga, 1990).

This fortunate set of circumstances has now ended; indeed it may have gone into reverse. If the net reproduction rate (the number of girls born to a cohort of women in their lifetime, where a figure lower than 1 is below population replacement) indicates underlying demographic trends early and accurately then Japan's future population decline was already apparent by the 1950s: Its net reproduction rate had fallen to 0.96 by 1955–1959 (Rostow, 1998, pp. 21–23). A more common measure is the total fertility rate (TFR; the average number of children born to a cohort of women in their lifetime, where a figure of less than approximately 2.1 for a developed country indicates a rate below population replacement level). After the period of high fertility following the Second World War, known as the 'baby boom,' Japan's TFR dropped rapidly to 2.04 in 1957 and hovered at about 2.1 till 1973, before dropping again in 1974. Since that time, the TFR has remained below replacement level, reaching a postwar low of 1.26 in 2005. The effect of this long period of low fertility, combined with increasing life expectancy, is that Japan's population is ageing rapidly. Moreover, looking backwards from the year 2011, 1974 was 37 years ago, and the number of women of child-bearing age is consequently also now declining, dealing a secondary blow to the population's capacity to replace itself or grow.

Reflecting these trends, in 2005 (or shortly thereafter) Japan's population began to shrink for the first time in the country's modern peacetime history. The government's 2006 medium variant population projection assumes that if present trends continue, the population will decrease by 7.9 percent to 117 million between 2010 and 2030 (NIPSSR, 2006). This is equivalent to losing about 490,000 people annually, the number of residents in a city the size of Nagasaki (population in 2008: 448,911) or Matsuyama (513,897) every year for 20 years (Statistics Bureau, 2010b). From 2030 the population is projected to decrease more rapidly, by about 1 million persons per year, due to the combined cumulative effects of long-term low fertility and ageing.

Taking the long view, two conclusions emerge from this rather bleak assessment for Japan. First, just as Japan's economic expansion was a purposive acceleration of developmental processes under a state-led industrial and modernisation policy that was underpinned by the country's 20th-century population trends, so the rate at which the country's population is ageing and the rate of its projected decline might be understood as an accelerated version of the second demographic transition (see Van de Kaa, 1987). That is, because the rate of fertility decline is to some degree a consequence of the rate of economic expansion, so the rapidity at which Japan is ageing and shrinking may be a consequence of the rapidity with which its government and people were able to deliver the country's so-called economic miracle. If this analysis is correct, it could have important implications for development goals across the world, particularly in Asia. This sea change in Japan's population structure and trajectory is already placing considerable strain on the nation's resources as the government seeks to maintain economic growth while simultaneously putting in place the necessary mechanisms and infrastructure to care for and manage Japan's ageing population. These problems could be magnified several times over in future decades if China and other Asian countries experience similar situations in the wake of their own accelerated development programmes.

The second conclusion is that Japan's current and projected demographic changes may be returning the country's population structure to its premodern state, with one important difference. The 20th century was unique in that it was probably the only period in human history in which the world's labour force outnumbered those—children, older people, and adults unable or unwilling to work—who depended on it for their survival and prosperity (Münz & Reiterer, 2009). This circumstance has provided a means by which to raise millions out of poverty worldwide and for the establishment of generous health-care systems and other state entitlements in developed countries—systems that themselves have contributed to longer, healthier, and more productive lives in an upward spiral of demographic and economic expansion. Indications are ominous, however, suggesting that in the 21st century the world may return to a situation in which dependents outnumber workers, and this time the majority of those dependents will not be children but rather older people; this will have important implications for state health and welfare entitlements (Münz & Rieterer, 2009; Rostow, 1998). Though Japan's dependency ratio of the number of people of working age (15–64) to those 65 and older was 12 to 1 in 1950, by 2030 that ratio is expected to shrink to approximately 2 to 1 (figure 11.1; United Nations Population Division, 2010; NIPSSR, 2006). If children are included and if adjustments are made for labour-force participation rates, the ratio becomes more problematic still. Figure 11.1 shows the proportion of the population of

FIGURE 11.1. Percentage of the Japanese Population by Age Groups, 1950–2008 (actual) and 2010–2030 (projected).

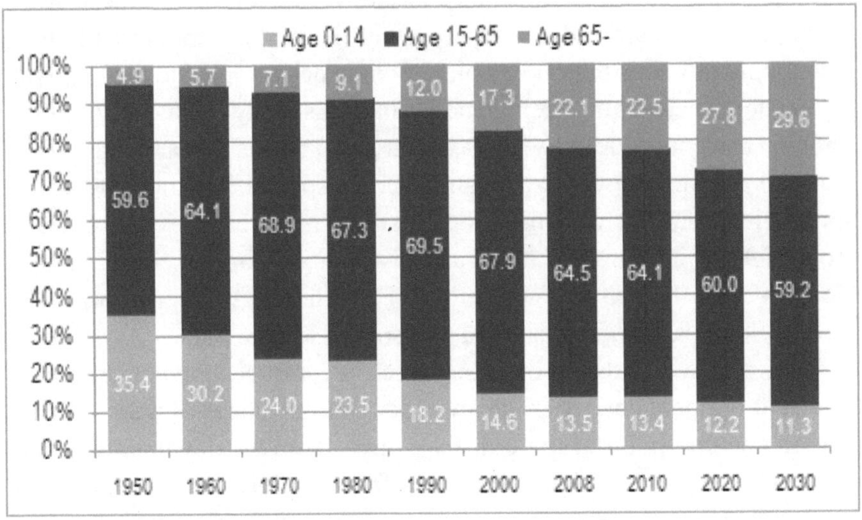

Sources. 1950-2008 (Statistics Bureau, 2010b); 2010-2030 (NIPSSR, 2006, 2010).

working-age people falling to 59.2 percent by 2030. In addition, despite increasing life expectancy and improving health among older people, the overall labour-force participation rate for all persons over 15 has been falling, to reach 60.2 percent in 2008; declining participation rates among older people are a principle cause of this decrease (Statistics Bureau, 2010b). Holding the 2008 labour-force participation rate as a constant, at current rates of population change projected through 2030, we calculate that, of a projected population of 117 million people, fully 68.7 million people—58.4 percent of the population—will not be working in 2030. It is doubtful, however, that the Japanese government and people will tolerate a deterioration in their circumstances to these levels; accordingly, significant changes in the way that Japanese people live, work, and depend upon each other are inevitable (Matsutani, 2006). At the time of writing, 2030 is just 19 years away.

These problems are coming at a particularly difficult time, when considerable resources will be required to manage and reverse the negative effects of many decades—even centuries—of accumulated human pressures on the natural environment. Japan, with the highest life expectancy and one of the lowest fertility rates in the world, and one of the world's most technologically advanced societies, is in the vanguard of these developments and is therefore a pioneer in experiencing and dealing with the consequences of an ageing and shrinking society (Matsutani, 2006). Though the consequences for Japan are worthy of research in and of themselves, we believe that Japan deserves special treatment by scholars in view of what we might anticipate in other countries, especially those in Asia and Europe that are already facing shrinking populations—Germany and the countries of central, Eastern, and southern Europe, as well as South Korea, Taiwan, and, before too long, China.

Our intention for this book is to provide a comprehensive treatment of rural and regional change in Japan under circumstances of national population decline. In order to do this we have taken the developments and processes just described as our overall frame of reference for analysing rural and regional shrinkage in terms of their characteristics, impacts, and implications and in terms of the responses of national, regional, and local actors to the problems they are experiencing. The next pages present a summary of the book's core narrative and its contributions to the academic literature on Japan's modern development, followed by four policy recommendations that have emerged from our research.

We bring together in this volume a theoretically and methodologically diverse set of data and case studies on the macro, mezzo, and micro scales to provide a comprehensive analysis of the processes and effects of regional shrinkage in Japan and to set this in the national and global contexts. Logistical limitations and resource constraints have limited many studies of rural and regional decline in Japan to a single-case-study approach, resulting in the accumulation of independent portraits of particular instances of rural change. Although they represent excellent ethnographic portraits, these studies necessarily lack both representative application beyond each case in question and cannot include a thorough consideration of the broader demographic context of regional decline. Because it seeks to provide evidence and examples of rural revitalisation and regrowth, the existing research literature tends not to address the fundamental truth that, in an era of national depopulation and in the absence of large-scale immigration from overseas, one region's growth requires another's shrinkage. Furthermore, single case studies of regional shrinkage do not generally fit the *exuberant and dynamic Japan* paradigm that has pervaded half a century of social-scientific enquiry into the country's development; therefore such research is easily rendered peripheral with respect to the standard narrative of Japan's successful postwar expansion. We seek to bridge these methodological constraints by combining our research into a single continuous narrative that, we believe, provides a geographically representative series of richly textured studies that reveal the microscopic processes of shrinkage unfolding at the local level and that, combined in this way, produce an overall account of Japan's regional decline that duly considers the macroscopic national and global contexts.

Part I describes how regional shrinkage is being experienced in developed societies worldwide. As a start, regional shrinkage can be characterised principally by a recursive downward spiral of demographic and economic shrinkage, the precise origins of which are often difficult to isolate and identify. In remote rural areas, the impacts of shrinkage have been experienced most visibly in the gradual deterioration of the built environment and in natural succession in areas formerly used for human activities. Less visible have been changes in the economic structure of regional communities with reduced economic output, which have steadily reduced the quality of employment and created both greater economic precariousness in employment and reductions in public and commercial service provision. Along with broad and deep changes in the national and global political economies, many towns and cities have experienced dramatic declines as their principal industries have collapsed, resulting in steep drops in economic activity, employment, and ultimately population. Government responses to the effects of shrinkage in many rural communities have resulted in huge public debts for the central, prefectural and municipal authorities, which are now compromising their financial flexibility and capacity to deal with the deepening crisis enveloping the country's regions.

Within this overall process, regional shrinkage in Japan can be divided into two basic types. The first is the steady, gradual, and somewhat imperceptible—at least over the short term—decline of rural areas experiencing a combination of reduced fertility and the continuous emigration of adolescents and young adults in search of employment, educational, and social opportunities in urban and metropolitan areas. The second is a more sudden community collapse in peripheral towns and cities that have lost their principal means of economic sustenance; this is often a failing heavy-industrial sector, such as mineral extraction and processing. Both of these patterns are to some degree consequences of the entrenchment of an extractive political economy in the national economic space intended to contribute to national growth and prosperity but that has actually benefited metropolitan areas at the expense of the periphery.

It is important to note that shrinkage has not been experienced uniformly among Japan's regional settlements in the postwar era; most regional urban centres have grown rapidly due to specific factors (such as the construction of advantageous transportation infrastructure), whereas other nearby communities have endured sustained depopulation and economic decline. Ominously, our research shows that regional shrinkage will almost certainly be experienced much more uniformly from now on as regional cities, and even some core metropolitan districts, begin to experience the kind of sustained long-term shrinkage that has hitherto been confined to rural locales. This consideration raises the question of what it really means to be Japanese for the residents of the various settlements that are scattered across the archipelago. If metropolitan regions have indeed advanced at the expense of rural areas, as we argue, then what does this reveal about the relative status of rural and urban dwellers within the Japanese national political space?

Part II of this study analyses the responses that actors at the national, regional, and local levels have brought to bear on shrinkage. Throughout the postwar era, the overall response has been the attempted reversal of prevailing trends and the reestablishment of growth through the application of various revitalisation measures. Principal among these has been the development of public infrastructure financed by a complex system of public subsidies at the national and local levels, which itself has encouraged the establishment of, we argue, a co-dependent relationship between rural regions and the national government based on financing public infrastructure of increasingly limited public utility and value. More recently, as traditional sources of regional sustenance have eroded under the intensification of global economic competition and the national government's reform measures, many areas have turned to tourism as a source of economic sustenance. Although tourism is emerging as the dominant response to regional shrinkage, however, it is a notoriously unstable source of income because it is seasonal and subject to distant and changing consumer tastes; moreover, it provides sometimes poor-quality employment. Tourism also has the potential to change a locale's cultural attributes and natural endowments in ways that local residents find disagreeable, thereby pushing them away from a sense of connectedness with their own places. Furthermore, as progressively more communities attempt to reinvent themselves in order to profit from tourism resources, competition between them is intensifying, and there is a growing element of risk, for developments may fail to deliver the expected returns; indeed, this is already occurring. Consequently, though there are and will undoubtedly be success stories to tell, tourism in and of itself will probably not be a sufficient foundation upon which to build a generalised nationwide recovery and a revitalisation of Japan's regions.

Aside from tourism there are other opportunities being explored in Japan's regions, though success is rather limited and constrained by overall conditions within the national and global economies. Some of these opportunities are based on existing comparative advantages in particular locales, and others are newer developments based on emerging circumstances and technologies. As with tourism, many economic revitalisation efforts in regional Japan often lack proper preparation and coordination in both the planning and implementation stages, which can lead to poor returns to investment and sometimes to spectacular losses. With a view to improving this situation, authorities and actors at all levels may wish to move towards greater regional integration of political and economic development activities, as is being done to positive effect in some shrinking regions in the European Union, with an emphasis on including local nongovernmental actors in decision-making processes. This is the first policy proposal to emerge from our research.

Our second recommendation is that municipal governments and other stakeholders in regional Japan might ultimately be better served if they develop professional brand-creation and brand-management capacity with the aim of extracting added value from their inherent cultural and natural assets. Beyond this, stakeholders should be aware that the exploitation of cultural and natural heritage via tourism carries the risk of damaging both the vibrancy of local cultural assets and the sensitive ecosystems in many rural areas. Sometimes visitor numbers need to be controlled, and this increases the requirement for effective planning and coordination between different local tourism and service providers so that fewer visitors will spend longer periods in the same locale, thus increasing local per capita visitor consumption. Hence the task of successfully reviving a local economy and reinvigorating its society and culture requires a detailed and well-researched plan for the coordinated development of a variety of different and complementary economic sectors that are based on a broad range of governmental, commercial, and nongovernmental or nonprofit actors identifying and reinventing local potential for consumption by highly segmented and rapidly changing markets.

Although immigration is being debated within Japan as a possible solution for stabilising shrinking regional communities, the numbers required and the probable dynamics of large-scale replacement migration almost certainly render it an unworkable policy solution in the Japanese context, at least on a national scale and as a principal policy tool. As the national population declines in size and vitality, it becomes a mathematical certainty that many communities will collapse and disappear in the years ahead; the majority of these will be small hamlets and villages situated in comparatively inaccessible coastal, mountainous, and island locales. These disappearing communities require careful and sensitive management so that the remaining residents may live contented and dignified lives. Furthermore, progressively more peripheral towns and cities will increasingly feel the impacts of economic and demographic shrinkage, and they may feel the need to draw on the previous experience and knowledge of rural communities as they, too, manage their declines.

Japan is also not the only country in the world experiencing regional shrinkage. Many regions and countries in the European Union and in East Asia are ageing, and many are either already shrinking or will begin to shrink within the coming decades (Komine & Kabe, 2009; Liu 2010; Longman, 2004). China, for instance, is ageing rapidly; its labour force is expected to decrease in size from about 2010, and its population is projected to commence its decline sometime between 2025 and 2050 (Liu, 2010; Lutz, Sanderson, & Scherbov, 2004; UNPD, 2010). The experiences of Japan's regional communities with the dynamics of national population decline might assist not only in the search for solutions to rural and urban shrinkage in Japan itself but also in countries across Europe and East Asia as they encounter similar situations. Our third policy recommendation, therefore, is the establishment of a specialist international clearing house of information, research, and advice on regional shrinkage, proposed by a body such as the United Nations, or, better still, the Japanese government, in order not only to minimise the disruption caused by the phenomenon but also to maximise any opportunities, particularly environmental ones, that shrinkage might confer.

Our fourth recommendation is to urge more research into the potential positive outcomes of shrinkage, including and especially the establishment of possible relationships between depopulation and reductions in human pressures on the natural environment. Although it is sometimes assumed that depopulation will automatically result in reduced anthropogenic pressures, this might not always be so in circumstances where per capita consumption of natural resources rises at a rate faster than the rate of population decline. Nevertheless, our research points to the possibility that depopulation may induce community members in peripheral areas to think differently about the desirability of continuous economic expansion. Should the causal relationship suggested by intuition be established by detailed empirical research, the implications will apply to environmental policy in shrinking regions and countries worldwide.

The impacts of depopulation on Japan's rural areas have been great, and for some communities they have been catastrophic. Entire villages have disappeared, or have even been 'sold' (BBC Radio 4, 2007), and thousands of municipalities have been judged nonviable and merged into larger entities. Thousands of businesses have collapsed, and hundreds of thousands of older people have been left to live solitary lives in communities with few neighbours as relatives have migrated away or died and as nearby families have abandoned their homes. Such a description might confound those who grew up appreciating the *dynamic and exuberant urban Japan* paradigm, but it is nonetheless accurate.

It is by no means certain, however, that in the long term depopulation will yield only negative results for Japan (or other countries), nor will it necessarily be as severe as current estimates imply—though it could also be worse. Still, properly managed, depopulation may result in improvements to citizens' lives. Living space may expand and the built environment may be reconfigured. Depopulation may reduce consumption of natural resources and result in less pressure on the natural environment. People may decide to spend less time at work and devote more of their energies to family and community. The Japanese government might wish to emulate the European Union and attempt a reconfiguration of the parameters of the nation-state so as to allow mass immigration from neighbouring countries in Asia. Nevertheless, if one wanders around some of the medium-sized towns and cities that make up what has become somewhat disparagingly known as *ura Nihon* (the *backwaters* of Japan), one gradually becomes aware that something is amiss. Although the built environment remains, for the most part, orderly and in fairly good repair, it feels deserted and is growing shabby around the edges. Though the odd convenience store or pharmacy still attracts (mostly older) customers, even at the peak of the day other shops remain closed and shuttered. Weeds increasingly compete for light in the open spaces that have appeared where businesses and residential properties once stood.

Economic recovery and community revitalisation do not just happen; they must be achieved, and as shown in this study, their achievement requires detailed research and planning, as well as inclusive and integrated implementation and coordination. Communities must collectively imagine and reinvent their futures and develop the necessary mechanisms to enact those futures in lived experience. The questions whether regional communities should abandon the expectation of revitalisation and growth and whether urban Japan can or should learn from the past experiences of rural Japan, and finally whether Japan's experience offers lessons for other countries, are difficult to answer. Indeed, the answers are likely to depend upon the precise circumstances of shrinkage in each locale. Many Japanese cities, however, are now decisively in the grip of shrinkage, and some will ultimately face collapse or merger with neighbouring municipalities. Rural villages and small towns have already experienced this, and they have a useful story to tell. It is, for example, becoming clearer with each passing day to some residents in such communities that, rather than struggle to grow in the face of increasingly improbable odds, it is perhaps more realistic to acknowledge and even embrace shrinkage as a fact of life.

Like climate change, population change is a process that takes place over a time horizon that is longer than either the electoral cycle or other periods that most ordinary people are used to dealing with. Hence there are built-in disincentives for governments in democratic countries to enact policies to address the negative impacts of shrinkage that may not manifest themselves until years, even decades, after the tipping point into depopulation has been passed. Indeed, societies are often unaware that such tipping points even exist until long after they have come and gone. Population projections are notoriously unreliable and, once made, have the capacity to alter the contexts of their own projection, thus rendering themselves inaccurate and subject to question. Governments are therefore vulnerable to critique, whatever action they take. If politicians take early action in response to dire projections and warnings from scientists, and the problem disappears, they are subject to the accusation that there was never a problem in the first place. If they ignore the projections and warnings because they believe claims that scientists are self-interested pessimists or simply wrong or because it is not politically expedient to take action, they are likely to be accused of doing too little too late once problems do begin to appear.

Preparing and putting together a book of this type and size has been a monumental task for all of us; but we think the result is worth the effort. In July 2008 a group of scholars gathered at the Yorkshire Art Space in Sheffield formed the Shrinking Regions Research Group and asked the simple question: What is happening right now in Japan's shrinking regions? This book is the product of that gathering, and it tells us that Japan's developmental state is no longer delivering what it once promised the nation and the regions. Villages are gradually disintegrating and disappearing and are being swallowed up by natural succession. Global postindustrial transformations are reaching deep into regional Japan and destroying entire communities, which are collapsing in all but name. In terms of its current responses to the problem, and to borrow a well-worn phrase from economics, the government—in all its various guises—is currently reduced to pushing on a piece of string. Perhaps it is now time for urban communities to listen to the residents of rural areas who have lived for decades with depopulation and who themselves are learning to embrace shrinkage by thinking and living 'beyond growth'; perhaps it is time to turn towards new ways of living rooted not in outmoded and rigid doctrines of maintaining permanent expansion but rather in notions of stability and sustainability.

Epilogue

Restoring Hope in Japan's Shrinking Regions

Lessons from Tōhoku

The Great East Japan Earthquake, Tsunami, and Nuclear Crisis of 2011

At 2.46 p.m. local time on 11 March 2011, a reverse-fault megathrust earthquake measuring 9.0 on the Richter magnitude scale struck 100 km east of Miyagi Prefecture, along the subduction zone under the northwest Pacific Ocean where the Pacific and North American tectonic plates meet (JMA, 2011a). It was the most powerful earthquake ever recorded in Japan and the fourth most powerful to have occurred anywhere on Earth since 1900 (JMA, 2011a; USGS, 2011a). The resulting upthrust and subsidence generated a tsunami with a simulated height of over 20 metres (Fujii & Satake, 2011); it swept over the low-lying coastal areas of the northeastern seaboard of Honshū, leaving debris and devastation in its wake. As of 23 April 2011, the National Police Agency had registered 14,238 deaths, as well as 12,228 missing persons and 5,314 injured persons, across 19 prefectures (NPA, 2011). Although areas as distant as Hokkaido, Tokushima, and Hawaii experienced flooding and damage, Miyagi, Iwate, and Fukushima Prefectures were the worst hit: some 8,618 deaths in Miyagi, 4,121 in Iwate, and 1,436 in Fukushima had been recorded by 23 April (NPA, 2011; Tsai, 2011). Aerial television footage showed entire towns and villages being swept away and many residential areas, fishing ports, and industrial and commercial zones have been severely damaged or completely destroyed.

The tsunami was high enough to breach the protective sea walls at the Fukushima Daiichi nuclear power plant in Okuma and Futaba Towns, Fukushima Prefecture, and to flood the facility, knocking out the main electricity supply as well as the backup generators that kept the six reactors' cooling systems functioning. The loss of cooling capacity set off a chain of events and led to radioactive leaks that extended into the environment beyond the plant's immediate vicinity. An evacuation zone was immediately established; this was widened to cover a 20 km radius around the plant, and residents of the areas 20–30 km from the plant were asked to remain indoors. Approximately 80,000 people either left voluntarily or were evacuated to emergency shelters in Fukushima and nearby prefectures; some moved farther afield. On 21 April the government declared the 20 km evacuation zone a 'no-go area' and those caught trespassing by the police, including residents, faced fines of up to JPY 100,000 or 30 days of detention (*Japan Times*, 2011b).

On 12 April 2011, Japan's Nuclear Industrial Safety Agency raised the level of the accident's seriousness on the International Nuclear and Radiological Event Scale (INES) to 7, placing it alongside the 1986 catastrophe at Chernobyl, in Ukraine. It needs to be stated, however, that the two accidents are different in character and that the quantity of radioactive material released at Chernobyl was much larger than that released thus far at Fukushima Daiichi (BBC, 2011a; NISA, 2011). At the time of this writing, radioactive leakage continues, and Tokyo Electric Power Company (TEPCO), owner of the plant, has estimated that a period of approximately nine months is needed to bring the release of radioactive materials under control (TEPCO, 2011b)—although what *under control* actually means is open to interpretation. The government and the International Atomic Energy Agency (IAEA) are monitoring the situation, and whether to evacuate citizens from areas outside the zone of concentrated radioactive deposits is a question constantly under review (IAEA, 2011).

In addition to the damage caused by the earthquake and tsunami, there has been major disruption to electricity supply, transportation infrastructure, and economic and social life across the Tōhoku and Kantō regions—indeed, in all of Japan. In addition to Fukushima Daiichi, all 15 reactors at the Fukushima Daini, Tokai Daini, Onagawa, and Higashidōri nuclear power plants either went into emergency shutdown or remained offline, and three reactors at the Kashiwazaki-Kariwa plant in Niigata Prefecture had been shut down for inspection prior to the earthquake. In total, 17 of the 21 reactors in the Tōhoku and Hokuriku regions of north-eastern Honshū were at a standstill as of late-April 2011 (Genden, 2011; TEPCO, 2011b; Tōhoku Denryoku, 2011). Some thermal power stations were also damaged and temporarily shut down, and water and gas supplies to more than 1.5 million households were cut off (NPR, 2011).

In the immediate aftermath of the so-called triple disaster, hundreds of thousands of homeless refugees were temporarily housed in emergency shelters across the whole of north-eastern Honshū; 7,000 were accommodated in neighbouring Niigata Prefecture alone.[1] Many endured freezing weather while sleeping for days on the floors of damp and cavernous gymnasiums, with little or no heating, food, water, gasoline, or medical supplies; essential deliveries were hampered by the destruction of transportation infrastructure and by the huge amounts of debris that the tsunami had dumped on roads and railway lines. Older people were particularly vulnerable under these circumstances. Bedridden individuals and those with restricted mobility required transfer from their homes under dangerous conditions, and many others were in need of medication

[1] E-mail communication from correspondent in Niigata.

and treatment for pre-existing illnesses or for conditions resulting from the disaster. Not all of these people survived the ordeal.

The Japan Self-Defence Force despatched 100,000 personnel to the affected area to provide emergency support, and the United States military provided additional labour, equipment, and expertise (Fujioka, 2011). The Royal Australian Air Force organised flights to deliver relief supplies and personnel (Oldaker, 2011), and many countries sent special equipment and emergency search-and-rescue teams; some of the first to arrive were from South Korea and China (Anderlini, 2011; *Reuters.com*, 2011). The runway at Sendai airport had been completely submerged by the tsunami and the terminal building had flooded above the ground floor, rendering electrical and other equipment useless. American soldiers succeeded in clearing away the sludge and opening the airport again for relief flights; limited commercial services resumed on 13 April (*Japan Times*, 2011a). JR East has also been rapidly restoring rail services in and around the area, though as of 23 April 2011 the Tōhoku Shinkansen remained suspended along the stretch between the Fukushima and Ichinoseki stations (JR East, 2011). Thousands have volunteered their efforts, and money has been collected from around the world to help the region's recovery. Nevertheless, the sheer scale of the disaster has been overwhelming, and the authorities have not been able to attend to all needs. Furthermore, the restrictions in place around the Fukushima Daiichi power plant have impeded efforts to recover bodies and clear debris.

Because of power-supply shortages and supply-chain stoppages, thousands of commercial and manufacturing operations were suspended or curtailed, with factories halting production, shops opening for shorter hours and not replacing stock, and transportation and communication services having to decrease operations. The number of foreign tourists to Japan was 50 per cent lower in March 2011 than for the same month in 2010 (NHK, 2011a), and thousands of foreign residents left Japan (especially the Kantō region) after the nuclear crisis began. The disaster has also had widespread impacts on farming and fishing communities across the Tōhoku region, which have seen decreased business and income due to the release of radiation into the atmosphere, soil, and ocean. The radiation has rendered some food products unsafe for consumption and public trust in food safety has been damaged.

Nuclear engineers from Toshiba and Hitachi, two of the three companies that built and installed the reactors and turbines at Fukushima Daiichi, estimate that it will take between 10 and 30 years to complete the decommissioning process that the Japanese government plans for the power plant (NHK, 2011b; *Nikkei.com*, 2011). The decommissioning of the Fukushima Daiichi plant that the government has ordered, the disposal and storing of nuclear materials and contaminated debris, restoration of the area around the plant, and payment compensatory damages to affected citizens will be a huge financial and moral burden on the Japanese state and people for decades to come.

Tectonic activity in north-eastern Japan continues. The main earthquake was preceded by a foreshock measuring 7.2 on the Richter scale and, as of 23 April, there have been more than 425 powerful aftershocks of magnitude 5.0 and above; of these, 73 had magnitudes greater than 6.0 and 5 registered magnitudes greater than 7.0 (JMA, 2011b). These earthquakes have caused additional deaths and injuries and material damage, have hindered the clearance of debris and the restoration of basic services, and have resulted in continued anxiety for people in affected areas. Tōhoku—and Japan—are located at the northwestern edge of the Pacific Ring of Fire and will experience earthquakes and tsunamis long after the effects of the March 2011 event have dissipated. Indeed, the Sanriku coast of Iwate Prefecture has endured many destructive tsunamis, some of these in living memory. On 15 June 1896, the Meiji-Sanriku earthquake generated a tsunami more than 30 m high in some areas that killed more than 20,000 people and destroyed nearly 9,000 homes (Nakao, 2005). On 2 March 1933, a magnitude 8.4 earthquake off the Sanriku coast caused a tsunami of up to 28.7 m that destroyed 5,000 houses and killed 3,000 people (USGS, 2011b). Given this history, it is not surprising that some question both the adequacy of TEPCO's protective measures at its Fukushima Daiichi power plant and the government regulations that framed and guided TEPCO's disaster planning.

* * *

The research, writing, and editing of this book were all conducted before the 11 March earthquake occurred, and the final draft was sent to the publisher in late January 2011—approximately six weeks before the disaster. The earthquake presented us with the dilemma of whether to publish the book without mentioning recent events or to include an epilogue discussing some effects that the disaster may have on future development in Japan's shrinking regions, of which Tōhoku is a major part. The former option would have dated the book and ignored the enormous scale of this event, whereas the latter option could provide only a very incomplete summary of a fast-changing situation. Nevertheless, we concluded that readers might wish to read our view—however limited by circumstances—of how this disaster may affect Japan and the Tōhoku region in the months and years to come.

All the authors of this book wish to express their deepest sympathies and condolences to those affected by this triple disaster. If only one thing is clear at this stage, it is that life in the Tōhoku region has been permanently altered by this crisis. People have lost loved ones and friends, homes, farmland, treasured possessions, and livelihoods. In this epilogue we share with readers our impressions of this major event in Japan's history and make some preliminary assessments about what the disaster and its aftermath may mean for Japan's shrinking regions; we write with the limitations already mentioned in mind. The information presented here is a snapshot of conditions at that time drawn from being resident in Japan throughout the crisis, reading and watching countless press and television reports, as well as from personal experiences and discussions that took place during and after the disaster.

THE IMMENSITY OF THE CRISIS

On 13 March 2011, prime minister Naoto Kan described the challenges presented by the Great East Japan Earthquake and its aftermath as the toughest crisis that the Japanese people have faced since the Second World War (BBC, 2011c). Japan has certainly overcome huge crises in the past; natural disasters, tragedies for those who experience them, are an inescapable part of the ebb and flow of life in this country. The Great Kantō Earthquake of 1923 killed more than 140,000 people; most of the infrastructure and built environment of the region was destroyed either in the earthquake itself or in the ensuing fires. Millions of Japanese lost their lives in the Second World War, and the American strategic bombing campaign not only destroyed Tokyo and Yokohama once more but also devastated large sections of more than 60 cities and killed over 500,000 people. For the Japanese the war culminated, of course, with the atomic bombs dropped on Hiroshima and Nagasaki in August 1945.

Japan's cities were rebuilt with remarkable speed after the war, and by the early 1950s the country had recovered its economic growth trajectory. In fact, by the 1980s Japan was being praised worldwide as the most vibrant and dynamic economy in the world. In 1995 the Great Hanshin-Awaji Earthquake killed more than 6,000 people and devastated the city of Kobe, requiring what has been estimated as the most expensive reconstruction operation in world history—costing approximately USD 64 billion in damage to capital stock—though the regional economy had almost completely recovered within 15 months of the disaster (Horwich, 2000).

It is not our intent to portray the Japanese people as victims on all these occasions; each time they have met adversity positively and with great energy. There is no doubt that the effects of the 11 March 2011 disaster will be acutely felt across the Tōhoku region; but the Japanese are resourceful and knowledgeable people, and they possess deep wells of self-discipline, determination, and dignity. These attributes will stand them and the region as a whole in good stead in the future. Indeed, Japan and Tōhoku will survive and prosper; the question is how and in what form, given that both the country and the region were shrinking before March 2011.

Japan undoubtedly has considerable economic and technological resources at its disposal, not least of which are the impressive resilience and fortitude of the Japanese people in responding to the disaster. But the affected area is broader and the reconstruction requirements much greater than those of the Great Hanshin-Awaji Earthquake. Moreover, the nuclear crisis and subsequent plant decommissioning present unique problems for recovery efforts; access restrictions are expected to remain in place for many months, perhaps years. Continued power shortages will slow reconstruction and restoration in the region.

The economic impacts on the Tōhoku region, and across the whole of Japan, will be substantial and are already being felt. In April 2011 the Bank of Japan (BOJ) downgraded its assessments for the economies of seven of Japan's nine regions, citing supply-chain and production difficulties as well as cautious consumer and business sentiment in the wake of the disaster (BOJ, 2011). The extent to which the crisis will affect the national economy over the medium to long term, however, remains to be seen—because this disaster is different in scope than previous events in Japan's more recent history. Preliminary estimates put the recovery cost at USD 200 billion (*Economist*, 2011). The actual costs are likely to be higher, for the nuclear cleanup and decommissioning of Fukushima Daiichi were not factored into these early calculations.

Prime minister Naoto Kan has ordered the formation of the Great East Japan Earthquake Reconstruction Design Council, which had its inaugural meeting on 14 April (Prime Minister's Office, 2011a). Headed by Makoto Iokibe, president of the National Defence Academy and professor emeritus at Kobe University, the council has been assigned the ambitious task of developing a 'grand vision' for the reconstruction of the Tōhoku region—a vision that is not 'stuck with[in] a traditional framework' and that will be 'highly regarded in history' (Prime Minister's Office, 2011b). Kan himself is a notable figure; he was a campaigner and activist before he became a politician, and his tenure as minister for health and welfare was marked by the unusual and courageous 1996 decision to publicly admit government involvement in the HIV-tainted blood products scandal. Based on the prime minister's record, it seems reasonable to surmise that he is sincere in the wishes he has expressed for the people of Tōhoku and for the direction and purpose of the region's reconstruction. For his part, Professor Iokibe was involved in city planning for Kobe in the wake of the great Hanshin earthquake. The council and subcommittees are composed of experts from relevant fields, including the renowned architect Tadao Ando, who also participated in the Hanshin reconstruction efforts (Prime Minister's Office, 2011). The council aims to issue its first major report on reconstruction in June 2011 (NHK, 2011c).

On 14 April, after the council's first meeting, Professor Iokibe announced that the group had devised a five-point outline of its basic approach; this is summarised here.

1. The council should not be partisan.
2. Discussions should have 'local ownership.'
3. Discussions should result in 'creative' outcomes.
4. Plans should have nationwide support.
5. Plans should give 'hope for the future.' (Prime Minister's Office, 2011a, p. 2)

In addition to organising the Design Council, the government has established an office for managing the economic impacts of the nuclear crisis in Fukushima; this office will be responsible for working with TEPCO to compensate those affected by the release of radiation. Thus far TEPCO has offered JPY 1 million to each affected household as a preliminary payment (TEPCO, 2011a), and the government office, together with TEPCO and the other electricity-generating companies, will establish a compensation fund. At the time of this writing, a nationwide disaster reconstruction tax to help pay for the recovery of the region has not been implemented, but the prime minister's argument for this measure is that the earthquake and its aftermath represent a *national* disaster in which all Japanese citizens have roles and responsibilities.

An initial assessment of the situation suggests that at regional and local levels some municipal boundaries will be redrawn and merged, and that destroyed communities in low-lying areas will be amalgamated into 'compact towns' and relocated to higher ground (NHK, 2011a). Public infrastructure—schools, hospitals, municipal offices, community centres, and so on—will be maintained, but it may be scaled down: These communities were shrinking prior to the earthquake, and the population has been further reduced by the disaster (NHK, 2011a). Residential and commercial areas will be rebuilt so that they are protected from the effects of future earthquakes and tsunamis, and ports and transportation infrastructure will be reconstructed. But greater attention must be paid to the fact that these communities have a high proportion of older residents (NHK, 2011a). At the moment it is still unclear how much of the original infrastructure will be rebuilt and to what extent and in what ways the built environment will be redesigned.

Minamisanriku in Miyagi Prefecture represents an example of current considerations at the local level. On 14 April 2011, NHK news presented a report from the town, which was almost completely destroyed by the earthquake and tsunami: Great swathes were swept away, and approximately 7,000 people have been registered dead or missing (NHK, 2011b). The report stated that the Miyagi prefectural government has drawn up two possible scenarios for the town's reconstruction and invited comments from residents and municipal officials. The plans describe the continued viability of the region's fisheries, and the proposals base economic and societal revival on marine industries. The prefecture plans to rebuild the port, turn the low-lying coastal area into a green belt and park, and rebuild residential and commercial zones on higher ground (NHK, 2011b). More parkland will be created on specially raised areas inland, and these areas will double as emergency evacuation points.

The same NHK report goes on to describe one precedent for such measures from the experience of Shimabara City in Nagasaki Prefecture, which was inundated with water and volcanic debris after the eruptions of Mt. Unzen during the 1990s. There, housing was either relocated or rebuilt on ground raised by approximately 9 m through a process of layering compacted debris and soil. But the report noted that the cost of these measures in Shimabara amounted to more than JPY 9 billion, for a part of a single settlement—an area far smaller than that affected by the Tōhoku tsunami (NHK, 2011b). It is doubtful, therefore, that land-raising and community reconstruction of this type will be employed across the whole Tōhoku region. More likely is that a variety of techniques will be implemented according to risk assessment and cost considerations. For example, many taller concrete structures, such as public buildings and offices, managed to survive even the fiercest aspects of the tsunami. Replacing densely packed low-level housing in port areas with widely spaced apartment blocks surrounded by gardens and devoting the two lowest floors of the new buildings to car parking may be more cost-effective than moving an entire community or raising the level of the land.

Another NHK report focused on the issues faced by Shichigahama Town in Miyagi Prefecture, which was also badly damaged by the tsunami (NHK, 2011c). Located on a small peninsula to the south of Matsushima, it is the smallest municipality by land area in the Tōhoku region. The town's mayor said that many of the town's residents whose homes were washed away would prefer to rebuild on higher ground, but that current government regulations prevent this because most of this higher land (60% of the town's land area) lies within an urbanisation-restricted area, protected by laws meant to preserve its natural beauty and ecosystems. This area is noted for its potential as a tourist attraction, a characteristic that local authorities wish to preserve and which might be compromised by the addition of residential communities to the area. There exists a tension in the community, therefore, between the need to rebuild safer homes and the wish to retain the area's natural heritage and develop its touristic potential (NHK, 2011c). The question, then, becomes this: To what extent should reconstruction authorities prioritise the long-term sustainability of human settlements that were shrinking even before the disaster over the preservation of the region's natural environment, on which the residents themselves depend for their survival and prosperity?

The same NHK report goes on to describe conditions in Yamada Town in Iwate Prefecture, where almost the entire built up area of the town was submerged in the 11 March tsunami; the town has effectively ceased to exist (NHK, 2011c). The fishing industry is gone, and Yamada lacks the finances to begin even modest rebuilding. The town's tax revenues total approximately JPY 1.2 billion in a normal year, but in 2011 condolence payments for deaths in the disaster will cost almost JPY 1 billion, leaving little for anything but basic services. The town's mayor said that bold measures are needed from the central government in order to help towns like Yamada survive, but that at present the structure of government regulations and taxes does not allow for the special measures that would be needed by these communities (NHK, 2011c). Again, these problems highlight the potential for conflict between national and local government over of the costs of maintaining viable settlements and the extent to which residents of shrinking communities can be coerced into moving to newly built compact towns—where they may be safer, but where the new location may not be to their liking.

Of the shrinking regions that feature in this book, one has been directly affected by the earthquake and tsunami. Like Yamada Town, Kamaishi City is located along the scenic Sanriku coast, which is characterised by a series of rias penetrating deep inland that provide natural harbours and shelter (at least from storms) for coastal communities; the rias provide ideal geographical and ecological conditions for marine-products industries. In Kamaishi the 11 March earthquake measured 6.1 on the Richter magnitude scale. The city had recently completed construction of a USD 1.5 billion defence breakwater, reputedly the deepest in the world, as part of its revitalisation plan. But the tsunami breached the breakwater, and the port area of the city, including more than 300 shops, was destroyed (BBC, 2011; Onishi, 2011a). The central populated area of the city, along with Kamaishi Steel Works, is located at the head of a ria, and it is almost certain that as the tsunami waters advanced into the harbour, they were constricted by the shape of the ria, which raised the height of the tsunami above that of the breakwater. Because the port community and buildings, limited by the narrow topography, were also compact and densely nestled on the valley floor, the water level may have been forced still higher as it advanced through the narrow streets, engulfing the low-lying one- and two-storey wooden houses. Reports from the town suggest that the tsunami measured 9 m in the port area, though a massive tsunami of 20 m or more appears to have inundated other bays in Kamaishi, including Tōni, Heita, Ryoshi, Unosumai and

Ōtsuchi.[2] Fujii and Satake's (2011) simulated-tsunami height calculations show the maximum height along the coast of Kamaishi twice rising off the scale and surpassing 25 m.

In all, it is estimated that approximately 1,300 people may be dead or missing in Kamaishi—that is, around 3.5 per cent of the city's population (Onishi, 2011b). Many local citizens housed in emergency shelters are doubtless currently pondering their futures; others will have decided to move away permanently. Low-lying parts of the city, including areas inundated in previous tsunamis, have been swept away. Substantial areas of farmland have been rendered unusable by flooding from seawater and ocean sludge, and the city's fishing fleet, on which much hope for community revitalisation had been placed, has been destroyed. Ships and boats have been dumped inland, and one 6,000-ton freighter, the MV *Asia Symphony*, was left straddling the port wall (Gilligan, 2011).

Despite the presence of so much damage and so many obstacles, the cleanup in Kamaishi and Tōhoku is progressing quickly, and rebuilding will follow. Roads are being speedily mended, utilities are being reconnected, and replacement housing is being brought in. Rural Japanese homes are often prefabricated and require little time to raise. Nippon Steel resumed production at its Kamaishi plant on 12 April using previously accumulated inventory, but it is unclear how long output will continue (*Mainichi Daily News*, 2011). Much of the plant was inundated and its power-generating facilities remain offline; many employees are dead or missing. Nevertheless, neither Kamaishi City nor the Tōhoku region as a whole have disappeared. Indeed, the majority of residents have survived the ordeal; the worst effects of the tsunami were largely limited to the low-lying coastal areas.

Beyond the immediate damage assessments, the earthquake and its aftermath are a grim reminder of the deep-seated and discomfiting questions that Japan's shrinking regions—indeed, the state and nation as a whole—have inherited from the decisions made in the postwar era supporting accelerated economic development. Of the 13,135 bodies

[2]Personal communication and field-work report, N. Nakamura, 22 April 2011.

identified and assigned a cause of death by 11 April, 65.2 per cent were aged 60 or over; drowning was the cause of 92.5 per cent of the deaths (*Daily Yomiuri*, 2011) . These numbers indicate that whatever the reasons, many older people were unable to reach safety in time, and it is reasonable to infer from this that a high proportion of disabled people also died in the tsunami. Clearly, the very high rate of older victims points to differentials within Japanese society in vulnerability to natural disasters, highlighting the question whether the state and society offer adequate care and protection to the country's most vulnerable citizens.

Furthermore, the nuclear crisis exposes the fragility of Japan's postwar energy policy, based as it is on the inaccurate premise that the country lacks other energy resources. The crisis also reveals the misplaced optimism that economic expansion and advanced technology alone could provide the necessary solutions to problems born out of the country's high-speed growth oriented political economy. Fukushima Daiichi is not the only nuclear facility in Japan that is vulnerable to tectonic activity. The massive Kashiwazaki-Kariwa complex in Niigata Prefecture, also owned by TEPCO, sustained damage when a magnitude 6.6 earthquake—its epicenter just 24 km from the plant—occurred on 6 July 2007. Worrying, too, is the fact that the Hamaoka complex in Shizuoka Prefecture, owned by Chūbu Electric Power Company, sits near a known major fault line where powerful earthquakes have regularly occurred in the past, and where an earthquake measuring 8.0 on the Richter scale is predicted to occur soon (Matsumura, 2010; McCormack, 2011).

In addition to its primary function of generating electricity, for much of the postwar era, nuclear energy has been used by the government and the energy industry to generate rural employment and to funnel state funds into the regions—a policy that has obvious long-term impacts on the vulnerability of these areas to natural disasters. Where, for example, should Japan put its nuclear waste, which remains hazardous for many thousands of years, when the country is so vulnerable to underground movements (see, Madsen, 2010)? It is almost certain that the development of expensive fast breeder facilities, the use of mixed oxide fuels, and the accumulation of large quantities of spent fuel in pools at the plants (nearly all of which are located in politically and economically weak rural regions) have been driven in part by the wish to delay the difficult decisions about waste disposal and ageing power plants. Japan possesses abundant and stable geothermal energy sources, receives an average of 1,800–2,100 hours of sunshine per year, and is home to some of the most plentiful wind, tidal, wave and ocean current energy resources in Asia; the statement that Japan lacks domestic sources of energy is simply not true. What is true is that Japan lacks fossil fuels, and therefore the state has invested huge sums of money in developing nuclear power as a substitute—in a country that since 1900 has experienced the greatest density of magnitude 8.0 and higher earthquakes than any other country in the world (USGS, 2011c).

Restoring Hope: Ten Lessons From Tōhoku

On 11 April, on the one-month anniversary of the earthquake, prime minister Kan issued an address to Japan and the world that was later extended in length and detail and printed in the *New York Times*, among other publications (Kan, 2011a; 2011b). In the address Kan thanked those who had helped the Japanese people face this historic crisis, and he expressed deep regret for the nuclear accident. In assuring the world that Japan would make earnest efforts to prevent such accidents in the future, Kan presented 'a two-pronged challenge: responding to rising global energy demand and striving to reduce greenhouse gas emissions to combat global warming' (Kan, 2011b). He continued: 'Going forward, I would like to present a clear vision to the world—that includes the aggressive promotion of clean energy—that may contribute to solving global energy issues' (Kan, 2011b).

Addressing the broader question of regional reconstruction, Kan wrote that this difficult period would provide a 'precious window of opportunity to secure the 'Rebirth of Japan'' and that he wished to 'realize a forward-looking reconstruction that gives people bright hopes for the future' (Kan, 2011b). The prime minister established three principles for the reconstruction plan:

1. To create a regional society that is highly resistant to natural disasters.
2. To establish a social system that allows people to live in harmony with the global environment.
3. To build a compassionate society that cares about people and, in particular, the vulnerable.

From the perspective of the themes and arguments presented in this book, it is significant that Kan did not directly mention the economy; instead, he prioritised societal recovery and environmental sustainability. Moreover, Kan saw potential in transforming the reconstruction of Tōhoku into an opportunity for a new vision for the revitalisation of the rest of Japan's rural regions. Kan's vision is ambitious, and coming at a low point in Japan's modern history, it is certainly inspiring and uplifting. But is it realistic?

Japan's rural regions will almost certainly not grow for the foreseeable future; indeed, they will continue to shrink, and the population will become progressively older. To be sure, the crisis in Tōhoku creates opportunities to think afresh about the achievement of rural and regional community reproduction and sustainability, the development of civil society, and the protection of vulnerable citizens throughout Japan. Likewise, the nuclear crisis affords a chance to reconsider the country's long-term energy needs and how these may be met. Here again, the concept of sustainability comes to the fore, this time in terms of conserving the environment and encouraging human beings to flourish alongside and as a part of nature. Nevertheless—and this is not to cast doubt on the sincerity of Prime Minister Kan's intentions—politics is replete with beautiful phrases unfulfilled. There will be others in Japan in the coming months and years who will wish, for various reasons, to change the direction of this process of creative destruction unleashed by the earthquake on 11 March 2011.

Therefore we support prime minister Kan's intentions for the reconstruction of Tōhoku, for Tōhoku's becoming an example for Japan—and for regions beyond—of successfully implemented measures supporting sustainable communities and a stable environment in the face of population shrinkage. To this end, and based on the research accumulated in the preparation and writing of this book, we present the following 10 objectives to the Reconstruction Design Council for building a stable, resilient and sustainable society in Japan's regions in the years and decades to come.

1. Population shrinkage: Full recognition should be made of population shrinkage in the overall reconstruction design phase, both in amalgamating communities into compact towns and cities and in providing sensible and noninvasive public infrastructure that does not despoil the environment.
2. Community ownership: Public consultation with local residents regarding the design of new communities should be thorough and exhaustive, and the locals' needs and wants should take priority over political and administrative interests. In particular, provisions for an ageing population must be incorporated into all community and infrastructure designs.
3. Sustainable local employment: Local businesses should be prioritised when the national and local governments tender reconstruction contracts, even if these are not always the lowest-cost providers. At all times, reconstruction investments should focus on fostering sustainable local employment as the foundation of sustainable regional prosperity.
4. Environmental sustainability: Assessments of the environmental effects of reconstruction plans should consistently be made at the design stage, in order to prioritise the emergence of an economically, socially, and environmentally sustainable region.
5. Renewable energy: Japan should aim to lead the world in the development of cost-effective, clean, and renewable energy sources. Moreover, small-scale local producers such as co-operatives and

individual households should be granted incentives to supply their own and their regions' energy needs. Redevelopment should emphasise solar, geothermal, wind, and tidal power sources. In addition, the government should, through the judicious use of incentives, encourage the Tōhoku region to become a national (and international) leader in the development of local green energy technologies.

6. Sustainable agriculture: Agricultural and fishing communities should be encouraged to pool resources, collaborate and innovate to produce food that is simultaneously economically and environmentally sustainable. Food production could then regain its place as the principal source of long-term vitality for rural communities, and agriculture would become attractive to new producers wishing to establish a permanent stake in the locale.
7. Vibrant and sustainable local culture: Arts, crafts, theatre, and music should be encouraged in rural regions through the establishment of galleries, museums, performance venues, and exhibition spaces that attract visitors from outside the area and give local communities a sense of their own place through the organic development and sharing of a flourishing, living culture. The Tōhoku region should again be encouraged to brand itself as a pioneer in the development of a regional cultural renaissance in Japan. Local groups should manage these facilities; collaboration with big-name urban galleries, museums, and artists would further assist in the re-establishment of cultural dynamism outside of Japan's urban centres.
8. Lifelong education for sustainability: Educational facilities should be developed with a special emphasis on lifelong learning and on a dynamic intergenerational sharing of knowledge and culture that has community sustainability as its ultimate goal. Facilities should focus on bringing older, middle-aged, younger people and children together to promote the organic development of their region. Centres for advanced education and research should focus on each area's unique attributes and on the scientific, economic,

and cultural bases of a socially and environmentally sustainable region.

9. Integrated, barrier-free space: Public infrastructure and private residential housing should be constructed according to barrier-free designs so that vulnerable and less able-bodied citizens can move about their local areas with ease and without embarrassment, and so that individuals of all attributes may gather, meet and develop relationships easily and without hindrance. In this way, barrier-free design would contribute to the development of a truly integrated civil society that benefits all citizens without favour or prejudice.
10. Support for local entrepreneurs: Proper recognition should be made of the difficulties that local businesses face in competing against national and multinational corporations. National and local government bodies should be encouraged and granted incentives to prefer small-scale local producers of goods and services to larger businesses based elsewhere.

In concluding this epilogue, we wish to reiterate our condolences to those affected by the great east Japan earthquake. We offer this brief piece as our modest contribution to the restoration of hope for a more vibrant, stable and sustainable society that we believe will emerge in the Tōhoku region—a society that will serve as an example for the rest of Japan.

25 April 2011

Notes

1. NUTS stands for Nomenclature of Units for Territorial Statistics and was created by Eurostat as a standardised classification of European spatial units. Although referred to as regions, in the UK context, NUTS 3 applies to single local authorities (e.g., Sheffield) or small groups of authorities (e.g., Barnsley, Doncaster, and Rotherham), whereas NUTS 2 applies to subregions (e.g., South Yorkshire).
2. Philomena de Lima would like to acknowledge the contribution of the coauthors of the study: Maariyah Masud Chaudhry, Robert Whelton, and Rowena Arshad.
3. Population figures in this paragraph taken from Niigata ken (2010) and include all municipal mergers up to that time.
4. For a detailed explanation of methods of calculation, refer to Matanle and Sato (2010).
5. Please see the epilogue to this volume, which gives a preliminary assessment of the impacts of the earthquake, tsunami, and nuclear crisis at Fukushima Daiichi power plant on Kamaishi City and the wider Tōhoku region.
6. Ecotourism can be defined here as tourism that seeks to leave an ecosystem unaltered by human intervention, and green tourism as tourism through comparatively ecologically benign activities, such as enjoying sustainable agricultural, marine and forest products.

References

Aaker, D. (1991). *Managing brand equity: Capitalizing on the value of a brand name*. New York, NY: Free Press.

Adachi, I. (1973). *"Mura' to ningen no hōkai–Nōmin ga asu ga aru ka'* Tokyo, Japan: Sanichishobo.

Adachi, N. (1998). *Shinrin Nippon*. Tokyo, Japan: Shinchō Sensho.

Aitken, A. (2006). Needs assessment of migrant workers. In National Resource Centre for Ethnic Minority Health (Ed.), *Case studies for change* (pp. 24–30). Glasgow, UK: NHS Scotland.

Akamatsu, K. (1962). A historical pattern of economic growth in developing countries. *The Developing Economies*, *1*(1), 3–25.

Akita ken (2010). *Kankō, Akita ken seiyōran*. Retrieved from http://www.pref.akita.lg.jp/www/contents/1260411310720/files/22_p.pdf. Accessed 11 November 2010.

Aldrich, D. (2008). *Site fights: Divisive facilities and civil society in Japan and the West*. Ithaca, NY: Cornell University Press.

Allen, M. (1994). *Undermining the Japanese miracle: Work and conflict in a coalmining community*. Cambridge, UK: Cambridge University Press.

Anderlini, J. (2011, 13 March). China sends rescue team to Japan. *Financial Times*. Retrieved from http://www.ft.com/cms/s/0/40510292-4d6e-11-e0-85e4-00144feab49a.html#axzz1JlE3Jnbe. Accessed 17 April 2011.

Anderson, B., Ruhs, M., Rogaly, B., & Spencer, S. (2006). *Fair enough? Central and Eastern European migrants in low-wage employment in the UK*. Oxford, UK: University of Oxford, Centre on Migration, Policy and Society [COMPAS].

Aoki, H. (2007). Kamaishi Seitetsu-sho no keieigōrika to rōdō-undō (Joint Research Discussion Paper No. 11). University of Tokyo, Institute of Social Science.

Aono, B. (1987). *Yūbarishichō machiokoshi funsenki: Kasoka kara no dasshutsu sakusen*. Tokyo, Japan: PHP Kenkyūjo.

Asahi Shimbun. (2005). *Japan Almanac 2004*. Tokyo, Japan: Asahi Shimbun.

Asahi Shimbun. (2008, 30 April). Nihon, hinkonritsu wāsuto 2 (Evening edition).

Ayabe shi. (n.d.). Rokudo-kankei shisetsu riyo jōkyō. Ayabe, Japan: Ayabe City Office.

Ayabe shi. (various years). Gyōseiku-betsu jūminkubun-betsu Shūkeihyō. Ayabe, Japan: Ayabe City Office.

Bailey, J. (1991). *Ordinary people, extraordinary lives: Political and economic change in a Tohoku village*. Honolulu, HI: University of Hawaii Press.

Bank of Japan. [BOJ]. (2011, April). Regional economic report (summary). Retrieved from BOJ website: http://www.boj.or.jp/en/research/brp/rer/rer110411.htm/. Accessed 16 April 2011.

Bassani, C. (2003). Social capital theory in the context of Japanese children. *electronic journal of contemporary japanese studies*. Article 1. Retrieved from http://www.japanesestudies.org.uk/articles/Bassani.html. Accessed 2 November 2010.

BBC. (2000). Changing the Japanese Way [Television series episode]. In W. Treharne Jones & M. Kiggell (Producers), *Bubble Trouble*, London: British Broadcasting Corporation.

BBC. (2006, 8 August). Council tax 'rises for migrants.' Retrieved from BBC News website: http://news.bbc.co.uk/1/hi/uk_politics/5255038.stm. Accessed 2 November 2010.

BBC. (2011a, 12 April). How does Fukushima differ from Chernobyl? Retrieved from http://www.bbc.co.uk/news/world-asia-pacific-13050228. Accessed 17 April 2011.

BBC. (2011b, 10 April) Japan: One town's struggle a month after the disaster. Retrieved from http://www.bbc.co.uk/news/world-asia-pacific-13029824. Accessed 16 April 2011.

BBC. (2011c, 14 March) Japan quake: Worst crisis since WWII, says PM. Retrieved from http://www.bbc.co.uk/news/world-asia-pacific-12726297. Accessed 17 April 2011.

BBC Radio 4 (2007, 16 February). The village that got too old. Retrieved from http://news.bbc.co.uk/2/hi/programmes/documentary_archive/6367949.stm. Accessed 7 December 2009.

Beck, U. (1992). *Risk society: Towards a new modernity*. London, UK: Sage.

Becker, H., Franke, T., Löhr, R.-P., & Rösner, V. (2002). *Socially integrative city programme—An encouraging three-year appraisal*. Federal Ministry of Transport, Building, and Urban Development website. Retrieved from http://www.sozialestadt.de/en/veroeffentlichungen/zwischenbilanz/1-socially-integrated-city-appraisal.shtml. Accessed 2 November 2010.

Bernstein, G. (2005). *Isami's house: Three centuries of a Japanese family*. Berkeley, CA: University of California Press.

Bloom, D., Canning, D., & Sevilla, J. (2003). *The demographic dividend: A new perspective on the economic consequences of population change*. Santa Monica, CA: Rand.

Blotevogel, H. (2000). Rationality and discourse in (post)modern spatial planning. In W. Salet & A. Faludi (Eds.), *The revival of strategic spatial planning*. Amsterdam, the Netherlands: Royal Netherlands Academy of Arts and Sciences.

Blotevogel, H., & Schmitt, P. (2006). 'European metropolitan regions' as a new discursive frame in strategic spatial planning and policies in Germany. *Die Erde*, *137*(1–2), 55–74.

BMVBS & BBR [Ministry of Transport, Building, and Urban Affairs & Federal Office for Building and Regional Planning]. (2006).

Perspectives of spatial development in Germany. Retrieved from http://www.bbr.bund.de/nn_26208/BBSR/EN/Publications/Special Publication/2006__2001/PerspectivesSpatialDevelopment.html. Accessed 7 December 2009.

Boorstin, D. (1992). *The image: A guide to pseudo-events in America.* New York, NY: Vintage.

Bothwell, R. (2003). The challenges of growing the NPO and voluntary sector in Japan. In S. Osborne (Ed.), *The voluntary and non-profit sector in Japan: The challenge of change*. London, UK: RoutledgeCurzon.

Bowen, R. (2003). *Japan's dysfunctional democracy: The Liberal Democratic Party and structural corruption.* Armonk, NY: M. E. Sharpe.

Braun, B. (2005). Economic restructuring and regional development in Germany. *Geographische Rundschau (International Edition)*, *1*(1), 16–22.

Brinton, M. (1996). *Women and the economic miracle: Gender and work in postwar Japan.* Berkeley, CA: University of California Press.

Broadbent, J. (2002). Comment: The institutional roots of the Japanese construction state. *ASIEN*, *84*, 43–46.

Bryden, J., & Munro, G. (2001). New approaches to economic development in peripheral rural regions. *Scottish Geography*, *116*(2), 111–124.

BSolutions. (2005). *An initial survey of migrant labour in the north east of Scotland.* Banff, UK: Banff and Buchan College of Further Education.

Bucher, H., & Mai, R. (2005). *Depopulation and its consequences for the regions of Europe*. Report Prepared for the Council of Europe, Directorate General III–Social Cohesion, DG3/CAHP10(2005) 7 final.

Burgess, C. (2007, 2 February). 'Loss' and 'recovery' of voice amongst Korean international marriage migrants: Discourses of Koreanness in contemporary Japan. *electronic journal of contemporary japanese studies,* Discussion Paper 1. Retrieved from http://www.japanesestudies.org.uk/discussionpapers/2007/Burgess.html. Accessed 7 December 2010.

Casio. (2009, 6 November). *Casio announces spin-off to establish a small and medium-size display business subsidiary and partial transfer of its shares* [Press release]. Retrieved from http://world.casio.com/corporate/news/2009/20091106e.pdf. Accessed 11 December 2010.

Casio. (2010a). Establishment of Kochi Casio Co., Ltd., in Nankoku City, Kochi. In *History of Casio* (chapter 4). Retrieved from http://world.casio.com/corporate/history/chapter04/index.html. Accessed 17 December 2010.

Casio. (2010b). *Annual Report 2010.* Retrieved from http://world.casio.com/ir/library/pdf/ar2010/annual_2010.pdf. Accessed 17 December 2010.

Central Intelligence Agency [CIA] (2010). *The World Factbook 2010.* Retrieved from https://www.cia.gov/library/publications/download/download-2010/factbook.zip. Accessed 11 November 2010.

Chalmers, N. (1989). *Industrial relations in Japan: The peripheral work force*, New York, NY: Routledge.

Chambers, E. (1997). *Tourism and culture: An applied perspective.* Albany, NY: State University of New York Press.

Chawla, M., Betcherman, G., & Banerji, A. (2007). *From red to gray: The 'third transition' of aging populations in Eastern Europe and the former Soviet Union*. Washington, DC: World Bank.

Chūgoku Shimbun (2000, 30 January). Urayama no jūnin.

Chūnichi Shimbun (1997, 12 October). Nishiasai no nōmin himei.

Citizens Advice Bureau [CAB]. (2005). *Home from home? Experiences of migrant workers in rural parts of the UK, and the impact on local service providers*. London, UK: Citizens Advice Bureau.

Coates, D. (2007). The rise and fall of Japan as a model of progressive capitalism. In D. Bailey, D. Coffey, & P. Tomlinson (Eds.), *Crisis or recovery in Japan: State and industrial economy* (pp. 179–196). London, UK: Edward Elgar.

Cole, D. (2004). Exploring the sustainability of mining heritage tourism. *Journal of Sustainable Tourism, 12*(6), 480–494.

Commission of the European Communities [CEC]. (2005). *Confronting demographic change: A new solidarity between the generations* [Green paper]. Communication from the Commission, COM(2005) 94 final.

Commission of the European Communities [CEC]. (2006). *The demographic future of Europe – From challenge to opportunity*. Communication from the Commission, COM(2006) 571 final.

Commission of the European Communities [CEC]. (2007). *Growing regions, growing Europe: Fourth report on economic and social cohesion.* Communication from the Commission, Luxembourg: CEC.

Commission for Rural Communities [CRC]. (2007). *A8 migrant workers in rural areas* [Briefing paper]. Cheltenham, UK: Commission for Rural Communities. Retrieved from http://www.ruralcommunities.gov.uk/files/A8%20migrant%20workers%20in%20rural%20areas.pdf. Accessed 17 October 2009.

Cornelius, W. (1994). Japan: The illusion of immigration control. In W. Cornelius, P. Martin, & J. Hollifield (Eds.), *Controlling immigration: A global perspective* (pp. 375–410). Stanford, CA: Stanford University Press.

Coulmas, F. (2007). *Population decline and ageing in Japan: The social consequences*. London, UK: Routledge.

Council of European Municipalities and Regions [CEMR]. (2006). *The impact of demographic change on local and regional government– Research project*. Brussels, Belgium: CEMR.

Crichton, T. (2004, 18 January). Where have all the people gone? *Sunday Herald*. Glasgow, UK.

Crooker, A. (2007). *Improved methodology for the commercialization of university intellectual property*. Unpublished master's thesis, University of Kentucky, Lexington, KY. Retrieved from http://archive.uky.edu/bitstream/10225/772/FinalThesisPackage.pdf. Accessed 17 December 2010.

Culter, S. (1999). *Managing decline: Japan's coal industry restructuring and community response*. Honolulu, HI: University of Hawaii Press.

Daily Yomiuri (2002, September 18). Salty source of income: Health conscious develop thirst for deep-sea water.

Daily Yomiuri. (2011, 21 April) 92.5% of Disaster victims drowned, NPA Finds. Retrieved from http://www.yomiuri.co.jp/dy/national/T110420005996.htm. Accessed 24 April 2011.

de Lima, P., Chaudhry, M., Whelton, R., & Arshad, R. (2007). *A study of migrant workers in Grampian*. Edinburgh, UK: Communities Scotland.

de Lima, P., Jentsch, B., & Whelton, R. (2005). *Migrant workers in the Highlands and Islands*, Inverness, UK: Highlands and Islands Enterprise.

de Lima, P., & Wright, S. (2009). Welcoming migrants? Migrant labour in rural Scotland. *Social Policy and Society*, *8*(3), 391–404.

Denholm, A. (2004, 1 May). Migrants help boost population figures in Scotland. *The Scotsman*. Retrieved from http://thescotsman.scotsman.com/latestnews/Migrants-help-boost-population-figures.2524940.jp. Accessed 2 November 2010.

Development Bank of Japan. (2001). *Revitalization of middle-aged and elderly workers in Japan's labor markets: Requiring the expansion of the vocational training functions* (Research Report No. 16). Retrieved from http://www.dbj.jp/en/reportshift/report/research/pdf_all/all_16e.pdf. Accessed 17 December 2010.

Dewit, A., & Yamazaki, Y. (n.d.). Flawed political economy of decentralization. *The Asia Pacific Journal: Japan Focus*. Retrieved from http://japanfocus.org/-Andrew-DeWit/1824. Accessed 14 December 2009.

Diamond, J. (2005). *Collapse: How societies choose to fail or succeed.* New York, NY: Viking.

Difu [German Institute of Urban Affairs] (Ed.). (2007). *Dritte bundesweite Befragung in den Programmgebieten der 'Sozialen Stadt'–Zentrale Ergebnisse und Empfehlungen.* Berlin, Germany: Arbeitspapiere zum Programm Soziale Stadt.

DiGaetano, A., & Strom, E. (2003). Comparative urban governance: An integrated approach. *Urban Affairs Review, 38*(3), 356–395.

Donmoyer, R. (2000). Generalizability and the single case study. In R. Gomm, M. Hammersley, & P. Foster (Eds.), *Case Study Method.* London, UK: Sage.

Dore, R. (2003). *Stock market capitalism: Welfare capitalism–Japan and Germany versus the Anglo-Saxons.* Oxford, UK: Oxford University Press.

Dusinberre, M. (2008). Unread relics of a transnational 'hometown' in rural western Japan. *Japan Forum, 20*(3), 305–335.

Dusinberre, M. (in press). *Hard times in the hometown: A history of community survival in modern Japan.* Honolulu, HI: University of Hawaii Press.

Dusinberre, M., & Aldrich, D. (2011) Hatoko comes home: Civil society and nuclear power in Japan. *The Journal of Asian Studies, 20*(3). In press.

East Japan Railway Company. [JR East]. (2011). Train status information. Retrieved from JR East website: http://traininfo.jreast.co.jp/train_info/e/shinkansen.aspx. Accessed 23 April 2011.

Economic and Social Research Council. [ESRC]. (2009). Why is Scotland's population shrinking and ageing?–A new research initiative tackles Scotland's key demographic issues. Retrieved from ESRC website:

http://www.esrcsocietytoday.ac.uk/ESRCInfoCentre/PO/releases /2005/april/index2.aspx. Accessed 2 November 2010.

Economic and Social Survey of Asia and the Pacific. [ESCAP]. (2008). ESCAP: Benefits but costs also in international migration in Asia-Pacific. Retrieved from http://www.unescap.org/survey2008/backgrounders/ 09_international_migration.asp?print=true. Accessed 7 December 2010.

Economist. (2011, 17 March). The cost of calamity. Retrieved from http://www.economist.com/node/18387016?story_id=18387016. Accessed 18 April 2011.

Eisenstadt, S. (1988). Beyond collapse. In N. Yoffee & G. Cowgill (Eds.), *The collapse of ancient states and civilizations* (pp. 236–243). Tuscon, AZ: University of Arizona Press.

Endo, H. (2005). Kankō to iu 'imeeji no orimono.' In H. Sudo and H. Endo (Eds.), *Kankō shakaigaku* (pp. 93–116). Tokyo, Japan: Akashi Shoten.

Entwicklungsgesellschaft Duisburg mbH. [EG DU]. (2008). EG DU Intern: Ziele und Aufgaben. Retrieved from http://www.duisburg.de/ micro/eg-du/egduintern/egdu_intern_ziele.php. Accessed 2 November 2010.

Er, L. (2005). Local governance: The role of referenda and the rise of independent governors. In G. Hook (Ed.), *Contested governance in Japan: Sites and issues* (pp. 71–89). London, UK: RoutledgeCurzon.

European Parliament. (2008). *Shrinking regions: A paradigm shift in demography and territorial development*. Brussels, Belgium: European Parliament.

European Spatial Planning Observation Network. [ESPON]. (2005). Project 1.1.4. *The spatial effects of demographic trends and migration final report*. Retrieved from http://www.espon.eu/main/Menu_Projects /Menu_ESPON2006Projects/Menu_ThematicProjects/demographic-trends.html. Accessed 2 November 2010.

European Spatial Planning Observation Network. [ESPON]. (2008). Territorial dynamics in Europe: Trends in population development. Retrieved from http://www.espon.eu/main/Menu_Publications/Menu_TerritorialObservations/trendsinpopulationdevelopment.html. Accessed 2 November 2010.

European Spatial Planning Observation Network. [ESPON]. (2010). DEMIFER – Demographic and migratory flows affecting European regions and cities (Draft final report, Annex 11 – Atlas of maps). Retrieved from http://www.espon.eu/main/Menu_Projects/Menu_AppliedResearch/demifer.html. Accessed 13 October 2010.

Eurostat. (2010a). Population projections—Statistics explained (2010/10/3). Retrieved from http://epp.eurostat.ec.europa.eu/statistics_explained/index.php/Population_projections#. Accessed 2 November 2010.

Eurostat. (2010b). Population change at regional level—Statistics explained (2010/10/3). Retrieved from http://epp.eurostat.ec.europa.eu/statistics_explained/index.php/Population_change_at_regional_level. Accessed 2 November 2010.

Federal Statistical Office. (2006). *Germany's population by 2050: Results of the 11th Coordinated Population Projection*. Wiesbaden, Germany: Statistisches Bundesamt.

Feldhoff, T. (2002a). Japan's construction lobby activities: Systematic stability and sustainable regional development. *ASIEN*, *84*, 4–42.

Feldhoff, T. (2002b). Japan's regional airports: Conflicting national, regional and local interests, *Journal of Transport Geography*, *10*(3), 165–175.

Feldhoff, T. (2005). *Bau-Lobbyismus in Japan: Institutionelle Grundlagen–Akteursnetzwerke–Raumwirksamkeit*. Dortmund, Germany: Dortmunder Vertrieb für Bau- und Planungsliteratur.

Feldhoff, T. (2007). Japan's construction lobby activities and the privatization of highway-related public corporations. In A. Sorensen & C. Funck (Eds.), *Living cities in Japan: Citizens' movements, machizukuri and living environments* (pp. 91–111). London, UK: Routledge.

Feng, X. (2008). Who benefits?: Tourism development in Fenghuang County, China. *Human Organization, 67*(2), 207–220.

Flüchter, W. (2005). Megalopolises and rural peripheries: Shrinking cities in Japan. In Project Office Philipp Oswalt (Ed.), *Shrinking cities, volume 1: International research.* Ostfildern-Ruit, Germany: Hatje Cantz.

Flüchter, W. (2008). Schrumpfende Städt als Herausforderung: Japan, Hokkaidō und der Fall der Stadt Yūbari. *Japanstudien, 20*, 69–102.

Forestry Agency. (2006). Shinrin oyobi ringyō no dōkō. *Shinrin ringyō hakusho*. Tokyo, Japan: Forestry Agency.

Fujii, Y., & Satake, K. (2011). Off Tōhoku-Pacific tsunami on March 11, 2011. International Institute of Seismology and Earthquake Engineering (IISEE), Building Research Institute. Retrieved from IISEE website: http://iisee.kenken.go.jp/staff/fujii/OffTōhokuPacific2011/tsunami.html. Accessed 18 March 2011.

Fujioka, C. (2011). Tsunami puts rare spotlight on Japan soldiers. Retrieved from Reuters website: http://www.reuters.com/article/2011/03/22/us-japan-soldiers-idUSTRE72L0FJ20110322. Accessed 23 April 2011.

Fujita, K. & Hill, R. (1989). Global production and regional 'hollowing out' in Japan. In M. Smith (Ed.), *Pacific Rim cities in the world economy: Comparative urban and community research*, vol. 2 (pp. 200–230). Piscataway, NJ: Transaction Books.

Fujita, M., & Tabuchi, T. (1997). Regional growth in postwar Japan. *Regional Science and Urban Economics, 27*(6), 643–670.

Funck, C. (1999). When the bubble burst: Planning and reality in Japan's resort industry. *Current Issues in Tourism, 2*(4), 333–353.

Gardenfors, P. (2000). *Conceptual spaces: The geometry of thought.* Cambridge, MA: MIT Press.

Gardenfors, P. (2004). Conceptual spaces as a framework for knowledge representation. *Mind and Matter*, *2*(2), 9–27.

Garside, W. (2005). A very British phenomenon?: Industrial politics and the decline of the Japanese coal mining industry since the 1950s. *Australian Economic History Review*, *45*(2), 186–203.

Gatzweiler, H.-P., Meyer, K., & Milbert, A. (2003). Schrumpfende Städte in Deutschland? Fakten und Trends. *Informationen zur Raumentwicklung*, *10/11*, 557–574.

Genda, Y. (2005). *A nagging sense of job insecurity: The new reality facing Japanese youth.* Tokyo, Japan: International House of Japan.

Genda, Y., & Nakamura, N. (Eds.). (2009). *Kibōgaku [2]: Kibō no saisei: Kamaishi no rekishi to sangyō ga katarumono*. Tokyo, Japan: Tōkyō Daigaku Shuppankai.

General Register Office for Scotland [GROS]. (2010). *Scotland's population 2009—The Registrar General's annual review of demographic trends.* Retrieved from http://www.gro-scotland.gov.uk/statistics/publications-and-data/annual-report-publications/rgar-2009/index.html. Accessed 2 November 2010.

Gerring, J. (2007). *Case study research: Principles and practice*. Cambridge, UK: Cambridge University Press.

Gilligan, A. (2011, 20 March). Japan earthquake: Calm after the storm. *Daily Telegraph.* Retrieved from http://www.telegraph.co.uk/news/worldnews/asia/japan/8393056/Japan-earthquake-calm-after-the-storm.html. Accessed 16 April 2011.

Gilpin, N., Henty, M., Lemos, S., Portes, J., & Bullen, C. (2006). *The impact of free movement of workers from Central and Eastern Europe on the UK labour market* (Department for Work and Pensions [DWP] Working Paper No. 29). Retrieved from DWP website: http://campaigns.

dwp.gov.uk/asd/asd5/report_abstracts/wp_abstracts/wpa_029.asp. Accessed 2 November 2010.

Green, A., & Hardill, I. (2003). *Rural labour markets, skills and training.* London, UK: Department for Environment, Food and Rural Affairs.

Groth, D. (1986). *Biting the bullet: The politics of grass-roots protest in contemporary Japan.* Unpublished PhD dissertation, Stanford University, Stanford, CA.

Groth, D. (1996). Media and political protest: The bullet train movements. In S. Pharr and E. Krauss (Eds.), *Media and politics in Japan* (pp. 213–242). Honolulu, HI: University of Hawaii Press.

Haimurubushi. (2009). Haimurubushi homepage. Retrieved from http://www.haimurubushi.co.jp/. Accessed 15 December 2009.

Hane, M. (1996). *Eastern Phoenix: Japan since 1945.* Boulder, CO: Westview Press.

Hao, S. (2006, 6 June). Isle seawater exports surge. *Honolulu Advertiser.*

Hara. (2007). Kokuritsu kōen to chiiki no shinkō—chihō bunken jidai no miryoku aru kokuritsu kōen zukuri. *Kokuritsu kōen, 659*, 12–15.

Harada, N., & Matsuhashi, H. (2008). Academic spin-offs in Japan: Institutional revolution and early outcomes. University of Tsukuba Department of Social Systems and Management Discussion Paper Series No. 1196. Retrieved from http://www.sk.tsukuba.ac.jp/SSM/libraries/pdf1176/1196.pdf. Accessed 11 December 2010.

Harris, C. (1982). The urban and industrial transformation of Japan. *Geographical Review, 72*(1), 50–89.

Hayashi, F., & Prescott, E. (2002). The 1990s in Japan: A lost decade. *Review of Economic Dynamics, 5*(1), 206–235.

Hayashi, Y. (2006). Chihō bunken to kokudo keisei keikaku. *Toshi Keikaku, 263*, 21–26.

Hein, C., & Pelletier, P. (2006). Decentralization policies—Questioning the Japanese model. In C. Hein & P. Pelletier (Eds.), *Cities, Autonomy, and Decentralization in Japan* (pp. 164–180). London, UK: Routledge.

Hein, L. (2008). The cultural career of the Japanese economy: Developmental and cultural nationalisms in historical perspective. *The Asia-Pacific Journal: Japan Focus*. Retrieved from http://japanfocus.org/-Laura-Hein/2792. Accessed 7 December 2009.

Heineberg, H. (2005). Cities in Germany–Between growth, shrinkage and restructuring. *Geographische Rundschau International Edition, 1*(1), 30–41.

Higashide, M. (2008). Zenkoku todōfuken-shikuchōson hensen rekishi jōhō: Todōfuken ichiran Niigata-ken. In Todōfuken-shikuchōson deeta to zatsugaku de manabō tabi. Retrieved from http://uub.jp/upd/niigata.html, Accessed 16 June 2009.

Highlands and Islands Enterprise. [HIE]. (2005). *A Smart, successful Highlands and Islands.* Inverness, UK: HIE.

Higuchi, N. (2006) *Brazilian migration to Japan: Trends, modalities and impact.* Paper presented to the Expert Group Meeting on International Migration and Development in Latin America and the Caribbean, Population Division. Department of Economic and Social Affairs, United Nations Secretariat, November–December 2005.

Hirotani, H. (2000). Seisho nihonzaru kotaigun no higai taisaku to hogo kanri ni tsuite. In Y. Yokomizo & S. Kimura (Eds.), *Nihonzaru no ima mukashi mirai—Yasei dōbutsu to no kyōson o kangaeru* (Research Report No. 10). Odawara: Kanagawa Kenritsu Hakubutsukan.

Hisada, T. (2007) Yūbari no sakebi. *Chizu chūshin, 416* (May), 22–23.

Hiwasaki, L. (2005) Toward sustainable management of national parks in Japan: Securing local community and stakeholder participation. *Environmental Management, 35*(6), 753–764.

Hobo, T., Kawai, H., Sasaki, T., & Hiraoka, K. (2007). *Yūbari, hatan to saisei*. Tokyo, Japan: Jichitai kenkyūsha.

Hokkaidō Shinbunsha (Ed.). (1999). *Hokkaidō no 20-seiki*. Sapporo, Japan: Hokkaidō Shinbunsha.

Hokkaidō Shinbunsha (Ed.). (2007). *Hokkaidō shichōson deetabukku*. Sapporo, Japan: Hokkaidō Shinbunsha.

Hongū-chō. (2003) Ippan Shitsumon, 76. *Gikaidayori*. Hongū Town: Hongū Town Office.

Hood, C. (2006). *Shinkansen: From bullet train to symbol of modern Japan*. London, UK: Routledge.

Hook, G., & Siddle, R. (Eds.). (2003). *Japan and Okinawa: Structure and subjectivity*. London, UK: RoutledgeCurzon.

Hornyak, T. (2004, 30 August). Ghost town: Japan's ill-fated Canadian theme park goes bust. Canadian Business Online. Retrieved from http://www.canadianbusiness.com/article.jsp?content=20040830_61548_61548. Accessed 27 September 2010.

Horwich, G. (2000). Economic lessons of the Kobe earthquake. *Economic Development and Cultural Change*, *48*(3), 521–542.

Howell, D. (1995). *Capitalism from within: Economy, society and state in a Japanese fishery*. Berkeley, CA: University of California Press.

Hsieh, P., & Li, Y. (2009). A cluster perspective of the development of the deep ocean water industry. *Ocean and Coastal Management*, *59*, 287–293.

Idei, N. (2005). *Shitei kanrisha seido*. Tokyo, Japan: Gakuyō shobō.

Igarashi, T. (1999). Public works at a crossroads. *Social Science Japan*, December, 3–5.

Iguchi, M. (1990). Okutama no nihonzaru tanpōki–2. *Monkey*, *34*(4), 11–14.

Ikuma, H. (2002). *Dai-san sekutā o risutora seyo*. Tokyo, Japan: Nikkan kōgyō.

Imamura, T. (1991). Dai-san sekutā no gainen to kokka shingi. In T. Imamura (Ed.), *'Dai-san sekutā' no kenkyū*. Tokyo, Japan: Chūō hōki.

Imura, H. (2005). Japan's environmental policy: Institutions and the interplay of actors. In H. Imura & M. Schreuers (Eds.), *Environmental Policy in Japan* (pp. 49–85). Cheltenham, UK: Edward Elgar.

Inoue, M. (2002). *Yama no hatake o saru kara mamoru*. Tokyo, Japan: Nōbunkyō.

Inoue, M., & Kanamori, H. (2006). *Yama to tahata o shika kara mamoru*. Tokyo, Japan: Nōbunkyō.

International Atomic Energy Agency. [IAEA]. (2011). Fukushima nuclear accident update blog. Retrieved from http://www.iaea.org/newscenter/news/tsunamiupdate01.html. Accessed 18 April 2011.

Irving, R. (1984). *Rural depopulation and levels of living in post war Japan: The case of Kyoto and Shiga Prefectures*. Unpublished PhD dissertation, University of Sheffield, Sheffield, UK.

Irving, R. (2005). *Environmental caretaker—Who wants the job?* Dubrovnik Conference on Sustainable Development of Energy, Water and Environment Systems, Dubrovnik, Croatia, June 2005.

Irving, R. (2006). Kusakabe revisited: The demise of a village community in the Tamba Uplands (I). *Journal of Policy Studies*, *22*(March), Kwansei Gakuin University, 57–66.

Irving, R.(2009). Kusakabe revisited: The demise of a village community in the Tamba Uplands (II). *Journal of Policy Studies*, *33*(November), Kwansei Gakuin University, 25–38.

Ishigaki shi. (2009). Yaeyama Islands tourist information. Retrieved from Ishigaki City website: http://www.city.ishigaki.okinawa.jp/International/tourist.html. Accessed 15 December 2009.

Ishigaki shi. (2010). Ishigaki City website. Retrieved from http://www.city.ishigaki.okinawa.jp/. Accessed 3 November 2010.

Ishiguro, K. (2008). Japanese employment in transformation: The growing number of non-regular workers. *electronic journal of contemporary japanese studies*, Article 10. Retrieved from http://www.japanesestudies.org.uk/articles/2008/Ishiguro.html. Accessed 28 October 2010.

Ishii, S. (2009). *Chihō shakai ni okeru ichiji sanpin wo chūshin to shita chiiki burando no keisei shuhō ni kansuru kenkyū: jiba sangyō no kasseika wo shiya ni ireta chiiki burando no kachi to keisei shuhō no kōsatsu wo chūshin ni.* Unpublished PhD dissertation, Hirosaki University, Hirosaki, Japan. Retrieved from http://hdl.handle.net/10129/2262. Accessed 29 November 2010.

Ishikawa, Y. (1992). The 1970s migration turnaround in Japan revisited: A shift-share approach. *Papers in Regional Science, 71*(2), 153–173.

Isomura, A. (2000). *Oga no tabi, michi, shuku–Oga no hosomichi*. Akita: Nihonkaiiki Bunka Kenkyūsho.

Itō, A. (2000). Kaihatsu no jinruigaku–Jinruigaku no kaihatsu. In M. Aoyagi (Ed.), *Kaihatsu no bunkajinruigaku*. Tokyo, Japan: Kokonshoin.

Ito, M. (2008). Measures for supporting regional job creation in Japan. *Japan Labor Review, 5*(1), 85–99.

Ito, R. (1996). Mohitotsu no kokusai rōdōryoku ido. In T. Iyotani & T. Sugihara (Eds.), *Nihon shakai to imin: Koza gaikokujin teiju mondai*, 1 (vol. 1). Tokyo, Japan: Akashi Shoten.

Iwate ken. (2010). *Heisei 21-nen Iwate ken kankō tōkei gaiyō*. Retrieved from Iwate Prefecture website: http://www.pref.iwate.jp/view.rbz?cd=27924. Accessed 29 September 2010.

Iwate ken kankō kyōkai. (2004). *Heisei 15-nen Iwate ken kankō tōkei gaiyō*. Retrieved from Iwate Prefecture Tourist Association website: http://www.iwatetabi.jp/page/association/statistics.html. Accessed 29 September 2010.

Iwate Tōkai Shimbun. (1995, 27 November). *Aonoki Shufu no Kai ni daijin shō.*

Iwate Tōkai Shimbun. (1998, 2 May). *Syujitsu eigyō ni noridasu.*

Iwate Tōkai Shimbun. (2006, 23 March). *Omoshiro tisan tishō taishō wo jushō.*

Iwate Tōkai Shimbun. (2007, 26 January). *Sōsaku nōka restoran cosmos.*

Jacob, A.L., Vaccaro, I., Sengupta, R., Hartter, J., & Chapman, C. (2008). Integrating landscapes that have experienced rural depopulation and ecological homogenization into tropical conservation planning. *Tropical Conservation Science, 1*(4), 307–320.

Jain, P. (2000). Jūmin tōhyo and the Tokushima anti-dam movement in Japan: The people have spoken. *Asian Survey, 40*(4), 551–570.

Jamieson, L. & Groves, L. (2008). Drivers of youth out-migration from rural Scotland: Key. Retrieved from the Scottish Government website: http://www.scotland.gov.uk/Publications/2008/01/22131922/0. Accessed 2 November 2010.

Japan Association of Travel Agents. [JATA]. (2009). Ryokōsha-sū no hensen. Retrieved from http://www.jata-net.or.jp/tokei/004/2009/01.htm. Accessed 24 November 2010.

Japan Corporate News Network. (2006). Ako Kasei confirms that high mineral water helps suppress helicobacter pylori. Retrieved from http://www.thefreelibrary.com/Ako+Kasei+Confirms+that+High+Mineral+Water+Helps+Suppress...-a0147113605. Accessed December 11, 2010.

Japan Economic Journal. (1986, 6 May). Foreign brides: Cure for 'lonely hearts' blues? Tax payers may fund foreign marriages.

Japan Economic Newswire. (2003, 18 September). Toyama Prefecture town eyes economic boost via deep seawater.

Japan Economic Newswire. (2007a, 15 May). Employment rate for high school graduates rises for 5th Year in a Row.

Japan Economic Newswire. (2007b, 19 September). National average of commercial land prices posts first rise in 16 years.

Japan Ecotourism Society. [JES]. (2007). *Ecotsūrizumu ni kan suru shōhisha neezu chōsa*. Tokyo, Japan: Japan Ecotourism Society.

Japan Federation of Construction Contractors. [JFCC]. (2010). *Kensetsugyō handobukku*. Tōkyō, Japan: Tanaka Insatsu.

Japan Forum on International Relations. [JFIR]. (2010). Prospects and challenges for the acceptance of foreign migrants to Japan. Retrieved from JFIR website: http://www.jfir.or.jp/e/pr/pdf/33.pdf. Accessed 7 December 2010.

Japan International Training Corporation Organization. [JITCO]. (2010, October). Ginōjisshūsei kenshūsei nikansuru JITCO gyōmu tōkei. Retrieved from JITCO website: http://www.jitco.or.jp/about/statistics.html. Accessed 1 December 2010.

Japan Meteorological Agency. [JMA]. (2011a). The 2011 off the Pacific coast of Tōhoku earthquake: First report. Retrieved from http://www.jma.go.jp/jma/en/News/2011_Earthquake_01.html. Accessed 17 April 2011.

Japan Meteorological Agency. [JMA]. (2011b). The 2011 off the Pacific coast of Tōhoku earthquake: Portal. Retrieved from http://www.jma.go.jp/jma/en/2011_Earthquake.html. Accessed 23 April 2011.

Japan Research Institute. [JRI]. (2007). Jichitai zaisei kenzenka hō to chihō zaisei e no eikyō. Retrieved from http://www.jri.co.jp/MediaLibrary/file/report/other/pdf/2915.pdf. Accessed 27 September 2010.

Japan Times. (2006). 20% of Japan's population over 65. Retrieved from http://search.japantimes.co.jp/cgi-bin/nn20060603a2.html. Accessed 24 September 2010.

Japan Times. (2009). Justifying a new airport. Retrieved from http://search.japantimes.co.jp/cgi-bin/ed20090619a2.html. Accessed: 3 November 2010.

Japan Times. (2011a, 14 April). Sendai airport partially resumes domestic flights after quake. Retrieved from http://search.japantimes.co.jp/cgi-bin/nn20110414a8.html. Accessed 17 April 2011.

Japan Times. (2011b, 22 April). No-go zone trespassers face fines, arrest. Retrieved from http://search.japantimes.co.jp/cgi-bin/nn20110422a1.html. Accessed 23 April.

Japan Tourism Agency. [JTA]. (2008). Significance of and recent progress towards becoming a tourism nation [Internal Memo]. Tokyo, Japan: Japan Tourism Agency.

Jiji Press. (1986, October 30). Mitsubishi plant starts producing LSIS.

Johnson, C. (1982). *MITI and the Japanese miracle: The growth of industrial policy, 1925–75*. Stanford, CA: Stanford University Press.

Johnston, E. (2008, 19 August). Doshusei: Regions not prefectures: Ruling coalition wants new system in step with administrative reforms. *Japan Times*. Retrieved from http://search.japantimes.co.jp/cgi-bin/nn20080819i1.html. Accessed 11 December 2009.

Jones, T., Yamamoto, K., & Aramaki, S. (2009). A comparative study of interpretation for Japanese and foreign climbers at Mt. Fuji. In *Proceedings of Japan Institute of Tourism Research Annual Conference 2009* (pp. 221–224). Tokyo, Japan: ACNet.

Kabashima, I. (2000, October). The LDP's 'kingdom of the regions' and the revolt of the cities. *Japan Echo*, pp. 22–28.

Kahoku Shinpō. (1996, 30 April). Nōsakumotsu no higai shinkoku, saru gundan ni sensenkyōkyō. Yamagata-Yamadera.

Kahoku Shinpō. (1998, 23 October). 'Engai' fusege! Borantiatai katsuyaku.

Kajita, S. (2001). Public investment as a social policy in remote rural areas in Japan. *Geographical Review of Japan*, *74*(Ser. B) 2, 147–158.

Kajita, T., Tanno, K., & Higuchi, N. (2005). *Kaō no mienai teijūka: Nikkei burazirujin to kokka, shijō, imin nettowaaku*. Nagoya, Japan: University of Nagoya Press.

Kamaishi shi. (2000). *Kamaishi-shi guriinu tsūrizumu moderu seibi koso sakutei jigyō hōkokusho*. Kamaishi, Japan: Kamaishi City Office.

Kamaishi shi. (2001). *Daigoji Kamaishi-shi sōgō keikaku: Sukuramu Kamaishi 21 puran*. Kamaishi, Japan: Kamaishi City Office.

Kamaishi shi. (2003). *Heisei 14-nendo Kamaishi-shi eco miujiamu jigyō chōsa gyōmu: Kamaishi gakuin kasshi (seibu chiku): Kaisshi no aru mono sagashi: hōkokusho*. Kamaishi, Japan: Kamaishi City Office.

Kamaishi shi. (2005). *Kamaishi-shi tōkeisho 2005 nen-do*. Kamaishi, Japan: Kamaishi City Office.

Kamaishi shi. (2006a). *A ando F guriin tsūrizumu no koremade no ayumi*. Kamaishi, Japan: Kamaishi City Office.

Kamaishi shi. (2006b). *Daigoji Kamaishi-shi sōgo keikaku: Sukuramu Kamaishi 21 puran: Kōki kihon keikaku*. Kamaishi, Japan: Kamaishi City Office.

Kamaishi shi. (2006c). *Kamaishi-shi chūki zaisei mitōshi (Heisei 18-nendo-22-nendo)*. Kamaishi, Japan: Kamaishi City Office.

Kamaishi shi. (2006d). *Kamaishi-shi kankō shinkō bijon (an) odense Kamaishi*. Kamaishi, Japan: Kamaishi City Office.

Kamaishi shi. (2007a). *A ando F guriin tsūrizumu jikkō iinkai 2007 nendo sōkai shiryō*. Kamaishi, Japan: Kamaishi City Office.

Kamaishi shi. (2007b). *Kamaishi-shi tōkeisho 2007 nen-do*. Kamaishi, Japan: Kamaishi City Office.

Kamaishi shi sōmu kikaku bu sōgō seisaku ka. (2004). *Heisei 16-nendo Kamaishi shi sōgōkeikaku kōkikihonkeikaku sakutei' ni kakaru jūmin ankeeto chōsa kekka*. Kamaishi, Japan: Kamaishi City Office.

Kamaishi Steel Works. (1986). *Tetsu to tomoni 100-nen*. Kamaishi, Japan: Kamaishi City Office.

Kaminoseki chōshi hensan iinkai. (1988). *Kaminoseki chōshi*. Kaminoseki, Japan: Kaminoseki Town Office.

Kan, N. (2011a). Kizuna: The bonds of friendship. Retrieved from Prime Minister's Office website: http://www.kantei.go.jp/foreign/kan/statement/201104/11kizuna_e.html. Accessed 17 April 2011.

Kan, N. (2011b, 15 April). Japan's road to recovery and rebirth. *New York Times*. Retrieved from http://www.nytimes.com/2011/04/16/opinion/16iht-edkan16.html?scp=2&sq=naoto%20kan&st=cse. Accessed 17 April 2011.

Kanai, T. (2007). Vectors of change in Japan's political and fiscal decentralization. *Social Science Japan, 37*, 7–11.

Kaneko, R., Ishikawa, A., Ishii, F., Sasai, T., Iwasawa, M., Mita, F., & Moriizumi, R. (2009). Commentary to population projections for Japan: A supplement to report of the 2006 revision. *The Japanese Journal of Population, 7*, 1–46. Retrieved from http://www.ipss.go.jp/index-e.html. Accessed 4 January 2010.

Kase, K. (1997). *Shūdan shūshoku no jidai*. Tokyo, Japan: Aoki shoten.

Kase, K. (2007). Kamaishi-shi: Kamaishi-shi ni okeru gyogyō (ISS Joint Research Discussion Paper No. 20). Institute of Social Science, University of Tokyo.

Kaso Taisaku Kenkyū Kai (Ed.). (2004). *Kaso taisaku dēta bukku: Heisei 15-nendo kaso taisaku no genkyō*. Tokyo, Japan: Marui Kōbunsha.

Katayama, Y. (2008). Nihon wo miru. *Sekai, 777*, 122–129.

Kato, H. (2007). Chihō-toshi ni okeru shakai-kankei. In Chūō daigaku shakai kagaku kenkyūsho (Ed.), *Chiiki shakai no hendo to shakai keikaku: Kamaishi shakai to Kamaishi-seitetsusho* (pp. 109–126). Tokyo, Japan: Chūō Daigaku Shakai Kagaku Kenkyūsho.

Kato, M. (2008). *National Park System of Japan*. Tokyo, Japan: Kokon.

Katz, R. (1998). *Japan, the system that soured: The rise and fall of the Japanese economic miracle*. Armonk, NY: M. E. Sharpe.

Kavaratzis, M., & Ashworth, G. (2005). City branding: An effective assertion of identity or a transitory marketing trick? *Tijischrift voor Economische en Sociale Geografie, 96*(5), 506–514.

Kelly, W. (1986). Rationalization and nostalgia: Cultural dynamics of new middle-class Japan. *American Ethnologist, 13*(4), 603–618.

Kerr, A. (2002). *Dogs and demons: Tales from the dark side of Japan.* New York, NY: Hill and Wang.

Kikkawa, T. (2006). Chihō ni okeru Kibō: Kamaishi-shi no keizai-kasseika to daisanji-sangyō (Joint Research Discussion Paper No. 5). Institute of Social Science, University of Tokyo.

Kikkawa, T. (2007). Kamaishi niwa kibō ga aru, demo, motto aruhazuda (Institute of Social Science Joint Research Discussion Paper No. 19). Institute of Social Science, University of Tokyo.

Kil, W. (2004). *Luxus der Leere, Vom schwierigen Rückzug aus der Wachstumswelt, Eine Streitschrift*. Wuppertal, Germany: Müller und Busmann.

Knight, J. (1994). Rural revitalization in Japan: Spirit of the village and taste of the country. *Asian Survey, 34*(7), 634–646.

Knight, J. (1996). Competing hospitalities in Japanese rural tourism. *Annals of Tourism Research, 23*(1), 165–180.

Knight, J. (2003). *Waiting for wolves in Japan: An anthropological study of people–wildlife relations*, Oxford, UK: Oxford University Press.

Knorr-Siedow, T. (2006). The activating state. In Project Office Philipp Oswalt (Ed.), *Shrinking cities, volume 2: Interventions*. Ostfildern-Ruit, Germany: Hatje Cantz.

Kōchi Prefecture Deep Seawater Laboratory. (2010). Retrieved from Kōchi Prefecture Deep Seawater Laboratory website: http://www.pref.kochi.lg.jp/soshiki/151407/eigo-top-page.html. Accessed 17 December 2010.

Kōchi Shimbun. (2006, 9 August). Shinsōsui Shōhin Hanbaiken.

Kōchi Shimbun. (2008, 28 March) Kōchiken Nai Kyūjin Bairitsu 0.52 Bai.

Komine, T., & Kabe, S. (2009). Long-term forecast of the demographic transition in Japan and Asia. *Asian Economic Policy Review*, *4*(1), 19–38.

Kondo, M. (2001). *Networking for technology acquisition and transfer*. United Nations Industrial Development Organization [UNIDO] forum on Management of Technology: Global Forum with Focus on the Arab Region, Vienna, Austria, 29–30 May. Retrieved from http://www.unido.org/fileadmin/import/userfiles/timminsk/featarabmotkondo.pdf. Accessed 12 December 2010.

Konno, S. (1984). Strengths and weaknesses of the bullet train. *Japan Echo*, *11*(3), 73–80.

Kōsoku Tetsudō Kenkyūkai. (2003). *Shinkansen: Kōsoku tetsudō no gijutsu no subete*. Tōkyō: Sankaido.

Kosugi, R. (2008). *Escape from work: Freelancing youth and the challenge to corporate Japan*. Melbourne, Australia: Trans Pacific Press.

Kumagai, F. (2007). Interracial marriage in Japan: A strategy to maintain rural farm households. Presented at the Fourth International Conference on Population Geographies, 10–13 July 2007, Hong Kong.

Kuta jikkō iinkai. (1977). *Kutakō hyakunenshi*. Kyoto, Japan: Kuta jikkō iinkai.

Kuta kinomi-kai. (1993). *Kyoto Kuta*. Kyoto, Japan: Nakanishiya.

Kutsuki mura. (2006). *Kutsuki-mura kaso chiiki jiritsu sokushin keikaku: Heisei 12 nendo–heisei 16 nendo*. Kutsuki, Japan: Kutsúki Village Office.

Landesamt für Datenverarbeitung und Statistik Nordrhein-Westfalen [LDS NRW], (Ed.). (2006). *Auswirkungen des demographischen Wandels, Teil 1*. Düsseldorf, Germany: Statistische Analysen und Studien Nordhrein-Westfalen.

Lankford, S. (1994). Attitudes and perceptions toward tourism and rural regional development. *Journal of Travel Research*, *32*(3), 35–43.

Leadbeater, C. (1997). *The rise of the social entrepreneur.* London, UK: Demos.

Lewis, M. (2000). *Becoming apart: National power and local politics in Toyama, 1868–1945.* Cambridge, MA: Harvard University Asia Center.

Liu, L. (2010). China's population trends and their implications for fertility policy. *Asian Population Studies, 6*(3), 289–305.

Longman, P. (2004). *The empty cradle: How falling birth rates threaten world prosperity and what to do about it.* New York, NY: Basic Books.

Lowndes, V. (2001). Rescuing Aunt Sally: Taking institutional theory seriously in urban politics. *Urban Studies, 38*(11), 1953–1973.

Lutz, W., Sanderson, W., & Scherbov, S. (2004). *The end of world population growth in the 21st century: New challenges for human capital formation and sustainable development.* London, UK: Earthscan.

Lützeler, R. (2008). Regional demographics. In F. Coulmas, H. Conrad, A. Schad-Seifert, & G. Vogt (Eds.), *The demographic challenge: A handbook about Japan.* Leiden, The Netherlands: Brill.

MacCannell, D. (1999). *The tourist: A new theory of the leisure class* (3rd ed.). Berkeley, CA: University of California Press.

Macnaughtan, H. (2005). *Women, work and the Japanese economic miracle: The case of the cotton textile industry, 1945–1975.* London, UK: Routledge.

Madsen, M. (Director). (2010). *Into eternity* [Documentary film]. http://www.intoeternitythemovie.com/.

Mainichi Daily News. (2011). Nippon Steel resumes production at disaster-hit plant in Iwate Prefecture. Retrieved from http://mdn.mainichi.jp/mdnnews/business/news/20110414p2g00m0bu046000c.html. Accessed 17 April 2011.

Masaki, H. (2006). Japan stares into a demographic abyss. *The Asia-Pacific Journal: Japan Focus.* Retrieved from http://japanfocus.org/products/details/1864. Accessed 1 July 2008.

Matanle, P. (2006). Organic sources for the revitalisation of rural Japan: The craft potters of Sado. *Japanstudien, 18*, 149–180.

Matanle, P. (2008). Shrinking Sado: Education, employment and the decline of Japan's rural regions. In Project Office Philipp Oswalt (Ed.), *Shrinking cities—Case study Japan* (chapter 6, pp. 42–53). Ostfildern-Ruit, Germany: Hatje Cantz.

Matanle, P., & Sato, Y. (2010). Coming soon to a city near you! Learning to live 'beyond growth' in Japan's shrinking regions. *Social Science Japan Journal, 13*(2), 187–210.

Matsubara, H. (2006). Shōshi kōreika jidai no chiiki saihen. *Keizai chirigaku nenpō, 52*(4), 1–17.

Matsuishi, Y. (2003). Kōdōseichō-ki no kigyō jōkamachi, Kamaishi ni okeru sangyō-kōzō. *Iwate kenritsu Miyako Tanki Daigaku kiyo, 14*(2), 38–56.

Matsumura, S. (2010). Gap between research and implementation: Prediction of Tokai earthquake. *Science and Technology Trends*. Retrieved from National Institute of Science and Technology Policy website: http://www.nistep.go.jp/achiev/ftx/eng/stfc/stt035e/qr35pdf/STTqr3503.pdf. Accessed 24 April 2011.

Matsutani, A. (2006). *Shrinking population economics: Lessons from Japan*. Tokyo: International House of Japan.

McCarthy, J., Lloyd, G., & Illsley, B. (2002). National parks in Scotland: Balancing environment and economy. *European Planning Studies, 10*(5), 665–670.

McClain, J. (1999). Space, power, wealth, and status in seventeenth-century Osaka. In J. McClain and O. Wakita (Eds.), *Osaka: The Merchants' Capital of Early Modern Japan*. Ithaca, NY: Cornell University Press.

McCormack, G. (2001). *The emptiness of Japanese affluence*. New York, NY: M. E. Sharpe.

McCormack, G. (2002). Breaking the iron triangle. *New Left Review, 13* (January–February), 5–23.

McCormack, G. (2003). Okinawa and the structure of dependence. In G. Hook & R. Siddle (Eds.), *Japan and Okinawa: Structure and subjectivity* (pp. 93–133). London, UK: RoutledgeCurzon.

McCormack, G. (2005). Koizumi's kingdom of illusion. *The Asia-Pacific Journal: Japan Focus*. Retrieved from http://japanfocus.org/-Gavan-McCormack/1924. Accessed 11 November 2010.

McCormack, G. (2011). Hubris punished: Japan as nuclear state. *Asia Pacific Journal*, *9*(16). Retrieved from http://www.japanfocus.org/-Gavan-McCormack/3517. Accessed 24 April 2011.

McCormick, K. (2006). Japanese engineers abroad: Challenge and opportunity in globalization. In P. Matanle & W. Lunsing (Eds.), *Perspectives on work, employment and society in Japan* (pp. 117–142). Basingstoke, UK: Palgrave.

McGranahan, D. (2003). How people make a living in rural America. In D. Brown and L. Swanson (Eds.), *Challenges for rural America in the 21st Century*. University Park, PA: Pennsylvania State University Press.

McKay, S., & Winkelman-Gleed, A. (2005). *Migrant workers in the east of England*. London, UK: London Metropolitan University.

Ministry of Agriculture, Forestry, and Fisheries. [MAFF]. (2007). *Annual report on food, agriculture and rural areas in Japan* FY2006. Tokyo: MAFF. Retrieved from MAFF website: http://www.maff.go.jp/e/annual_report/pdf/fy2006_rep.pdf. Accessed 1 July 2008.

Ministry of Agriculture, Forestry, and Fisheries. [MAFF]. (2010). *Shichōson no sugata–Akita-ken, Oga-shi*. Retrieved from MAFF website: http://www.machimura.maff.go.jp/machi/map2/05/206/fisheries.html. Accessed 20 November 2010.

Ministry of Economy, Trade, and Industry. [METI]. (2008). *Census of manufacturers 2005*. Retrieved from http://www.meti.go.jp/english/statistics/tyo/kougyo/index.html. Accessed 8 November 2010.

Ministry of Economy, Trade, and Industry. [METI]. (2010a). *Census of manufacturers 2010*. Retrieved from http://www.meti.go.jp/english/statistics/tyo/kougyo/index.html and http://www.meti.go.jp/statistics/tyo/kougyo/result-2.html.

Ministry of Economy, Trade, and Industry. [METI]. (2010b). *Indices of industrial production.* Retrieved from http://www.meti.go.jp/english/statistics/tyo/iip/h2afdlde.html. Accessed 26 September 2010.

Ministry of Education, Culture, Sports, Science and Technology. [MEXT]. (2005). *Support for university educational reform*. Retrieved from MEXT website: http://www.mext.go.jp/english/org/struct/021.htm. Accessed 15 December 2010.

Ministry of Education, Culture, Sports, Science and Technology. [MEXT]. (2006). *Japan's education at a glance*. Tokyo, Japan: MEXT.

Ministry of Environment. [MOE]. (2010). *Kanren hōrei-kakushu shiryō.* Retrieved from MOE website: http://www.env.go.jp/park/doc/data/index.html. Accessed 7 July 2009.

Ministry of Health, Labour, and Welfare. [MHLW]. (2009). *Mandatory notification of the status of employment of foreign workers*. Retrieved from MHLW website: http://www.mhlw.go.jp/bunya/koyou/gaikoku-jin12/pdf/english_0004.pdf. Accessed 7 December 2010.

Ministry of Internal Affairs and Communications. [MIC]. (2006). *Chihōsai no gaiyō to saikin no jōkyō*. Retrieved from MIC website: http://www.soumu.go.jp/main_sosiki/c-zaisei/chihosai/. Accessed 6 December 2010.

Ministry of Internal Affairs and Communications. [MIC]. (2008). *Kuni – chihōsai no saimu zandaka (GDP hi) no kokusai hikkaku [2008]*. Retrieved from MIC website: http://www.soumu.go.jp/main_sosiki/c-zaisei/chihosai/. Accessed 6 December 2010.

Ministry of Internal Affairs and Communications. [MIC]. (2010). *White paper on local public finance* (FY2008 Settlement). Retrieved from MIC Website: http://www.soumu.go.jp/menu_seisaku/hakusyo/index.html. Accessed 6 December 2010.

Ministry of Justice. [MOJ]. (2008). *Shutsunyū-kokusha, 1950–2005*. Retrieved from http://www.e-stat.go.jp/SG1/estat/List.do?lid=000001035550. Accessed 24 November 2010.

Ministry of Justice. [MOJ]. (2009a). *2009 Immigration control, Part 1: Immigration control in recent years*. Retrieved from Ministry of Justice website: http://www.moj.go.jp/nyuukokukanri/kouhou/nyukan_nyukan91.html. Accessed 7 December 2010.

Ministry of Justice. [MOJ]. (2009b). *2009 Immigration control, Part II: Primary measures related to immigration control administration in FY 2008*. Retrieved from Ministry of Justice website: http://www.moj.go.jp/nyuukokukanri/kouhou/nyukan_nyukan91.html. Accessed 6 December 2010.

Ministry of Justice. [MOJ]. (2010a). *Heisei 21 nenmatsu genzai ni okeru gaikokujin tōrokusha tōkei nitsuite*. Retrieved from Ministry of Justice website: http://www.moj.go.jp/nyuukokukanri/kouhou/nyuukokukanri04_00005.html. Accessed 10 October 2010.

Ministry of Justice. [MOJ]. (2010b). *Basic plan for immigration control, 4th edition, March 2010*. Retrieved from Ministry of Justice website: http://www.immi-moj.go.jp/seisaku/keikaku_101006_english.pdf. Accessed 10 October 2010.

Ministry of Justice. [MOJ]. (2010c). *Kokuseki-betsu nūkoku gaikokujin no kokuseki*. Retrieved from http://www.e-stat.go.jp/SG1/estat/List.do?lid=000001064568. Accessed 24 November 2010.

Ministry of Land, Infrastructure, Transport, and Tourism. [MLIT]. (2003). *Heisei 15-nendo kokudo kōtsū hakusho*. Tokyo, Japan: Gyōsei.

Ministry of Land, Infrastructure, Transport, and Tourism. [MLIT]. (2006a). *Kokudo keisei keikaku sakutei no tameno shūrakuno jyōkyōni kansuru genjyō haaku chōsa saishū houkoku ni tsuite* [Final report on the assessment of the present situation concerning the villages for the national land development planning]. Retrieved from http://www.mlit.go.jp/kisha/kisha07/02/020817_.html. Accessed 29 October 2010.

Ministry of Land, Infrastructure, Transport, and Tourism. [MLIT]. (2006b). *The new national land sustainability plan*. Retrieved from http://www.mlit.go.jp/english/2006/b_n_and_r_planning_bureau/01_duties/New_NLSP_060515.pdf. Accessed. 11 December 2009.

Ministry of Land, Infrastructure, Transport, and Tourism. [MLIT], National and Regional Planning Bureau. (2007). *Kokudo keisei keikaku zenkoku keikaku (chūkan torimatome) nit tsuite, Hito to kokudo*, *21*(1), 20–27.

Ministry of Land, Infrastructure, Transport, and Tourism. [MLIT], National and Regional Planning Bureau. (2009). *Kōiki chihō keikaku ni tsuite*. Retrieved from http://www.mlit.go.jp/common/000046729.pdf. Accessed 14 September 2010.

Miyairi, K. (2003). *Isahaya-wan kantaku-jigyō no sho-mondai to seikangyō-yuchaku-kōzō*. Unpublished manuscript.

Miyazaki, N. (1994). *Toppasu no kaze—Chiisai na kuni no ōkina chōsen*. Tokyo: Shichiken Shuppan.

Mochida, N. (2001). Taxes and transfers in Japan's local finance. In M. Muramatsu, F. Iqbal, and I. Kume (Eds.), *Local Government Development in Postwar Japan* (pp. 2–35). Oxford, UK: Oxford University Press.

Mochizuki, Y. (2000). *Tsugaru nuri*. Tokyo, Japan: Rikogakusha.

Moon, O. (1989). *From paddy field to ski slope: The revitalisation of tradition in Japanese village life*, Manchester, UK: Manchester University Press.

Mori, T. (2005). Atarashii shakai kiban seibi keikaku no rinen to sono jitsugenka ni kan suru kenkyū. *Nihon daigaku daigakuin sōgō shakai jōhō kenkyūka kiyō, 6*, 315–323.

Mort, G., Weerawardena, J., & Carnegie, K. (2003). Social entrepreneurship: Towards conceptualisation. *International Journal of Nonprofit and Voluntary Sector Marketing, 8*(1), 76–88.

M. Setek. (2009). *Kaisha Annai*. Retrieved from M. Setek website: http://www.msetek.com/jp/profile/index.html. Accessed 17 December 2010.

Mulgan, A. (2006). *Agriculture and political reform in Japan: The Koizumi legacy* (Pacific Economic Papers No. 360, Australia-Japan Research Centre, Australian National University). Retrieved from http://www.eaber.org/intranet/documents/41/774/AJRC_Mulgan_2006.pdf. Accessed 28 October 2010.

Münz, R., & Rieterer, A. (2009). *Overcrowded world? Global population and international migration*. London, UK: Haus Publishing.

Murakushi, N. (2005). *Kokuritsu kōen seiritsushi no kenkyū*. Tokyo, Japan: Hōsei University.

Murphy, P. (1985). *Tourism: A community approach*. New York, NY: Methuen.

Mutai, S. (2008, 5 July). *The shrinking regions of Japan: National strategies for adapting to demographic change*. Paper presented at the symposium on Japan's Regional Society: Community Sustainability under Demographic Shrinkage, Yorkshire Art Space, Sheffield, UK.

Myrskyla, M., Kohler, H.-P., & Billari, F. (2009). Advances in development reverse fertility declines. *Nature, 460*, 741–743.

Nakajima, M. (2005). Chiiki Burando Gaku Josetsu. *Chiiki Burando Kenkyū, 1*, 33–49.

Nakamura, H. (1989). Ajiajin hanayome no shōhinka. In K. Sakamoto (Ed.), *Ningen ni totte nōgyō towa*. Tokyo, Japan: Gakuyō Shobō.

Nakamura, K. (2007). Suitai kara saisei he: seizō-gyō ni chakumoku-shite. In Y. Genda & N. Nakamura (Eds.), *Kamaishi ni kibō wa aruka: Kamaishi chōsa kōkai shimpojiamu zen-kiroku* (pp. 34–49). Tokyo, Japan: Tōkyō Daigaku Shuppankai.

Nakanishi, S. (2009). *Umi no fugō no shihonshugi: kitamaebune to Nihon no sangyōka*. Nagoya: Nagoya Daigaku Shuppankai.

Nakao, M. (2005). Meiji Sanriku Dai-tsunami. Retrieved from: Hatamura sōzō kōgaku kenkyūjo website: http://www.sozogaku.com/fkd/hf/HA0000616.pdf. Accessed 18 April 2011.

National Institute of Population and Social Security Research. [NIPSSR]. (1996). *The fourth migration survey general results*. Retrieved from NIPSSR website: http://www.ipss.go.jp/ps-idou/e/msc_4th/jinko5.pdf. Accessed 1 July 2009.

National Institute of Population and Social Security Research. [NIPSSR]. (1997). *Population projections by prefecture*. Retrieved from NIPSSR website: http://www.ipss.go.jp/pp-fuken/e/ppp_h9/gaiyo.html. Accessed 1 November 2010.

National Institute of Population and Social Security Research. [NIPSSR]. (2002). *Nihon no to-do-fu-ken betsu shōrai suikei jinkō (Heisei 14-nen 12-gatsu suikei) ni tsuite*. Retrieved from NIPSSR website: http://www.ipss.go.jp/. Accessed 1 November 2010.

National Institute of Population and Social Security Research. [NIPSSR]. (2003). *Nihon no shi-ku-chō-son betsu shōrai suikei jinkō (Heisei 15-nen 12-gatsu suikei) ni tsuite*. Retrieved from NIPSSR website: http://www.ipss.go.jp/. Accessed 1 November 2010.

National Institute of Population and Social Security Research. [NIPSSR]. (2006a). *Population statistics of Japan 2006*. Retrieved from NIPSSR website: http://www.ipss.go.jp/p-info/e/PSJ2006.pdf. Accessed 1 November 2010.

National Institute of Population and Social Security Research. [NIPSSR]. (2006b). *Population projections for Japan: 2010–2050*. Retrieved from NIPSSR website: http://www.ipss.go.jp/pp-newest/e/ppfj02/top.html. Accessed 4 December 2010.

National Institute of Population and Social Security Research. [NIPSSR]. (2007). *Nihon no to-do-fu-ken betsu shōrai suikei jinkō (Heisei 19-nen 12-gatsu suikei) ni tsuite*. Retrieved from NIPSSR website: http://www.ipss.go.jp/. Accessed 1 November 2010.

National Institute of Population and Social Security Research. [NIPSSR]. (2008). *Nihon no shi-ku-chō-son betsu shōrai suikei jinkō (Heisei 20-nen 12-gatsu suikei) ni tsuite*. Retrieved from NIPSSR website: http://www.ipss.go.jp/. Accessed 1 November 2010.

National Institute of Population and Social Security Research. [NIPSSR]. (2010). *Jinkō tōkei shiryō shū*. Retrieved from NIPSSR website: http://www.ipss.go.jp/syoushika/tohkei/Popular/Popular2010.asp?chap=0. Accessed 28 November 2010.

National Parks Association of Japan. [NPAJ]. (2004). *National Parks Handbook 2004*. Tokyo, Japan: National Parks Association of Japan.

National Police Agency. [NPA]. (2011, 15 April). Heisei 23-nen (2011-nen) Tōhoku chihō Taiheiyō oki no higai jōkyō to keisatsu sochi. Retrieved from http://www.npa.go.jp/archive/keibi/biki/higaijokyo.pdf. Accessed 15 April 2011.

National Public Radio. [NPR]. (2011, 14 March). Millions of stricken Japanese lack water, food, heat. Retrieved from http://www.npr.org/2011/03/18/134527591/millions-of-stricken-japanese-lack-water-food-heat. Accessed 24 April 2011.

Natural Environment Agency. [NEA]. (2005). *Sekai isan chiiki hozen taisaku hi*. Natural Environment Agency, Tokyo, Japan: Ministry of the Environment.

Nihon Genshiryoku Hatsuden Kabushiki Kaisha [Genden]. (2011). Nihon genshiryoku hatsuden kabushiki kaisha. Retrieved from Japan

Electric Power Company website: http://www.japc.co.jp/. Accessed 23 April 2011.

Nihon Hōsō Kyōkai [NHK]. (2011a, 13 April). NHK News Watch 9, NHK General.

Nihon Hōsō Kyōkai [NHK]. (2011b, 14 April) NHK News 7, NHK General.

Nihon Hōsō Kyōkai [NHK]. (2011c, 23 April). NHK News 7, NHK General.

Nihon Keizai Shimbunsha (Ed.). (2007). *Chihō hōkai: Saisei no michi wa aru ka?* Tokyo, Japan: Nihon Keizai Shinbunsha.

Nihon Tetsudō Kensetsu Kōdan. (2002). *Kyūshū Shinkansen* [Pamphlet from Kyūshū Railway Company].

Niibari, H. (2004). Kamaishi Kyōjō Ichiba. In Tōhoku Toshi Gakkai (Eds.), *Tōhoku toshi jiten* (pp. 75–76). Sendai: Sendai Kyōdō Insatsu.

Niigata ken. (1963). *Niigata ken jinkō no ugoki*. Niigata shi: Niigata ken Tōkeikyoku.

Niigata ken. (1964–2009). *Niigata ken no jinkō idō*. Niigata shi: Niigata ken Tōkei Kyōkai.

Niigata ken. (2011a). *Niigata ken tōkei nenkan*. Retrieved from Niigata Prefecture website: http://www.pref.niigata.lg.jp/tokei/1196871357582.html. Accessed 1 November 2010.

Niigata ken. (2009). *Heisei 20 Niigata ken tōkei nenkan*. Niigata shi: Niigata ken Tōkei Kyōkai.

Niigata ken. (2010). *Niigata ken suikei jinkō (geppō)*. Retrieved from Niigata Prefecture website: http://www.pref.niigata.lg.jp/tokei/1194797750548.html. Accessed 1 November 2010.

Niigata ken. (2011b). *Niigata ken tōkei nenkan 2010*, Retrieved from Niigata Prefecture website: http://www.pref.niigata.lg.jp/tokei/1300827699746.html. Accessed: 10 May 2011.

Niigata shi. (2008). *Jinkō no suii, Heisei 20-nendoban niigata shi tōkeisho*. Retrieved from Niigata City website: http://www.city.niigata.jp/info/somu/toukei/toukeisho20/3kokutyou20.htm. Accessed 8 December 2009.

Nikkei.com. (2011, 13 April) Hitachi submits long-term plan to decommission Fukushima Daiichi plant. Retrieved from Nikkei.com website: http://e.nikkei.com/e/fr/tnks/Nni20110413D13JF895.htm. Accessed 17 April 2011.

Nikkei Weekly. (1999, 11 October). Deep-sea water finding its way into food, drinks, cosmetics.

Nikkei Weekly. (2000, 17 July). Sea water makes splash in the market.

Nikkei Weekly. (2002, 7 October). Science project leader looks to put Kansai on the map.

Nikkei Weekly. (2008, 10 March). Regional wage gaps spark jump in worker migration.

Nippon Hōsō Kyōkai (NHK). (2008). Daihensai jidai: shakkin 200-chō en, hajimatta jūmin futan, NHK Special, 21 April.

Nippon Kodoshi Corporation. [NKK]. (2010). *Uriage*. Retrieved from NKK website: http://www.kodoshi.co.jp/0502-psd/uriage.pdf. Accessed 17 December 2010.

Nitta, H. (2006). *Capitalizing on retirement of Japan's first baby-boomers* (Japan External Trade Organisation Japan Economic Report, April–May). Tokyo: JETRO. Retrieved from http://www.jetro.go.jp/en/reports/market/pdf/2006_18_u.pdf. Accessed 14 December 2009.

Nuclear Industrial Safety Agency. [NISA]. (2011, 12 April). International Nuclear and Radiological Event Scale (INES) Rating on the events in Fukushima Dai-ichi nuclear power station by the Tōhoku District: Off the Pacific Ocean earthquake [News release]. Retrieved from Ministry of Economy, Trade, and Industry website: http://www.nisa.meti.go.jp/english/files/en20110412-4.pdf. Accessed 15 April 2011.

Office for National Statistics. [ONS]. (2009). *National projections: UK population to exceed 65m by 2018*. Retrieved from ONS website: http://www.statistics.gov.uk/cci/nugget.asp?id=1352. Accessed 2 November 2010.

Office for National Statistics. [ONS]. (2010a). *Population change: UK population increases by 394,000*. Retrieved from ONS website: http://www.statistics.gov.uk/cci/nugget.asp?ID=950. Accessed 2 November 2010.

Office for National Statistics. [ONS]. (2010b). *Ageing: Fastest increase in the 'oldest old.'* Retrieved from ONS website: http://www.statistics.gov.uk/cci/nugget.asp?ID=949. Accessed 2 November 2010.

Office for National Statistics. [ONS]. (2010c). *Fertility: UK fertility remains high*. Retrieved from ONS website: http://www.statistics.gov.uk/cci/nugget.asp?ID=951. Accessed 2 November 2010.

Oguma, E. (2002). *The genealogy of 'Japanese' self-images*. Trans. David Askew. Melbourne, Australia: Trans Pacific Press.

Ohno, A. (2005). *Sanson kankyo shakaigaku jyosetsu*. Tokyo, Japan: Nōsan Ryōson Bunka Kyōkai.

Ohori, K. (2007). Kamaishi no guriinu tsūrisumu to toshi imeegi. In Y. Genda and N. Nakamura (Eds.), *Kamaishi ni kibō wa aruka: Kamaishi chōsa kōkai shimpojiamu zen-kiroku* (pp. 72–88).Tokyo, Japan: Tōkyō Daigaku Shuppankai.

Okinawa ken. (2006). *Hitori atari shichōsonmin shotoku*. Retrieved from Okinawa Prefecture website: http://www.pref.okinawa.jp/toukeika/ctv/2006/ctv.html. Accessed 2 November 2010.

Okinawa ken. (2009a). *Latest indicators*. Retrieved from Okinawa ken tōkei shiryō website, Okinawa Prefectural Government website: http://www.pref.okinawa.jp/toukeika. Accessed 14 December 2009.

Okinawa ken. (2009b). *Shin Ishigaki kūkō ga dekitara*. Retrieved from Okinawa Prefecture website: http://www.pref.okinawa.jp/shin-ishigaki/newishigaki/kukoudekitara.html. Accessed 14 December 2009.

Okinawa ken chiiki ritō ka. (2009, 21 February). *Honken ritō no genjō to kadai*. Unpublished internal briefing paper.

Okinawa ken kankō kikaku ka. (2008). *Daisanji Okinawa-ken kankō shinkō keikaku gaiyō*. Retrieved from Okinawa Prefectural Government website: http://www3.pref.okinawa.jp/site/contents/attach/16570/gaiyou.pdf.

Okinawa-ken kankō kikaku ka. (2009). *Okinawa-ken kankō no genjō to kadai (haikei)*. Retrieved from Okinawa Prefectural Government Website: http://www3.pref.okinawa.jp/site/contents/attach/5413/1–1.haikei.pdf. Accessed 15 December 2009.

Oldaker, A. (2011). RAAF C-17 flying around the clock in Japan. Retrieved from Yokota Air Base website: http://www.yokota.af.mil/news/story.asp?id=123247518. Accessed 23 April 2011.

Omran, A. (2005). The edpidemiological transition: A theory of the epidemiology of population change. *The Milbank Quarterly*, *83*(4), 731–757.

Onishi, N. (2011a). In Japan, seawall offered a false sense of security. *New York Times*. Retrieved from http://www.nytimes.com/2011/04/02/world/asia/02wall.html. Accessed 16 April 2011.

Onishi, N. (2011b). At age 84, a city's last geisha defies time and a fourth tsunami. *New York Times*. Retrieved from http://query.nytimes.com/gst/fullpage.html?res=9A00E1DB1739F936A35757C0A9679D8B63&ref=japan. Accessed 16 April 2011.

Organisation for Economic Co-operation and Development [OECD]. (2010). *Share of value added in services*. Retrieved from http://stats.oecd.org/Index.aspx. Accessed 26 September 2010.

Oswalt, P. (2005). Introduction. In Project Office Philipp Oswalt (Ed.), *Shrinking cities, volume 1: International research* (pp. 12–18). Ostfildern-Ruit, Germany: Hatje Cantz.

Ota, I. (2002). The shrinking profitability of small-scale forestry in Japan and some recent policy initiatives to reverse the trend. *Small-scale Forest Economics, Management and Policy, 1*(1), 25–37.

Ozawa, T. (2003). Japan's dual industrial structure as a welfare system: 'The lexus and the olive tree' and 'the vulture.' *Journal of Economic Issues, 37*(2), 519–526.

Palmer, E. (1983). *Rural depopulation in post-war Japan: With reference to remote rural settlements of the Tajima Region.* Unpublished PhD dissertation, School of Oriental and African Studies, University of London, London, UK.

Partner, S. (2000). Brightening country lives: Selling electrical goods in the Japanese countryside, 1950–1970. *Enterprise and Society, 1*(4), 764–784.

Pempel, T. (1998). *Regime shift: Comparative dynamics of the Japanese political economy*. Ithaca, NY: Cornell University Press.

Pergams, O., & Zaradic, P. (2008). Evidence for a fundamental and pervasive shift away from nature-based recreation. *Proceedings of the National Academy of Sciences, 105*, 2295–2300.

Pretes, M. (2002). Touring mines and mining tourists. *Annals of Tourism Research, 29*(2), 439–456.

Prime Minister's Office. (2011a, 14 April). Press briefing at the prime minister's office for members of the foreign press. Retrieved from http://www.kantei.go.jp/foreign/incident/pdf/foreign-press-briefing-20110414-script-e.pdf. Accessed 17 April 2011.

Prime Minister's Office. (2011b, 11 April). Press briefing at the prime minister's office for members of the foreign press. Retrieved from http://www.kantei.go.jp/foreign/incident/pdf/foreign-press-briefing-20110411-script-e.pdf. Accessed 17 April 2011.

Project Office Philipp Oswalt. (Ed.). (2008). *Complete works 3: Japan, shrinking cities*. Retrieved from http://www.shrinkingcities.com/digital.0.html?&L=1. Accessed 3 September 2008.

Rainisto, S. (2003). *Success factors of place marketing: A study of place marketing practices in northern Europe and the United States*. Unpublished PhD dissertation, Institute of Strategy and International Business, Helsinki University of Technology, Helsinki, Finland.

Rausch, A. (2005a). Municipal mergers in rural Japan: Easy on the powerful, severe on the weak. *electronic journal of contemporary japanese studies*. Retrieved from http://www.japanesestudies.org.uk/discussionpapers/2005/Rausch.html. Accessed 11 November 2010.

Rausch, A. (2005b). Tsugaru *nuri* lacquerware: Nation-state patronage and the constructed, contested and reconstructed meaning and representation of a local craft. In N. Guo, S. Hasegawa, H. Kawanishi, K. Kitahara, H. Johnson, & A. Rausch (Eds.), *Tsugaru: Regional identity on Japan's northern periphery* (pp. 99–119). Dunedin, NZ: Otago University Press.

Rausch, A. (2006). The Heisei Dai Gappei: A case study for understanding the municipal mergers of the Heisei Era. *Japan Forum*, *18*(1), 133–156.

Rausch, A. (2010). Post-Heisei merger Japan: A new realignment in the Doshu system. *electronic journal of contemporary japanese studies*, Discussion Paper 2. Retrieved from http://www.japanesestudies.org.uk/discussionpapers/2010/Rausch.html. Accessed 9 August 2010.

Ray, C. (1998). Culture, intellectual property and territorial rural development. *Sociologia Ruralis*, *38*(1), 3–20.

Reuters.com. (2011, 15 March). South Korea to send boron to stabilize Japan reactor. Retrieved from http://www.reuters.com/article/2011/03/16/us-japan-quake-boron-idUSTRE72F0KG20110316. Accessed 17 April 2011.

Rieniets, T. (2005). Global shrinkage. In P. Oswalt (Ed.), *Shrinking cities, volume 1: International research.* Retrieved from http://www.shrinkingcities.com/fileadmin/shrink/downloads/pdfs/SC_Band_1_eng.pdf. Accessed 21 October 2010.

Roca, Z. (2000). *Local identity, globalisation and rural development: Searching for empirical evidence.* International conference: European Rural Policy at the Crossroads, University of Aberdeen, 29 June–1 July. Retrieved from http://www.abdn.ac.uk/irr/arkleton/conf2000/papers/roca-z.doc. Accessed 14 December 2009.

Roggenthin, H. (2001). Stadtteile mit besonderem Entwicklungsbedarf – die Soziale Stadt. In H. Roggenthin (Ed.), *Stadt—der Lebensraum der Zukunft? Gegenwärtige raumbezogene Prozesse in Verdichtungsräumen der Erde* (pp. 79–87). Mainz, Germany: Geographisches Institut, Johannes Gutenberg-Universität Mainz.

Rolfe, H., & Metcalf, H. (2009). *Recent migration into Scotland: The evidence base.* Retrieved from the Scottish Government website: http://www.scotland.gov.uk/Publications/2009/02/23154109/0. Accessed 2 November 2010.

Roosevelt, T. (1903). At laying of cornerstone of gateway to Yellowstone National Park (speech, 1903, 24 April). Retrieved from http://www.theodore-roosevelt.com/images/trenvpics/tryellowstonearchspeech.pdf. Accessed 15 February 2011.

Rostow, W. (1998). *The great population spike and after: Reflections on the 21st century.* New York, NY: Oxford University Press.

Rudiger, A., & Spencer, S. (2003). *Social integration of migrants and ethnic minorities: Policies to combat discrimination.* Presented at the Economic and Social Aspects of Migration Conference, European Commission and the Organization for Economic Cooperation and Development (OECD). Brussels, Belgium, 21–22 January 2003. Retrieved from http://www.oecd.org/document/1/0,

2340,en_2649_37415_15582209_1_1_1_37415,00.html. Accessed 2 November 2010.

Sado shi. (2006). *Tōkei shiryō shū—sō mokuji* [Statistics—General Contents]. Retrieved from Sado shi website: http://www.city.sado.niigata.jp/admin/toukei/index/index.html. Accessed 1 July 2008.

Sado shi. (2009). *Tōkei shiryō shū*. Retrieved from Sado City website: http://www.city.sado.niigata.jp/admin/stat/index/index.shtml.Accessed 7 December 2010.

Sado shi. (2010). *Tōkei shiryō shū*. Retrieved from Sado City website: http://www.city.sado.niigata.jp/admin/stat/index/index.shtml.Accessed 1 November 2010.

Sado Shichō-shitsu. (2008). *Toki to kurasu sato-zukuri seido, Shichō no hitokoto: Dai yon kai*. Retrieved from Sado City website: http://www.city.sado.niigata.jp/mayor/i_v/log/04.shtml. Accessed 10 December 2009.

Samuels, R. (1983). *The politics of regional policy in Japan:Localities incorporated?* Princeton, NJ: Princeton University Press.

Sankei Shimbun.. (2008, 15 August). Nōsagyō ni asesuru Chūgokujin kenshūsei Nagano Kawakamimura.

Sato, I. (2008). *Kankō to Hokkaidō keizai: chiiki wo ikasu maaketingu*. Sapporo, Japan: Hokkaidō Daigaku Shuppankai.

Schaper, M. (2002). Understanding the green entrepreneur. In M. Schaper (Ed.), *Making ecopreneurs: Developing sustainable entrepreneurship*. Aldershot, UK: Ashgate.

Schebath, A. (2006). Financial stress in the Japanese local public sector in the 1990s: Situation, structural reasons, solutions. In C. Hein & P. Pelletier (Eds.), *Cities, autonomy, and decentralization in Japan* (pp. 81–100). London, UK: Routledge.

Schwartz, G. (2006). From collapse to regeneration. In Schwartz, G. & J. Nichols (Eds.), *After collapse: The regeneration of complex societies* (pp. 3–18). Tucson, AZ: University of Arizona Press.

Schwartz, G., & Nichols, J. (Eds.). (2006). *After collapse: The regeneration of complex societies*. Tucson, AZ: University of Arizona Press.

Scott, S. (2010, 3 August). Dying to work: Japan Inc.'s foreign trainees. *Japan Times*. Retrieved from http://search.japantimes.co.jp/cgi-bin/fl20100803zg.html. Accessed 7 December 2010.

Scottish Economic Research [SER]. (2006). *The Tayside migrant labour population: Scale, impacts and experiences* (Study No. 79). Edinburgh, UK: Communities Scotland.

Scottish Executive. (2004, January). Fresh Talent: Working in Scotland Scheme. Retrieved from http://www.scottish.parliament.uk/business/officialReports.

Scottish Executive. (2005, 22 June). Fresh Talent student scheme officially launched [Press release]. Retrieved from the Scottish Government website: http://www.scotland.gov.uk/News/Releases/2005/06/16102727. Accessed 2 November 2010.

Scottish Government. (2007). *The government economic strategy*. Retrieved from the Scottish Government website: http://www.scotland.gov.uk/Publications/2007/11/12115041/0. Accessed 2 November 2010.

Scottish Government. (2010). *Rural Scotland key facts 2009: People and communities, services and lifestyle, economy and enterprise*. Retrieved from the Scottish Government website: http://www.scotland.gov.uk/Publications/2009/09/24095407/1. Accessed 2 November 2010.

Seaton, P. (2010). Depopulation and financial collapse in Yūbari: Market forces, administrative folly, or a warning to others? *Social Science Japan Journal, 13(2)*, 227-240.

Select Committee on Economic Affairs. (2008). *The economic impact of immigration*. London. 1st Report of Session 2007–2008, House of Lords. Retrieved from UK Parliament website: http://www.publications.parliament.uk/pa/ld200708/ldselect/ldeconaf/82/82.pdf. Accessed 1 November 2010.

Sellek, Y. (2001). *Migrant labour in Japan*. Basingstoke, UK: Palgrave Macmillan.

Semmens, P. (2000). *High speed in Japan: Shinkansen—The world's busiest high-speed railway* (2nd ed.). Sheffield, UK: Platform 5.

Shibasaki, S. (2007). Sekai shizen isan tōroku ga chiiki shigen kanri taikei ni oyobosu eikyō—Satoichi/Satoumi chiiki no bunseki, oyobi Yakushima zentai kara no tenbō. *Ringyō Keizai*, *60*(3), 1–16.

Shibata, K. (2008). *The origins of Japanese planning culture: Building a nation-state, 1868–1945*. Research papers in Environmental and Spatial Analysis, 128. London School of Economics and Political Science Retrieved from http://eprints.lse.ac.uk/21682/. Accessed 11 November 2010.

Shiga ken. (2007). Dōrō keikaku-ka (Kairyō keikaku tantō). Retrieved from Shiga Prefecture website: http://www.pref.shiga.jp/h/o-doboku/kairyou.html. Accessed 6 December 2010.

Shimotori, S. (1981). Trends and some problems of private forestry in Hokkaido since World War II. In R. Handa & I. Nomiya (Eds.), *The current state of japanese forestry: Its problems and future*. Contributions to the 17th International Union of Forestry Research Organizations (IUFRO) World Congress, Kyoto, Japan: IUFRO.

Shinano Mainichi Shinbunsha (Ed.). (1969). *Shinano dōshokubutsuki*. Nagano, Japan: Shinano Mainichi Shinbunsha.

Shin-Nippon Seitestu. (2005). *Shin-Nitetsu gaido*. Tokyo, Japan: Shin-Nippon Seitestu Kabushiki Kaisha.

Shirai, S. (2005). Growing problems in the local public finance system of Japan. *Social Science Japan Journal*, *8*(2), 213–238.

Shizuoka Shimbun. (2002, 10 December). *'Nozomi' Tsūkōzei, Kangaetai*, p. 1.

Shoji, Y., Yamaguchi, K., & Yamaki, K. (2004). Understanding visitor flows in Daisetsuzan National Park: A case study in fall trekking season. In T. Ito and N. Tanaka (Eds.), *Social roles of forests for urban population: Forest recreation, landscape, nature conservation, economic evaluation and urban forestry*. Utsunomiya, Japan: Japan Society of Forest Planning Press.

Siddle, R. (2003). Return to Uchinā: The politics of identity in contemporary Okinawa. In G. Hook & R. Siddle (Eds.), *Japan and Okinawa: Structure and subjectivity* (pp. 133–147). London, UK: RoutledgeCurzon.

Slater, T. & Higgins, J. (2000). What is urban decline: Desolation, decay and destruction, or an opportunity? In T. Slater (Ed.), *Towns in Decline AD 100–1600* (pp. 1–24). Aldershot, UK: Ashgate.

Smith, R.J. (1978). Foreword: The eclipse of communal ritual in Japan. In Y. Yamamoto, *The Namahage: A festival in the northeast of Japan* (pp. 1-8). Philadelphia, PA: Institute for the Study of Human Issues.

Smith, T. (1973). Pre-modern economic growth: Japan and the West. *Past and Present*, *60*(1), 127–160.

Smith, T. (1988). *Native sources of Japanese industrialization, 1750–1920*. Berkeley, CA: University of California Press.

Soranaka, I. (1997). Obama: The rise and decline of a seaport. *Monumenta Nipponica*, *52*(1), 85–102.

Sorensen, A. (2007). Changing governance of shared spaces: Machizukuri as institutional innovation. In A. Sorensen & C. Funck (Eds.), *Living Cities in Japan: Citizens' Movements, Machizukuri and Local Environments* (pp. 56–90). London, UK: Routledge.

Sorensen, A., & Funck, C. (2007a). Living cities in Japan. In A. Sorensen & C. Funck (Eds.), *Living cities in Japan: Citizens' movements, machi-zukuri and local environments* (pp. 1–36). London, UK: Routledge.

Sorensen, A. & Funck, C. (2007b). Conclusions: A diversity of machi-zukuri processes and outcomes. In A. Sorensen & C. Funck (Eds.), *Living cities in Japan: Citizens' movements, machizukuri and local environments* (pp. 269–278). London, UK: Routledge.

Sriskandarajah, D. (2006, 23 August). Pulling up the drawbridge will damage our economy. *Guardian*. Retrieved from http://www.guardian.co.uk/commentisfree/2006/aug/23/comment.immigrationandpublicservices. Accessed 2 November 2010.

Statistics Bureau. (2004). *Survey on service industries*. Retrieved from Ministry of Internal Affairs and Communicafions website: http://www.stat.go.jp/english/data/service/index.htm. Accessed 8 November 2010.

Statistics Bureau. (2005). *Population census of Japan* [CD-ROM], vol. 3. Tokyo, Japan: Ministry of Internal Affairs and Communications.

Statistics Bureau. (2006). *Population by prefecture and sex (1884–2006)*. Retrieved from Ministry of Internal Affairs and Communications website: http://www.stat.go.jp/english/data/chouki/02.htm. Accessed 1 July 2009.

Statistics Bureau. (2008). *Shutsunyūkokusha*. Retrieved from Ministry of Internal Affairs and Communications website: http://www.e-stat.go.jp/SG1/estat/List.do?lid=000001035550. Accessed 7 December 2010.

Statistics Bureau. (2009). Persons who entered or departed from Japan by nationality. *Japan statistical yearbook*. Retrieved from Ministry of Internal Affairs and Communications website: http://www.stat.go.jp/english/data/nenkan/1431–02.htm. Accessed 7 December 2010.

Statistics Bureau. (2010a). *Labour force survey historical data*. Retrieved from Ministry of Internal Affairs and Communications website: http://www.stat.go.jp/english/data/roudou/lngindex.htm. Accessed 26 September 2010.

Statistics Bureau. (2010b). *Japan statistical yearbook 2010*. Retrieved from Ministry of Internal Affairs and Communications website: http://www.stat.go.jp/english/data/nenkan/backdata/index.htm.

Statistics Bureau. (2010c). *Statistics handbook of Japan 2010*. Retrieved from Ministry of Internal Affairs and Communications website: http://www.stat.go.jp/english/data/handbook/index.htm. Accessed 29 September 2010.

Statistics Bureau. (2010d). *Historical statistics of Japan*. Retrieved from Ministry of Internal Affairs and Communications website: http://www.stat.go.jp/english/data/chouki/index.htm.

Statistics Bureau. (2010e). *Population census [2005 and 2010 Census]*. Retrieved from Ministry of Internal Affairs and Communications website: http://www.stat.go.jp/english/data/kokusei/index.htm, Accessed: 8 November 2010.

Statistics Bureau. (2010f). *Population estimates* [1 October 2010]. Retrieved from Ministry of Internal Affairs and Communications website: http://www.e-stat.go.jp/SG1/estat/ListE.do?lid=000001063433. Accessed 1 November 2010.

Statistics Bureau. (2010g). *Table 4: Changes of general index*. Retrieved from Ministry of Internal Affairs and Communications website: http://www.stat.go.jp/english/data/cpi/158c.htm. Accessed 2 November 2010.

Statistics Bureau. (2010h). *Todōfuken – Kokuseki betsu nenmatsu genzai gaikokujin tōroku jinin*. Retrieved from Ministry of Internal Affairs and Communications website: http://www.e-stat.go.jp/SG1/estat/List.do?lid=000001064588. Accessed 7 December 2010.

Statistics Bureau. (2010i). *2004 Survey on service industries*. Retrieved from Ministry of Internal Affairs and Communications website: http://www.stat.go.jp/english/data/service/index.htm.

Sterngold, J. (1995, 17 January). Japan's cedar forests are man-made disaster. *New York Times*.

Suto, I. (1991). *Yama no hyōteki—Inoshishi to yamabito no seikatsushi.* Tokyo, Japan: Miraisha.

Tachibana, S. (2009). Ringyō no chiiki kōzō. In H. Mochida & K. Shiga (Eds.), *Nihon ringyō no kōzō henka to sensus taikei no saihen—2005-nen ringyō sensus bunseki*. Tokyo, Japan: Nōrin Tōkei Kyōkai.

Tainter, J. (1990). *The collapse of complex societies*. Cambridge, UK: Cambridge University Press.

Taira, N. (2006). Jinkō genshō shita no kokudo keikaku. *Toshi Keikaku, 263*, 31–36.

Takahashi, S. (1995). *Yasei dōbutsu to yaseika kachiku*. Tokyo, Japan: Taimeidō.

Tamaki, Y. (1996). 'Jizoku kanō na' kankō kaihatsu rizōto no hikari to kage. In S. Yamashita (Ed.), *Kankō jinruigaku* (pp. 66–73). Tokyo, Japan: Shinyōsha.

Tamura, S. (2007). *Jichitai kakusa ga kuni o horobosu*. Tokyo, Japan: Shūeisha shinsho.

Tanji, M. (2003). The dynamic trajectory of the post-reversion 'Okinawa struggle': Constitution, environment and gender. In G. Hook & R. Siddle (Eds.), *Japan and Okinawa: Structure and subjectivity* (pp. 167–187). London, UK: RoutledgeCurzon.

Tanno, K. (2010). The economic crisis and foreign workers in Japan: Why does Japan treat migrant workers as second class citizens? *Japan Labour Review*, *7*(3), 109–126.

Tanozaki, A. (2007). Kamaishi shakai no hendo to 'Kamaishi chōsa.' In Chūō daigaku shakai kagaku kenkyūsho (Ed.), *Chiiki shakai no hendo to shakai keikaku: Kamaishi shakai to Kamaishi-seitetsusho* (pp. 3–12). Tokyo, Japan: Chūō Daigaku Shakai Kagaku Kenkyūsho.

Tauninfo. (2009). *Saku-shi no kihon jōhō*. Retrieved from Tauninfo website: http://www.towninf.co.jp /p/20/20217/100.htm. Accessed 15 April 2009. Page no longer active.

Taylor, J. (2000). Authenticity and sincerity in tourism. *Annals of Tourism Research, 28*(3), 7–26.

Tews, H. (1993). Neue und alte Aspekte des Strukturwandels des Alters. In G. Naegele & H. Tews (Eds.), *Lebenslagen im Strukturwandel des Alterns. Alternde Gesellschaftt—Folgen für die Politik* (pp. 478–491). Opladen: Westdeutscher Verlag.

Thompson, C. (2003). Depopulation in rural Japan: 'Population Politics' in Tōwa-chō. In W. Traphagan & J. Knight (Eds.), *Demographic change and the family in Japan's aging society* (pp. 89–106). Albany, NY: State University of New York Press.

Thompson, C. (2006). Preserving the Ochiai deer dance: Tradition and continuity in a Tōhoku hamlet. In C. Thompson & J. Traphagan (Eds.), *Wearing cultural styles in Japan: Concepts of tradition and modernity in practice* (pp. 124–150). Albany, NY: State University of New York Press.

Thompson, W. (1929). Population. *American Journal of Sociology, 34*(6), 959–975.

Tōhoku Denryoku. (2011, 23 April). Genshiryoku jōhō. Retrieved from Tōhoku Electric Power Company website: http://www.Tōhoku-epco.co.jp/genshi/. Accessed 23 April 2011.

Tokida, K. (2001). Chōjū hogo seido to inoshishi kanri. In S. Takahashi (Ed.), *Inoshishi to ningen—tomo ni ikiru* (pp. 244–257). Tokyo, Japan: Kokon Shoin.

Tokyo Electric Power Company [TEPCO]. (2011a, 15 April) Payment of temporary compensation for damages caused by evacuation. Retrieved from http://www.tepco.co.jp/en/press/corp-com/release/11041501-e.html. Accessed 23 April 2011.

Tokyo Electric Power Company [TEPCO]. (2011b, 17 April). Roadmap towards restoration from the accident at Fukushima Daiichi nuclear power station. Retrieved from http://www.tepco.co.jp/en/press/corp-com/release/11041707-e.html. Accessed 18 April 2011.

Tokyo Metropolitan Government [TMG]. (2010). *Tōkyō-to no jinkō (suikei)*. Retrieved from Tokyo Metropolitan Government website: http://www.toukei.metro.tokyo.jp/jsuikei/js-index.htm. Accessed 1 November 2010.

Tominaga, K. (1990). *Nihon no kindaika to shakaihendo*. Tokyo, Japan: Kodansha.

Traphagan, J. (2000). *Taming oblivion: Aging bodies and the fear of senility in Japan*. Albany, NY: State Univeristy of New York Press.

Traphagan, J., & Knight, J. (Eds.). (2003). *Demographic change and the family in Japan's aging society*. Albany, NY: State Unitersity of New York Press.

Tsai, M. (2011, 11 March). Waves bring flooding on Maui, damage in Kailua-Kona. *Star Advertiser*. Retrieved from http://www.staradvertiser.com/news/breaking/Waves_peaked_on_Maui_there_are_some_reports_of_flooding.html. Accessed 24 April 2011.

Tsujita, M. (2007a). Koyō sōshutsu kara shin-sangyō no sōzō ni mukete. In Y. Genda & N. Nakamura (Eds.), *Kamaishi ni kibō wa aruka: Kamaishi chōsa kōkai shimpojiamu zen-kiroku* (pp. 50–71). Tokyo, Japan: Tōkyō Daigaku Shuppankai.

Tsujita, M. (2007b). Chiiki-sangyō no shinko ni kibō wa arunoka. *Nikkei Gurocal*, January, 40–45.

Uchino, T. (1983). *Japan's postwar economy: An insider's view of its history and its future*. Tokyo, Japan: Kodansha International.

Ue, T. (1983). *Yama ni sumu nari*. Tokyo, Japan: Shinjuku shobō.

Uekami, T. (2007). Survey of Kamaishi City Assembly members. *Social Science Japan*, *36*, 25–27.

Umehara, J. (2002). *Shinkansen no Nazo to Fushigi*. Tokyo, Japan: Tōkyōdō Shuppan.

United Kingdom Border Agency. [UKBA]. (2010). *Fresh talent: Working in Scotland*. Retrieved from UK Border Agency website: http://

www.ukba.homeoffice.gov.uk/workingintheuk/tier1/freshtalent/freshtalentscotland/#. Accessed 2 November 2010.

United Nations Population Divison. [UNPD]. (2001). *Replacement migration: Is it a solution to declining and ageing populations?* Retrieved from http://www.un.org/esa/population/publications/migration/migration.htm. Accessed 10 December 2009.

United Nations Population Division. [UNPD]. (2002). *World population ageing: 1950–2050*. New York, NY: United Nations.

United Nations Population Division. [UNPD]. (2004). *World population to 2300*. New York, NY: United Nations.

United Nations Population Division. [UNPD]. (2007). *World population prospects: The 2006 revision, highlights* (Working paper No. ESA/P/WP.202). Retrieved from UNPD website: http://www.un.org/esa/population/publications/wpp2006/WPP2006_Highlights_rev.pdf. Accessed 28 October 2010.

United Nations Population Division. [UNPD]. (2010). *World population prospects: The 2008 revision population database*. Retrieved from UNPD website: http://esa.un.org/unpp/p2k0data.asp. Accessed 4 December 2010.

United Nations Population Fund. (UNFPA). (2009). *State of world population 2009: Facing a changing world—Women, population, and climate*. New York, NY: United Nations Population Fund.

United States Geological Survey. [USGS]. (2011a). USGS updates magnitude of Japan's 2011 Tōhoku earthquake to 9.0. Retrieved from http://www.usgs.gov/newsroom/article.asp?ID=2727&from=rss_home. Accessed 17 April 2011.

United States Geological Survey. [USGS]. (2011b). Historic earthquakes: Sanriku, Japan 1933 March 02 17:31 UTC Magnitude 8.4. Retrieved from http://earthquake.usgs.gov/earthquakes/world/events/1933_03_02.php. Accessed 18 April 2011.

United States Geological Survey. [USGS]. (2011c). Magnitude 8 and greater earthquakes since 1900. Retrieved from http://earthquake.usgs.gov/earthquakes/eqarchives/year/mag8/magnitude8_1900_date.php. Accessed 24 April 2011.

Usui, C. (2003). Japan's aging dilemma? *Asia Program Special Report, 107*, 16–22.

Van de Kaa, D. (1987). Europe's second demographic transition. *Population Bulletin, 42*(1), 1–59.

van Houtum, H., & Lagendijk, A. (2001). Contextualising regional identity and imagination in the construction of polycentric urban regions: The cases of the Ruhr Area and the Basque Country. *Urban Studies, 38*(4), 747–767.

van Wolferen, K. (1990). *The enigma of Japanese power: People and politics in a stateless nation*. New York, NY: Vintage Books.

Vertovec, S. (2006). The emergence of super-diversity in Britain (Working Paper No. 25). Centre on Migration, Policy and Society [COMPAS], University of Oxford. Retrieved from COMPAS website: http://www.compas.ox.ac.uk/fileadmin/files/pdfs/Steven%20Vertovec%20WP0625.pdf. Accessed 2 November 2010.

Wada, K. (1994). *Saru wa dono yō ni fuyu o kosu ka—yasei nihonzaru no seitai to hogo*. Tokyo, Japan: Nōbunkyō.

Waley, P. (2000). Tokyo: Patterns of familiarity and partitions of difference. In P. Marcuse & R. Van Kempen (Eds.), *Globalizing cities: A new spatial order?* (pp. 127–156). Oxford, UK: Blackwell.

Warabi-za. (2005). *The mission*. Retrieved from Warabi-za website: http://www.warabi.jp/english/index.html. Accessed 11 December 2009.

Ward-Perkins, B. (2005). *The fall of Rome and the end of civilization*. Oxford, UK: Oxford University Press.

Washida, K. (2007). *Yūbari mondai*. Tokyo, Japan: Shōdensha shinsho.

Watanabe, H. (2010). Concerning revisions in the foreign trainee and technical intern system. *Japan Labour Review*, *7*(3), 43–67.

Watanabe, K. (1995). Chiiki ni okeru yasei nihonzaru hogo kanri no mondaiten to kongo no kadai. *Reichōrui Kenkyū*, *11*, 47–58.

Weiner, M. (Ed.). (2004). *Race, ethnicity and migration in modern Japan* (Vol. 1). 1. London, UK: Routledge.

Weiner, M. (2009). *Japan's minorities: The illusion of homogeneity* (2nd ed.). London, UK: Routledge.

Whittaker, E. (1997). The town that debates tourism: Community and tourism in Broome, Australia. In E. Chambers (Ed.), *Tourism and culture: An applied perspective* (pp. 13–30). Albany, NY: State University of New York Press.

Wigen, K. (1992). The geographic imagination in early modern Japanese history: Retrospect and prospect. *The Journal of Asian Studies*, *51*(1), 3–29.

Wigen, K. (1995). *The making of a Japanese periphery, 1750–1920.* Berkeley, CA: University of California Press.

Wiles, G. (2008, 12 May). Deep-sea water exports up 16%. *Honolulu Advertiser*.

Wood, D. (1999). *Ancestral land, inheritance, and the revitalization of rural Japan: The case of Ogata village.* Unpublished master's thesis, College Station, Texas.

Wood, D. (2003). Fragmented solidarity: Commercial farming and rice marketing in an experimental Japanese village. *Research in Economic Anthropology*, 22, 145–167.

Wood, D. (2004). *From paper to practice: Social solidarity, political economy, and change in a planned Japanese village* (Unpublished PhD dissertation). University of Tokyo, Tokyo, Japan.

Wood, D. (2005). The Polder museum of Ogata-mura: Community, authenticity, and sincerity in a Japanese village. *Asian Anthropology*, *4*, 29–58.

Wood, D. (2009). Children as a common-pool resource: Change and the shrinking kindergarten population market in a Japanese city. In D. Wood (Ed.), *Economic Development, Integration, and Morality in Asia and the Americas* (pp. 341–379). Research in Economic Anthropology, vol. 29. West Yorkshire, UK: Emerald Group Publishing.

Woodall, B. (1996). *Japan under construction: Corruption, politics, and public works*. Berkeley, CA: University of California Press.

Wright, R. (2006, 6 November). *Devolved immigration policy: Will it work in Scotland?* Department of Economics, Strathclyde Business School. Retrieved from http://www.gla.ac.uk/media/media_51213_en.pdf. Accessed 2 November 2010.

Yamaha (2007, 23 March). Yamaha to sell four resort businesses and the shares of their management companies [press release]. Retrieved from Yamaha Global Gateway website: http://www.global.yamaha.com/news/2007/20070323.html. Accessed 15 December 2009.

Yamamoto, S. (2007). Kokuritsu kō en to shinrin kanri: sono seiritsu, rinen to jissai [Panelist comment]. Sixth Symposium of Forest Economic Research Institute. *Ringyō Keizai*, *59*(12), 7.

Yamamoto, Y. (1978). *The Namahage: A festival in the northeast of Japan*. Philadelphia, PA: Institute for the Study of Human Issues.

Yamanouchi, S. (2000). *If there were no Shinkansen*. JR East. Translation of Yamanouchi S. (1998) *Shinkansen-ga nakattara*. Tokyo, Japan: Tōkyō Shimbunsha.

Yano Tsuneda Kinenkai (Eds.). (2006). *Kensei 2007 dai 15 ban*. Tokyo, Japan: Yano Tsuneda Kinenkai.

Yoffee, N. (2006). Notes on regeneration. In G. Schwartz & J. Nichols (Eds.), *After collapse: The regeneration of complex societies* (pp. 222–228). Tucson, AZ: University of Arizona Press.

Yokoi, M. (2007, 30 March). Saru mo tanan, nokoru mo kunan. *Hokkaidō Shimbun*.

Yomiuri Shimbun (2007, 11 May). Sennnin tōge dōro, Kamaishi ni onkei. Yomiuri Shimbun Iwate Prefecture Edition.

Yomiuri Shimbun Hokkaidō Shisha (Eds.). (2008). *Genkai jichi Yūbari kenshō*. Tokyo, Japan: Gotōshoin.

Yoshioka, H. (2003). Citizens' activities toward revitalization of the Sorachi coalmining region. Proceedings of the Sixth International Mining History Congress, Akabira City.

Yūbari City History Editorial Board [YCHED]. (1991). *Tsuiho Yūbari shishi*. Yūbari, Japan: Yūbari City Office.

Yūbari shi. (2007). *Yūbari-shi zaisei saiken keikaku sōan*. Yūbari, Japan: Yūbari City Office.

Yūbari shi. (2010). *Jinkō suii*. Retrieved from Yūbari City website: http://www.city.yubari.lg.jp/contents/download/jinko/suii/index.html. Accessed 9 November 2010.

Yukawa, Y. (1988). Sato ni chikazuku yama—Shiba mura Omae no minzoku henyō [Mountain descends to the village: The transformation of folkways in Omae, Shiba Village]. *Kokuritsu Rekishi Minzoku Hakubutsukan Kenkyū Hōkoku, 18*, 341–368.

Zaidan Hōjin Dentōteki Kōgeihin Sangyō Shinkō Kyōkai [ZHDKSSK]. (2006). *Dentōteki kōgeihin sanchi chōsa-shindan jigyō hōkokusho (sanchi tokubetsu chōsa-shindan: shikki)*. Tokyo, Japan: Zaidan Hōjin Dentōteki Kōgeihin Sangyō Shinkō Kyōkai.

INDEX

About the Authors (The Shrinking Regions Research Group)

Peter Matanle is Lecturer at the University of Sheffield's School of East Asian Studies, where he also gained his PhD. His research interests are in the economic sociology and cultural geography of work in Japan and the United Kingdom. Dr Matanle is the author of several publications in these fields, including *Japanese Capitalism and Modernity in a Global Era: Refabricating Lifetime Employment Relations* (RoutledgeCurzon, 2003) and *Perspectives on Work, Employment, and Society in Japan* (Palgrave, 2006; coedited with Wim Lunsing). He has also published articles in *Social Science Japan Journal*, *Local Environment*, *Japan Forum*, *Asian Business and Management*, and *Organization*, and he is the founding general editor of the *electronic journal of contemporary japanese studies*.

Anthony S. Rausch is Associate Professor in the Faculty of Education at Hirosaki University, Aomori Prefecture, Japan. He holds a degree in geography from the University of Minnesota, an MS from Hirosaki

University, and a PhD from Monash University. His research interests focus on rural Japanese society, and he has published on themes related to rural volunteerism, education, media, culture and revitalization. He is author of *A Year with the Local Newspaper: Understanding the Times in Aomori, Japan* (University Press of America, 2001) and *Cultural Commodities in Japanese Rural Revitalization: Tsugaru Nuri Lacquerware and Tsugaru Shamisen* (Brill, 2010).

Andrew David works at the US International Trade Commission (ITC). He holds master's degrees in public affairs and Asian studies from the University of Texas at Austin and a bachelor's degree from Duke University. He was a Next Generation Fellow at the National Bureau of Asian Research, and he also worked at the Food Bank of Contra Costa and Solano, The Cadmus Group, and taught English in Japan on the JET Programme. He is the author of two publications on wind turbine manufacturing and trade.

Philomena deLima is Director of the Centre for Remote and Rural Studies at the University of the Highlands and Islands, Scotland. Philomena graduated in Sociology from the University of Edinburgh and gained her PhD at the University of Stirling. Her research interests include equalities and social justice in rural communities with a particular focus on migration, ethnicity, belonging, poverty, and the impacts of climate change. Her publications include 'Welcoming Migrants: Migrant Labour in Rural Scotland' (*Social Policy and Society*, 2009, with Sharon Wright) and 'Migrant Workers in Rural Scotland: Going to the Middle of Nowhere' (*International Journal on Multicultural Societies*, 2007, with Birgit Jentsch and Brian MacDonald).

Martin Dusinberre is Lecturer in Modern Japanese History at Newcastle University in the United Kingdom. He received his DPhil from the University of Oxford. His first book, *Hard Times in the Hometown: A History of Community Survival in Modern Japan*, is forthcoming from the University of Hawai'i Press, and he has also published in *Japan Forum* (2008) and the *Journal of Asian Studies* (2011). His research focuses on the social history of modern Japan, particularly from the perspective of the regions, and on the maritime history of nineteenth-century Japan.

Neil Evans is Senior Lecturer in Human Geography and Planning, School of the Built Environment, Leeds Metropolitan University, UK. He obtained his PhD from the School of East Asian Studies at the University of Sheffield. His research interests and publications have been concerned with community participation in urban regeneration within Japan, planning for sustainable waste management and the concept of territorial governance in relation to European spatial planning.

Thomas Feldhoff is Academic Coordinator of the Interdisciplinary Centre for East Asian Studies at Goethe-University Frankfurt, Germany, and he gained his PhD and *habilitation* from the University of Duisburg-Essen. With an academic background in human geography and East Asian area studies, his research focus is on processes of demographic ageing and shrinking and their consequences with regard to regional development, planning and policy-making. He received the 2006 JaDe Award of the Association for the Promotion of Japanese-German Cultural Relations and a 2008 Book Prize of the European Association for Japanese Studies for his publication *Bau-Lobbyismus in Japan: Institutionelle Grundlagen – Akteure - Raumwirksamkeit* (Dortmunder Vertrieb für Bau- und Planungsliteratur, 2005).

Christopher P. Hood is Director of the Cardiff Japanese Studies Centre at Cardiff University. His research interests are the Shinkansen and disaster responses in Japan. His publications include: *Dealing with Disaster in Japan: Japanese and Global Responses to the Flight JL123 Crash* (Routledge, 2011), *Shinkansen: From Bullet Train to Symbol of Modern Japan* (Routledge, 2006), 'From polling station to political station? Politics and the shinkansen' (*Japan Forum,* 2006), *Japanese Education Reform: Nakasone's Legacy* (Routledge, 2001) and *The Politics of Modern Japan* (editor, 4 volumes, Routledge, 2008).

Richard Irving is Professor at the School of Policy Studies, Kwansei Gakuin University in Hyogo, Japan. He previously taught in the Department of Geography and Geology at the University of Hong Kong. In 1991 he walked from Kyoto to Tokyo along the old Nakasendo highway, which led to a collaboration with Dr Tom Stanley to produce a CDRom called *Journey to the Heart of Japan* and to cofound the tour company 'Walk Japan'. Richard gained his PhD at the Department of Geography at the University of Sheffield; his research was on the topic of rural depopulation in Japan and he has maintained his data base on population change in the villages of the Kanbayashi Valley ever since. He is currently researching the life of William Adams in Japan.

Thomas Jones is Assistant Professor at the Graduate School of Governance Studies at Meiji University. He gained his PhD in Forest Science from Tokyo University, after which he carried out fieldwork for Matsumoto City in the Japan Alps. His research revolves around social science approaches to natural resource management, focusing on national parks and other protected areas. He has published on themes related to nature-based tourism, place branding and regional revitalization.

John Knight is Reader in Anthropology at Queen's University Belfast. He completed his doctorate at the London School of Economics on the theme of social change in Japanese mountain villages and has held research fellowships in Japanese Studies at the University of Oxford and at Leiden University in the Netherlands. He has undertaken extensive field research in rural Japan on a range of topics, including migration, forestry, and tourism, and has published widely in these areas. He is the editor of *Natural Enemies* (Routledge, 2000), *Wildlife in Asia* (Routledge Curzon, 2004) and *Animals in Person* (Berg, 2005), the coeditor (with John Traphagan) of *Demographic Change and the Family in Japan's Aging Society* (SUNY, 2003), and the author of *Waiting for Wolves in Japan* (OUP, 2003) and *Herding Monkeys to Paradise* (Brill, 2011).

Sachie Mizohata is the cofounder of social-issues.org, a collaborative online community platform for social scientific research. Her research interests include multidimensional measures of well-being, quality of life in old age, the capability approach, eResearch, and rural Japan. Recent publications include 'Development of a Platform Dedicated to Collaboration in the Social Sciences' (with Raynald Jadoul) in the CELDA 2007 proceedings, as well as articles on feminism and women's issues in Japan. Sachie Mizohata holds a PhD in sociology from Paris Descartes University and two MAs, one in social service administration from the University of Chicago and the other in sociology from Loyola University Chicago.

Naofumi Nakamura is Professor in the Institute of Social Science at the University of Tokyo and gained his PhD from Kyūshū University. He is the author of several publications in the economic and business history of Japan, including *Nihon Testudō-gyō no Keisei* (The Formation of the Japanese Railway Industry, Nihon Keizai Hyōronsha, 1998) and *Chihō karano Sangyō-kakumei* (The Japanese Industrial Revolution from a Local Perspective, Nagoya University Press, 2010).

Ken Ohori is Research Associate at the Institute of Social Science (ISS) at the University of Tokyo. He has an MS from the University of Tokyo and specializes in regional and community studies. His research focuses in particular on the revitalization of Japanese local communities. He is a member of ISS's project 'The Social Sciences of Hope' and is the coauthor of *Kibōgaku 2 & 3* (*Studies of Hope vols. 2 & 3*, edited by ISS, Y. Genda and N. Nakamura, University of Tokyo Press, 2009).

Philip Seaton is Associate Professor in the Research Faculty of Media and Communication at Hokkaido University. He gained his DPhil from the University of Sussex. His research interests include World War II history and memory in Japan, as well as local history and tourism in Hokkaido. He is the author of *Japan's Contested War Memories: the 'memory rifts' in historical consciousness of World War II* (Routledge, 2007) and the translator of *My Father's Dying Wish: Legacies of War Guilt in a Japanese Family* (Paulownia Press, 2009). He was awarded the Daiwa Japan Forum Prize in 2006 for his article 'Reporting the 2001 textbook and Yasukuni Shrine controversies: Japanese war memory and commemoration in the British media'(*Japan Forum*, 2005).

Yoko Sellek is an affiliate of the White Rose East Asia Centre at the University of Sheffield. She was Lecturer in International Sociology and Japanese Studies at Sheffield's School of East Asian studies between 1990 and 2005. She specialises in international migration and focuses on Japan. Her publications include *Migrant Labour in Japan*, (Palgrave, 2001), 'Migration and the Nation-State: Structural Explanations for Emigration from Okinawa', in G.D. Hook and R. Siddle (eds), *Japan and Okinawa, Structure and Subjectivity* (Routledge, 2003), and 'Foreign Migration into Contemporary Japan under Globalisation', in H. Hasegawa and G.D. Hook (eds), *The Political Economy of Japanese Globalization* (Routledge, 2001).

Richard Siddle is Professor in the Research Faculty of Media and Communication at Hokkaido University, Japan. He received his PhD from the University of Sheffield for work on Japan's indigenous Ainu people. He has continued to research and publish on issues concerning Ainu, Okinawa, minorities and multiculturalism in Japan. Dr Siddle is the author of *Race, Resistance and the Ainu of Japan* (Routledge, 1996) and coeditor of *Japan and Okinawa: Structure and Subjectivity* (Routledge, 2003).

Donald C. Wood is Associate Professor in the Department of Medical Information Science at Akita University Graduate School of Medicine in Japan. He received his PhD in cultural anthropology from the University of Tokyo and holds BA and MA degrees in anthropology from Texas A&M University. He is especially interested in cultural change and development as well as center-periphery relations in Tōhoku, the economics of health and wellness, and the recent history of Akita. He has been researching the Hachirōgata reclaimed land area since 1995 and has been editor of the *Research in Economic Anthropology* (REA) book series since 2005.

www.ingramcontent.com/pod-product-compliance
Lightning Source LLC
LaVergne TN
LVHW101452200926
848483LV00001B/109

* 9 7 8 1 6 0 4 9 7 7 5 8 5 *